Quality of Life
in Mental Disorders

Quality of Life in Mental Disorders

Edited by

Heinz Katschnig

Chairman, Department of Psychiatry, University of Vienna, Austria

Hugh Freeman

Honorary Visiting Fellow, Green College, Oxford, UK

and

Norman Sartorius

Professor of Psychiatry, University of Geneva, Switzerland

JOHN WILEY & SONS

Chichester • New York • Weinheim • Brisbane • Singapore • Toronto

National   01243 779777
International (+44) 1243 779777
e-mail (for orders and customer service enquiries): cs-books@wiley.co.uk
Visit our Home Page on http://www.wiley.co.uk
or http://www.wiley.com

Reprinted February 1998, February 1999

Other Wiley Editorial Offices

John Wiley & Sons, Inc., 605 Third Avenue,
New York, NY 10158-0012, USA

WILEY-VCH Verlag GmbH, Pappelallee 3,
D-69469 Weinheim, Germany

Jacaranda Wiley Ltd, 33 Park Road, Milton,
Queensland 4064, Australia

John Wiley & Sons (Asia) Pte Ltd, 2 Clementi Loop #02-01,
Jin Xing Distripark, Singapore 129809

John Wiley & Sons (Canada) Ltd, 22 Worcester Road,
Rexdale, Ontario M9W 1L1, Canada

Library of Congress Cataloging-in-Publication Data

Quality of life in mental disorders / edited by Heinz Katschnig,
   Hugh Freeman and Norman Sartorius.
         p.   cm.
   Includes bibliographical references and index.
   ISBN 0-471-96643-6 (hardcover)
   1. Mentally ill—Medical care.   2. Quality of life.
   3. Social adjustment.
   I. Katschnig, Heinz   II. Freeman, Hugh L. (Hugh Lionel)
   III. Sartorius, N.
   RC455.4.S67Q34   1997
   616.89–dc21
   DNLM/DLC
   for Library of Congress   97–23241
                                                   CIP

British Library Cataloguing in Publication Data

A catalogue record for this book is available from the British Library

ISBN 0-471-96643-6

Typeset in 10/12pt Times from the editors' disks by MHL Typesetting Ltd, Coventry
Printed and bound in Great Britain by Biddles Ltd, Guildford and King's Lynn.
This book is printed on acid-free paper responsibly manufactured from sustainable forestation,
for which at least two trees are planted for each one used for paper production.

Contents

Contributors

Dr Michaela Amering
Department of Psychiatry, University of Vienna, Währinger Gürtel 18–20, A-1090 Vienna, Austria

Prof. Matthias C. Angermeyer
Chairman, Department of Psychiatry, University of Leipzig, Johannisallee 20, D-04317, Leipzig, Germany

Daniela Barge-Schaapveld
Department of Psychiatry & Neuropsychology, Brain & Behavior Institute, University of Maastricht, P.O. Box 616, 6200 MD Maastricht, The Netherlands

Dr Margaret Barry
Department of Health Promotion, University College, Galway, Ireland

Dr Marion Becker
Department of Health and Human Issues, 610 Langdon St., Room 325, Lowell Hall, Madison, Wisconsin 53703-9942, USA

Prof. Julio Bobes
Chairman, Department of Psychiatry, University of Oviedo, Julián Clavaria 6, 33006 Oviedo, Spain

Dr Philippe Delespaul
Department of Psychiatry & Neuropsychology, Brain & Behavior Institute, University of Maastricht, P.O. Box 616, 6200 MD Maastricht, The Netherlands

Mag. Ulrike Demal
Department of Psychiatry, University of Vienna, Währinger Gürtel 18–20, A-1090 Vienna, Austria

Prof. Marten deVries
Department of Psychiatry & Neuropsychology, Brain & Behavior Institute, University of Maastricht, P.O. Box 616, 6200 MD Maastricht, The Netherlands

Prof. Ronald Diamond
Department of Psychiatry, University of Wisconsin, 600 Highland Ave, Madison, Wisconsin 53792-2475, USA

Prof. Asmus Finzen
Department of Psychiatry, University of Basel, Wilhelm Klein-Strasse 27, CH-4025 Basel, Switzerland

Prof. Hugh L. Freeman
21 Montagu Square, London W1H 1RE, UK

Maria Paz González
Department of Psychiatry, University of Oviedo, Julián Claveria, 6, 33006 Oviedo, Spain

Prof. Barry Gurland, *Columbia University, Center for Geriatrics and Gerontology, 100 Haven Avenue, Tower 3-30F, New York, New York 10032, USA*

Dr Ulrike Hoffmann-Richter
Department of Psychiatry, University of Basel, Wilhelm Klein-Strasse 27, CH-4025 Basel, Switzerland

Prof. Heinz Katschnig, *Professor and Chairman, Department of Psychiatry, University of Vienna, Währinger Gürtel 18–20, A-1090 Vienna, Austria. Director, Ludwig Boltzmann-Institute for Social Psychiatry, Spitalgasse 11, A-1090 Vienna, Austria*

Prof. Sidney Katz
Columbia University, Center for Geriatrics and Gerontology, 100 Haven Avenue, Tower 3-30F, New York, NY 10032, USA

Dr Reinhold Kilian
Department of Psychiatry, University of Leipzig, Johannisallee 20, D-04317, Leipzig, Germany

Prof. Julian Leff
Institute of Psychiatry, De Crespigny Park, Denmark Hill, London SE5 8AF, UK

Prof. Anthony F. Lehman
University of Maryland, Department of Psychiatry, 645 West Redwood Street, Baltimore, Maryland 21201-1549, USA

Prof. Gerhard Lenz
Department of Psychiatry, University of Vienna, Währinger Gürtel 18–20, A-1090 Vienna, Austria

Prof. David Mechanic
Director, Institute for Health, Health Care Policy, Aging Research, Rutgers University, 30 College Avenue, P.O. Box 5070, New Brunswick, New Jersey 08903-5070, USA

Prof. Juan E. Mezzich
Professor of Psychiatry and Head Division of Psychiatric Epidemiology and International Center for Mental Health, Box 1093, Mt Sinai School of Medicine of the City University of New York, Fifth Avenue and 100th Street, New York, New York 10029-6574, USA

Dr Nancy A. Nicolson
Department of Psychiatry & Neuropsychology, Brain and Behavior Institute, University of Maastricht, P.O. Box 616, 6200 MD Maastricht, The Netherlands

Prof. Fritz Poustka
Chairman, Department of Child Psychiatry, Johann Wolfgang Goethe-Universität, Deutschordenstr. 50, D-60590 Frankfurt, Germany

Prof. Luis Salvador-Carulla
Department of Neurosciences, University of Cadiz, Fragela s/n., Cadiz 11003, Spain

Prof. Norman Sartorius
Professor of Psychiatry, University of Geneva, HUG, 16–18 Boulevard de St Georges, CH-1205 Geneva, Switzerland

Dr Klaus Schmeck
Department of Child Psychiatry, Johann Wolfgang Goethe-Universität, Deutschordenstrasse 50, D-60590 Frankfurt, Germany

Dipl.Psych. Margit M. Schmolke
Dynamisch-Psychiatrische Klinik, Menterschwaige, Geiselgasteig Str. 203, D-81545 Munich, Germany

Prof. Franklin Schneier
Associate Professor of Clinical Psychiatry, College of Physicians & Surgeons, Columbia University, 722 West 168th Street, New York, New York 10032, USA

Dr Maria D. Simon
Ludwig Boltzann Institut für Sozialpsychiatrie, Spitalgasse 11, A-1090 Vienna, Austria

Prof. Peter Stastny
Associate Professor of Psychiatry, Albert Einstein College of Medicine, 1300 Morris Park Ave., Bronx, New York 10461, USA

Dr Durk Wiersma
Department of Social Psychiatry, University of Groningen, P.O. Box 30.001, 9700 RB Groningen, The Netherlands

Preface

Quality of Life has only recently been recognised as the central purpose of health care. While a widely-valued concept, there is still insufficient agreement about the definition of quality of life, about its measurement, particularly in the field of mental health, and about the manner in which the results of assessing quality of life can best be used.

Since the term embraces a whole spectrum of uses and meanings, and is employed both as a fashionable catch-phrase and a scientific concept, it needs careful scrutiny. All too easily it can become a vague label for a state of subjective well-being, with doubtful scientific value. The annual publication of more than 2000 quality of life publications in medical journals – and the number is steadily increasing – documents both the enormous interest in this field and the wide range of uses of the term. A common denominator to these papers seems to be their emphasis on the long-neglected, subjective view of the patient.

This book brings together chapters that examine the definitions and limits of the concept of quality of life. The authors explore it both as it is now and as it could be applied to the field of mental health in the future. Because well-being and subjective satisfaction with various life domains are a core feature of most quality of life definitions, the relationship between psychopathological symptoms and quality of life had to be carefully considered. This is especially salient when it comes to practically measuring quality of life, because many instruments contain psychopathological symptoms. Some of these are, in fact, psychopathological rating scales with the addition of a new label "Quality of Life", but with little additional heuristic value.

When applying the "Quality of Life" concept to mental health the strengths and weaknesses of the concept become especially obvious. Its strengths lie in its potential for integrating the views of different players in the mental-health-care field, while its weaknesses reside in its openness – it still designates a *field of interest* rather than a clearly defined *scientific concept*. More than readers might expect, therefore, the contributions to this book deal with conceptual and methodological issues. Indeed, ten of the twenty-four chapters do address such issues. Some arguing mainly that quality of life research has generally been too much concerned with psychometrics and too little with conceptual issues.

What about a depressed patient who sees himself as deprived of all social support, while objectively sufficient support actually exists? How are we to judge a schizophrenic patient's assessment of his quality of life as good, while he is living on the streets of New York? And, finally, if a manic patient feels on top of the world, his subjectively experienced "Quality of Life" is excellent, but he will soon suffer from the consequences of his manic misjudgements of reality. These few examples show that while taking the subjective view of the patient into consideration signifies a tremendous progress in somatic medicine this is not enough in psychiatry. Therefore, most authors in this volume stress that the quality of life concept should be multidimensional, with role functioning and environmental living conditions – material and social – as additional dimensions to subjective well-being and satisfaction. It is argued that this multidimensionality is especially salient in the area of community psychiatry, where quality of life assessment is necessarily action-orientated.

These, and related topics, are discussed in the six conceptual and four measurement chapters of this book, while in the subsequent five chapters, results of quality of life research on specific psychiatric disorders – depression, anxiety, schizophrenia, childhood, and old-age disorders – are presented. In the following section, issues concerning treatment and management are discussed; with the acceptance of quality of life as an outcome measure in clinical trials and health services research, this has become a fast-growing area in recent years. This section also includes chapters on patients', relatives' and staff's perception of quality of life. Articles on broader issues, like cost analysis, service planning, and health policy conclude the volume. All references are contained in a single bibliography at the end of the book, presenting a comprehensive compilation of the most important existing publications.

We would like to extend our gratitude to Mrs Johanna Bewry for her careful secretarial work on the manuscripts, to Professor Scott Henderson and his staff of the Australian National University in Canberra for providing hospitality to one of us (HK) during the last stages of preparing the book and to Hilary Rowe and Lewis Derrick, of John Wiley & Sons, for handling the production of the book so effectively.

Heinz Katschnig, Vienna
Hugh Freeman, Oxford
Norman Sartorius, Geneva

August 1997

INTRODUCTION

CHAPTER ONE

How Useful is the Concept of Quality of Life in Psychiatry?

Heinz Katschnig

THE RISE OF THE QUALITY OF LIFE CONCEPT IN MEDICINE

The concept of quality of life is not yet defined in a uniform way, lacks clarity and even creates confusion. Nevertheless, quality of life publications are booming in medicine. A MEDLINE search shows slowly increasing numbers of these articles during the 1970s and 1980s, but a steep rise in the nineties to over 2000 publications in 1995. In 1992, a scientific journal devoted entirely to health-related quality of life research was founded, and an "International Society of Quality of Life Research" is already holding its fourth annual meeting in 1997. "Quality of life" is clearly a definite issue in medicine.

Psychiatry is lagging somewhat behind in this development. Psychiatrists are probably hesitating because the mainstream concept of quality of life in medicine, with its emphasis on subjective well-being and satisfaction of the patient, is less separated from psychiatric concepts of mental disorders than it is from medical concepts of somatic diseases. In the latter case, quality of life is welcomed by many as a humanistic addendum to a more and more technocratic practice of medicine. But as far as psychiatry is concerned: Isn't the subjective well-being of the patient the very topic of psychiatry or isn't it at least intimately related to psychopathology? The present chapter will explore these and related issues.

In the 1960s and 1970s, social scientists, philosophers, and politicians began showing interest in the concepts of "quality of life" and "standard of living". This was mainly in response to perceived inequalities in the distribution of resources and well-being in society and because of concern with population growth and developmental problems in poor countries (Albrecht & Fitzpatrick, 1994). In addition, the evolution of the welfare state stimulated research on social indicators and well-being, especially on the quality of work, family life, and leisure (Erickson, 1974; Drewnowski, 1974; Andrews & Withey, 1976; Campbell et al, 1976).

But what is quality of life? It seems that in medicine, the term has become a bandwagon concept for all those human needs which are often neglected in a health care field increasingly dominated by technology. As a rule, "quality of life" is used in medicine for characterising an individual patient's quality of life from his or her own subjective perspective. This is somehow in contrast to social indicator research, where subjective well-being is just one of many different indicators of the quality of life of the population under study, and where indicators of standard of living are regarded as equally important, assuming that well-being is strongly influenced by the latter.

One reason for the rise of the quality of life movement in medicine – with its emphasis on the patient's subjective view – was the growing consumer dissatisfaction with medical treatment in the 1960s and 1970s. This was also a cause of the development of the self-help movement. A specific aspect of this dissatisfaction was that in the effort to prolong life at any price, and by focusing exclusively on treatment needs, medicine tended to overlook the basic human needs of its patients, such as well-being, autonomy and a sense of belonging.

This issue was first brought into the forefront in oncology, where the question arose whether one should trade-off a longer survival time for a better quality of life. "I'd rather die with my own hair on" says a character in David Lodge's novel *Paradise News* (Penguin Harmondsworth 1992, p. 26), when asked why she refuses chemotherapy for cancer. In psychiatry, similar issues have been prevalent for a long time. The question whether "the cure is worse than the disease" arose in asylum psychiatry, as well as in the treatment of schizophrenia with conventional neuroleptics. There are quite a few patients who would rather experience their hallucinations than suffer from extrapyramidal side-effects, which are not only unpleasant but also socially visible and stigmatising.

Today, the term "quality of life" has become a rallying cry for all those who strive to integrate the patient's experience of his or her life during illness into clinical care – by using the patient's subjective assessment of his or her quality of life. It has become an umbrella catchword for non-physiological aspects of disease, which have been described before – but less successfully by other concepts.

Albrecht and Fitzpatrick (1994) have identified four uses of the quality of life concept in medicine. It is used: (1) for the planning of clinical care of individual patients; (2) as an outcome measure in clinical trials and health services research; (3) for health needs assessments of populations; and (4) for resource allocation. Most applications concern chronic and severe disorders.

The most promising use of the quality of life concept is as an outcome measure in clinical trials (Spilker, 1996) and health services research (Oliver et al, 1996).

There are problems, however, with the application of such measures in short-term clinical trials of psychotropic drugs, as will be discussed below. The use of quality of life instruments in everyday clinical practice to improve clinicians' awareness of patients' disabilities and general well-being remains uncommon (Deyo & Carter, 1992). The health needs assessment of populations by quality of life measures has not yet produced results which are specific enough to indicate the requirement for specific health care interventions (Donovan et al, 1993). Finally, resource allocation by means of quality of life measures is highly controversial, not least because simplified global measures tend to be employed in this area (Carr-Hill, 1991; see also Salvador-Carulla, Ch. 22, this volume).

While the developments described above are fairly recent, it has to be stressed that interest in non-physiological aspects of disease has existed for a long time. The World Health Organization has been especially creative in promoting this issue. Shortly after the Second World War, this organisation put forward its well-known definition of health, which stressed that "health is a state of complete physical, mental and social well-being and not merely the absence of disease or infirmity" (WHO, 1948). Fifty years later, this sounds like a definition of health-related quality of life. In 1980, the World Health Organization published its "International Classification of Impairments, Disabilities and Handicaps (ICIDH)" (WHO, 1980), but this was too complex for widespread use and was never widely adopted (it is actually being revised and simplified). More recently, WHO has jumped on the quality of life "bandwagon" and has just completed work on a generic assessment instrument for quality of life (WHOQOL; Orley & Kuyken, 1994).

Psychiatry has been especially prolific in assessing non-disease aspects of its patients by using concepts such as "impairment", "disabilities", "handicap", "social functioning", "social adjustment", "satisfaction", "social support", and so on. A fair number of instruments to measure these aspects have been in existence for some time, though without having been called "quality of life" instruments. In fact, there was a rich literature on defining and measuring such non-medical aspects of psychiatric disorders already some 20 years ago (for a review see Weissman et al, 1981b and Katschnig, 1983) – but these concepts did not come to the forefront to the same extent as quality of life has now done. Also, the structured assessment of psychopathological symptoms, which are integral items of most quality of life instruments, is a long-standing practice in psychiatry. Furthermore, the World Health Organization has recently published an easy-to-use multi-axial presentation of the ICD-10 Classification of Mental and Behavioural Disorders which includes one axis on disabilities and another on contextual factors (Janca et al, 1996; World Health Organization, 1997; see also Mezzich & Schmolke, Ch. 9 this volume). With this background, the question seems not irrelevant as to whether psychiatry needs the quality of life concept at all.

Although the concept of quality of life is vague, or perhaps because this is so, it has an intuitive appeal for many different parties who are involved in managing health and disease. Quality of life seems to be understood by everyone: patients, their family members, professionals – biologically orientated as well as psychosocially and sociologically orientated – the pharmaceutical industry and regulatory bodies, by politicians and the general public. Who does not strive for a good quality of life? Politicians know this, as the 1964 election campaign statement by Lyndon B. Johnson illustrates ("These goals cannot be measured by the size of our bank balances, they can only be measured in the quality of life that our people lead"; Rescher, 1972).

The concept of quality of life may thus have a large integrative potential in a health care environment which is characterised by ever increasing conflicts and debates on costs and outcome. It provides a "potential breath of fresh air in our understanding of health, illness and health care institutions" (Albrecht & Fitzpatrick, 1994). This is especially true for psychiatry, where in the case of patients with persistent mental illness living in the community, burn-out in their carers and professionals can occur fairly quickly (see Simon, Ch. 19 and Kilian, Ch. 21 this volume). The concept of quality of life as a primary aim of helping activities – as opposed to just symptom reduction and prevention of relapse – can help to unite forces and strengthen working alliances. In this respect, therefore, we can conclude that the concept of quality of life is potentially useful in psychiatry.

HEALTH-RELATED QUALITY OF LIFE

Despite this, the concept of quality of life has a number of disadvantages, since it is still confusing and lacks an agreed definition (see e.g. Hunt, 1997). It is justifiable to say that it is a term describing a field of interest rather than a single variable – much like the term "disease" – and that there is no simple way of measuring quality of life, just as there is no simple way of measuring disease. In social indicator research it has many different meanings, ranging from the notion of the welfare of a whole nation at one end to the concept of individual happiness at the other. In medical quality of life research, the term refers to a loosely related body of work on psychological well-being, social and emotional functioning, health status, functional performance, life satisfaction, social support and standard of living, whereby normative, objective and subjective indicators of physical, social and emotional functioning are all used.

GENERAL QUALITY OF LIFE (QoL) AND HEALTH-RELATED QUALITY OF LIFE (HRQL)

There are widely valued aspects of life that are not generally regarded as health, including income, freedom, and social support. Although low income, lack of freedom and poor social support may be relevant to health, there is a tendency to exclude such general aspects when dealing with quality of life and health problems and to focus on directly disease-related aspects of functional capacity (e.g. mobility in pulmonary disease) and well-being (Guyatt et al, 1993). For this purpose, the term "Health-Related Quality of Life (HRQL)" has been coined.

For the practice of somatic medicine, the use of this narrow concept can be regarded as progress – in comparison with the traditional tendency to focus exclusively on the disease and its symptoms. However, for the mental health field, the quality of life concept is only useful if it encompasses the aforementioned and other environmental factors, since income, lack of autonomy (e.g. because of lack of money) and low social support are all intrinsically related to psychopathology. What is required in the field of mental health is a broad and multi-dimensional concept which includes most aspects of life. Rather than using a single index, a profile is more appropriate here (Bullinger, 1993).

INSTRUMENTS FOR MEASURING HEALTH-RELATED QUALITY OF LIFE

In a first phase of health-related quality of life research in the 1970s and early 1980s, already available psychological well-being scales were used or new ones were specifically developed for this purpose. Examples are the "Affect Balance Scale (ABS)" by Bradburn (1969), the "Quality of Well-Being Scale (QWBS)" by Kaplan et al (1976) and the "Psychological General Well-Being Index (PGWB)" by Dupuy (1984). This particular development has connections to the "happiness research" tradition within psychology, where well-being is discussed not only in terms of the absence of negative factors (such as depressed mood), but as a positive concept (Diener, 1984; Ryff, 1995; see also Barge-Schaapveld et al, Ch. 8, and Katschnig & Angermeyer, Ch. 11 this volume).

From the 1980s onwards, in addition to the assessment of well-being and satisfaction, instruments for assessing functioning in daily life were developed. This development is subsumed under the term "health status research" (see Barge-Schaapveld et al, Ch. 8 this volume, for a more detailed discussion of the three roots of modern quality of life research – the social indicators, happiness, and health status research traditions). Well-known examples of "health status research" instruments are the Sickness Impact Profile (SIP: Bergner et al, 1981), the Nottingham Health Profile (NHP: Hunt & McEwen, 1980) and the SF-36 (Ware & Sherbourne, 1992). Although these instruments do not use the term "quality of life", studies employing them are today generally regarded as belonging to health-related quality of life research.

Later – in contrast to these "generic" instruments – disease-specific quality of life instruments were developed. Today, literally hundreds of such instruments are available, so that it is difficult to keep an overview and to evaluate the quality of these instruments. In fact, the content of most of them seems to be quite arbitrary and not linked to any theory of quality of life, so that it is often impossible to know what is being measured. (Updated overviews of these instruments have been regularly published in *Quality of Life Research* and are now available on diskette.)

USING THE QUALITY OF LIFE CONCEPT IN PSYCHIATRY: SOME SENSITIVE ISSUES

In the early 1980s, psychiatry was at the forefront of quality of life research in conducting studies on patients with chronic mental illnesses living in the community (Malm et al, 1981; Baker & Intagliata, 1982; Bigelow et al, 1982; Lehman et al, 1982; see also Angermeyer & Kilian, Ch. 2, and Lehman, Ch. 7 this volume). Later on, the momentum was rather lost, before renewed interest appeared in the 1990s. The remainder of this chapter will focus on sensitive issues which arise in applying the quality of life concept and its measurement techniques – primarily developed for somatically ill patients – to those with psychiatric illnesses. Topics to be discussed include: (1) the issue of "subjective" versus "objective" measures; (2) the three components – "well-being/satisfaction – functional status – contextual factors"; (3) the question of multi-area assessment and the needs of psychiatric patients; (4) the problem of the inclusion of psychopathological symptoms in many quality of life scales; and (5) aspects of the relationship between time and quality of life.

"SUBJECTIVE" AND "OBJECTIVE" MEASURES

The criticism has been made that quality of life research has so far been overconcerned with measurement issues and psychometrics at the expense of theoretical and conceptual development (Cox et al, 1992; Hunt, 1997). This theory deficit becomes especially apparent when the aim is to assess quality of life in mental disorders, since the widely accepted position of concentrating on the subjective perspective of the patient (Gill & Feinstein, 1994; Schipper et al, 1996) is prone to measurement distortions. Barry (Ch. 3 this volume) and Leff (Ch. 18 this volume) show convincingly that in psychiatry, such subjective assessment has to be complemented by objective evaluation.

The focus of health-related quality of life research on patients' subjective experience is logically echoed by the predominant use of self-report scales in this field – although research requirements are also a major reason for this predominance of self-assessment methods. In psychiatric patients, this method of data collection adds to the problems arising from the subject-centred approach of quality of life research. While the exclusively subjective approach to data collection is beginning to be regarded as problematic (Jacobson et al, 1997), it is still dominant today.

In psychiatry, reports about subjective well-being tend simply to reflect altered psychological states, as Katschnig et al (1996) and Atkinson et al (1997) have shown for depression. In addition, reports about functioning in social roles and about material and social living conditions may be distorted for several reasons, described here as *psychopathological fallacies*. There are at least three such fallacies which may distort both the perception by a psychiatric patient of his/her quality of life and the communication of his/her perception to others: they are the *affective fallacy*, the *cognitive fallacy*, and the *reality distortion fallacy*.

The most important of these fallacies is the *affective* one. It has been shown that people use their momentary affective state as information in making judgements of how happy and satisfied they are with their lives (Schwarz & Clore, 1983). A depressed patient will usually see his or her well-being, social functioning and living conditions as worse than they appear to an independent observer (Kay et al, 1964) or even to patients themselves after recovery (Morgado et al, 1991). The opposite is true for a manic patient who, quite naturally, rates his subjective well-being as very good, but also evaluates his social functioning and his environmental living conditions as unduly favourable. Mechanic et al (1994) have shown that depressed mood (in addition to perceived stigma) is a powerful determinant of a negative evaluation of subjective quality of life in schizophrenic patients. Both in research and in clinical practice, the affective fallacy can lead to wrong conclusions. For instance, in internal medicine, quality of life measures might disguise the presence of a comorbid depression, which as a consequence, might not be discovered and will not be treated (Jacobson et al, 1997).

The *reality distortion* and *cognitive fallacies* are less problematic, since they are more readily recognised. At times, patients suffer from delusions and hallucinations, whereby perception of oneself and of one's surroundings is distorted by these very symptoms. Accepting a deluded or hallucinating patient's judgement on his/her quality of life at face value would constitute the reality distortion fallacy. The cognitive fallacy concerns wrong evaluations by patients who are unable to assess their life situation intellectually, as is the case, for instance, in dementia and mental retardation.

Thus, while the patient's own view seems to be necessary, the question arises whether it is sufficient. Becker et al (1993; see also Becker & Diamond, Ch. 10 this volume) contend that in the field of psychiatry, quality of life assessment has to be carried out not only via the patient but also via professional helpers and key informants – as a rule family members and friends of the patient. Becker et al (1993) accordingly provide a "professional" and a "carer" version of their Wisconsin Quality of Life Index (W-QLI). There is empirical evidence for this position: Sainfort et al (1996) have demonstrated that such assessments differ between patients and their relatives, and Barry and Crosby (1996; see also Barry,

Ch. 3 this volume) have shown that schizophrenic patients, when moved from a mental hospital to the community, showed no improvements in life satisfaction ratings, despite improved living conditions and increased leisure activities, which were assessed objectively. Chronic schizophrenic patients obviously tend to overestimate their level of functioning and environmental assets, while depressives tend to underestimate both (Kay et al, 1964; see also Katschnig & Angermeyer, Ch. 11 this volume).

These observations warrant the conclusion that additional evaluations by professionals and by family members and friends are necessary to complement the patient's own subjective assessment. However, assessment by other persons is not per se objective and the term may be misleading. The term "external assessment" is probably more appropriate than "objective assessment", since such assessment might reflect the subjective view of the assessors themselves.

The quality of life assessment issue brings into the forefront a basic problem of psychiatry – it reflects the different viewpoints which exist in society about whether a psychiatric disorder is present or not and whether something should be done about it or not. Most often there is disagreement in this matter between the patient, his family and professionals, and such disagreement should at least be documented.

THREE COMPONENTS OF QUALITY OF LIFE: SUBJECTIVE WELL-BEING/SATISFACTION – FUNCTIONAL STATUS – CONTEXTUAL FACTORS

Calman (1984) has elegantly defined quality of life as "the gap between a person's expectations and achievements", which is basically a subjective concept. However, "achievements" do not depend only on subjective factors, but also on the environmental possibilities offered. Assessing functioning in social roles, as is done by health status instruments, takes the environment partly into consideration. What is lacking in today's quality of life research is more of the social indicator research tradition which builds environmental factors, social and material, into quality of life measures.

The need to include such contextual factors into the assessment of quality of life research is especially pressing in the case of psychiatric patients, where such factors interact with the patient's disorder more than in somatic problems. Income, social support and living conditions may be intimately related to psychopathology. There are signs of a move towards going beyond subjective well-being and satisfaction by including assessment of functional status and environmental factors (Romney & Evans, 1996). However, research on quality of life, both in medicine in general and in psychiatry, is still largely dominated by assessing subjective well-being and the patient's subjective view of his/her functioning in and satisfaction with different life domains, as the review by Lehman (Ch. 7 this volume) shows.

Katschnig and Angermeyer (Ch. 11 this volume) have developed an action-orientated framework for assessing quality of life in depressed patients which includes well-being, satisfaction, functioning and contextual factors and can easily be applied to other diagnostic categories. They show that helping actions have to be differentiated, since some act on psychological well-being (e.g. antidepressants), some on role functioning (e.g. social skills training) and some on environmental circumstances (e.g. providing money). If quality of life assessment is to be action-orientated, it has to be differentiated at least according to the three components of psychological well-being/satisfaction, functioning in social roles, and contextual factors.

MULTI-AREA ASSESSMENT AND THE NEEDS OF PSYCHIATRIC PATIENTS

One could argue that the way society has dealt with the mentally ill over most of the last hundred years interferes with basic human needs. While locking patients up in large mental hospitals at the turn of the last century might have had the advantage of fulfilling the most basic human needs (Maslow, 1954) – physiological needs such as food, and security needs such as shelter – higher human needs such as that for autonomy were neglected in this setting. On the other hand, at the end of the twentieth century, in the era of community psychiatry, patients do have the possibility of gaining autonomy, but at the possible expense of not having fulfilled the most basic human needs.

Psychiatric patients have the specific problem of being stigmatised when they declare themselves as being mentally ill, which seems necessary if they want to obtain the means for survival including their additional needs for treatment (drugs, social security benefits, etc.). Such stigma jeopardises autonomy, since patients are excluded from society, while they want "to be one of us", as qualitative research shows (Barham & Hayward, 1991). Many psychiatric patients are thus in a no-win situation as far as the fulfilment of their needs is concerned – and many give up some of their expectations and "cut their coat to their cloth" (see Finzen & Hoffmann-Richter, Ch. 6, and Mechanic, Ch. 23, this volume).

In addition to having specific additional needs for treatment, psychiatric patients are disadvantaged since they usually have fewer resources to cope with life problems, fewer social and cognitive skills and fewer environmental assets, especially money. In many studies on the quality of life of schizophrenic patients in the community, the lack of money is a prominent complaint, probably because it stands for autonomy, which they strive for.

A salient issue which becomes especially important in psychiatry is the use of single quality of life index-measures, as opposed to a quality of life profile (Bullinger, 1993). Both for the planning of interventions and for assessing outcome in a single patient and in clinical trials, a structured multi-area use of the quality of life concept is necessary which covers different specific life domains, such as work, family life, money, and so on, since quality of life might be satisfactory in one domain and not in another, and different life domains might be of different importance to different people (see Becker & Diamond, Ch. 10 this volume). Some psychiatric quality of life instruments separate such domains from each other (e.g. the Q-LES-Q by Endicott et al, 1993, and the W-QLI by Becker et al, 1993), while others do not. For economic evaluations, a single index might be convenient, but this approach simplifies matters to such a degree that it becomes difficult to understand what the figure obtained actually means (see Salvador-Carulla, Ch. 22 this volume).

Recently developed instruments for assessing patients' needs, like the CAN (Camberwell Assessment of Need; Phelan et al, 1995) and the NCA-MRC (Needs for Care Assessment instrument of the MRC-Unit in London; Brewin et al, 1987), follow this multi-area approach, implying that different actions are necessary for different needs in different life areas. A specific "Management Orientated Needs Assessment" instrument (MONA) following these lines has actually been developed by Amering et al (1996) in Vienna. This instrument also covers the possibility that the patient regards one life area as less important than another in terms of actions to be taken.

THE NECESSITY OF EXCLUDING PSYCHOPATHOLOGICAL SYMPTOMS FROM QUALITY OF LIFE INSTRUMENTS

One theoretical issue that becomes especially salient in the mental health field is the fact that most quality of life instruments used in medical patients – besides assessing functioning and satisfaction with different life domains, such as work, leisure, and sexual functioning – also contain "emotional" items, such as depression and anxiety. Some authors even speak of an "emotional-function" domain. Here, the psychological tradition of measuring quality of life by "well-being measures" becomes tautological, since quality of life measures are necessarily correlated with measures of psychopathology, if the item content of both measures is largely overlapping – a clear case of measurement redundancy (Monroe & Steiner, 1986; see also Katschnig & Angermeyer, Ch. 11 this volume).

The use of quality of life as an outcome measure in clinical trials and evaluative studies has increased over recent years but – given the lack of a clear-cut definition and the very broad concept of quality of life – there is a danger that therapeutic strategies are promoted on the basis of ill-demonstrated benefits for quality of life. One typical problem in assessing the influence of psychotropic drugs is the inclusion of symptoms in quality of life measures. For instance, the "Quality of Life Scale" (QLS) by Heinrichs et al (1984), which was used in recent clinical trials of the new atypical neuroleptics, largely reflects the presence of negative symptoms. Another example is the Quality of Life in Depression Scale (QLDS) by Hunt and McKenna (1992a), which contains many depressive symptoms (see

Katschnig & Angermeyer, Ch. 11 this volume). Such "measurement redundancy" is not uncommon in psychiatry. A remarkable example is the Global Assessment of Functioning (GAF) Scale, included as Axis V in DSM-IV (American Psychiatric Association, 1994). Meant to be used for assessing "functioning", it nevertheless contains psychopathological symptoms in such a manner that it is not possible to find out whether a specific score is due to a high level of symptomatology or to dysfunction in daily life.

QUALITY OF LIFE AND TIME

Each of the three different components of quality of life – subjective well-being and satisfaction with different life aspects, objective functioning in social roles, and environmental living conditions (standard of living, social support) – has different time implications.

Subjective well-being, which is largely dependent on the actual affective state, can fluctuate quickly; functioning in social roles may break down rather quickly, but this usually takes some time. Finally, environmental living conditions – both material and social – change only slowly in most cases. Thus, a depressed patient, whose subjective well-being declines quickly while depression is worsening, may still go on to function in his or her social roles. Even if this person does break down in functioning, the material living conditions and social support might still be unchanged for some time. On the other hand, once social functioning has deteriorated due to the long duration of the disease – environmental assets, both material and social, have diminished, a patient might recover quickly in his psychological well-being, but not recover quickly in social role functioning. Also, it might take some time before environmental living conditions, both material and social, are re-established, if they are at all.

If "quality of life" is equated with "subjective well-being", then "changes in quality of life" might be observed after short psychopharmacological interventions. However, if functioning in social role is regarded, the chances are less clear-cut that drugs alone might lead to quick improvement; and finally, if social support and material living conditions are to improve again, it will probably take much longer and need other than psychopharmacological interventions.

A second, more complex time issue can best be described by Calman's (1984) gap between a person's expectations and achievements. Which is more important – a good quality of life today or one tomorrow? In Calman's terms: keeping the gap narrow now or tomorrow? There are numerous ways of achieving a short-term harmony between expectations and achievements, the use of psychotropic substances being the most common of these. In the long term, of course, substance abuse leads to a widening of this gap, following a vicious circle which implies decreased psychological well-being, loss of functioning in social roles and deteriorating environmental and social living conditions. In psychiatry, it is known that the chronic use of neuroleptics, while causing unpleasant side-effects, decreases relapse frequency, so that many patients are in the dilemma of having to choose between sustaining the side-effects "now" or having an increased risk of relapse "tomorrow". Quite a few reject neuroleptic treatment since they prefer the "better quality of life now" versus the "better quality of life tomorrow". The new neuroleptics might change this situation.

A final quality of life issue in relation to time concerns the influence of a long duration of a disorder on the subjective assessment of quality of life. It has been repeatedly observed that such patients adapt their standards downwards. One could call this phenomenon the *standard drift fallacy*: if one cannot possibly achieve one's aims, these aims are changed. Such patients remind us of the fox in the fable, with regard to the grapes he cannot reach. Barry et al (1993; see also Barry, Ch. 3 this volume) have demonstrated that patients who have lived for a long time in a psychiatric hospital are more or less satisfied with their lives (when satisfaction is assessed by a self-rating scale). Leff (Ch. 18 this volume) reports that a substantial proportion of patients in two psychiatric hospitals were satisfied to stay there, but after having moved to community homes, did not want to go back into the hospital – probably because of the increased autonomy they re-experienced in the community, after having "forgotten" it while in hospital. Wittchen and Beloch (1996) have shown that persons suffering from social phobia rate their quality of life as worse in the past than in the present, probably because they tend to be satisfied with what they have achieved, although this is far below the standards of the general population. A similar finding is reported by Davidson et al (1994) on persons meeting only subthreshold criteria for social phobia – a closer look at the data showed that they were disadvantaged in many respects, but did not find it worth while reporting this.

CONCLUSION

The first documented use of the term "quality of life" in a medical journal can be found in the *Annals of Internal Medicine* of 1966, where J.R. Elkinton published an editorial with the title "Medicine and the Quality of Life", discussing problems of transplantation medicine. In the introduction, Elkinton quotes Francis Bacon's view that "*the office of medicine is but to tune this curious harp of man's body and reduce it to harmony*", and criticises today's medicine as doing the tuning with unprecedented skill but having trouble with the harmony. Elkinton goes on to ask: "What is the harmony within a man, and between a man and his world – the quality of life – to which the patient, the physician, and society aspire?"

Both in its brevity and in its comprehensiveness, this is a most remarkable definition of quality of life. It stresses not only "well-being" and "satisfaction" ("the harmony within a man"), but also the relationship of a person to the environment ("harmony between a man and his world"), which would correspond to "functional status" and "environmental living conditions" in our terms.

I would like to follow this definition and conclude that the use of the quality of life concept in psychiatry is only meaningful if its assessment is carried out in a complex and differentiated way which includes the interaction with the environment. It should keep to the following guidelines:

1. Whenever feasible, at least three assessments should be carried out: (1) one by the patient, (2) one by a family member or friend, and (3) one by a professional.
2. Three components of quality of life should be distinguished, (1) subjective well-being/satisfaction, (2) functioning in (social) roles and (3) external living conditions (material, i.e. "standard of living", and social, such as social network and social support).
3. Different life domains should be assessed separately ("multi-area-assessment"), since a person's quality of life might be excellent in one (e.g. family) and inferior in another life area (e.g. work); also, helping actions have to address those segments of life which are most in need of assistance.
4. The inclusion of psychopathological symptoms in quality-of-life instruments should be made explicit.
5. The assessment of change of quality of life should consider the different "speeds" of change inherent in the different components (well-being/satisfaction, functional status, contextual factors) and the possible downward drift of standards to which patients with persistent mental illness compare their actual situation.

Many of the chapters in this volume address these and similar issues, and some are perhaps more theory- and method-laden and less result-orientated than the reader might wish. However, it is only if these conceptual and methodological requirements are taken into consideration that quality of life measures will be useful in psychiatry; and only then can the potential "breath of fresh air" which accompanies the concept be used in a profitable way for the whole mental health field.

In psychiatry, the art and science of quality of life assessment consist in capturing a patient's quality of life midway between the two extremes of writing a novel on the one hand and summarising the phenomenon into a single index on the other. It also has to take a position between objective assessments on the one hand and the indispensable subjective view of the patient on the other. Also, despite the caveats described in this chapter, the subjective view of the patient should become a prominent voice in discussing the aims of intervention in psychiatry, both on the individual and on the service/political level. The concepts of "empowerment" (Stastny & Amering, Ch. 20 this volume) and of the "trialogue" (Amering et al, in press) should be given more prominence, especially in the case of persons with persistent mental illness living in the community. (In a trialogue, patients, caregivers and professionals discuss – outside the traditional familial therapeutic and institutional context – the experiences and consequences of psychosis and ways to cope with them.) A sense of control and participation is, after all, one of the aspects of quality of life which is most valued by psychiatric patients (Mechanic, Ch. 23, and Leff, Ch. 18, this volume).

The future will show whether quality of life research was a fashionable and transient movement at the end of the twentieth century or a serious endeavour with profound implications for the daily practice of medicine, for outcome assessment in clinical trials and health services research, for health needs assessment of populations, and for resource allocation.

CONCEPTUAL ISSUES

CHAPTER TWO

Theoretical Models of Quality of Life for Mental Disorders

Matthias C. Angermeyer and Reinhold Kilian

INTRODUCTION

In 1969, Fairweather et al published a study evaluating a community treatment programme which, in addition to the objective outcome measures – such as relapse rates, work performance, compliance with medical treatment, duration of stay in the community – also included a number of questions directed at the subjective perspective of the patients. "One of the five scales concerned the individual's satisfaction with his living conditions, the second his satisfaction with leisure activity, the third his satisfaction with community living, and the fourth his satisfaction with the job he held" (Fairweather et al, 1969, p. 201). Several years later, the scales of Fairweather et al were adopted by Test and Stein (Test & Stein, 1978; Stein & Test, 1978, 1980) in their evaluation of the "Training in Community Living Program" (TCL) of the Medota Mental Health Institute. Though in both studies the term "quality of life" was not mentioned explicitly, the measurements used are largely comparable with those instruments used today.

It was during the early 1980s that assessment of the subjective experience of psychiatric patients was first put on a theoretical basis with the introduction of the concept of quality of life (Malm et al, 1981; Lehman et al, 1982; Lehman, 1983a,b; Baker & Intagliata, 1982; Bigelow et al, 1982; Tantam, 1988). In contrast to the former ad hoc development of subjective measures, these authors introduced theoretical considerations of the meaning of quality of life in general and in the field of psychiatry in particular. A common feature of these is the assumption that the scope of quality of life goes beyond the classical disease-related measures, such as symptoms, impairments, and disabilities, to include patients' subjective experience of their objective living conditions.

> As we see it, the challenge is to describe and assess our patients' patterns of existence. A wide range of factors in the social and material environment, together with the subjective, contribute to their overall QoL. We must assess this full range of factors to have a comprehensive view of our patients. Existence is more than symptoms and behaviour, more than happiness; more than adjustment; role performance, and social skills; more than admissions, relapses, days in hospital, and burden on the family. These are parts of existence, but they are not all. (Malm et al, 1981, p. 478)

Notwithstanding these common basic assumptions, there are considerable differences with regard to the question of how objective conditions are related to subjective perceptions and by which additional factors this relationship might be influenced. There are at least three distinct models for the specification of this relationship, which can be identified: (1) The satisfaction model; (2) The combined importance/satisfaction model; and (3) The role functioning model.

THE SATISFACTION MODEL

According to the *satisfaction model* developed by Lehman et al (1982) and by Baker and Intagliata (1982) – with reference to the work of Campbell, Converse and Rodgers (1976) and Andrews and Withey (1976) – quality of life (QoL) consists of three components: "personal characteristics, objective life conditions in various life domains and the satisfaction with life conditions in these various domains" (Lehman, 1988). Although the theoretical background of the model has not been explained by the author, it is apparently based on the supposition that the level of quality of life experienced by an individual depends on whether or not his actual living conditions comply with his needs, wants, and wishes. Unfortunately, this model neglects the question of which needs, wants, and wishes people in the target population really have. For that reason, if a patient has a high degree of satisfaction with a particular domain of life, there could be at least three possible interpretations. First, it can be interpreted as a good fit between what he wants and what he gets within this particular life domain; second, it may result from the fact that this life domain carries such little importance for the patient that his satisfaction is not affected by the objective conditions; and third, it might be that the patient had adapted his wants and wishes to his perceived opportunities, and that in this case the apparent satisfaction really represents resignation.

Only if the first of these is correct can the measuring of satisfaction be accepted as a valid indicator of QoL. Therefore, the two other possibilities must first be systematically excluded, in order to be able to draw unequivocal conclusions from the data.

THE COMBINED IMPORTANCE/ SATISFACTION MODEL

One step towards solving the problem of the pure satisfaction model is the *combined importance/satisfaction model,* which incorporates both the subjective satisfaction of the patients and with an assessment of the importance which a particular life domain carries for him/her. According to Becker et al, "existing scoring systems [of quality of life] do not allow for cultural diversity or reflect the fact that various aspects of life are not equally important to everyone [because] giving equal weight to different individual domains implicitly assumes that all the domains have equal value" (Becker et al, 1993, p. 240). In as much as people differ in their individual values and preferences, the objective conditions of particular aspects of life will also affect their subjective quality of life in different ways. Thus, for a person with low aspirations for occupational advancement, promotional opportunities will not be an important criterion of job satisfaction, whereas for one with high aspirations, it will be the most important criterion. Hence, the same degree of job satisfaction will carry a completely different subjective meaning for these two persons. Without an assessment of the importance which a specific life domain or a single part of this domain holds for the patient, it will be impossible to explain why those living under totally different conditions express the same degree of satisfaction.

Even though the combined importance/satisfaction model considerably enlarges the predictive power of the quality of life concept, it does not solve all the problems of interpretation mentioned above. While emphasising the significance of individual values and preferences, this model disregards the dynamic character of these attitudes. From social-psychological research in the area of cognitive dissonance, it is well known that persons are able and willing to change their values and preferences in the face of environmental pressure. Like the fox in the famous fable of Aesop, who devalues the grapes which he cannot reach, many people try to avoid or reduce cognitive dissonance by devaluing those things or goals which subjectively seem unattainable. Therefore, one cannot exclude the possibility that the low importance of a certain life domain, as mentioned by a patient during a quality of life interview, does in fact represent a resigned adaptation to his deprived living conditions.

THE ROLE-FUNCTIONING MODEL

In contrast to the approaches described above, the *role-functioning model* of quality of life is explicitly based on the theory that "happiness and satisfaction are related to the social and environmental conditions required to fill basic human needs" (Bigelow et al, 1982, p. 349). Proceeding on Maslow's assumption (1954) that human needs include such basic requirements as food, shelter, and safety, as well as such higher order needs as affiliation, esteem, autonomy, and self-actualisation, the authors develop a person–environment model of quality of life. "The environment consists of opportunities through which the individual may satisfy his or her needs. The opportunities are such material opportunities as housing and food, but, more important, they are social opportunities" (Bigelow et al, 1982, p. 350). These social opportunities are embedded into social roles such as friend, spouse, employee or parent, which on the one hand can be used by the individual to satisfy his psychological needs, but which on the other hand are associated with demands or performance requirements. "For example, in the parent role, one must protect, nurture, defend, and instruct. In the work role, one must concentrate, be able to withstand stress, get along with colleagues without excessive conflict, be punctual etc." (Bigelow et al, 1982, p. 350). Because of this link between environmental opportunities and demands, the degree to which an individual can satisfy his needs depends on his cognitive, affective, behavioural, and perceptual abilities to meet the demands of different social roles.

> Thus we have an exchange economy in which, (a) it is demanded that each individual performs, using his or her abilities, and (b) it is provided that the individual will also have opportunities to have his or her needs satisfied. To the extent that adequate satisfaction and performance are achieved, the individual is adjusted to his or her environment and enjoys a good quality of life. (Bigelow et al, 1982, p. 351)

With the incorporation of role theory into the concept of quality of life, Bigelow et al increased theoretical comprehension of the association between subjective well-being and environmental conditions. Nevertheless, there are some critical points, particularly with regard to the application of the model to assessment of the QoL of mentally ill people. One problem seems to be that the model supposes that human needs are universal and stable properties, even though Maslow had emphasised the dynamic nature and culture-boundedness of these needs. Within his theory of the hierarchical nature of human needs, it was suggested that the emergence of the higher-order psychological needs depends on the satisfaction of the basic ones, especially that for safety (Maslow, 1954). Moreover, as a consequence of the permanent non-satisfaction of a basic need, as perceived by an individual, for example for safety, this one may come to dominate the need structure of this individual in a pathological manner. Since many forms of mental illness are associated with such pathological domination of the need for safety, it seems inadequate to focus any theory of quality of life of the mentally ill only on the satisfaction of higher-order needs.

A second problem results from the implicit assumption that only conventional roles provide opportunities for the satisfaction of the needs of the mentally ill. However, since mentally ill people have particular needs due to their illness, for example for nurturing, protection, financial benefits, medication, therapy, and so on, they are obliged to meet some of the demands of the sick role (Parsons, 1951;

Arluke, 1988; Segall, 1988), such as seeking the help of an expert, compliance with treatment, adaptation to the rules of treatment facilities, and last but not least, proving their inability to secure their own subsistence.

Therefore, for the role-theory as a concept of QoL, it seems necessary to include questions about the illness-related needs of mentally ill people and the degree to which these particular needs can or cannot be satisfied by conventional role performance within such a concept. Further, it seems to be important to assess the patient's engulfment in the sick role (Lally, 1989) and the degree to which the subjectively perceived demands of this role restrict his/her capability to meet the demands of conventional roles (Scheff, 1966).

TOWARD A DYNAMIC PROCESS MODEL OF QUALITY OF LIFE IN MENTAL DISORDER

Summarising the above-mentioned criteria, even though all existing theoretical concepts of QoL of the mentally ill will emphasise the central importance of patients' subjective assessments of their objective living conditions, the dynamics and factors influencing these subjective assessment processes have been largely neglected. The starting point for the analysis of these dynamics must be a developmental model of subjective human need satisfaction, which takes into consideration both socio-cultural factors and those influential factors based on individual personality development (Figure 2.1).

This model is based on the assumption that subjective quality of life represents the result of an ongoing process of adaptation, during which the individual must continuously reconcile his own desires and goals with the conditions of his environment and his ability to meet the social demands associated with the fulfilment of these desires and goals. Within this model, satisfaction will not be regarded as the outcome, but rather as the steering mechanism of this process. When examining the findings of QoL research founded on the measurement of subjective satisfaction, these appear to support the fundamentally trivial fact that most people possess a relatively great ability to keep their level of satisfaction relatively stable by means of cognitive and conative activities – at least in the long run – even in the light of constantly changing environmental circumstances. This means that if an individual feels dissatisfied because he perceives a discrepancy between his individual values and preferences and his actual living conditions, he can in fact reduce this dissatisfaction either by changing his environmental conditions or by changing his values and preferences. From everyday experience, we know that humans continuously use both strategies in different combinations. Because of this non-recursive nature of the need-satisfaction process, using measurements of subjective satisfaction as indicators of QoL will not permit us to differentiate between the quality of life of an individual who reduces his expectations to such an

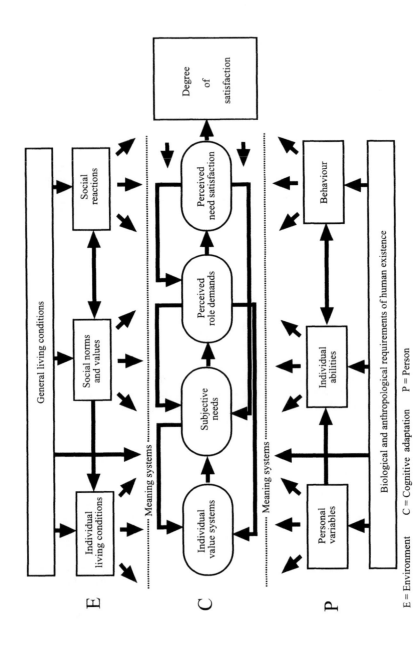

Figure 2.1 Dynamic process model of quality of life in mental disorder

extent that he will be satisfied with very poor circumstances, objectively speaking, and that of someone who is satisfied with life due to the realisation of all aspired-to goals.

In the light of the intentions initially associated with the concept of QoL of the mentally ill – to attach more emphasis to the subjective perspectives of the persons afflicted when assessing their living conditions (Lamb, 1982; Baker & Intagliata, 1982; Diamond, 1985) – reducing this subjective dimension to simply measuring expressed satisfaction seems of little value. The studies described above indicate that the ability to maintain a particular level of satisfaction remains largely intact, even in the presence of mental illness, so that the question arises under which conditions and in which form it is indeed meaningful and necessary to consider subjective perspectives, when assessing the QoL of the mentally ill.

However, clarification of this question first demands the outlining of the general requirements for assessing the quality of human living conditions. The first prerequisite for such an assessment is the supposition of a universal system of basic human needs (Maslow, 1954; Gasiet, 1981; Griffin, 1986), and, secondly, taking a normative setting as the basis for those modes of satisfying these basic needs which can be considered adequate. If we look at the different theoretical models of human needs which have been developed by philosophers, political and social scientists, and anthropologists, despite their theoretical differences, all of these systems include the following need categories:

1. Physiological needs, which consist of all those resulting from the biological constitution of human beings, i.e. for food, water, air, shelter from natural forces, sexuality, etc.
2. The need for emotional relationships with other people.
3. The need for social acceptance.
4. The need for accomplishment and meaning.

Even though these four categories can be accepted as the framework for a general conceptualisation of quality of human life, they do not constitute a sufficient basis for its assessment. When assessing an individual's living conditions, it is not enough to assume an abstract need for food or emotional relationships. Instead, explicit standards must be defined with regard to the particular living arrangement by which these needs might be satisfied adequately. Such standards of quality, however, can rarely be established solely on the basis of objective needs, but must largely be guided by commonly accepted norms and value systems. From an objective point of view, the assessment of QoL will be possible by comparing the objective living conditions of an individual with these general standards of need satisfaction within the society to which the individual belongs.

The purpose of including the subjective view, when assessing QoL, lies mainly in the fact that an individual's system of values and preferences is not determined entirely by the general normative system of his surrounding society. Individual systems of values and preferences are always shaped also by personal characteristics and individual experiences. Disregarding this subjective aspect of QoL would neglect the fundamental principle that in pluralistic societies, everyone has the right to achieve happiness in his own fashion. The central problem of including the subjective viewpoint in the assessment of QoL is that due to the dynamic nature of the need satisfaction process described above, individual systems of values and preferences can be the result of coercive environmental or personal conditions which are also incompatible with the principle of personal freedom. If, for example, an individual who has grown up under deprived material or psychosocial conditions expresses a very low aspirational level, it would be inappropriate to interpret his/her relative satisfaction with these conditions as an expression of the individual value system, and therefore to assess the quality of the living arrangements as good. To solve this problem, it seems necessary to define criteria which assess the quality of the adaptational process of individual need satisfaction itself. If we accept the universal nature of the need categories presented above, it seems plausible to assess the quality of the adaptational process of human need satisfaction against the background of how a personal system of values and preferences enables the individual to satisfy the basic needs included in these categories. In general, there will be two ways in which an individual's ability to satisfy the basic human needs might be limited by his personal system of values and preferences. Firstly, by the complete suppression of one or more of these basic needs, and secondly, by using strategies for the satisfaction of one need which lead to restrictions on the ability to satisfy others. The first form of a maladaptive need satisfaction process might be a rare phenomenon emerging only under very unfavourable developmental circumstances, but could, nevertheless, be of great importance in the case of chronic mental illness. The second form, on the other hand, will be found to a greater or lesser degree within the need structure of most people. Referring to the development of restrictive need structures as "maladaptive" does not imply that delaying the satisfaction of a particular need in favour of the satisfaction of another one will generally be maladaptive. On the contrary, in the course of their life, people must continuously use such strategies in order to deal with conflicting needs. Instead, speaking of a "maladaptive" restrictive need structure would suggest that an individual loses his ability to re-establish the balance between the different basic needs.

Before discussing the general methodological consequences of these theoretical notions for the assessment of subjective QoL, the developed model will be applied to the particular situation of the chronically mentally ill.

APPLICATION OF THE MODEL TO MENTAL DISORDER

Taking the situation of a chronically mentally ill person as the starting-point, his/her objective opportunities of achieving a high level of quality of life, measured against general normative standards, will clearly be more or less limited. Adjusting the individual aspirational level to actual opportunities in life is thus a prerequisite for the afflicted individual to be able to lead, in his/her own view, a tolerable life despite the handicaps. The development of this adaptational process will be very important for the subjective assessment of chances in life by the mentally ill person. At best, this adaptational process will enable the patient to take advantage of those opportunities for improving the overall life situation which are objectively available, in spite of the degree of impairment. At the worst, this process will lead to an extreme reduction in aspirational level, which limits the patient's ability to satisfy even the most elementary human needs.

When considering the possible influencing factors this adaptational process, it is important to differentiate between the factors directly resulting from mental illness and those resulting from environmental conditions, including social reactions to the mentally ill. Factors directly related to the illness, such as the time of first onset or the frequency and severity of psychiatric symptoms, will affect the adaptational process primarily through the impairment of the individual's perceptual, physical, and social abilities to fulfil the demands of conventional social roles. How a patient adapts his aspirational level to these impairments will depend largely on social reactions to such impairments. Commonly, people with reduced abilities for fulfilling social role demands will nevertheless be able to satisfy their needs, since every society supplies particular role patterns for such people. As described by Parsons (1951), most modern societies have institutionalised *sick role patterns* for those members who are not able to fulfil conventional role demands because of physical or mental illness. As with conventional role patterns, sick role patterns link particular rights concerning the satisfaction of needs with particular duties, which must be fulfilled by the afflicted individual. But in contrast to conventional roles, sick role patterns correspond with the particular needs and abilities of ill people. As an example, conventional role patterns commonly connect the satisfaction of material needs with the fulfilment of occupational role demands. In contrast, sick role patterns release the individual from the demands of the worker's role by substituting the demands of the patient role, including the duty to comply with medical treatment. Depending on how the duties and the rights of the sick role are defined, the mentally ill patient can expect to be supplied with the means for the satisfaction of his material needs without fulfilling occupational duties, for example by social benefits, if he is willing to accept the duties associated with that right, such as the need to prove his mental impairment through the expertise of a psychiatrist.

The influence of sick role patterns on the aspirational level of mentally ill patients has been analysed in an ethnographic study by Estroff (1981), who found that while the rights attached to the sick role, for example for financial benefits from the social security system, enable patients to satisfy their material needs, the duties connected with these rights, such as the requirement to prove their inability to work regularly, also restrict the satisfaction of their need for social acceptance:

> The customary acquainting interrogative in our culture soon focuses on work or on what one does. How could a client converse with a stranger for more than a moment without revealing the disability-connected means of income? The client was caught in but another Catch-22. If he or she revealed being on SSI (Social Security Disability Insurance), others presumed differentness, and more particularly, inadequacy. If he exposed the source of his income but did not appear disabled (or even denied problems), others became resentful, even hostile, at the life of leisure lived at the taxpayer's expense. (Estroff, 1981; p.169f)

This example illustrates that the influence of sick role patterns on the patient's aspirational level depends not only on formal rights and duties, but also on informal social attitudes concerning these patterns. Because the utilisation of the rights of the sick role, despite its legitimacy, is often coupled with negative social attitudes, afflicted individuals are frequently forced to choose between waiving their rights or accepting stigmatisation or social devaluation. Irrespective of which alternative a patient will choose, his choice will result in a reduction of his aspirational level below the degree directly determined by the severity of his illness-related impairment.

Beyond the example of social security benefits, this general dynamic can also be demonstrated in connection with the utilisation of psychiatric care, complementary psychosocial services, and medical treatment. Despite the fact that all of these facilities have been created for the purpose of reducing the burden of mental illness, in particular by enabling patients to live outside mental hospitals, they often produce unintended outcomes which restrain the realisation of objective opportunities for need satisfaction. Based on their qualitative study on the living situation of mental patients in the community Barham and Hayward observed that

> in participants' experience of services the significant questions that concerned them about the value and direction of their lives were left unaddressed or obscured. Medication was judged to be beneficial but delivered crudely, as the primary form of intervention, it became a currency that devalued participants' efforts to re-establish their personhood and resist entrapment in an unremitting state of mental patienthood. For the most part services appeared to offer participants a form of protective containment within the identity of a community mental patient. As our participants saw it, such containment did not generally provide a means or stepping-stone to a more meaningful form of inclusion in social life as much as confirmation of their own marginalisation and lack of social worth. (Barham & Hayward, 1991, p. 69)

These conclusions, like those of Estroff, suggest that mentally ill patients must often cope with a conflict between their illness-related needs, such as for psychiatric care, medical treatment, or complementary services, and their need for maintaining at least a partial normal social identity. As one possible way of coping with this conflict, many patients reduce their aspirations to a very low level. While some of the patients observed by Barham and Hayward (pp. 46ff) and by Estroff preferred to live under very poor material and psychosocial conditions because they refused to accept their dependency on community mental health services, others accepted dependency and the duties of the patient role, but relinquished their efforts at living a normal life.

These empirical examples generally suggest that the subjective quality of life of chronically mentally ill people depends to a great extent on the degree to which they are able to satisfy their illness-related needs, such as psychiatric care or medication, without interfering with the satisfaction of universal basic human needs, such as social acceptance or emotional relationships. Therefore, in order to assess the quality of life of these people, it will be necessary to combine measures of their objective living conditions and their subjective degrees of satisfaction with an in-depth analysis of their subjective meaning system and need structures. Such comprehensive data should enable us to ascertain what strategies people with chronic mental disabilities have developed for satisfying their different needs, despite their objective deprivations, and for dealing with conflicts between illness-related needs and general human needs. The next step must be to examine how the development of these strategies has been influenced by both environmental and personal factors. Against the background of this information, it should be possible to assess whether or not these individual strategies for need satisfaction enable patients to take full advantage of their objective opportunities, and through which interventions, either on the environmental or on the personal level, this ability might be improved.

METHODOLOGICAL CONSEQUENCES

From a methodological point of view, it seems necessary that we first overcome the classic polarisation between quantitative and qualitative research methods, when analysing quality of life of the mentally ill. Standardised quantitative methods should allow for a more-or-less objective recording of the various aspects of the objective living conditions of mentally ill persons. The analysis of the subjective dimension of QoL, on the other hand, requires a methodological instrument which would allow the recording of subjective meaning structures and the conditions of their emergence. Such an instrument is provided by the various methodologies used in qualitative social research, with its broad spectrum of elaborate survey and evaluation methods (Strauss, 1987; Denzin & Lincoln, 1994). Based on the fact that qualitative research methods in the field of psychiatry have a long tradition, dating back to the early 1930s (see also Stanton & Schwartz, 1954) and have given rise to a number of far-reaching and, with regard to psychiatric reforms, important findings concerning the situation of patients in mental institutions, it is surprising that research on quality of life of extra-mural mental patients so far has been limited to using standardised quantitative methods. It seems equally incomprehensible that already existing qualitative studies (Edgerton & Bercovici, 1976; Edgerton et al, 1984; Edgerton, 1967; Edgerton, 1984; Edgerton, 1990; Estroff, 1981; Estroff et al, 1991;

Scheper-Hughes, 1981; Jodelet, 1991; Barham & Hayward, 1991; Prior, 1993; Hatfield & Lefley, 1993), dealing with the living conditions of this steadily growing group of mental patients, are hardly considered within the scope of quantitative quality of life research.

CHAPTER THREE

Well-being and Life Satisfaction as Components of Quality of Life in Mental Disorders

Margaret M. Barry

INTRODUCTION

This chapter focuses on the theoretical conceptualisation and measurement of the subjective quality of life of people with chronic mental health problems. Despite the increasing importance of quality of life in the planning, delivery, and evaluation of community mental health services, the theoretical conceptualisation of this concept for people with long-term psychiatric problems remains poorly developed. While substantial progress has been made in the last 15 years in developing scales and measures of subjective well-being, the more fundamental question of how people with these chronic problems come to assess their subjective well-being remains largely unexplored. The growing number of research studies in this area have generated little theory, and few of the empirical findings have been related to an overall theoretical framework. As a result, there are major theoretical gaps in the literature and many of the core conceptual and methodological issues remain unresolved.

The lack of theoretical development may be attributed to the fact that much of the research work has been concerned with the development of quality of life scales for use as outcome measures. Quality of life is increasingly identified as a key outcome measure for evaluating community mental health services, but its use in this context highlights the importance of accurately defining and measuring its determinants, and of gaining an understanding of how patients perceive this aspect of their lives. As pointed out by Fabian (1990), the appropriate use of quality of life as a programme evaluation tool entails an understanding of the theoretical and methodological issues underpinning the relevant measures. To date, however, there has been relatively little attention directed to such theoretical development.

The need for a more coherent theoretical conceptualisation of quality of life for long-term patients is evidenced by the fact that many of the basic concepts remain ill-defined, thereby limiting their usefulness in practical application. There is a need to have a clearer understanding of the defining characteristics of concepts such as subjective well-being and life satisfaction, and to examine the nature of their interrelationship within a formulated theoretical model. Likewise, we need to examine the theoretical assumptions underlying the measures used to operationalise these constructs. As Cheng (1988) points out, how one approaches the measurement of such a broad concept as subjective quality of life can very much influence the nature of the results obtained. A coherent theoretical framework is necessary in order to guide research development in this area, both in terms of methodology and in facilitating the use of quality of life measures as effective tools in service planning and evaluation.

THEORETICAL MODELS OF SUBJECTIVE WELL-BEING

The theoretical base for quality of life research with chronic psychiatric patients derives mostly from the seminal work of Campbell et al (1976) as well as that of Andrews and Withey (1976), in their large-scale national surveys of quality of life in the USA. This approach to measuring quality of life involves assessing both global well-being and life quality in specific life areas, incorporating both subjective and objective indicators. Andrews and Withey's "domains-by-criteria model" outlines a life domain structure, and sets out a number of criteria by which each of these domains are evaluated. In operationalising their model, these authors employed a combination of satisfaction ratings and affect scales in several life domains, to measure subjective quality of life.

This approach has been adapted by researchers in relation to chronic psychiatric populations, most successfully by Lehman (1983a, 1988), who developed a general model based on the original national survey data, and adapted many of the measures originally used by Andrews and Withey (1976) and Campbell et al (1976). According to Lehman's model, quality of life is ultimately "a subjective matter, reflected in a sense of global well-being" (Lehman, 1983a, p. 369). The experience of general well-being is viewed as being a product of three types of variables: personal characteristics, objective quality of life in various life domains, and subjective quality in the same domains. Lehman's Quality of Life Interview (1988), which is one of the best validated and most widely used instruments, is based on this conceptual model and includes a structured interview format, collecting objective and subjective data covering nine aspects of life, in addition to measures of general well-being.

Both Lehman's model and Andrews and Withey's "domains-by-criteria model" place much importance on subjective well-being in their conceptualisation of quality of life, and both models rely heavily on ratings of life satisfaction as a means of assessing perceptions of subjective well-being. This raises the issue of whether life satisfaction is indeed the critical dimension along which to measure subjective well-being. Are the two concepts equivalent? Do life satisfaction measures give an understanding of how individuals arrive at their judgements of quality of life? What are the methodological implications of employing satisfaction measures in the context of service evaluation? Given the increasing use of quality of life measures based on these models, it is timely to consider whether the existing empirical findings validate the models, and to examine critically the findings concerning the key determinants of subjective well-being for chronic psychiatric patients.

In examining these issues, this paper will draw on the findings of a recent prospective longitudinal study evaluating the impact of changes in the setting and delivery of care on the quality of life of long-term psychiatric patients. As the details of this study are reported in full in Barry and Crosby (1995a), they will be summarised and selective here, in order to illustrate points raised. Likewise, this paper will draw on key issues raised in recent review papers (Cheng, 1988; Fabian, 1990, 1991) in relation to the difficulties in using quality of life measures with a chronic psychiatric population for the purposes of service evaluation. Reference to relevant research is therefore selective, and the issues discussed are intended to question current assumptions rather than provide conclusive answers at this stage.

METHODOLOGICAL ISSUES CONCERNING THE USE OF LIFE SATISFACTION MEASURES

Life satisfaction measures have become an increasingly popular means of understanding and measuring subjective well-being; the approach of operationalising subjective quality of life as life satisfaction has also been applied to long-term psychiatric patients. Many of the quality of life scales currently used with psychiatric populations employ life satisfaction ratings as measures of subjective quality of life (Lehman, 1983a; Baker & Intagliata, 1982; Malm et al, 1981). Current findings show that these scales can be reliably used with a psychiatric population, and that the measurement of subjective quality of life in psychiatric patients behaves similarly to such measurements in the general population (Bigelow et al, 1982; Lehman, 1988). However, the majority of studies using these measures have not been very successful in identifying predictors of life satisfaction or in delineating the relationship between life satisfaction and the more general concept of subjective well-being. Thus, in reviewing the life satisfaction data from studies of people with chronic mental health problems, a number of anomalies or discrepancies arise in the research findings.

The majority of studies report that most demographic characteristics show only modest relationships, if any, to measures of life satisfaction (Lehman, 1983a; Baker & Intagliata, 1982) – a conclusion that is also drawn from quality of life research with general populations (Andrews & Withey, 1976; Campbell et al, 1976; Zautra & Goodhart, 1979). The relationship between the objective and subjective indicators also appears to be weak – a finding that also corresponds to general population data (Campbell et al, 1976). The nature of the relationship between these two kinds of indicators is obviously complex, and there would not appear to be one-to-one mapping between objective conditions and their subjective evaluation. Glatzer (1991) reports that individuals may experience feelings of satisfaction and deprivation at the same time. The occurrence of this disjunction between the objective and subjective components of quality of life points to the need for further exploration of the mediating mechanisms by which these different constituent elements are appraised. As current theoretical models do not help to explain the nature of the interrelationship between objective conditions and their subjective evaluation, it would seem important to examine the possible mediators of subjective well-being for long-term clients, and to delineate those factors which determine how individuals perceive and judge their quality of life.

If satisfaction levels are unrelated to objective conditions, the question arises as to how satisfaction measures should be interpreted. Studies of the life satisfaction of chronic psychiatric patients typically report high levels of satisfaction, with the majority of patients reporting being "mostly satisfied" in most life areas (Lehman et al, 1982; Baker & Intagliata, 1982). Whether these high levels of satisfaction can be accepted at face value as an expression of satisfaction with current quality of life, or whether they may be attributed to other factors is unclear. To use the terms applied by Campbell et al (1976), there may be difficulty in distinguishing between the satisfaction of success and the satisfaction of resignation. This may be especially the case when patients' objective life conditions fall below generally acceptable standards.

Yet despite the clustering of positive responses, life satisfaction measures do succeed in highlighting those areas where most dissatisfaction exists for chronic psychiatric clients, such as finance, health (Lehman, 1983a; Baker & Intagliata, 1982) and frequency of contact with family (Barry et al, 1993). However, the assumptions inherent in the use of satisfaction scales with a chronic psychiatric population have been questioned. Assessing satisfaction may involve a cognitive judgement concerning the discrepancy between one's current situation and one's aspirations (Michalos, 1985); this judgement is likely to be affected by expectation levels, aspirations, and comparison with others. Fabian (1991) points out that restricted life experiences can constrain the ability to draw the comparisons required for making subjective evaluations of life quality, and that reported satisfaction may be more indicative of prior experience and current expectations.

This point is particularly important in relation to long-term psychiatric patients, many of whom may have suffered severe role constriction in their lives as a result of disabling mental health problems or of having spent large portions of their life in psychiatric institutions. Low aspirations and depressed levels of expectation may lead individuals to report satisfaction with life conditions which are considered inadequate by social norms. Quality of life research in the general population has examined the effects of aspirations, expectations, and values on an individual's quality of life evaluations (Andrews & Withey, 1976; Campbell et al, 1976), but this area has not been explored with psychiatric populations. Understanding the link between these internal standards and satisfaction outcomes will lead to a better understanding of how individuals attach meaning to their experiences, as well as how these internal standards shift in response to external changes.

In addition, there are a whole host of factors, such as social desirability effects and acquiescent response set, affecting the reporting of life satisfaction. Currently, relatively little is known about the dynamics of reporting satisfaction among psychiatric populations. Most studies have been cross-sectional in nature and not informative about changes in levels of life satisfaction over time or the accommodation of internal standards to changes in external conditions.

Another critical issue is the sensitivity of satisfaction measures to changes in external or internal life circumstances. Life satisfaction measures have been found to be sensitive to the effects of psychiatric state (Lehman, 1983b), but the issue of how improvements in adaptive or clinical functioning interact with improvements in overall life satisfaction over time is not well documented (Barry & Crosby, 1996). Concerning changes in external life circumstances, Cheng (1988) critically reviews the extent to which subjective quality of life measures are capable of reflecting the impact of therapeutic interventions. Cheng argues that the effects of such interventions may not be readily captured by life satisfaction scales, which tend to demonstrate stability over time and across situations. Large-scale interventions may be needed in order to bring about any change in satisfaction measures, so that the appropriateness of using satisfaction measures in evaluating interventions, particularly on a smaller scale, may need to be carefully considered. Cheng's review calls for longitudinal studies to test the sensitivity of these measures empirically, and for further development in the theoretical conceptualisation of subjective quality of life. These methodological issues highlight the difficulties that may be encountered when using life satisfaction scales for the purpose of programme evaluation. This point will now be discussed in relation to the findings from a recent prospective longitudinal quality of life study.

NORTH WALES QUALITY OF LIFE STUDY

Employing a repeated measures design, Barry and Crosby (1995a, 1996) examined the sensitivity of quality of life measures in evaluating the impact of changes in the setting and delivery of care on the quality of life of long-term psychiatric patients discharged to community settings. This longitudinal study employed an adapted version of Lehman's Quality of Life Interview (Barry et al, 1993) to determine the specific changes brought about as a result of the move from hospital. Quality of life was one of a number of outcome and process measures used in the evaluation project to assess the impact of community resettlement on the well-being of patients. Three baseline measures were collected at three-monthly intervals from 62 long-stay patients on the hospital wards prior to discharge, and there were three repeat assessments of 34 of the original cohort who were moved to residential facilities in the community. Interviews were carried out at six weeks, six months, and twelve months post-discharge, monitoring the impact of community living on perceived quality of life.

Given the scale of the changes brought about as a result of the resettlement programme, this study may be considered a good test of the sensitivity of quality of life measures in registering the impact of change in services. The other evaluation measures in the study registered a number of significant changes following resettlement in the community, including improved social and behavioural functioning, improved care environments, and a more liberal and client-orientated care philosophy by the service (Crosby et al, 1993). An important objective of the study was to determine the sensitivity of the quality of life measures in reflecting these and other changes, brought about by the change in service provision. The pattern of reported levels of well-being over the time period of the study was analysed by means of repeated measures analysis of variance (MANOVAs) across the hospital and community phases of the study.

One of the most striking findings from the hospital phase of the study was the high levels of reported satisfaction by patients on long-stay wards. The hospital baseline findings (Barry et al, 1993) suggested that in-patients' quality of life rated low on the objective indices (e.g. living conditions, social relationships, finance, leisure activities), yet the majority rated their life satisfaction in a positive manner. Satisfaction ratings across life domains ranged from 52% to 73%, with relatively little expressed dissatisfaction, apart from finance and amount of contact with family. As discussed earlier, the lack of correlation between the subjective and objective indices raised the question of how the data should be interpreted and how much weight should be given to each set of indices for evaluation purposes. A fuller discussion of these issues is reported in Barry and Crosby (1995b). If the subjective indices were considered alone, movement from hospital would not have been supported by the hospital baseline findings, despite the poor quality of life indicated by the objective indicators. However, examination of responses to open-ended questions on the quality of life interview suggested that the levels of expressed satisfaction were more indicative of the satisfaction of resignation, rather than that of achieved goals. Expressed aspirations were quite low; many seemed resigned to life in hospital and expressed uncertainty concerning what life outside the hospital might have to offer them.

The follow-up results of the move to the community are reported in detail in Barry and Crosby (1995a), so that only the main findings will be summarised here. Repeated measures analysis (MANOVA) of the composite life domain indices, before and after discharge, revealed that the impact of the move to the community on patients' quality of life was most clearly observed in relation to the objective life domain indices, registering improvements in living conditions, social relationships, and increased leisure activities. However, the impact of these changes on patients' sense of well-being was not apparent from the satisfaction measures. The life satisfaction ratings registered no significant changes across the hospital and community phases of the study, apart from an increase in satisfaction with the living situation. Both the general life satisfaction measures and life domain satisfaction measures, with the exception of living situation, remained relatively stable across the pre-discharge and post-discharge assessment points. Therefore, the subjective quality of life indices did not indicate the extent to which the improvements in the objective life domain scores were being translated into increased levels of subjective well-being.

Analysis of the open-ended data again proved useful in interpreting the life satisfaction measures. Clients' responses to questions concerning their reactions to the move from hospital clearly showed that the movement to the community was having a considerably positive impact on their lives. Patients commented on the changes in their outlook, "*I see the future as good*", "*I'm enjoying life like never before*", and how they valued being "*treated with decency and respect*" in the community settings. However, these critical changes were not being identified by the satisfaction measures, which did not register any significant improvements in life satisfaction. The qualitative data also revealed that one of the biggest changes in clients' lives was the increased freedom and independence afforded by the care regimes in the community settings. Constructs such as autonomy and perceived control emerged as important determinants of subjective well-being for respondents in the present study. They made quite strong statements concerning how their lives had changed, such as: "*I feel I'm in control*", "*I can be my own boss*". Awareness of the importance of these constructs seems to have been triggered by the change in care regime from hospital to the community. However, since neither of these constructs was measured directly by the life domain indices, an appreciation of this change in the client's life view would not have been evident from examination of the satisfaction ratings alone. These constructs also provide an important link between the process and outcome measures, in showing how the changes observed in the settings and the process of care had impacted on patients' lives. Their reports of increased freedom and independence matched the findings from the study concerning improved care environments and more liberal and client-orientated care regimes (Crosby et al, 1995).

These findings underscore the need to consider issues of personal autonomy and perceived control as being central to the effort of assessing perceived quality of life, as they are clearly of considerable importance to people with chronic mental health problems who are service-dependent. However, evidence for this outcome in the present study emerges largely from the qualitative data, rather than from the life domain indices. Future studies of the quality of life of chronic patients may aim to assess perceptions of individual autonomy and to include a measure of perceived control. Although implied in some of the life domain scales, the addition of items specifically dealing with independence or freedom would increase the content validity of the quality of life scales for a chronic population.

Consideration of these findings has a number of important methodological and theoretical implications for future work in this area. There is a need to develop a fuller understanding of the appraisal process involved in self-assessed judgements of quality of life by this client group. It is important that further developments in the measurement of quality of life be informed by a coherent theoretical model of the process of appraisal and the type of mediating variables which need to be taken into account. There is a need to study the factors which mediate changes in subjective quality of life, and the criteria that are being used to measure subjective well-being may also need to be re-examined. Despite the emphasis given to the concept of life satisfaction in the quality of life literature, it may be advisable to move away from a reliance on satisfaction as the sole dimension along which subjective well-being should be measured. As discussed earlier in relation to the hospital baseline findings, the construct of satisfaction is influenced by a whole host of cognitive and affective factors, many of which directly affect the lives of chronic psychiatric patients: restricted life experiences, low aspirations, limited expectations, atypical social comparison standards as a result of institutional living, and generally a life history hampered by chronic psychiatric problems and high levels of dependency. It would therefore seem critical at this stage to review how the concept of subjective well-being is operationalised. While life satisfaction may indeed be an important component of subjective well-being, we may need to explore other dimensions and consider the role of other constructs which might act as mediators of subjective well-being for chronic patients. The present study highlights the importance of concepts such as perceived control and personal autonomy in mediating the impact of changes in external life conditions on the subjective experience of clients' well-being.

MEDIATORS OF SUBJECTIVE QUALITY OF LIFE

In seeking to understand the process of how people arrive at their judgements of quality of life, there is some theoretical and empirical justification for exploring broader psychological concepts as possible mediators of perceived quality of life. Abbey and Andrews (1985) examined the link between perceived well-being and a range of psychosocial concepts, in considering how people come to feel as they do about their well-being. Data collected from a longitudinal study of 675 out-patient pharmacy users supported the hypothesis that concepts relating to quality of life include stress, control over one's life, social support, and performance in personal life. The results of causal modelling indicated that stress and depression relate negatively to perceptions of life quality, while internal control, performance, and social support relate positively. Abbey and Andrews therefore advise quality of life researchers to include such psychological concepts in their instruments, in order to obtain a better understanding of how respondents' life quality assessments are made. Gutek et al (1983) also explored the relationship between life satisfaction and psychological concepts which they termed "internal referents". In a study using survey data from members of the general population, they reported that level of aspiration, comparison level, and perceived control were significant situation-specific predictors of satisfaction ratings. Gutek et al suggest that a more general social psychological model of quality of life, which employed such concepts, could be useful in determining the predictors of life domain satisfaction. In the mental health literature, there is also a move to examine possible mediators of quality of life within the context of evaluating programme intervention.

Two recent studies have examined the role of self-related concepts in mediating the effects of rehabilitation programmes on the quality of life of chronic psychiatric patients. Concepts of perceived control, self-esteem, and self-efficacy emerge from this work as significant mediating factors in the success of rehabilitation interventions and their impact on the well-being of patients. Rosenfield (1992) outlines a theoretical framework for identifying the critical components of rehabilitation programmes that enhance the quality of life of chronic psychiatric patients. The proposed framework suggests that the critical elements of psychosocial rehabilitation programmes are those components which provide actual and perceived control for clients, and that these are effective because they facilitate an increase in patients' sense of mastery. Evaluation of a model programme offering intensive rehabilitative care for chronic psychiatric patients supports the view that vocational rehabilitation, an empowerment approach to service delivery, and (to a lesser extent) financial support services are the components significantly related to life satisfaction. It was also shown that these service components affect life satisfaction because they are associated with patients' greater perceptions of mastery. These results underscore the importance of factors such as perceived control for chronic psychiatric patients and their role in mediating the impact of professional intervention on subjective quality of life.

Arns and Linney (1993) also assessed the impact of psychosocial rehabilitation programmes on the life satisfaction and self-concept of participants. Their model suggests that psychosocial rehabilitation affects community tenure, residential status, and vocational status, and that it is the change in status which affects life satisfaction, through its impact on subjective states such as self-efficacy and self-esteem. Analysis of data from 88 psychiatric patients participating in three psychosocial rehabilitation programmes supported the view that change in vocational status has a greater impact on outcome than change in residential status or community tenure. Regression analysis also showed that the impact of change in vocational status on life satisfaction was mediated by its effect on participants' self-efficacy, which in turn affects life satisfaction through its impact on self-esteem.

Drawing from the models proposed by Rosenfield (1992) and Arns and Linney (1993), together with the findings from Barry and Crosby (1995a), a proposed mediational model of quality of life is outlined in Figure 3.1. This model focuses on the link between self-related constructs and subjective evaluations of quality of life. It suggests that intervening between objective conditions and their subjective evaluation is an appraisal process involving a judgement of life quality which is influenced by variables such as expectations, aspirations, and social comparison standards. It is hypothesised that this appraisal process is mediated by a number of interrelated variables, among which are self-related constructs which mediate the impact of both internal and external life changes on perceived quality of life. The proposed model incorporates the variables identified by Rosenfield (1992) and Arns and Linney (1993) as being significant predictors of life satisfaction. This model is currently being empirically tested by Zissi and Barry (1997) in examining the quality of life of long-term psychiatric patients in community hostels throughout Greece.

Support for exploring the relationship between quality of life and psychological concepts related to the self is found in the relevant literature. Flanagan (1978) included a self-development category in his quality of life measures, while Campbell (1981) reported that satisfaction with self was a better predictor of global satisfaction than any other aspect in a national sample. Cheng (1988) also suggests that inclusion of the self domain may be capable of more effectively capturing the personal meaning that is attached to life satisfaction. However, the area of quality of life regarding the self has not so far been widely explored in relation to chronic psychiatric patients.

A broad literature in psychology has developed around the issues of human agency, mastery, and control, which appears directly relevant to the psychosocial rehabilitation literature. The power of self-related concepts such as self-esteem (Robson, 1988), self-efficacy (Gecas, 1989), and perceived control (Pearlin et al, 1981) on psychological well-being and specific health-related behaviour is well documented. The studies by Rosenfield (1992) and Arns and Linney (1993) also point to the importance of evaluating self-perceptions among chronic psychiatric patients. However, the application of these concepts in the evaluation of psychiatric rehabilitation has not been extensive. This may be partly due to problems concerning the measurement of these concepts for chronic psychiatric patients and perhaps also to difficulties in approaching the concept of the self for people with psychotic problems. However, the importance of considering the self-concept of people with schizophrenia and other forms of psychosis was highlighted in a 1989

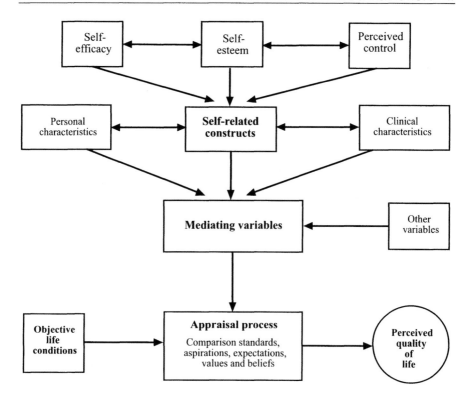

Figure 3.1   Mediational model of quality of life

special issue of the *Schizophrenia Bulletin*. Here, writers such as Estroff (1989) emphasised the importance of concepts of personhood and subjectivity, in understanding the experiences of people with psychiatric disorders such as schizophrenia.

Too little is known about how the components and processes of services affect patients' self-perceptions and bring about changes in their life view. While self-esteem and self-efficacy have long been recognised as critical intervening factors in the long-term success of rehabilitation (Shaffer & Gambino, 1978; Rosenfield, 1987), the impact of rehabilitation programmes on the self-concept of chronic psychiatric patients has received relatively little empirical study. As outlined in Figure 3.1, the use of subjective self-reported constructs such as perceived control, self-esteem, and self-efficacy can be incorporated across different life domains in order to assess how changes in quality of life are mediated by self-related experiences. In order to achieve this, the measurement of these constructs is being carefully developed, since the existing global scales, devised for use with members of the general population, may not always be very appropriate. Current work is examining the components of these constructs, as they apply to different aspects and experiences of the life of chronic psychiatric patients. The approach adopted is to ground the constructs in the everyday experiences and life issues which have significant implications for the self-view and life-view of a chronic psychiatric population.

The overall framework of the model links quite well with a psychosocial rehabilitation model of intervention, and may prove quite useful in exploring how service input impacts on patients' self-perceptions, and thereby affects their sense of well-being. This model proposes a direction along which to build an integrated model of quality of life, in order to provide a theoretical and empirical foundation upon which the measures can be applied in planning and evaluation.

CHAPTER FOUR

Role Functioning as a Component of Quality of Life in Mental Disorders

Durk Wiersma

INTRODUCTION

The multi-dimensional concept of quality of life contains aspects of physical, psychological and social well-being, but is not yet well defined. Any broad consensus on the definition and explanation of quality of life is lacking. There is nevertheless the recognition that social well-being or social function is an important dimension, although many disagree as to how this dimension should be conceptualised and operationalised. "Social function" is indeed an ambiguous term, carrying different meanings which are partly individually, partly collectively focused (see Tyrer & Casey, 1993). This is expressed by such terms as "co-operation", "affability" and "bonding" vs "community", "status" and "social class". Tyrer and Casey define social function as "the level at which an individual functions in his or her social context, such function ranging between self-preservation and basic living skills to the relationship with others in society". They point to various factors that affect social function but should not be confused with it, such as personality, intellect, symptoms, or circumstances. Mental disorders are strongly associated with social dysfunctioning, which is particularly the case with schizophrenia and the major affective disorders, but also with personality disorders.

For a long time, social dysfunctioning was considered as an epiphenomenon and a part of the disease process; criteria for the diagnosis of a mental disorder were, and still are, often derived from the domains of work and social relationships. However, there are at least two related reasons why social functioning deserves a closer look: Firstly, growing evidence that the courses of symptomatology and social dysfunctioning may vary relatively independently (Casey et al, 1985; Hurry & Sturt, 1981; De Jong et al, 1986; Wohlfarth et al, 1993). A well-known example is the patient with paranoid psychosis or manic-depressive psychosis who may function well in his social roles. Another example is the social disablement of a schizophrenic patient which is characterised more by his social disabilities than by his persistent psychiatric symptoms; the former may require a different kind of intervention from usual; for example, psychosocial rehabilitation focusing on cognitive and social abilities of the patient that are crucial for a more independent life. Therefore, separate measurement of these disabilties would be justified, so that the right choice of treatment could be made.

Secondly, there is an increasing trend to treat patients in the community instead of in mental hospitals (Freeman & Henderson, 1991; Wiersma et al, 1994), but this changing orientation needs careful evaluation with respect to its consequences. To what extent is survival in the community possible and what is the quality of life there? Are community programmes better than hospital treatment, and for whom? Therefore, separate measurement is justified for the evaluation of outcome as well as costs and benefits.

Social dysfunction as a consequence of disease or disorder has been conceptualised in terms of (social) disabilities and (role) handicaps, but the usual diagnostic systems of the ICD (WHO, 1992a,b) and the DSM (American Psychiatric Association, 1987; Skodol et al, 1988) offer no adequate solution to the problem of classification and assessment of social dysfunctioning. This chapter will discuss two conceptual models of role functioning that characterise a person's integration into the community – an aspect which is of the utmost importance for psychiatry and mental health care.

CONCEPTUAL MODELS OF DISABILITY AND HANDICAP IN ROLE PERFORMANCE

The WHO (1980; see also Badley, 1993) has produced the International Classification of Impairments, Disabilities & Handicaps (ICIDH), which offers a conceptual framework to study their long-term consequences, in terms of functional disabilities and social handicaps that are experienced, as well as the effectiveness of health care to handle these kind of problems. The ICIDH has been developed in order to improve the quantity and quality of information on the effects of health care systems on individuals, and in particular to evaluate the outcome of treatment. This classification distinguishes three levels of experiences and of consequences of *disease or disorder* (i.e. intrinsic, pathological changes in the structure or functioning of the body) for the individual: *impairment* (i.e. loss or abnormality of psychological, physiological, or anatomical structure or function, representing the exteriorisation of the pathological state), *disability* (i.e. restriction or lack of ability to perform an activity – this represents objectification of an impairment and reflects the disturbances at the level of the person), and *handicap*. Handicaps represent the disadvantages experienced by the individual as a result of the impairments and/or disabilities that limit or prevent the fulfilment of social roles. They reflect the interaction with the social environment. The dimensions of handicap are characterised as survival roles with respect to orientation, physical independence, mobility, occupation, social integration and economic self-sufficiency. The conceptual model of this classification is linear and relatively simple. It is assumed that impairments may cause disabilities, which in turn may give rise to handicaps; sometimes impairment may cause a handicap directly, without the intermediate steps of disability, for example in the case of a social stigma.

Although this classification has to some extent been welcomed as a tool for policy evaluation, assessment, and research, it has already been criticised because of conceptual problems relating to the distinction between the three main concepts (e.g. Wiersma, 1986; Wiersma & Chapireau, 1991). There is a lack of internal coherence within the framework with respect to the way the concepts are defined. One problem refers to the distinction between role disability and handicap. Both classifications of disability and handicap deal with social functioning (in work, household, with partner, children) and use the concept of role – the one in regard to the category "disabilities in relationships", and the other in regard to "occupational handicap" and "social integration handicap". For example, social integration with respect to family, work colleagues, spouse, peers, and other customary social relationships is considered in a unidimensional scale in the handicap classification, while family and marital role functioning are put in several categories of the disabilities classification. Another problem is that the individual's social relationships and social functioning on both levels of disability and handicap have to be assessed against normative standards and expectations, while the concept of disability is claimed as value-free. Finally, handicap also refers to physical and social barriers outside the individual and to circumstances that place individuals at a disadvantage. What should be taken into account here: the individual's abilities and competence, his circumstances, or both? Thus, the ICIDH is ambiguous and confusing with respect to social functioning, the use of the concepts of role, values and norms, and the issue of circumstances.

An alternative conceptual model has been developed by Nagi (1969, 1991). This is more coherent and consistent with respect to comparable, but slightly different terms of: (1) *active pathology* (i.e. the condition involving interruption of normal processes and simultaneous efforts of the organism to regain a normal state), (2) *impairment* (i.e. loss or abnormality of anatomical, physiological, mental or emotional nature), (3) *functional limitation* (i.e. functional impairment on the level of the organism as a whole), and (4) *disability*. This latter term is defined as inability or limitation in performing socially defined roles and tasks that are expected within a sociocultural and physical environment, such as those in the family, in work, education, recreation, and self-care. The word "handicap" has been left out, mainly because it is felt to be a stigma. Disability in this model is explicitly focused on role functioning (Pope & Tarlov, 1991). As role functioning is central in both models, I will delineate its theoretical structure and summarise the status of social role theory.

SOCIAL ROLE THEORY

Sociologists, psychologists, and anthropologists have used the concept of "role" to study both the individual and the collectivity within a single conceptual framework. Anthropologists, such as Ralph Linton (1936) have traditionally treated role as a culturally derived blueprint for behaviour. In this sense, it is an external constraint upon an individual, and a normative rather than a behavioural concept. Roles are always linked to a status or a position in a particular pattern or social structure, which consists of a network of social relations and communications. A role represents the dynamic aspect of a status. These anthropologists, however, made no distinction between behavioural and normative aspects of role: both actual and ideal behaviour were used to describe the people studied, and a uniform mode of behaviour was assumed in regard to status. However, empirical research showed that these assumptions are not valid and that a consensus concerning status-role behaviour is lacking.

Psychologists such as Newcombe (see Gordon, 1966) have relied heavily on interactional theory, and were interested in roles more in relation to the self and to the personality. They treated role and status as a given, and not as a variable, defining role as the subjective perception of direct interaction. This comes close to the symbolic interactionism which regards self-consciousness and the continuous interpretations of the actions of others as the motive of human action. Their focus is on the individual response, based on the meaning attached to certain actions of other people. This interactionistic role concept, however, may not properly take into account the pathological changes in experience and behaviour due to mental disorders.

In contrast, sociologists such as Parsons (1958), described as the structural functionalists, considered the reciprocal relationship or the socially preconditioned interaction of two or more persons as the core of the analysis. Parsons regarded a role as the organised system of participation of an individual in a social system, and defined it in terms of reciprocal orientations. Thus, status and role were the building blocks or means by which individuals are able to engage in the reciprocal relationship. Essential parts of such a relationship are expectations which, according to Dahrendorf (1965), could have the character of *"kann"* (can), *"soll"* (shall) or *"muss"* (must), implying the application of positive or negative sanctions in order to promote conformity to the prevailing norms and values. However, other people are important here, to define whether an individual is behaving in a "normal", "deviant", or "maladjusted" way.

There is, unfortunately, no clear consensus as to how to define a social role (see also Biddle, 1979). The following description, composed of common elements found in most of the definitions, may be helpful: *"a social role is a complex of expectations which people have as to the behaviour of a person who takes up a certain position in society."* A position is a location in a social structure which is associated with a set of social norms or expectations, held in common by members of a social group. Such a group consists mainly of people with whom the individual frequently interacts, such as family members, friends, and colleagues. There are many positions in the social structure of a group, an association, a profession, a community, or society as a whole, with a corresponding number of social roles. Role performance therefore refers to the actual behaviour of the individual in the context of a particular role.

A social disability or a role disability could now be defined as: *"a deficiency in the ability to perform activities and manifest behaviour, as these are expected in the context of a well-defined social role."* The deficiency can be inferred from violations of or deviations from norms and expectations, but it is important to understand that anyone's behaviour should always be assessed against the background of how other people expect the individual to behave. It also means that such an assessment pertains above all to the individual's capacity for interpersonal functioning.

CLASSIFICATION OF ROLE PERFORMANCE

Social role theory does not produce a standard classification of roles which could be taken into account, in order to give an adequate description of the individual's overall functioning or integration in the community. We therefore rely on what researchers put into their scales, schedules, and instruments, but the number and content of roles in existing instruments vary. There is an overwhelming number of schedules and instruments, reviewed by Weissman (1975), Weissman et al (1981b), Katschnig (1983), Wing (1989), and Tyrer and Casey (1993). Others have considered instruments for specific use: Hall (1980) with respect to ward behaviour, Wallace (1986) and Rosen et al (1989) with respect to schizophrenia, and Tyrer (1990) with respect to personality disorders. The instruments for measuring social function or role performance show a reasonable level of agreement on a number of roles (see Table 4.1).

These are all more or less well-known instruments, described with data on reliability and validity, but it is striking that different terms are used to describe the role behaviour; some instruments use terms with a negative connotation (maladjustment, disability) and others neutral terms (adjustment, performance). Nevertheless, the content of these terms and concepts is to a large extent similar, although great differences remain as to the precise wording, description, assessment, anchor points, scaling, and so on. Most instruments also measure

Table 4.1.   Selection of scales for social role function

Scale	Authors
Social Role Performance (SRP)	Hurry and Sturt, 1981
Groningen Social Disabilities Schedule (GSDS)	Wiersma et al, 1988, 1990
Psychiatric Disability Assessment Schedule (DAS)	World Health Organization, 1988a
Role Activity Performance Scale (RAPS)	Good-Ellis et al, 1987
Social Adjustment Scale (SAS)	Weissman and Paykel, 1974
Social Behaviour Assessment Schedule (SBAS)	Platt et al, 1980
Social Role Adjustment Instrument (SRAI)	Cohler et al, 1968
Standardised Interview to Assess Social Maladjustment	Clare and Cairns, 1978
Structured and Scaled Interview to Assess Maladjustment (SSIAM)	Gurland et al, 1972

other concepts such as social support, psychiatric symptoms, burden of the illness on the family, satisfaction, or attitudes. However, there seems to be a consensus of opinion on eight areas of role behaviour (see Table 4.2).

These areas describe general domains of roles and status which apply to every individual in the community. Each area could be subdivided into smaller behavioural domains, for example in instrumental tasks and affective or attitudinal aspects. The description of expected behaviour is of course different in various communities or cultures: for example, doing nothing is highly undesirable in Western countries, but may be less so in Eastern countries; similarly, taking part in the household by doing some cooking or household chores has a quite different meaning for young men in various European countries. The applicability of the role concept seems to be culturally universal, but it is essential to establish that the norms and values of the local community or of the people with whom the individual is interacting are decisive in the assessment. We should not assume the existence of general norms and values which apply to everybody; there is no general or objective standard of behaviour. Norms and values vary from community to community and the acceptability of particular behaviour will sometimes be the result of negotiations between those involved. Therefore, *ideal norms* with respect to what should be done are not relevant here: empirical research has shown that their applicability in practice hardly exists (cf. Platt, 1981). Neither *statistical norms*, nor *personal norms* are sufficient and adequate: they do not take into account the sociocultural context of the individual and do not reflect the actual differences between social and cultural environments. On the other hand, reliance

Table 4.2.   Description of eight roles and role behaviour

Role area	Role behaviour with respect to
OCCUPATION	Performance and routine in work, education, household, and other daily activities
HOUSEHOLD	Participation in and contribution to the household and its economic independence
PARTNER AND MARRIAGE	Emotional and sexual relationship with partner or spouse
PARENTHOOD	Contacts and affective relationship with children, including their caring
FAMILY OR KINSHIP	Contacts and affective relationship with parents and siblings
SOCIAL RELATIONSHIPS	Contacts and relationships in the community: friends, acquaintances, and neighbours
GENERAL INTEREST AND PARTICIPATION	Interest in society and participation in societal organisations, including spare-time activities
SELF-CARE	Personal care and hygiene and self-presentation of appearance

on individual norms runs the risk that one is measuring merely the coping style, personality, or symptomatology of a person. It is preferable to speak about the norms of the *"reference group"*. This consists of people who are in social or other respects of great importance to the individual; people in his close environment, such as the partner, members of the family, and those with whom the individual comes into direct contact while performing the different roles: colleagues at work, friends, neighbours. The composition of the reference group will be dependent partly on the role to be assessed. It is important to note here that the concept of reference group is not defined in sociological terms; that would imply that the person strives to be a member of a group to which he does not yet belong (Dahrendorf, 1965).

ISSUES IN THE ASSESSMENT OF DISABILITY OF ROLE PERFORMANCE

The measurement of social function and social adjustment has been heavily criticised, not only because of its normative perspective, but also with respect to independence of psychopathology, actual role behaviour, opportunities, criteria of assessment, source of information, and method of measurement (Platt, 1981; Katschnig, 1983; Link et al, 1990). These crucial issues in the assessment of disability in role performance will now be briefly reviewed.

In the context of the models of disabilities of ICIDH and of Nagi, it has been argued that a clear distinction between signs and symptoms of psychopathology or psychological functioning on the one hand, and social functioning on the other is necessary for reasons of causal vs consequential reasoning and of evaluation of mental health intervention. Thus, hearing voices or feeling depressed should not automatically be linked to a social or role disability. Their measurement should be separated, and not mixed, as it is in the Global Assessment of Functioning Scale (GAFS, Endicott et al, 1976) in the DSM-III-R.

However, it should also be stressed here that a role disability has been caused, demonstrably or plausibly, by physical, psychological, and/or psychopathological impairment or functional limitation. The assessment has to take place in the context of health experience or health problem. If there is no health problem, then there is no disability. One has to keep in mind that a person may not be working, not be married, could have a bad relationship with his family, or have financial problems for other reasons than a mental disorder. The existence of a social problem does not in itself presuppose a mental health problem: such a relationship should be demonstrated or made plausible. Therefore, the assessment of role disability has to be based on the actual performance of activities, actual manifestation of behaviour, or actual execution of tasks over a defined period (e.g. the last month). The focus is on observable phenomena, and not on inferences from abstract concepts such as competence or abilities that are assumed to be present.

Each community or society has developed more or less defined criteria for entering or exiting from social roles, such as the marital role, occupational or parental. The eligibility for sickness benefits, disability pensions, sheltered work or accommodation, social assistance, and so on is based on norms and regulations which define the individual's level and quality of functioning to a certain extent, and are thus a first guideline for the assessment. Other criteria are the frequency of contacts, number of completed tasks, degree of conflict, depth of involvement, or strength of motivation. Decisive criteria for the assessment of a role disability are: (1) the frequency and duration of the deviations; (2) the damage inflicted to the person himself or to others; and (3) the desirability or necessity of help. This means, for example, that not having a job or being divested of parental authority because of mental disorder, that is not fulfilling the occupational or parental role, implies a severe or maximum role disability.

The reduction in or the lack of performance should not result from personal or social circumstances that are beyond the control of the individual. There must be a freedom of action at the disposal of the individual to make it possible for the expected behaviour to be displayed. This points to the possibility of deviations in role behaviour which do not result from the individual's physical and/or psychological impairments, but which are the consequences of external factors over which the individual has no control. Examples of such factors are lack of financial resources, unfavourable living conditions, geographical distance, behaviour of others, illness in the family, formal or informal rules precluding an (ex-)patient from normal role performance (as to civil rights or getting a driving licence), social stigma, and the state of the labour market. All of these can influence the individual's role behaviour negatively. An example is the hospitalised patient who cannot demonstrate certain behaviours because of the rules prevailing on the ward (e.g. visiting friends or family). It is evident that these factors should not lead to a disability per se. The assessment has to take into account the influence of such circumstances or barriers in assessing role performance.

There are three main sources of information: the patient himself, an informant (the partner, or a parent or other family member), and an expert or mental health professional. Each source has its advantages and disadvantages, which could influence the validity and reliability of the assessment. The assessment of role performance should preferably rely on several sources, and not only on one. The patient should always be interviewed, although the severity of symptoms may sometimes negatively influence his behavioural report. Patients' own opinions are important for the observer to become informed on their perceptions, feelings, and satisfactions with social situations, as well as actual behaviour. The informant – partner, parent, or friend – is also influenced by the patient's symptoms to a certain extent. Information on (dis)agreements and on the evaluation of the patient's behaviour is of value, for example if an informant is mostly acquainted with only some roles. One has to find out the normative standards of the people with whom the patient is interacting, although that may be difficult for certain groups, such as those who live alone. An expert or a mental health professional has to be chosen as informant if a (hospital) treatment or long stay in hospital is being evaluated, but there are disadvantages in using these as informants: the difference in education, lack of opportunity to observe the patient outside the treatment setting, and conceptions of normal and abnormal social behaviour. In research on the Groningen Social Disability Schedule in psychiatric patients (Kraaijkamp, 1992) we found that the influence of the informant on the ratings is substantial: an 8–29% change in the ratings, mostly in the direction of greater disability, compared to those based on the patient's report only. This occurred more often in the role areas of family, parenthood, and social relationship with friends and acquaintances. It was felt that the use of an informant rectified social desirable response of the individual and made social expectations more explicit. The change in ratings was not influenced by such variables as age, sex, diagnosis or setting of care (hospital vs community). In many cases disability ratings were also reduced by the additional information.

For the assessment of social or role disabilities, the semi-structured investigator-based interview is to be preferred, because it is the most flexible method, although more costly (in training) and time-consuming. The advantages of this method are the direct observation of the patient's behaviour, the possibility of getting more precise information (probing), and the possibility of taking into account the biographical and sociocultural context of the individual. Another implication of this method is that the investigator (or in some cases the clinician) and not the individual (patient or family member) decides the presence or absence of a disability. This method might therefore be called "objective", in contrast to the "subjective" approach of the patient's self-report or response to standardised scales.

SOME EMPIRICAL CONSIDERATIONS

Platt (1981) and Katschnig (1983) were fairly pessimistic about the state of the art with respect to measuring social adjustment, because of the lack of agreed social norms, and the unwarranted assumptions, variability of expectations, number of relevant roles, and lack of validity. However, this is not so much the case now. Reliability research (using the Groningen Social Desirability Schedule in psychiatric patients) on social role disabilities among a stratified sample of 131 patients from various mental health services and 26 control persons from general practice (Kraaijkamp, 1992) showed a high level of agreement on the assessment of disabilities. The interrater (observation as well as audiotape) and test–retest reliability (observation) as measured by Kappa, intraclass correlation, Finn's r and proportion of agreement demonstrated that all eight social role areas (see Table 4.2) were rated as reliable (all $K > 0.40$) and that these results were robust. The use of an informant influenced the reliability of the ratings only marginally. Factor-analysis and (Mokken) hierarchical scaling methods (dichotomy and trichotomy) indicated the reliability and validity of one score for overall role disability. Furthermore, indicators of the biographical and sociocultural context of the individual such as age, sex, education, and occupation were hardly related to role disabilities. There were minor exceptions: women do function slightly better in the social role ($N = 157$; t-test; $p = 0.03$); older ($r < -0.23$) and higher professional ($r < -0.18$) people appear to have less general (and some specific) role disabilities, which means that only a small part of the variance could be explained by age and profession. This signifies also that the sociodemographic background of the patients has been adequately taken into account, and that the assessment is not being biased by factors of intellect or social class.

An important finding in this reliability study was that neither specific nor general role disabilities differentiated between four "broad" diagnostic groups (alcohol and drug dependency, affective and non-affective psychoses, neurosis and personality disorders), but did so between settings of care. The intensity of care ranged from a psychiatric hospital (most intensive), via a psychiatric department of a general hospital, a day hospital, and out-patient care to general medical practice (for the control patients as the least intensive): disability scores decreased significantly in that order ($F = 20.1$, $p < 0.001$). This indicates that treatment is probably more related to social dysfunctioning than to diagnosis per se. A final point to stress is that role disabilities are amenable to change due to treatment. But it has also been demonstrated that for many patients, these disabilities are much more persistent than symptoms and therefore typify their situation of disablement. This latter finding is obvious among patients with schizophrenia and affective psychoses (two-year follow-up; Wiersma et al, 1995) or with alcohol amnestic disorder (three-year follow-up; Blansjaar et al. 1992), but also among patients with "minor" psychiatric disorders in primary care (Ormel et al, 1994).

CONCLUSION

Disability in social role functioning or role performance deserves its own place in a classification of (consequences of) diseases, for its significance in the study of the origins and course of psychiatric symptoms, in the choice of treatment and rehabilitation and in the evaluation of the use of mental health services. For the sake of clarity, it should not be mixed with other concepts such as symptoms, social support, adverse social circumstances, unemployment, homelessness, or personality. A preliminary axis of social function has been recently introduced by the WHO (1997) which covers four distinct areas: (1) personal care and survival; (2) occupational functioning (role of worker, student or homemaker); (3) functioning with family (interaction with spouse, parent, children, other relatives); and (4) broader social behaviour (other roles and activities). Essentially, this comprises all the areas listed in Table 4.2, but condensed into four categories.

The extended model of disability – combining the framework of Nagi (1969, 1991) and the WHO/ICIDH – may be useful in this context, because it also comprises the concept of risk factors (biological, environmental, and lifestyle) and that of quality of life (Pope & Tarlov, 1991). Both have an interaction with the disabling process of pathology, impairment, functional limitation, and resulting disability. The concept of quality of life has been loosely described as total well-being, with reference to the WHO definition of health as a state of complete physical, mental, and social well-being. Components or dimensions are the performance of social roles, the physical and emotional status, social interactions, the intellectual functioning, economic status, and subjective health status, as well as aspects of personal well-being not related to health. Work by the WHO (1993a; Kuyken & Orley, 1994) concerning the instrumental development of quality of life, which is defined as *an individual's perception of their position in life in the context of the culture and value systems in which they live and in relation to their goals, expectations, standards and concerns,* is currently in progress. This instrument covers six broad domains: (1) physical; (2) psychological; (3) levels of independence; (4) social relationships; (5) environment; and (6) spiritual. It focuses upon the individual's "perceived" quality of life. This "subjective" approach is in contrast to our concept of role disabilities, which relies on "objective" assessments.

About 15 years ago, social adjustment was considered an umbrella concept encompassing areas such as skills, competence, integration, impairment, disability and inadequacy. Now, it seems to have been replaced by the paradigm of quality of life. Role performance which, more than anything else, typifies the individual's integration and participation in the local community or society at large should be a key dimension when assessing a patient's quality of life.

CHAPTER FIVE

"Standard of Living" and Environmental Factors as a Component of Quality of Life in Mental Disorders

Hugh L. Freeman

Material environmental factors determine to a large degree the limits which can be achieved in the level of individuals' quality of life (QoL). With a few voluntary exceptions, such as religious orders, the fulfilment of a certain basic level of standards of environmental circumstances is necessary if an adequate QoL is to be attained. In addition to the physical environment, though, social support and social networks are also relevant to this question, as is the factor of social control autonomy. Institutional life inevitably involves the reduction of personal autonomy (though this need not be to a marked extent), but in the general community, the only control on such autonomy is from the norms of society. The environmental aspects of QoL have been generally neglected, and very few studies have obtained objective data which could allow these matters to be reliably assessed.

Personal autonomy assumes that an individual will not just adapt to a particular environment or to constant environmental changes, but will sometimes seek to change these conditions. Angermeyer and Kilian (Ch. 2 this volume) refer to the role-functioning model of quality of life, in which happiness and satisfaction are related to the social and environmental conditions required to fill basic human needs. Using Maslow's well-known hierarchy of human needs, Bigelow et al (1982) have developed a person–environment model of QoL in which the environment is seen as consisting of opportunities (both material and social) through which an individual's needs may be satisfied. The social opportunities are associated with requirements for performance, so that the degree to which an individual's needs can be satisfied may depend largely on his/her ability to meet the demands of different social roles. However, there are a number of problems about this model, which Angermeyer and Kilian discuss fully.

In the study of resettlement reported by Barry (Ch. 3 this volume), one of the biggest changes recorded in patients' lives was the increased freedom and autonomy resulting from their move from hospital to community settings. Constructs such as "autonomy" and "perceived control" were found to be important determinants of subjective well-being, and awareness of their importance seemed to have been triggered by the environmental change. The same point is made by Leff (Ch. 18 this volume) about the reprovision of accommodation for long-stay mental hospital patients in London – "they were living under much freer conditions and greatly appreciated the increased freedom". It also appeared that this freedom has been appreciated by them even more with the passage of time.

There is in fact an interaction between the coping behaviour of individuals and environmental circumstances. The WHO International Pilot Study of Schizophrenia (World Health Organization, 1979) found that affected people showed a better overall adjustment in developing than in industrialised countries. The reasons for this environmental effect remain unproven, but it is not difficult to accept that moderately handicapped individuals (who constitute at least one-third of those affected by schizophrenia) would adjust better to the extended families and simple employment of agrarian societies than to the complex and impersonal surroundings of an industrial city. However, as urbanisation increases rapidly in developing countries, this advantage may be gradually lost. Where the social environment is fragmented by suspicion and hostility, as in many Western public housing developments, social support is lost and the opportunities for adaptive behaviour are greatly reduced. Newman (1972) showed that where a single entrance was used by a large number of people, social behaviour deteriorated, whereas semi-public spaces – used by a limited number of residents – had the opposite effect.

The influence of environmental factors on mental health in general is also a much neglected issue, in spite of the salience of the environment as a political and social issue for several decades past. Although an attempt has been made to examine and summarise existing knowledge of the subject (Freeman, 1984), there is still a marked shortage not only of empirical data but also of well-defined concepts for it. Yet this is surprising, considering that psychiatry operates on the basis of a multi-factorial model in which genetic factors interact with those which are of environmental origin. If these caveats apply to the attempts to relate specific psychiatric disorders to environmental factors, they would apply even more to the rather "softer" phenomena which make up "Quality of Life". Neither "mental health" nor "the environment" is a unitary factor; both are often discussed in vague terms which may apply more to an ideal than to reality, and the same tends to be true of QoL. Scientific study, though, can only make progress through the deconstruction of all these categories into discrete items which are capable of measurement. There also has to be concern with social values, since what is seen as a "good" environment by any population may depend as much on cultural or aesthetic values as on the extent to which it promotes physical or mental health.

Halpern (1995) distinguishes four channels of environmental influence through which mental health may be affected. The first of these is environmental stress (pollution, noise, heat, adverse weather, high social densities), which may lead to annoyance or overt symptoms. The second is social support, which is not necessarily gained from the proximity of others; the quality of neighbouring relationships may be strongly influenced by the physical environment (e.g. the presence of many strangers makes positive relationships less likely). Thirdly, there are symbolic aspects of the environment, whereby residents may be affected by social labelling, for example of a "respectable" or a "bad" area. Fourthly, planning or redevelopment may cause forced relocation with adverse effects on mental health (Fried, 1963), or may separate people geographically from employment or essential services. An example of the last of these influences is that long-stay patients being discharged from mental hospitals may have to take whatever accommodation is available in public housing, which may well be the least desirable; exposure to harassment, crime, or social isolation may then worsen their psychiatric condition.

The question of social roles deserves some attention at this point; it is dealt with at length elsewhere (Wiersma, Ch. 4 this volume). Though there is no clear consensus about the meaning, Wiersma defines it as "a complex of expectations which people have as to the behaviour of a person who occupies a certain position in society". Such expectations depend on the norms of the individual's reference group, particularly those present in the close environment. Whilst some deviations in role behaviour result from the individual's own impairment (physical or mental), others are the consequence of external factors which the individual cannot control. These environmental circumstances include unfavourable living conditions, geographical distance from social support, and the availability of employment. Wiersma refers to the development of an extended model of disability which assumes the presence of risk factors including biological, environmental, and those relating to lifestyle. The use of such a model should result in environmental factors being more widely recognised than in the past.

COMPARISON OF ENVIRONMENTS

A landmark study by Wing and Brown (1970) examined the adverse effects on schizophrenic patients of a prolonged stay in three varying British mental hospitals, with the object of finding ways in which these effects could be counteracted and prevented. They concluded that a substantial proportion of the morbidity shown by such patients was a product of their environment, and that the social pressures which acted to produce this extra morbidity could be counteracted to some extent by the efforts of the hospital staff. "Environmental poverty" (e.g. lack of personal possessions, interesting activities, and contacts with the outside world) was very highly correlated with the "clinical poverty syndrome" of social withdrawal, flatness of affect, and poverty of speech. Both types of poverty became more intense with increased length of stay, while the longer a patient had been in hospital, the more likely it was that he or she would wish to remain there or would be indifferent about leaving.

These authors defined "institutionalism" as the gradual acceptance of and contentment with the values and routine of an institution, so that the person no longer wishes to live any other sort of life. Whilst this can sometimes be an adaptive attitude, it can also prevent individuals from improving their level of functioning and cause them to remain more dependent than is really necessary. In principle, institutionalism in mental hospitals is no different from that in other institutions, such as hostels or group homes, but it might be seen in its most severe form in long-stay schizophrenic patients, because of their vulnerability to social understimulation. If they are living in wards containing large numbers, this process is likely to be reinforced, because it becomes very difficult for staff to care for them in an individual way.

Brown et al (1972) then extended this research to community settings, concluding that the optimal social environment for chronically handicapped schizophrenic patients was one which was structured and mentally stimulating, but without situations requiring complex decision-making. However, if the patient was living with relatives, emotional overinvolvement, critical comments, and hostility were strongly associated with symptomatic relapse.

In most countries, long-term residence in mental hospitals by patients with chronic psychoses is now relatively uncommon, but it cannot be assumed that this environmental change is necessarily a favourable one. Smaller institutions, such as "nursing homes", may offer even greater environmental poverty than many mental hospitals, while patients discharged to live on their own may be equally deprived of social support and stimulation. Rather than being concerned primarily with the run-down of psychiatric hospitals, true "deinstitutionalisation" should have as its major objectives the improvement of patients' clinical state and quality of life, through resettlement in the community. One of the unfortunate results of these changes, with the loss of long-stay or medium-stay accommodation, is that chronically handicapped patients may remain for long periods on admission wards. As Bridges et al (1994) point out, this is a very unsuitable environment for such people: the ward atmosphere will often be too arousing and disruptive, so that relapse may be provoked; ward staff may concentrate their time and interest on the acute patients; and the maintenance of a consistent rehabilitation programme may be impossible. However, "deinstitutionalisation" has been an expression of major cultural and political processes, and is unlikely to be influenced by any evidence that it is often working badly.

Shepherd et al (1996) point out that over the past 30 years, there have been profound changes in the pattern of residential care for people with long-term psychiatric problems. These changes have been mainly associated with the reduction of beds in mental hospitals, which usually results in the less disabled patients leaving hospital first, so that those with the most severe difficulties fill the remaining accommodation. At the same time, in Britain and most other industrialised countries, there has been a considerable expansion of residential care in the community, though in a great variety of settings. Whilst it has been argued (Davidge et al, 1993) that the overall result of these changes is to leave the number of beds available to the mentally ill unaltered, this assumes that a bed in a fully staffed hospital is equivalent to one in a home operated for profit by unqualified persons. Any such assumption is clearly wrong, but in most countries, little systematic information is available about the range of alternative accommodation for the mentally ill outside hospitals.

Shepherd et al (1996) compared a random sample of community residential homes with a sample of hospital rehabilitation wards, both in outer London; the "general acceptability of the environment" was assessed in each case. The hospital wards were all in old buildings, which had mostly been neglected; basic provision for privacy and the care of personal possessions was generally absent. In the community homes, standards were variable, but they were generally clean and pleasant, with a more "homely" atmosphere than any of the hospital wards. Overall, the most disabled residents were still living in hospital, in the worst accommodation, receiving the poorest quality of care, and often expressing the most dissatisfaction with their living situation. Those who had recently moved from long-stay hospitals particularly appreciated the improved quality of their new accommodation, especially in non-private-sector homes. The usual restrictions of hospital settings may result partly from their having to look after a very disabled group of residents, but may also be related to the training and attitudes of staff. Therefore, better training could result in an improved quality of life for the patients in their care.

Amongst those affected by chronic mental illness in every population, there is a relatively small number of people who are disabled by chronic psychosis or organic brain syndromes and who cannot be safely managed in any community setting. They need 24-hour nursing care for prolonged periods, as well as an appropriate rehabilitation programme, but do not need to be resident within a hospital. Some will be long-stay patients from mental hospitals, some may come directly from the community, and others will have failed to settle in sheltered accommodation. It is necessary for these people to remain in a hospital unit, where they can receive intensive rehabilitation and where disturbed or violent behaviour can be controlled without danger to other patients, staff, or the general community. Here, extra nursing or medical help can be obtained quickly, some secure accommodation is available, and there is spatial separation from the local community (which benefits both them and the patients).

One facility designed to meet this need in Britain is the "hospital hostel". These units have been developed in domestic settings within the community – usually a large old house – and may be operated by health services alone or in partnership with voluntary organisations. No time limit is specified for a resident to remain, but if any shows severe behavioural problems which cannot be safely managed there, a return to hospital may be unavoidable. Oliver (1991a) compared the QoL of "hospital hostel" residents with that of similar people residing in group homes, conventional hostels, or supervised lodgings. As people moved from hospital to a less restrictive setting, there was a trend for aspects of their QoL to improve; most residents were generally satisfied with their current living conditions. It was concluded that all these forms of residential support should be seen as elements in a spectrum of provision for patients with varying needs.

As mentioned above, it is undesirable for patients of this kind to be housed on acute psychiatric wards, but a long-stay unit of this kind can still show special concern for their QoL. Space around the unit should allow some freedom of movement, without risk to people outside the hospital, and the accommodation should be more of a domestic than an institutional type. There should be ready access to the occupational and recreational activities of a rehabilitation service, as well as to community accommodation (e.g. a hospital hostel) when any patient is ready to try resettlement outside.

Simpson et al (1989) point out that when the populations of different kinds of facilities are being compared, there must be control for their levels of severe psychopathology; otherwise, apparent benefits from living in one or another "may be illusory, reflecting only differing population characteristics". Also, "very severe forms of psychopathology affect the cognitive processes involved in the perception and evaluation of personal experiences" (Oliver et al, 1996), so that in these cases, greater importance may have to be given to the objective assessments of staff or independent observers than to patients' subjective ratings. Nevertheless, some interesting findings emerged from a comparison of patients' assessments of their QoL in a general hospital-based service in Manchester (UK) with those of patients treated by the community mental health service in Boulder (USA). The significant differences (at the 0.05 level) were that hospital patients in Manchester were significantly less happy about their personal safety than those in the acute treatment unit in Boulder, which is a converted house. These Manchester patients were also less happy about their living situation than those receiving out-patient case management in Boulder, as well as group home residents in Manchester (Warner & Huxley, 1993).

ENVIRONMENT OF DISCHARGED PATIENTS

Until the 1970s, there had been little research on the effects either of physical characteristics of the environment or of the conditions within different living settings on discharged patients' level of functioning and length of stay within the community. However, it is now widely recognised that these latter have been found to be influenced by the social–emotional circumstances of the home, such as social support and interpersonal stress. Wing (1986) has emphasised that the quality of life of those affected by chronic psychoses is often undermined by material disadvantages which tend to accumulate over time. These can include poverty, poor housing, homelessness, unemployment or poor opportunities for meaningful activities (work-related or recreational), as well as lack of a supportive social network and appropriate services. A study of discharged patients from the psychiatric hospitals in York, in the north of England, found that different kinds of facilities fulfilled different needs for these individuals. Mental hospitals were the best at providing for patients' basic survival needs, for their health care, and for their general activities (Jones et al, 1986).

Focusing on the question of living environments, Oliver et al (1996) point out that people who suffer from schizophrenia over a long period have a range of needs for accommodation, which arise in various ways – "There are those who are actually homeless; those who are inappropriately hospitalised; those lodging in inappropriate residential settings; and some who are at risk of eviction because of the consequences of intolerable and persistent forms of psychopathology and disability." Whilst it may be generally agreed that any given area covered by a psychiatric service should have a spectrum of residential provision for those suffering from chronic mental illness, the degree to which this actually exists anywhere will clearly depend on many factors, both local and national.

However, the residential accommodation will be unable to function effectively for long unless closely linked to a clinical service which also has a range of facilities, capable of dealing with even the most severely disabled and disturbed patients. These will include acute admission and long-term, high-dependency units in hospital, while in the community, there should be "hospital hostels", conventional hostels, group homes, supervised lodgings, and residential units with only part-time support staff (Oliver & Mohamad, 1992).

It was pointed out earlier that the community-based accommodation available to many severely disabled people is usually sited in inner-city areas. Oliver et al (1996) comment that the advantages of this policy may include cheaper rents and lower costs for travelling to various amenities and services. "However, the disadvantages may include having to live in poorly maintained and substandard buildings, coping with neighbourhood problems, and difficulties in getting household insurance. Even when residential units are available, their design, size, operational policies and forms of care may not be appropriate for the needs of their residents."

A linkage between social support and the course of serious psychiatric disorder is proposed by Goldstein and Caton (1983), who followed-up for one year 119 schizophrenic individuals with a history of multiple admissions, returning to a variety of living arrangements in poor areas of New York City. In this study, patients' living arrangements were separated into six categories (e.g. with parents, or alone in the patient's own flat), but these categories were found to have no significant differential effect on the rate of readmission, level of clinical functioning, or degree of adjustment in the community. Similarly, no major social or clinical differences were found between those living with their families and those who had a solitary domestic environment: the latter experienced less interpersonal stress, but clearly had poorer social support. Although some patients changed their home during the course of the year, the new environments tended to be quite similar to the old ones.

In this study, outcome over the year was more strongly predicted by social support and interpersonal stress within the home than by the use of available treatment services, those patients who were in high stress/poor social support environments having the highest risk of readmission. Goldstein and Caton conclude that since interpersonal stress and degree of social support are strong predictors of rehospitalisation, regardless of the patient's type of living arrangement, the most valuable community care resource might be natural support environments such as families. In that case, help to improve these family situations should perhaps have more priority for resources than is usually the case. These results were open to some selection bias, for instance through living arrangements not being randomly assigned, and it is possible that more effective treatment services than the ones available to these particular patients would have shown a stronger effect on outcome. Nevertheless, this New York study does indicate an important direction for further research.

Also in New York, Cohen and Sokolovsky (1978) found that for schizophrenic patients with few manifest symptoms, small social network size predicted readmissions, but this was not so for those with severe symptoms. This may be because in a small network, the patient depends on one person for medication, and other needs and will deteriorate if that person becomes dysfunctional. Also, readmission was more frequent for patients with few instrumental relationships (i.e. doing things for other people), but many dependent ones.

Discharged schizophrenic patients in the English industrial city of Salford (Cotterill, 1993) were found to have impoverished social networks (in terms of size and density), which also varied significantly with gender and age. Elderly males tended to be socially isolated, whereas females were not. On average, females had larger, denser networks, which were composed of a higher proportion of kin, and younger patients had larger, slightly less dense networks, composed of a higher proportion of non-kin.

Also in the north of England, Oliver and Mohamad (1992) undertook a pilot survey comparing three types of resettlement facility for chronic psychiatric patients – publicly provided hostel, private boarding-out, and voluntary group-home. Social relations were greatest in the first and least in the third, so far as total and within-residence contacts were concerned, whereas for outside the residence, the ratio was 1:3:2. However, these findings were complicated by the fact that personal characteristics of the residents varied considerably between the three settings. For most of these people with severe, long-standing psychiatric disabilities, global well-being or QoL was essentially positive across all the forms of accommodation, but the life satisfactions of this sample could not be explained simply by their underlying mental health, since some dimensions of it showed marked differences between the residential settings.

Hamilton and Hoenig (1966) investigated social isolation in a selected group of new patients of two district services in the north of England, followed-up over four years. At inception, 84.7% were more or less confined to the home; 16.8% died during the 4 years. At follow-up, 53% were still partly or wholly confined to the home. The over-65 age-group in which, not unexpectedly, organic psycho-syndromes and concomitant physical illness were overrepresented, was most vulnerable to isolation. It was concluded that mental health services needed to do more to counteract the socially isolating results of psychiatric illness, particularly the severe, chronic forms.

Very few studies have attempted to relate the quality of care provided in residential homes or hostels for the mentally ill to the quality of life, as experienced there by residents. However, Lehman et al (1986) in the USA investigated the QoL of four groups of chronic patients. These were divided along the following two dimensions: (1) in-patients of a state mental hospital or residents of a supervised community home; (2) with a current length of stay that had been greater or less than six months. Irrespective of length of stay, the community residents perceived their living conditions more favourably than the hospital patients, had more financial resources, and were less likely to have been assaulted in the past year.

Similarly, Simpson et al (1989) compared patients in three different living situations in Manchester – general hospital ward, hospital hostel, and group home – for both QoL and psychopathology. Their placement within the spectrum of care was found to correspond well to the severity of their psychopathology. There was an overall tendency for QoL to be better in the group homes, with higher levels of general well-being, subjective satisfaction with the living situation and social contacts, and greater comfort. Residents of the hospital hostel occupied an intermediate position for QoL, while those in the acute ward complained particularly about lack of safety (from disturbed patients) and lack of comfort.

The role of a hospital hostel in a rural community was evaluated by Simpson (1996), who surveyed the ten patients admitted to a new, five-bed unit. There was particular concern whether such a small hostel, with care assistants sleeping in at night (but no awake staff) could manage a group of severely mentally ill patients. Assessment was made of QoL (Lehman, 1983a), mental state and behaviour, and staff attitudes and practices. Despite this being a "hospital" unit, staff were found to be geared towards individual care of the residents, rather than the running of the facility. There was a general trend in improvement of the QoL scores, compared with the patients' previous circumstances, particularly in respect of comfort and residents' cohesion. The hostel was shown to be taking a very disturbed group of patients, similar to those described in 1989 by Simpson et al, and their QoL in the two units was similar. The residents were also thought to be similar to patients treated in the US in a form of case management programme (Warner & Huxley, 1993) in one urban area.

In the very different setting of pre-communist Laos, Westermeyer (1980) found that the chronic mentally ill had social networks that were reduced in size, in spite of the fact that they had generally lived in the same agrarian village all their lives. Without the ability to exchange goods or labour, they mostly became dependent on a few family members or altruistic others to care for them.

Although, as mentioned above, schizophrenia is usually considered to run a generally benign course in non-industrialised societies (World Health Organization, 1979), these important findings show that the more severe forms can be as disabling there as in communities with a modern way of life.

Discussing the economic aspects of this question, Baines et al (1995) report on the reprovision of services from two mental hospitals in London, which they have studied since 1985 through the Team for Assessment of Psychiatric Services (TAPS) project. They have found an upward trend in the costs of providing care for each successive group of leavers over time, since each one has a wider range of problems than its predecessors. Out of 751 former long-stay patients, 72 eventually had to be accommodated either in other hospitals or in purpose-built facilities in or near the hospital grounds. Accommodation dominates the cost of reproviding care in the community, and in Britain, this cost has been shifted from being mainly borne by the National Health Service to become the responsibility of local authority social services, acting as purchasers. However, this study has shown that a comprehensive and unusually well-financed programme of reprovision has by no means eliminated the need for hospital services among the complete cohort of in-patients – quite apart from new and relapsed patients who will emerge from the local population year by year.

Baines et al state that:

> The variety of accommodation types used by former hospital residents reflects their different demands and needs but, over and above the care offered in these facilities, a range of other services is required to provide comprehensive support. Even were it desirable, the most highly staffed accommodation units cannot provide all the components of care packages in-house: psychiatry, psychology, chiropody, and social work services are usually supplied on a peripatetic basis; and recreational and leisure activities are still required. Emphasising that a first-class service cannot be provided on the cheap, Baines et al conclude that: "Higher cost care packages are significantly correlated with improvements in mental health and quality of life in a number of dimensions". In other words, one gets what one pays for, and no more than that.

METHODOLOGICAL ISSUES

Awad (1994) states that not much attention has been given to systematic evaluation of the quality of life of schizophrenic patients taking neuroleptics. Thus, the lack of an integrative conceptual model for QoL when medication is being taken on a long-term basis may have slowed the progress of research in this important area. As in other chronic illnesses, a serious problem in assessing schizophrenic patients' QoL is to define the critical factors that compose the quality of life profile. It is important that only significant factors that make clinical sense or are supported by research evidence should be incorporated in such conceptual models. On the other hand, evaluating quality of life has to be more than merely the assessment of symptomatic improvement or deterioration. In Awad's view, the three major determinants of the QoL of schizophrenic patients on continuous medication are the number and severity of schizophrenic symptoms, the number and severity of side-effects of the medication, and patients' psychosocial performance. Such determinants are not merely baseline conceptual factors for judging the quality of life; these are also factors influencing therapeutic outcome. Symptoms may improve with neuroleptic therapy, but even dramatic symptomatic improvement may not necessarily allow the patient to become self-sufficient or productive.

Discussing the relationship of neuroleptics to QoL, Weiden (1994) states that compared to self-report by the patient, family report of extra-pyramidal symptoms (EPS) seems to be a better indicator of the impact EPS have on global distress. This paper proposed, therefore, that family observation should be used when studying the adverse impact of neuroleptics on QoL, though of course, not all patients have available relatives. It adds to the widespread view that more objective data are needed to assess various aspects of the QoL of patients with severe mental illness.

So far as the relationship between psychopathology and QoL in schizophrenia is concerned, Packer (1994) states that in addition to medication, other methods that may lessen symptoms must be explored. These include psychosocial and psychoeducational interventions. Improved housing, for example, while objectively enhancing quality of life, may also positively influence the individual's sense of satisfaction and well-being. Family psychoeducational approaches may help to enrich these relationships, while supportive psychotherapy may enhance self-esteem. However, symptoms may recur or become exacerbated even under the most supportive and positive circumstances. Nevertheless, intervention of this sort may indirectly modify symptoms by decreasing stress, and so further improving quality of life.

Considering problems in assessing quality of life in clinical trials, Lehman (1994) proposed that: (1) psychiatric symptoms are significantly correlated with QoL experiences; (2) changes in psychiatric symptoms correlate with changes in quality of life; (3) in the USA, QoL experiences are correlated with patients' gender and race; (4) symptoms and QoL experiences are both significant and are predictors of hospital readmission; and (5) "objective" life conditions and life satisfaction are at best only modestly correlated. The QoL interview of Lehman et al (1982) seeks data on nine life domains, including "living situation". The data are divided into "objective" (i.e. obtained by asking direct questions) and "subjective" (from patients rating their satisfaction with any of these domains). However, the degree of "objectivity" is very limited, since it may be influenced by the individual's mental state, so that the description "objective" is better kept for information from other people or from documents. Alternatively, Sainfort et al (1996) contrast "subjective" perceptions of life satisfaction, happiness, social relations, physical health, and psychological well-being with "objective" indicators such as income, quality of housing, and physical functioning.

In Britain, Oyebode (1994) has stated that there are problems with the application of quality of life measurements such as Quality-Adjusted Life Years (QALYs) to psychiatry. For instance, the emphasis on the extension of life as one of the major components of outcome is probably not appropriate to psychiatry (Wilkinson et al, 1990; Oyebode et al, 1992). As a method, QALY is likely to favour treatment of acute fatal conditions which effect a full recovery characterised by a good quality of life. On the other hand, treatment for either fatal or non-fatal conditions which produce only minimal or no extension of life and only moderate improvement in quality of life may be unjustifiably disfavoured. Treatments for conditions such as schizophrenia may fall into this category, although those for the major mood disorders which can be shown to prevent fatality (suicide), such as long-term lithium treatment, may be favoured (Boyle & Callaghan, 1993). Nonetheless, there may still be a formalised structural disadvantage for psychiatric treatment if the QALY were to be accepted as a principal method for allocating resources.

Rather similarly, McGill (1995) claims that most measurements of quality of life seem to aim at the wrong target. That is, most investigators, while professing to measure QoL, are in fact measuring various aspects of health status. What distinguishes QoL from all other measures of health is the need to obtain and incorporate patients' values and preferences into the final assessment. McGill also states that the absence of instruments suitable for measuring quality of life can be explained, in part, by two distinct, but related phenomena: the use of psychometric, as opposed to clinical measurement techniques, and a failure to recognise the fundamental importance of patients' individual values and preferences. Emphasising that most of the instruments for assessing QoL that are used in mental health rely on a single respondent, Sainfort et al (1996) gave two QoL instruments both to 37 schizophrenic patients and to their primary clinicians. The judgements of the two groups coincided more on clinical aspects, such as symptoms, than on social aspects; there was in fact little agreement between the two on patients' social relationships and the occupational aspects of their QoL.

As QoL may encompass not only health-related factors, but also many non-medical phenomena, such as work, religion, and interpersonal relationships, investigators could ask patients to give two global ratings – one for overall QoL and the other for "health-related" quality of life. In McGill's view, multiple-term indices that measure quality of life may differ substantially in content amongst themselves, but their design should be guided by three general principles. First, patients should be allowed to identify the items that affect their quality of life.

Second, the severity of the identified items should be rated. Third, patients should be invited to rate the relative importance of these items to their QoL. He maintains that only after investigators acknowledge the fundamental importance of patients' values and preferences will quality of life be measured, not just with statistical elegance, but with convincing face validity.

Keilen et al (1994) propose that inferences about overall quality cannot be drawn without actually measuring the health profile with a generic QoL instrument. In the Rosser–Kind Index, which has been used for the calculation of QALYs, all the data for an individual, and then for a set of individuals, are collapsed to form a single measure to be used in comparative calculations.

Oliver et al (1996) have developed the Lancashire Quality of Life Profile (LQOLP), which includes a number of well-known indicators of QoL; when used for assessing chronically mentally ill people, this has appeared to be useful under a variety of conditions. The Profile's internal reliability coefficients for multi-item scales have been consistently above 0.5, which is regarded as acceptable for group comparisons, though specific mental symptoms such as loneliness or boredom can be associated with inaccuracy. The validity of the Profile has also appeared to be satisfactory, though it is still in an extended process of development. Amongst the operational uses to which QoL assessment is well suited, Oliver et al mention the monitoring of patients' life conditions, which are related to the outcomes of medical and social services.

CONCLUSION

As the opportunities and the costs of medicine grow, society is being asked to provide ever more resources for it, and in turn is demanding that health care professionals become more accountable in the way they work. Swales (1995) states that the medical "issues of the day" are in fact largely social issues – areas of activity where the doctor or other health professional meets those of the society in which he/she works. Conflict under such circumstances often results from a failure of understanding between the health professional and those responsible for public policies. Sainfort et al (1996) emphasise that, whatever the difficulties of definition and measurement, QoL has become an important feature of outcome in mental health care. However, not only do patients differ from professionals in their views on the different aspects of QoL, but individual patients vary between themselves. Therefore, mental health services and treatment strategies should be concerned with a wide range of needs, reflecting different domains of QoL, which are perceived as being important by individual patients. Ultimately, "Quality of Life is a personal and subjective value" (Sainfort et al, 1996).

The question of resources is clearly a key issue in relation to the environment of those affected by mental illness. This chapter has illustrated ways in which individuals can be matched to appropriate environmental settings, with a view to encouraging the optimal result that is possible in view of the clinical and social handicaps that may affect them. To provide the required range of these settings will make big demands on the resources of any community, but it is a necessary expenditure if there is genuine concern for the quality of life of the mentally ill.

CHAPTER SIX

Stigma and Quality of Life in Mental Disorders*

Asmus Finzen and Ulrike Hoffmann-Richter

The quality of life of the mentally ill is adversely affected not only by the illness and the disabilities it engenders, but also by the reactions of their fellow beings: through social prejudices, assignments of blame, rejection, and defamation. Patients suffer not only from their nameable mental disorder, but also from the consequences of the stigmatisation of their suffering and from the damage to their identity (Goffman, 1963). This is especially true for patients with psychoses pertaining to the group of schizophrenias, whose impairment through stigmatisation will be portrayed here as an example. Mechanic et al (1994) have recently shown that attributing one's problems to a mental illness is associated with reduced subjective quality of life among persons with schizophrenia and that a substantial proportion of the negative effect of illness is explained by perceived stigma. This chapter explores the implications of stigma for the life of mental patients.

Stigmatisation begins with the statement: "Everybody who deals with psychotic patients and their relatives knows what fear the mere mention of the word schizophrenia produces. He has learned to use it with utmost caution or not at all." According to Katschnig (1989), the term has apparently "developed an individual existence that in no way corresponds to the present-day reality of the illness schizophrenia". This is not a result of the failure of psychiatry in dealing with its principal illness, but a direct consequence of a conversion of the term into a defamatory metaphor. For schizophrenia is not merely a name for an illness. Like cancer, AIDS and formerly tuberculosis, it is at the same time a metaphor. The notion represents everything else possible, none of which is good. The word "schizophrenia" thus becomes a metaphor of defamation.

The American essayist Susan Sontag has devoted two books to this problem. In the introduction to the first one – *Illness as a Metaphor* (1979) – occasioned by her own bout of cancer, she outlines the dilemma. On the one hand, she insists "that

---

* Translated from the German by William Kieffer.

illness is *not* a metaphor, and that the most truthful way of regarding illness – and the healthiest way of being ill – is one most purified of, most resistant to metaphoric thinking." On the other hand, she has to conclude: "Yet it is hardly possible to take up one's residence in the kingdom of the ill unprejudiced by the lurid metaphors with which it has been landscaped."

At the end of the second book – *AIDS and its Metaphors* (1989) – she maintains:

> For the time being, much in the way of individual experience and social policy depends on the struggle for rhetorical ownership of the illness: how it is possessed, assimilated in argument and in cliché. The age-old, seemingly inexorable process whereby diseases acquire meanings (by coming to stand for the deepest fears) and inflict stigma is always worth challenging, and it does seem to have more limited credibility in the modern world. ... With this illness, one that elicits so much guilt and shame, the effort to detach it from these meanings, these metaphors, seems particularly liberating, even consoling. But the metaphors cannot be distanced just by abstaining from them. They have to be exposed, criticized, belabored, used up.

This is all the more urgent, because the stigmatisation of certain groups of patients may not be accidental; Sontag (1989) suspects that it is a question of satisfying a basic need of society: "It seems that societies need to have one illness which becomes identified with evil, and attaches blame to its 'victims'." Apparently schizophrenia, like cancer and AIDS, is especially suited for this. The illness eludes understanding. Many people find it uncanny, and this has consequences:

> Any disease that is treated as a mystery and acutely enough feared will be felt to be morally, if not literally, contagious. Thus, a surprisingly large number of people with schizophrenia find themselves being shunned by relatives and friends and are the object of practices of decontamination by members of their household, as if schizophrenia, like TB, were an infectious disease. Contact with someone afflicted with a disease regarded as a mysterious malevolence inevitably feels like a trespass; worse, like the violation of a taboo. The very names of such diseases are felt to have a magic power. (Sontag, 1989; the word cancer has been replaced by us with the word schizophrenia – it fits)

Stigmatisation is tragic, because those afflicted themselves – at least up until the time their illness breaks out and they become aware of it – share the opinions, judgements, and prejudices of the society to which they belong. This is one of the reasons why the word schizophrenia is so dreadful to those who are stricken by the illness. One feels like Susan Sontag, who writes from her own sorrowful experience:

> Twelve years ago, when I became a cancer patient, what particularly enraged me – and distracted me from my own terror and despair at my doctors' gloomy prognosis – was seeing how much the very reputation of this illness added to the suffering of those who have it. ... Many fellow patients evinced disgust at their disease and a kind of shame. They seemed to be in the grip of fantasies about their illness by which I was quite unseduced. And it occurred to me that some of these notions were the converse of now thoroughly discredited beliefs about tuberculosis.

Numerous testimonies by relatives (for example Seelhorst, 1984) and by persons affected (for example Anonymous, 1981; Fuchs, 1986; Mittleman, 1985) underline the extent to which stigmatisation impairs the patients' quality of life. An investigation by Wahl and Harman (1989), which comprises nearly 500 members of the National Alliance for the Mentally Ill (NAMI), showed to what extent the stigmatisation and its consequences afflict the relatives as well, the way in which they are subjected to processes of social isolation. A study by Angermeyer (1987) reveals that moving the patients to protective quarters in the community in itself has no effect on the stigmatisation and its individual experience. On the other hand Barrowclough et al (1987) and Penn et al (1994) show that clarification and confrontive discussion about illness can be a first step towards the management of stigmatisation for relatives and patients.

Tuberculosis has lost its terror. For a metaphor of evil, it is now unsuitable. We have learned to deal with the illness cancer openly and more aggressively, with the word cancer more carefully. Schizophrenia as a metaphor of derogation and withdrawal has in some respects taken its place – as also recently has AIDS.

CONCEAL THE ILLNESS?

Whoever attempts to understand schizophrenic patients will be bewildered to discover in what an unfortunate way the general public's view of the illness adds to the suffering. It distorts patients' self-perception, undermines their self-confidence, and influences the detrimental way in which healthy individuals should deal with them. The patients and their relatives are thus obliged to come to the conclusion that they deal cautiously with information about the illness with respect to the extended family circle of acquaintances and place of occupation – that they would rather conceal the illness when in doubt. But this leads to new problems. A concealed illness is unavoidably veiled in secrecy. Its image is already imbued with a negative meaning, because those who have surmounted it, those for whom the illness has taken a mild course, and those who have learned to live with it go unnoticed in public.

Ronald Reagan announced that he is suffering from Alzheimer's disease. The coverage of Klaus von Amsberg's depressive illness occupied the newspapers for years. Artists and athletes reveal that they are suffering from AIDS and thereby arouse sympathy. What does not occur is that someone makes public: "I am Friedrich Hölderlin; I suffer from Schizophrenia."

Yet there are many people who are ill with schizophrenia. One recent exception should not go unmentioned. The Nobel prize for economics in 1994 was awarded to the mathematician John Forbes Nash. As a very young man, Nash had written a pioneering doctoral thesis on the games theory that later became highly important for economic theory. Nash is a Nobel prize laureate; he is also ill with schizophrenia. He was incapacitated by his psychosis for a long time before his condition finally improved. A news item comments thus:

> Perhaps the nightmare at the beginning of the eighties was dissipated thanks to the shelter of a particular social surrounding: Nash started very slowly to work again. Even if his best years are perhaps behind him, some colleagues feel that he is still capable of providing a surprise or two. And with its choice the Nobel prize committee made one thing clear: "A mental illness is to be regarded in no different way than for instance cancer".

"GETTING WELL AGAIN EXCLUDES HAVING BEEN SCHIZOPHRENIC"

Even in a decade characterised by openness, it is still highly improbable that the schizophrenic psychosis of a prominent contemporary would be made public. Occasionally, the opposite seems to be true. If the completely cured schizophrenic illness of a prominent contemporary becomes known, the sequel is not a story of disclosure, for instance, as is customary in today's media, but a denunciation of the doctors who made this diagnosis. The diagnosis must have been incorrect; otherwise, the person so affected could not have been so capable and successful. To illustrate this, a recent article in the *Frankfurter Allgemeinen Zeitung* honoured the works of the New Zealand author Janet Frame, who had spent eight years in psychiatric hospitals; it stated that she had been falsely – because she was not incurable – diagnosed as schizophrenic (Lueken, 1995).

The myth of incurability is ineradicable. Even in a concrete individual case, it appears to be wellnigh insurmountable. The American Lori Schiller, ill with schizophrenia, conveys an impressive example of this in her exceptionally valuable life and illness history (Schilles and Bennett, 1996). She reports that people often simply cannot understand her. When she speaks about her illness, they do not believe her. Once she showed an article she had written about her experience to a man she met and had a pleasant time with. He reacted with disgust. He did not believe that she had suffered from schizophrenia. He accused her of having made up a story.

Whoever appears healthy cannot have schizophrenia. Whoever masters life cannot ever have had it. This reasoning is false; it distorts reality. For those who suffer from schizophrenia, it becomes a twofold trap. It throws them back on themselves, even after they have overcome their suffering. It makes them appear to be untrustworthy if they reveal themselves when they are doing well. It hinders the development of their own identity with respect to their experience of illness.

HISTORICAL PERSONALITIES WITH SCHIZOPHRENIA

Since the schizophrenic illnesses of contemporaries are taboo, it is necessary to go back to reports about historical personalities in the field of literature, which the Swiss psychiatrist Christian Müller (1993) has gathered and published. There is Jakob Michael Reinhold Lenz, Goethe's friend, whose schizophrenic crises were dramatised by Büchner. There is the French poet Gérard de Nerval, who endured a series of schizophrenic episodes and had to undergo in-patient treatment several times; Benedetti wrote about this in his *Psychiatric Aspects of Creativity* (1975): "In Nerval's case, a fusion of work and psychosis takes place, which is unfortunately of rare occurrence. According to an older concept, Friedrich Hölderlin's and Robert Walser's psychosis leads to an impoverishment of creative power and to a dwindling of poetic activity. However, recently documents have appeared – above all by Walser – which question this point of view. August Strindberg developed a paranoid schizophrenia. The classification of Virginia Woolf remains open."

We usually learn about a psychosis only if its course leads to an unfortunate outcome, when the illness throws the affected person off the ordered path of life. How the many others – possibly like Janet Frame – manage to overcome the disorder remains hidden to us. We also do not know for the most part how it is that people live and suffer with their psychotic illness and nonetheless remain creative and capable. Thus, for example, it is hardly known that Rilke – at least according to the opinion of Ernst Kretschmer (1966) – was one of these.

IDENTIFICATION – WITH WHOM?

Nothing would be more important for young schizophrenic patients than models with whom they can identify, who announce: "I am schizophrenic – or I was. I live with the illness. I have overcome it. To be sure, it was sometimes hell. But I can and want to live with it. Look, it is my life. I have to show it. I am just as good as anyone else." But for that we shall presumably have to wait for a long time.

Until then, autobiographical reports by people who have experienced and endured schizophrenia and other mental illnesses are of all the greater importance. In the meantime, a number of such reports do exist. Impressive examples are Sylvia Plath's *The Bell Jar*, Stuart Sutherland's *Break Down*, Hanna Green's *I Never Promised You a Rose Garden*, Mary Barnes's *Two Accounts of a Journey Through Madness*, or Janet Frame's *An Angel at My Table*.

The books either have to do with reports about life and the struggle with psychiatric illnesses or are novels with pronounced autobiographical traits, whereby it is not always evident which mental illnesses caused the author's suffering. Scholars argue about Mary Barnes, Hanna Green, and Sylvia Plath.

Stuart Sutherland, who wrote one of the most impressive books, suffered from a severe manic-depressive psychosis. His step into the open – like that of the Hamburg sculptor Dorothea Buck under the pseudonym Sophie Zerchin – is also of particular importance, because as an active professor of experimental psychology who has overcome the illness, he can assume the function of a model for identification. The same applies to the severely depressed emeritus professor of psychiatry Piet Kuiper.

The latest document about a successful struggle with a schizophrenic psychosis stems from the American Lori Schiller, who fell severely ill with schizophrenia at the age of 17 and endured persistent and sometimes extremely oppressive phases of the illness, until after the age of 30. Supplemented by chapters written from the point of view of her relatives, friends, and attending doctor, it relates movingly, yet without sentimentality, a history of suffering, whose mild outcome was not foreseeable for a long time. Her book can be a source of encouragement both for patients and for their relatives. It additionally dispels a multitude of prejudices about the illness and reveals the types of reactions that confront patients and relatives. It offers a valuable contribution to the understanding of the illness and the ill people. It can help patients to find and consolidate their identity.

"I AM SCHIZOPHRENIC; I SEEK WORK"

What happens when someone admits that he is or was schizophrenic, that he even still takes medication? Probably people retreat; an inner alarm goes off. All the prejudices and reservations that are associated with the word "schizophrenia" become aroused: unpredictability, dangerousness, unreliability, being distant from reality, strangeness, confused thinking, uncanny expression, crazy laughter. ... If one is lucky, the person takes the communication for an inappropriate joke, like Lori Schiller's friend in the example given above.

The acknowledgement of a schizophrenic illness still leads far too often to a social catastrophe. The mere idea that someone applies for a job with the following words seems contradictory: "I was schizophrenic. I am now healthy again. I would like to work for you".

Whoever is schizophrenic is well advised to use information about the illness sparingly when dealing with third parties. He runs the danger of losing his friends and his job. He does well by telling a pack of lies as far as his illness is concerned. To be sure, this can also lead to difficulties if he is applying for a job, for if he conceals the diagnosis, he is committing employment fraud. If it subsequently becomes known, it can cost him his job. But if he mentions it beforehand, he will in all probability not even get the job. Therefore, he may lie, but according to the circumstances this may be the wrong thing to do. Lying is fully justified only if the illness has been reliably overcome, if the state of health is stable, if residual symptoms have either completely subsided or at least are fully under control. It is the wrong thing to do if the illness persists, if the patient's capacity to cope with stress is reduced, if he or she is seeking a social or occupational niche or a sheltered job, if he or she falls ill out of their processional activity, has to be admitted to hospital, and seeks the way back.

Under such circumstances, it is often sensible to tell the employer and colleagues the plain truth. Two arguments speak in favour of this. First, on returning to work after having overcome a psychosis, one is probably less capable of coping with stress than usual and, in some respects, is not the same person as one used to be prior to the manifestation of the illness. Being truthful facilitates the further enlightenment and engagement of one's workmates and superiors, and this can become an important contribution for the rehabilitation and re-establishment of health. Second, both superiors and workmates know one from days of health. As a rule they esteem one or surely at least feel themselves bound by loyalty. With respect to earlier performance, they are prepared to give one a vote of confidence and in a more or less adequately functioning enterprise to lend one their support. After all, anyone can fall ill sometime. Anyone can sometime need help in a similar or in some other way.

Finally, openness remains the only solution if the illness is not overcome, if residual symptoms persist, if handicaps or a partial invalidity have ensued. Whether in the search for a sheltered job or an occupational niche, or for a place specialising in occupational rehabilitation, information for the employer and the workmates is a basic prerequisite for the success of the enterprise. Mental handicaps are not to be regarded like a walking handicap or a hearing aid. Handicaps of any kind require specifically appropriate consideration in the social and occupational environments. Information is necessary in order to evaluate what consideration is appropriate with respect to mental handicaps. Otherwise, the venture unavoidably winds up through too little or too much being expected of the handicapped, with misunderstandings and avoidable suffering.

STIGMA MANAGEMENT

According to the classical definition, stigma is a visible sign, but mental illness is in principle not visible. Mental patients are not openly discredited because of their stigma, but they are discredited. For this reason, regulating the amount of information about their illness becomes a central problem:

> To display or not to display; to tell or not to tell; to let on or not let on; to lie or not to lie; and in each case, to whom, how, when and where.

In the process, they encounter complex problems. For instance, if a mental patient has kept his information to himself:

> It is not that he must face prejudice against himself, but rather that he must face unwitting acceptance of himself by individuals who are prejudiced against persons of

the kind he can be revealed to be. Wherever he goes his behaviour will falsely confirm for the other that they are in the company of what in effect they demand but may discover they haven't obtained, namely, a mentally untainted person like themselves. By intention or in effect the ex-mental patient conceals information about his real social identity, receiving and accepting treatment based on false suppositions concerning himself. (Sontag, 1989)

Such management can succeed, but it can be associated with great hardship and brutality, if "normal" people reveal their prejudices in the presence of individuals hiding their stigmas. Moreover, it carries the risk of discovery and rejection. Yet for bearers of hidden stigma, subterfuge appears to be a suitable form of stigma management. The difficulties of maintaining the subterfuge, in the occupational setting, for example, have been described above. Concealment is even more difficult to maintain among one's family and friends, where the disorder responsible for the hidden stigma can be more easily recognised and noticed than among one's fellow-employees. The desire to confide in others becomes greater with increasing emotional proximity. Goffman even believes that the disclosure of disagreeable and disadvantageous things about oneself to someone else is really a sign of intimacy in our society.

Indeed, people who are or were mentally ill need to exchange views concerning their disorder, their treatment, and the problems associated with other people because of it. Social life in a world of deception can be oppressive and facilitate relapse. All the same, finding people beyond the inner family circle who can be trusted without fear of abuse or rejection appears to constitute one of the most difficult social challenges for convalescent mental patients. Precisely what they wanted to avoid can be the consequence of a mistaken action: disrepute through their disclosure of the stigma and betrayal through the propagation of their secret.

ASSESSMENT AND MEASUREMENT

CHAPTER SEVEN

Instruments for Measuring Quality of Life in Mental Illnesses

Anthony F. Lehman

INTRODUCTION

Mental illnesses exert a wide range of effects on persons' lives, which include psychiatric symptoms as well as changes in functional status, access to resources and opportunities, subjective well-being, family burden, and sometimes community safety (Attkisson et al, 1992). Because of this broad array of relevant outcomes and because of a prevailing concern that assessments of these should include the patient's perspective, increased attention has been paid to the development of measures of their "quality of life" (QoL).

Over the past decade, several measures have been developed to assess the QoL experiences of persons with mental illnesses, in particular severe and persistent psychoses, but more recently also with depression and anxiety disorders. These are in addition to the more generic QoL measures that have been developed in general health care and which, to a limited extent, have been applied to persons with psychiatric disorders (Revicki & Murray, 1994).

This chapter reviews the published instruments available to assess quality of life for persons with mental disorders. It is based on a computerised search of MEDLINE and PSYCLIT for the years 1984–1995 which crossed "quality of life" with "depression", "bipolar disorder", "anxiety disorders", "mental disorders", "schizophrenia", "neurotic disorders", "adjustment disorders", "personality disorders", and "paranoid disorders". Citations were restricted to the English language, due to the author's limitations. Additional citations were identified through review of bibliographies of articles and the author's prior reviews of the topic.

Although definitions vary, the "quality of life" concept encompasses three over-arching dimensions: (1) what a person is capable of doing (*functional status*);

(2) *access to resources and opportunities* to use these abilities to pursue interests; and (3) *sense of well-being*. The former two dimensions are often referred to as *objective quality of life* and the latter as *subjective quality of life*. Within these overarching dimensions, certain *life domains* have been identified, such as health, family, social relations, work, financial status, and living situation. Quality of life is thus a complex notion. Three perspectives can be identified to frame core issues regarding QoL assessment in health care: (1) the *general quality of life framework*; (2) the *health-related quality of life framework*; and iii) the *disease-specific quality of life framework*.

The *general QoL framework* underlies the considerable research that has been done with the general population – work which for the most part preceded the more recent development of such research in the health care context (Andrews & Withey, 1976; Campbell et al, 1976). The intent of this line of research has been to derive a social perspective about the status and well-being of various groups of people, and the values that they and their societies place upon various aspects of life experience. Such a perspective may provide insights into what people strive for, why they choose as they do, and how different societies and subgroups within a society fare, relative to others, in their life aspirations. These insights may help to guide decisions about how to improve quality of life. Measures based on this approach typically cover functional status, access to resources and opportunities, and sense of well-being across multiple aspects of life domains, necessarily directly affected by health care (e.g. housing).

The *health-related quality of life framework (HRQL)* emphasises the specific impacts that the prevention and treatment of disease and injury have on the value of survival (Patrick & Erickson, 1993). The concept of HRQL acknowledges the limited, but often vital influences that disease and health care have on QoL, and holds health care accountable only for those aspects that it may directly affect. The health-related quality of life framework focuses on functional status and sense of well-being, but within these dimensions covers only those aspects directly related to health (e.g. functional role limitations *due to* emotional or physical illness as opposed to limitations due to poverty or limited social opportunities). Such HRQL measures offer generic health-related quality of life assessments that can be used across most medical conditions.

The *disease-specific quality of life framework* presses for an even narrower definition of QoL in health care evaluations, tailored to the potential impacts or quality of life of a specific disorder and its treatment.

SPECIFIC MEASURES

The vast majority of QoL measures that were identified in this survey were designed for mixed diagnostic groups of persons with severe and persistent mental illnesses, primarily schizophrenia, but also including chronic and disabling affective disorders and a variety of other seriously disabling mental disorders in the DSM system. More recently, QoL measures for less disabling, common psychiatric disorders, particularly acute depression and anxiety disorders have been developed. These measures will be discussed according to the illness(es) they target: (1) severe and persistent mental illnesses; (2) schizophrenia; and (3) depression and anxiety disorders. Most include the general QoL framework, but a few disease-specific measures are becoming available. Each measure is summarised in terms of its name, key reference(s), original purpose, types of patients studied, type of instrument, number of items, length of administration, summary content, and data on reliability and validity.

SEVERE AND PERSISTENT MENTAL ILLNESSES

Quality of life assessments for persons with chronic mental illnesses have typically assumed a general QoL perspective, assessing multiple life domains and including measures of functional status, access to resources and opportunities, and sense of well-being (Lehman & Burns, 1996). The fact that QoL assessments for the chronic disorders have taken this tack reflects the social and economic impacts that these disabling conditions have on patients, as well as the policy context in which they evolved. Assessments for persons with chronic mental illnesses arose in the era of deinstitutionalisation and the need to develop strategies to care for these persons in the community. In this regard, it was not only the patients' medical needs that were of concern (proper pharmacotherapy, psychiatric care, and medical care), but also social support needs (decent housing, income support, safety, and integration into families and communities) (Schulberg & Bromet, 1981). Therefore, a wider social perspective was chosen to assess these broader issues and to inform policy makers and service providers about how well comprehensive *service programmes,* not just *treatments*, were meeting these needs.

Community Adjustment Form (CAF) (Stein & Test, 1980; Hoult & Reynolds, 1984)

This semi-structured self-report interview was developed to assess life satisfaction and other QoL outcomes in a randomised study of an experimental system of community-based care for the severely mentally ill vs standard care in Dane County, Wisconsin. It consists of 140 items, and requires approximately 45 minutes to complete. The areas assessed include: Leisure activities; Quality of living situation; Employment history and status; Income sources and amounts; Free lodging and/or meals; Contact with friends; Family contact; Legal problems; Life satisfaction (21 items); Self-esteem; Medical care; and Agency utilisation. No psychometric data have been reported. The original sample that was studied consisted of 130 patients seeking admission to a state mental hospital; over half were men (55%) and their mean age was 31 years. Half carried a diagnosis of schizophrenia. They were treated both in the state hospital and in a community-based assertive community treatment programme. The results of the original Wisconsin study were replicated in Australia, using the same measures (Hoult & Reynolds, 1984).

Quality of Life Checklist (QLC) (Malm et al, 1981)

This checklist was developed to provide information about which aspects of quality of life are particularly important both to patients and to clinical raters, to assist in therapeutic planning. It is a 93-item rating scale, completed by a trained interviewer after a one-hour semi-structured interview. Scoring for all areas assessed is dichotomised as "satisfactory" or "unsatisfactory". The areas assessed include: Leisure activities, Work, Vocational rehabilitation, Economic dependency, Social relationships, Knowledge and education, Psychological dependency, Inner experience, Housing standard, Medical care (Psychiatric and General), and Religion. No psychometric data are collected, but analyses report simple frequencies of "satisfactory" vs "unsatisfactory" by items. The patients studied included 40 with chronic schizophrenia from a Swedish out-patient clinic; they ranged in age from 18 to 50 and 68% were men.

Satisfaction with Life Domains Scale (SLDS) (Baker & Intagliata, 1982; Johnson, 1991)

This instrument was developed to evaluate the impact on the quality of life of chronically mentally ill patients of the Community Support Program (CSP) in New York State. It is administered to the subject by a trained interviewer, consists of 15 items, and requires approximately 10 minutes. Its individual items cover: satisfaction with housing, neighbourhood, Food, Clothing, Health, People lived with, Friends, Family, Relations with other people, Work/day programming, Spare time, Leisure, Local services and facilities, Economic situation, and the Place lived in now compared to the state hospital. These can be summed into a total life satisfaction score, which correlates at $r = 0.64$ with the Bradburn Affect Balance Scale (Bradburn, 1969) and at $r = 0.29$ with the Global Assessment Scale (Endicott et al, 1976). No other psychometric data are provided. The frequencies and means on these items can be compared with item scores in a national QoL survey of the general population (Andrews & Withey, 1976). The patients studied were 118 chronically mentally ill out-patients, aged 18 to 86, in two community support programmes. They had a mean age of 53.3 years, 61% were women, and 84% lived in supervised residential settings. Diagnoses included 56% schizophrenia, 14% affective disorders, 5% substance use disorders, and 3% organic mental syndromes.

Oregon Quality of Life Questionnaire (OQLQ) (Bigelow et al, 1982; Bigelow et al, 1990; Bigelow et al, 1991a,b; Bigelow & Young, 1991)

The OQLQ was originally based on the Denver Community Mental Health Scale, but has undergone a series of developments since 1981. The original purpose was to assess QoL outcomes among clients served by community mental health programmes, especially those developed under the NIMH CSP initiative. The OQLQ has been updated with more recent psychometric data, alternative versions, and further programme applications.

This instrument exists in two versions: a structured self-report interview (263 items) and a semi-structured interviewer-rated interview (146 items). Both are administered by a trained (not necessarily clinical) interviewer. The underlying theory states that QoL derives from the social contract between an individual and society: individuals' needs are met to the extent that persons fulfil the demands placed upon them by society. Most of the items use fixed, ordinal response categories, and the interview requires approximately 45 minutes to administer. The OQLQ yields 14 scale scores: Psychological distress, Psychological well-being, Tolerance of stress, Total basic need satisfaction, Independence, Interpersonal Interactions, Spouse role, Social support, Work at home, Employability, Work on the job, Meaningful use of time, Negative consequences of alcohol use, Negative consequences of drug use.

The data on reliability and validity of the OQLQ have been evaluated extensively. Cronbach's alpha for the 14 scales on the self-report interview versions range from 0.05 to 0.98 with a median of 0.84. Eight of the scales have excellent reliability (alpha > 0.8), two have intermediate reliability (alpha between 0.8 and 0.4) and four have poor reliability (< 0.4). Test–retest reliabilities (interval not specified) ranged from 0.37 to 0.64 with a median of 0.50. The interrater reliability for the interviewer-rated version has been assessed in a small sample study ($N = 6$) and produced interrater agreement levels between 58% and 100% on the interviewer judgements. More than half of the items showed greater than 90% agreement, and Cronbach's alpha ranged from 0.32 to over 0.80 (more than half over 0.80). The predictive validity of the OQLQ has been evaluated by comparing: (1) clients in different types of community mental health programmes (CSP, drug, alcohol, and general psychiatric clinics); (2) general community respondents from economically distressed and non-distressed communities; and (3) changes in community mental health clients over time. Results of these analyses support the overall predictive validity of the questionnaire.

The OQLQ has been applied both to out-patients of mental health programmes and to samples of the general population. The out-patient samples included patients at intake to community mental health programmes in Oregon (including chronically mentally ill, drug abusers, alcoholics, and general psychiatric patients); their mean age was 33.8 years (range 18–85), and there were 60% men and 96% "non-Hispanics". The community sample had 43% men, a mean age of 36.8, and was 92% non-Hispanic.

Lehman Quality of Life Interview (QOLI) (Lehman et al, 1982; Lehman, 1983a,b; Lehman et al, 1986; Lehman, 1988; Franklin et al, 1987; Simpson et al, 1989; Levitt et al, 1990; Lehman et al, 1991; Sullivan et al, 1992; Huxley & Warner, 1992; Rosenfield & Neese-Todd, 1993; Rosenfield, 1992; Mechanic et al, 1994; Lehman et al, 1995)

The QOLI assesses the life circumstances of persons with severe mental illnesses, both in terms of what they actually do and experience ("objective" quality of life) and in their feelings about these experiences ("subjective" quality of life). This interview provides a broad-based assessment of the recent and current life experiences of the respondent in a wide variety of life areas of potential interest, including living situation, family relations, social relations, leisure activities, finances, safety and legal problems, work and school, and health (as well as religion and neighbourhood in some versions).

The QOLI is a structured self-report interview, administered by trained lay interviewers. Its original version consists of 143 items and requires approximately 45 minutes to administer, but it has undergone a variety of revisions over the past ten years, primarily to improve its data on reliability and validity and to shorten it. The core version contains a global measure of life satisfaction, as well as measures of objective and subjective QOL in eight life domains: living situation, daily activities and functioning, family relations, social relations, finances, work and school, legal and safety issues, and health. Each section is organised such that information is obtained first about objective quality of life and then about level of life satisfaction in that area. This pairing of objective and subjective quality of life indicators is essential to the QoL assessment model (Lehman, 1988).

All the life satisfaction items in the interview use a fixed interval scale, which was originally developed in a national survey of the quality of American life (Andrews & Withey, 1976). The types of objective QoL indicators used vary considerably across the different aspects. In general, they can be viewed as of two types: measures of functioning (e.g. frequency of social contacts or daily activities) and measures of access to resources and opportunities (e.g. income support or housing type). The QoL indicators include both individual items (e.g. monthly income support) and scales (e.g. frequency of social contacts).

The variables generated by the QOLI include: (1) *Objective QoL Indicators:* Residential stability, Homelessness, Daily activities, Frequency of family contacts, Frequency of social contacts, Total monthly spending money, Adequacy of financial supports, Current employment status, Number of arrests during the past year, Victim of violent crime during past year, Victim of non-violent crime during the past year, General health status; and (2) *Subjective QoL Indicators*: Satisfaction with: Living situation, Leisure activities, Family relations, Social relations, Finances, Work and school, Legal and safety, and Health.

The data on reliability and validity of the QOLI have been extensively assessed. Internal consistency reliabilities range from 0.79 to 0.88 (median = 0.85) for the life satisfaction scales, and from 0.44 to 0.82 (median = 0.68) for the objective quality of life scales. These reliabilities have been replicated in two separate studies of persons with severe mental illness. Test–retest reliabilities (one week) have also been assessed for the QOLI: life satisfaction scales: 0.41–0.95 (median = 0.72); objective quality of life scales: 0.29–0.98 (median = 0.65). Construct and predictive validity have been assessed as good by confirmatory factor analyses and multi-variate predictive models. The QOLI also differentiates between patients living in hospitals and supervised community residential programmes both in the US and in Britain (Lehman et al, 1986; Simpson et al, 1989). Individual life satisfaction items clearly discriminate between persons with severe mental illness and the general population (Lehman et al, 1982). Further construct validation has been assessed in studies of the predictors of QoL among day-treatment patients in Britain (Levitt et al, 1990) and the relationship between QoL and feelings of empowerment among persons with severe mental illness in the United States (Rosenfield & Neese-Todd, 1993). A variety of methodological papers have explored such other issues as the relationship between QoL and clinical symptoms (Lehman, 1983b); gender, race, and age (Lehman et al, 1992; Lehman et al, 1995), and housing type (Slaughter et al, 1991; Lehman et al, 1991).

The QOLI has been used almost exclusively with persons with severe mental disorders. The samples in published studies have included approximately equal numbers of men and women, about 75% Caucasian, ranging in age from 18 to 65. The predominant diagnosis in these studies, ranging from 57% to 76% of patients, has been schizophrenia. General population norms for individual life satisfaction items are available (Andrews & Withey, 1976).

A brief version of the QOLI is now available (Health Services Research Institute, 1995). As with the core version, this provides a broad-based QoL assessment and consists of 78 questions, taken from the full version. It too is a self-report interview, administered by trained lay interviewers. It requires an average of 16 minutes and measures the same life domains as the core version, including the global measure of life satisfaction as well as measures of objective and subjective QoL in the eight life domains.

This brief QOLI has been tested on a sample of 50 individuals with severe and persistent mental illness from a local psychosocial rehabilitation programme who participated in this pilot study. Diagnoses included schizophrenia ($n = 17$), major depression ($n = 17$), and other severe and persistent mental illness ($n = 16$). Internal consistency reliabilities for the brief QOLI life satisfaction are comparable to those for the full version, ranging from 0.70 to 0.87 (median = 0.83). Internal consistency reliabilities for the objective brief QOLI scales range from 0.56 to 0.82 (median = 0.65).

Client Quality of Life Interview (CQLI) (Mulkern et al, 1986; Goldstrom & Manderscheid, 1986)

The CQLI was developed as part of a battery of instruments to assess outcomes among persons with severe mental disorders who were served by the NIMH Community Support Program (CSP). These instruments include the Uniform Client Data Instrument (UCDI), the UCDI-Short Form, the CSP Participant Follow-up Form, and the CQLI, the contents of which overlap to a considerable degree. All but the CQLI are completed by case managers or other professionals serving the clients and generally focus on functioning, services, and clinical outcomes. Only the CQLI asks clients directly about the quality of their lives and therefore only it is reviewed here. The conceptual model underlying the CQLI assumes that certain life essentials are necessary precursors to a good quality of life. One major purpose of the Community Support Program was to provide these essentials, and thus to enhance QOL.

The CQLI is a structured self-report interview, administered by a trained lay interviewer. It consists of 46 items rated by the respondent, as well as 19 interviewer ratings; ratings are done on fixed, ordinal scales. The content areas covered include: Essentials of life (food, clothing, shelter, health and hygiene, money, and safety), Job training and education, Daily activities and Recreation, Privacy, Social support, Social time, Self-reliance, and Peace of mind. In each area, questions generally cover both the quantity of resources or activity, as well as the respondent's subjective feelings about these resources and activities. Many of the item sets lend themselves readily to composite scales, although their development or scoring is not available for the CQLI. Some of the scales parallel the UCDI, for which both scale computation guidelines and data on reliability and validity are available.

No formal psychometric analyses of the CQLI are available; correlations of items rated by the clients with comparable items from the UCDI rated by the case manager were quite low. The CQLI ratings remained stable over a 14-month follow-up period. The subsample in the CSP study who completed the CQLI were 109 severely mentally ill clients from six exemplary CSP programmes. They comprised 51% men; 82% Caucasian, 11% Black, 6% Hispanic, and 1% other; and had a mean age of 41.5.

California Well-Being Project Client Interview (CWBPCI)
(Campbell et al, 1989)

The California Well-Being Project was a three-year initiative, funded by the California Department of Mental Health, to develop a better understanding of the health and well-being concerns of persons who have been treated for mental illness (the "psychiatrically labeled"). The most unique aspect of this initiative is that it was designed and conducted entirely by consumers of mental health care. It consisted of three components: (1) research and analysis of well-being factors for individuals assessed through a structured survey of consumers, family members, and professionals; (2) production of educational materials based upon this survey; and (3) dissemination of these educational materials to consumers, family members, and mental health providers.

Three versions of the survey questionnaire on well-being were developed for consumers (151 items), family members (76 items), and mental health professionals (77 items). The time required for its administration has not been indicated. The questionnaires consist predominantly of Likert-scaled questions, but with some open-ended items interspersed. The questionnaires are designed to be either administered in face-to-face interviews (conducted by trained consumers), self-administered by mail, or self-administered in groups, with an interviewer available to answer questions. The instrument is thus designed for flexibility in administration to provide the multiple perspectives of consumers, family members, and professionals.

In the California survey, the CWBPCI was administered to 331 persons who were "psychiatrically labeled" and living in various settings, including psychiatric hospitals (non-state), skilled nursing facilities, board-and-care homes, satellite houses, single occupancy hotels, community residential treatment centres, drop-in centres, client self-help groups, organisations serving people identified as "homeless mentally ill", and on the streets. The final sample consisted of 61 randomly selected members of the California Network of Mental Health Consumers (surveyed by mail), 249 volunteer respondents from various facilities in California (face-to-face interviews, not randomly selected), and 21 randomly selected Project Return clients. Project Return was a programme designed to help ease the transition of clients from the hospital to the community. The sample was 52% men, 67.5% Caucasian, 14.7% Black, and 4.6% Hispanic. They were predominantly young with 41% below the age of 35 and 75% below age 45, and the authors describe them as predominantly chronically mentally ill, but no further clinical details are given.

No information is provided on the instrument's data on reliability and validity, most data from individual items having been reported as frequencies (or percentages) in a narrative section about the concerns of the respondents. The instrument covered a broad range of topics; a few examples include Adequate resources, Aspirations, Children, Family relationships, Freedom, Homelessness, Income, Patients' rights, Stigma, and Warmth and Intimacy.

A key measure derived from the interview is the Well-Being Quotient. This is derived from two questions providing information about the relative importance assigned to various factors that may affect well-being, and whether the respondent currently lacks these factors. The questions read: (1) "Below is a list of things that some people have said are essential for their well-being. Please mark all of those things that you believe are *essential* for your well-being"; (2) "Of the things that people have mentioned that are essential for well-being, which of the following, if any, do you lack in your everyday life?" The response factors include happiness, health, adequate income, meaningful work or achievement, comfort, satisfying social life, satisfying spiritual life, adequate resources, good food and a decent place to live, satisfying sexual life, creativity, basic human freedoms, warmth and intimacy, safety, and other. Besides rank-ordering these factors according to the percentages of respondents who identify each factor in each of the question, four well-being profiles are computed: (1) for each factor, the proportion of respondents who indicate that they lack a well-being factor that they consider essential; (2) the proportion of respondents who do not lack a factor they consider essential; (3) the proportion of clients who consider a factor essential, regardless of whether they have it; and (4) the proportion of respondents who lack a given factor regardless of its essentialness.

The most noteworthy aspect of this instrument is that it was entirely consumer-generated. This enhances its face validity, even though no formal psychometric analyses were conducted. However, the researchers consider this instrument to be still in a developmental stage.

Lancashire Quality of Life Profile (LQOLP) (Oliver, 1991b; Oliver & Mohamad, 1992)

The LQOLP was developed in the United Kingdom during the late 1980s by Oliver et al in response to a request by the British government that community care programmes serving persons with severe mental disorders assess the impact of their services on patients' quality of life. The LQOLP is based on the Lehman QOLI, and uses the same underlying theory, but is modified to reflect cultural variations and the broader wish for service-based evaluation of QoL.

The LQOLP is a structured self-report patient interview, designed for administration by clinical staff in community settings. It consists of 100 items and requires approximately one hour to administer. It assesses objective QoL and life satisfaction in nine life domains: Work/education, Leisure/participation, Religion, Finances, Living situation, Legal and safety, Family relations, Social relations, and Health. It also includes a measure of General Well-Being and Self-Concept. Objective QoL information is collected by means of categorical or continuous measures, depending on the content area. Life satisfaction ratings are on a seven-point Likert scale.

Data on reliability and validity of the life satisfaction have been evaluated in a series of pilot studies (Oliver, 1991b). Test–retest reliabilities for life satisfaction scores range from 0.49 to 0.78, depending upon the patient sample, while internal consistency reliabilities (Cronbach's alpha) of these scales range from 0.84 to 0.86. Content, construct, and criterion validities were also assessed using a variety of techniques and judged to be adequate.

The LQOLP has been used with chronically mentally ill patients in a variety of community care settings in both the United Kingdom and Colorado, but details of the sample characteristics are not available. A briefer version of the LQOLP is currently being piloted in 12 European countries and is being considered by the World Health Organization in conjunction with their broader studies of QOL. (See also p. 67 above.)

Quality of Life Self-Assessment Inventory (QLSAI) (Skantze, 1993)

The QLSAI provides information about which aspects of quality of life are particularly important to patients and natural raters to assist in therapeutic planning. It is an updated version of the QOL Checklist (Malm et al, 1981) and has been used with out-patients with chronic schizophrenia ($N = 66$). The QLSAI is a 100-item self-report inventory completed by the patient, followed by a semi-structured interview with a clinician to check the patient's ratings of satisfaction and dissatisfaction and to discuss the implications for treatment planning. It requires approximately 10 minutes for the patient to complete the self-rated inventory, plus 40–50 minutes for the semi-structured clinical interview.

The aspects assessed include: Physical health, Finances, Household and self-care, Contacts, Dependence, Work and leisure, Knowledge and education, Inner experiences, Mental health, Housing, Housing environment, Community services, and Religion. For all these, ratings are "satisfactory" or "unsatisfactory". The test–retest (7–10 days) correlation for the overall scale is 0.88. Comparative data are available from healthy university students.

Quality of Life Index for Mental Health (QLI-MH) (Becker et al, 1993)

The QLI-MH provides a patient-focused assessment of quality of life that is intended to be responsive to the needs and constraints of clinical practice and research, and which incorporates the multiple perspectives of patients, families, and clinicians. It is designed as a self-administered questionnaire, with which assistance may be given to more severely impaired patients. Versions exist for patients, families, and clinicians. It consists of 113 items; the patient version requires about 20–30 minutes, and the provider version 10–20 minutes. It has been tested with a sample of 40 out-patients meeting DSM-III-R criteria for schizophrenia.

The QLI-MH produces eight scaled scores on the following aspects: Life satisfaction (using 15 items from Andrews & Withey, 1976); Occupational activities; Psychological well-being (using the Bradburn Affect Balance Scale) (Bradburn, 1969); Physical health; Activities of Daily Living (using the Life Skills Profile) (Rosen et al, 1989) and the QL Index (Spitzer et al, 1981); Social relationships (using items from the International Pilot Study of Schizophrenia)

(Strauss & Carpenter, 1974); Economics (adequacy and satisfaction with finances); Symptoms (using the Brief Psychiatric Rating Scale) (Overall & Gorham, 1962). The QLI-MH also includes some open-ended questions to generate individual goals for improvement with treatment. Finally, the instrument includes ratings of the importance of each aspect in relation to subjects' overall QoL.

Test–retest reliabilities have been assessed on a subsample of 10 patients with schizophrenia over 3–10 days. The "percentage match" for the various aspects ranged from 0.82–0.87. Content validity is supported by some previously developed scales and a scale development process that uses key informants, including patients, family members, and providers. Criterion validity has been assessed through correlations between patient QLI-MH scores and provider ratings on the Uniscale and the Spitzer QL-Index (0.68 and 0.58, respectively).

Quality of Life Interview Scale (QOLIS) (Holcomb et al, 1993)

The QOLIS is designed as a QoL measure for assessing severely mentally ill persons. It is a semi-structured interview, administered by trained clinical interviewers, and consists of 87 items. The length of time required to administer it is not reported. The QOLIS was used with 201 patients, including 100 long-term in-patients and 101 in surrounding community residences. Diagnoses were: 45% schizophrenia, 16% organic mental disorders, 11% major affective disorders, 16% other. QOLIS items are rated on a Likert scale from "strongly agree" to "strongly disagree" and generate eight factors: Autonomy, Self-esteem, Social support, Physical health, Anger/hostility, Emotional autonomy, and Personal fulfilment.

Factor analysis of an initial pool of 148 items yielded the proposed eight factors, with 87 items. Alpha coefficients for these factors range from 0.72 to 0.93 (median = 0.77). Step-wise multiple regression analyses were used to predict self-reported life satisfaction using the Baker and Intagliata SLDS (Baker & Intagliata, 1982) and Global Assessment of Functioning Scale (GAF) (Endicott et al, 1976) ($p < 0.0001$ for both analyses). All of the QOLIS scales significantly discriminated between the in-patient and community-based samples. Canonical analysis of the QOLIS scales and the scales from the Heinrichs–Carpenter QLS (Heinrichs et al, 1984) showed substantial correlation.

SCHIZOPHRENIA

Although all the QoL measures reviewed above have been used with samples which had a predominance of schizophrenic patients, none was specifically developed as a disease-specific QoL measure. Only one schizophrenia-specific QoL measures exists.

Quality of Life Scale (QLS) (Heinrichs et al, 1984)

The QLS was developed to assess the deficit syndrome in patients with schizophrenia; it is a semi-structured interview rated by trained clinicians. Its 21 items are rated on fixed interval scales, based on the interviewer's judgement of the patient's functioning in each of the 21 areas. The interview requires approximately 45 minutes. The 21 items of the QLS cover: Commonplace activities, Occupational role, Work functioning, Work level, Possession of commonplace objects, Interpersonal relations (household, friends, acquaintances, social activity, social network, social initiative, social withdrawal, sociosexual functioning), Sense of purpose, Motivation, Curiosity, Anhedonia, Aimless inactivity, Empathy, Emotional interaction, and Work satisfaction. These items reduce to four scales: Intrapsychic Foundations, Interpersonal Relations, Instrumental Role, and Total Score.

The interrater reliabilities on conjointly conducted interviews range from 0.84 to 0.97 on summary scales. Individual item intra-class correlations range from 0.5 to 0.9, and confirmatory factor analysis has been undertaken. This scale is widely used in the evaluation of psychopharmacological treatments for schizophrenia, but predominantly in out-patients (e.g. see Meltzer et al, 1990).

AFFECTIVE AND ANXIETY DISORDERS

Work on QoL measures for use with persons with mental illnesses that do not fall into the traditional definition of "severe and persistent" has been quite recent. This has been stimulated by current pressures to assess the QoL impacts of pharmaceuticals, as well as by a broadening general interest in such outcomes, paralleling the earlier work on severe and persistent mental illnesses. These newer measures are closer to being "disease-specific" or "health-related" than the measures developed for severe and persistent mental illnesses, which follow the "general" QoL framework. This trend probably reflects both the focus on short-term pharmacological effects and the less disabling nature of these disorders over the long run.

Quality of Life Enjoyment and Satisfaction Questionnaire (Q-LES-Q) (Endicott et al, 1993)

The intent of the Q-LES-Q is to provide an easy-to-use assessment of patients' enjoyment and satisfaction with their lives. It is a self-administered, 93-item questionnaire; the length of time to complete it has not been reported. The Q-LES-Q has been used with 95 out-patients meeting DSM-III-R criteria for major depression. It yields eight summary scale scores. Five of these are relevant to all subjects: Physical health, Subjective feelings, Leisure time activities, Social relationships, and General activities. Three can be scored for appropriate subgroups: Work, Household duties, and School/course work. Items are posed as questions, and respondents rate their degree of enjoyment or satisfaction on a five-point scale. The Q-LES-Q also includes single items assessing satisfaction with medication and overall life satisfaction.

Test–retest reliabilities (interval not specified) were assessed on 54 stable out-patients; these intraclass correlations ranged from 0.63 to 0.89 (median = 0.74) on the various scales. Internal consistency reliabilities all exceeded 0.90 (median = 0.92). Validity has been assessed with correlations of the Q-LES-Q scales with illness severity and depression measures. The correlations of the Q-LES-Q scales ranged from −0.34 to −0.68 (median = −0.54) with the Clinical Global Impressions Scale (CGI)(National Institute of Mental Health, 1985) and showed comparable correlations with the Hamilton Rating Scale for Depression (HAM-D) (Hamilton, 1960), the Beck Depression Inventory (Beck & Beamesderfer, 1974), and the Symptom Checklist-90 (Derogatis et al, 1973). Changes in the Q-LES-Q correlated with changes in the CGI and the HAM-D (correlations of change scores ranged from −0.30 to −0.54; median = −0.46).

SmithKline Beecham Quality of Life Scale (SBQOL) (Stoker et al, 1992)

The SBQOL was specifically designed to provide a method for assessing QoL in patients with affective disorders. It is a 28-item self-report questionnaire (time to complete has not been specified). It was developed with data from 129 out-patients who presented in general practice and met criteria for either DSM-III-R major depression or generalised anxiety disorder. The items in the SBQOL are rated on a ten-point scale, anchored by positive and negative extremes of the various constructs. Aspects covered include psychic well-being, physical well-being, social relationships, activities/interests/hobbies, mood, locus of control, sexual function, work/employment, religion, and finances. To provide an idiographic component, the respondent is asked to rate him or herself on these constructs from three perspectives: Self Now, Ideal Self, and Sick Self. A summary score is then generated across the aspects for the differences between Self Now and either Ideal Self or Sick Self.

Changes in the Self Now/Sick Self and Self Now/Ideal Self paralleled improvements in clinical depression (measured by the Hamilton Depression Rating Scale) over a 12-week therapeutic period. The Self Now/Sick Self and Self Now/Ideal Self "distances" correlated with the Sickness Impact Profile (Bergner et al, 1981) and the General Health Questionnaire (Goldberg, 1979), two generic health-related QoL measures. One-day test–retest reliabilities for the Self Now, Sick Self, Ideal Self, Self Now/Sick Self and Self Now/Ideal Self scores ranged from 0.66 to 0.83 (median = 0.70). Internal consistency reliabilities for these scores ranged from 0.85 to 0.95 (median = 0.90).

Quality of Life in Depression Scale (QLDS) (Hunt & McKenna, 1992a,b; Gregoire et al, 1994)

The QLDS was designed to assess the impact of depression on the QoL of patients. It is a 34-item, self-report questionnaire (time to complete has not been specified). It has been used in a study of 74 patients with depression in the United Kingdom. The QLDS generates a summary score encompassing six dimensions: Domestic activities, Interpersonal relationships, Social life, Cognition, Personal hygiene, Leisure activities and relaxation. The two-week test–retest reliability coefficient was 0.81 and the internal consistency reliability 0.93. The QLDS score had a correlation of 0.79 with the General Well-Being Index (Dupuy, 1984). These results have been replicated on samples of non-elderly and elderly Dutch patients with major depression (Gregoire et al, 1994).

DISCUSSION

Measurement of QoL among persons with mental disorders is currently a very active and fertile field of assessment research. Several of the measures reviewed here are reasonably well developed from a psychometric standpoint and have been used in various types of clinical studies. However, the apparent proliferation of newer measures suggests that no current measure fulfils the needs of most researchers and clinicians.

The choice of a QoL measure should be determined by the intended application and in turn by the framework (general, health-related, or disease-specific) appropriate for the task. In developing an assessment of quality of life in a mental health care context, one must consider both the breadth and the specificity of the measures. No single QoL measure will meet all needs. A general QoL approach may raise quality of life issues that mental health care cannot reasonably be expected to address (e.g. decent and affordable housing or access to good jobs) and hence may be insensitive to the effects of treatment on quality of life. A disease-specific approach, while sensitive to the quality of life issues of concern to patients with a specific diagnosis, lacks generalisability and comparability to other patient groups. General HRQL measures, such as the Duke Health Profile (Parkerson et al, 1990) and the Medical Outcome Study Short Form-36 (Ware and Sherbourne, 1992), permit fruitful comparisons across conditions (Wells et al, 1988), but may lack sufficient specificity to guide improvements in care for persons with specific mental disorders. The information derived from HRQL measures may be too narrow to adequately reflect the needs of persons who are chronically disabled and socially disadvantaged due to medical problems.

Quality of Life assessments can prove useful in assessing needs, developing intervention strategies, and evaluating outcomes of interventions at both the system and individual patient levels. At the system or policy level, the development of services and the deployment of resources must derive from a clear understanding of the needs of those being served and the priorities of these needs. Regarding system planning for persons with chronic mental illnesses, QoL assessment provides important information about how patients are experiencing their current life circumstances (not just their health status), and permits some estimation about the priorities that they place on these needs. Such information may be vital for allocating resources within service systems that are based on patients' priorities. Although the ultimate allocation of resources must take into account the needs and perceptions of multiple constituencies (e.g. families, providers, and communities), a patient-based QoL assessment provides the opportunity for systematic input from service recipients who often lack access to this decision-making process. Also at the system level, QoL assessment can provide continuous feedback from these recipients about the outcomes of services, and thus influence the further development of services and resource allocation.

At the individual patient level, QoL assessment can similarly be used to assess needs and to monitor the impact of treatment interventions and services. Malm et al (1981) used a QoL assessment to guide treatment planning in a mental health clinic. Diamond (1985), Awad (1992), and Revicki and Murray (1994) have discussed the use of QoL assessment in the context of psychopharmacology for patients with mental illnesses. Liberman (1988) has proposed that in a rehabilitation context, QoL assessments can be used to identify those life areas with which a patient is most dissatisfied and which therefore may be most fruitful to address in a behavioural treatment programme. Finally, Oliver et al (1992) in Great Britain have used QoL assessments in developing and assessing a national policy which includes case management services (renamed "care management").

In summary, the development of QOL assessment procedures that are appropriate for various subgroups of persons with mental disorders in various contexts remains a worthwhile endeavour. Considerable progress towards this objective has already occurred. There have been thoughtful adaptations of currently available measures, as well as development of new ones to fill certain gaps in order to meet the growing demand for efficient, reliable, valid, and sensitive QoL information for research, clinical decision-making, and policy development.

ACKNOWLEDGEMENT

Preparation of this chapter was supported by NIMH grant MH43703.

CHAPTER EIGHT

Assessing Daily Quality of Life with the Experience Sampling Method

Daniela Q.C.M. Barge-Schaapveld,
Nancy A. Nicolson,
Philippe A.E.G. Delespaul
and Marten W. deVries

INTRODUCTION

Over the second half of this century, evolving medical, governmental, and industrial perspectives on health care have encouraged an optimisation of treatment that reaches beyond standard medical outcome variables. Traditional indicators of the severity of illness have helped to clarify the disease pathophysiology and effects of therapy, but they do not provide insight into whether or not a particular treatment helps from the patient's perspective (Read et al, 1987). To meet these needs, a new concept has emerged in medicine: "Quality of Life" (QoL).

Current methods of assessing QoL have developed out of three main research traditions: "Happiness", "Social Indicators", and "Health Status". Each tradition has placed a different emphasis on affective, cognitive-appraisal, and behavioural dimensions. In this paper, the three QoL conceptualisations are briefly reviewed, (for more detailed reviews see Wilson, 1967; Diener, 1984; de Neeling, 1991), and some conceptual and methodological issues that appear to be either unexplored or unresolved, including the rationale for investigating QoL at the level of daily life experience, are discussed. Time-sampling techniques, such as the Experience Sampling Method (ESM), are proposed and illustrated, with examples of how ESM has been applied in research on QoL in mental disorders.

DEVELOPMENT OF THE QoL CONCEPT

HAPPINESS

The "happiness" research tradition developed primarily out of the interests of psychologists and personality researchers. QoL is defined subjectively as "feeling happy" (see, e.g. Gurin et al, 1960; Bradburn & Caplovitz, 1965; Costa & McCrae, 1980; Diener et al, 1991a). "Happiness" was first defined as a psychological construct in the 1950s (Jones, 1953), opening the way for research into its nature and determinants. In 1960, the first national study to assess the happiness of the population was carried out in the USA (Gurin et al, 1960), but it became clear later that "happiness" and "well-being" should not be restricted to the extent of the positive mood one feels. There is also increasing agreement on the relevance of negative affect as a second independent dimension, related to the overall concept of well-being (Bradburn, 1969). Evidence for the independence of positive and negative affects stems from findings that both constructs correlate with different variables (Costa & McCrae, 1980; Abbey & Andrews, 1985): positive affect with internal control, performance, social support, and extroversion, and negative affect with stress, depression, and neuroticism. Another current discussion focuses on the importance of distinguishing between short- and long-term components of happiness in models of subjective well-being (Kozma et al, 1990).

SOCIAL INDICATORS

Social indicators research originated at the beginning of this century and reflects the interest of social scientists in economic and social determinants of well-being. The measurement of material well-being dates back to 1930, when King produced the first rough estimates of National Product to compare the living standards of different countries. In the following three decades, the definition of well-being using material indicators was refined (see, e.g. Kuznets, 1941). In the 1950s, the term "quality of life" was introduced for the first time in this context (Ordway, 1953, p. 52). Even more influential was the use of the term by President Johnson during the American election campaign of 1964: "These goals cannot be measured by the size of our bank balances. They can only be measured in the *quality of life* that our people lead" (Rescher, 1972). These political statements were confirmed in several studies that found little or no relationship between objective indicators and subjective appraisals in terms of satisfaction with life (e.g. Cantril, 1965; Campbell, 1976; Rodgers & Converse, 1975; Andrews & Withey, 1976). This led to a divergence into two lines of research. One group continued with the idea that objective indicators such as use of time (time-budgets) could also be used as social indicators of well-being (Robinson, 1977, 1987; Juster et al, 1981; Milbrath, 1982; Grønmo, 1982). Others focused on subjective indicators: Cantril (1965) asked subjects to evaluate their current life situation on a ladder from 1 (worst possible) to 10 (best possible). The idea was that one's QoL reflects the size of the gap between an individual's actual situation and that to which he aspires. In other words, perceived QoL is thought to result from a cognitive-appraisal process and reflects current life satisfaction. Whether this satisfaction should be measured globally or with respect to specific life domains is still the subject of debate (Lance et al, 1989; Headey et al, 1991; Feist et al, 1995).

HEALTH STATUS

"Health status" QoL research originated in the World Health Organization Charter of 1948. Health was defined as "a state of complete physical, mental and social well-being and not merely the absence of disease or infirmity". Traditionally, the health status of a population was measured by the mortality rate or life expectancy. However, in the 1950s, the mortality rate reached a balance in Western countries, mainly due to a decrease in life-threatening diseases. It was therefore no longer a sensitive measure to differentiate the health status of different countries. On the other hand, due to the growing proportion of individuals with chronic diseases and the development of medical technology that diminished pain and discomfort without extending life, other sensitive outcome measures were needed. This led to the development of integrated and comprehensive health status indices in the late 1970s (e.g. the Sickness Impact Profile, Bergner et al, 1981; the Nottingham Health Profile, Hunt & McEwen, 1980; the SF-36, Ware et al, 1981). The "health status" tradition has contributed a behavioural dimension to the concept: QoL represents the effect of an illness and its consequent therapy upon the patient's ability to function in daily life circumstances (Schipper et al, 1990).

THE QUALITY OF DAILY LIFE EXPERIENCE

Across the three research traditions that have played an important role in the operationalisation of the QoL concept, a number of issues appear to be still unresolved or unaddressed. The first concerns the stability of QoL over time – more specifically, whether QoL reflects a top-down or a bottom-up process (Lance et al, 1989; Headey et al, 1991; Feist et al, 1995). If we are interested in changes in QoL resulting from either the natural course or the treatment of an illness, we would like to understand, for example, how the illness impinges on daily experiences of positive emotions, rewarding situations, and the satisfying use of productive and leisure time – inherently a bottom-up approach. However, while such daily experiences are made up of states that vary from moment to moment, it is clear that a QoL index should be a summary measure of experiences over some representative period of time.

A second issue concerns the reliability of the available QoL measures. In "health status" studies, individuals are asked to evaluate how the illness and its therapy affect their lives. However, traditional retrospective assessments of objective as well as subjective QoL dimensions are prone to a number of potential biases. Prospective monitoring of behaviour in time–budget research allows more accurate measures of frequencies and duration of activities than is possible with retrospective questionnaires (Juster, 1985). For subjective QoL data (emotions), retrospective bias has been well documented, and the effects of social desirability (Milbrath, 1982; Diener et al, 1991b; Veenhoven, 1991) and recall errors (Lehman & Burns, 1990) have been reported. Moreover, beyond the reliability issues involved, the emotional states occurring in natural environments are not necessarily the same as those elicited during traditional assessment situations such as clinical interviews. Thus, the problem here is one of ecological validity (Hormuth, 1992).

MODELS OF DAILY QoL

The problems described in the previous section have stimulated a search for models and methods for assessing daily QoL. For example, parameters of daily life experience such as the diversity of different activities or the variability of behaviour carried out from moment to moment has been related to QoL (Delespaul, 1995). According to this formulation, QoL will be higher when individuals have contact with a variety of different persons and carry out a wider variety of activities. QoL is also expected to be higher when social contacts are distributed over time, instead of, for example, being concentrated all in one day, with social isolation the rest of the week. Similarly, QoL will be low when the same activities have to be performed for extended periods of time without a break.

But QoL is not an objective state. While it might be true that most people prefer variability to continuously performing the same task, the concept of QoL points to the crucial role of subjective experience. Daily QoL is not then restricted to what subjects actually do in reference to some absolute norm, but incorporates the concurrent assessment of the individual's mood state. For example, "being alone" most of the time is only a problem if a person experiences his worst mental states in that context. Nor, obviously, does being in social contexts improve QoL if these are experienced as negative. Knowledge of individual preferences and experiences is thus vital for understanding QoL.

The "Flow" model conceptualises optimal experience as a state in which positive mood, motivation, alertness, concentration, and control are high, while negative mood is low. According to the model's theory, this state is most likely to be attained in the context of activities that are challenging and in which the individual is skilled (Massimini & Carli, 1988; Csikszentmihalyi, 1990). The subjects who contributed to the development of "Flow" theory were primarily artists, mountain climbers, and high achievers in school, but one might question whether mentally ill patients pursue optimal experience by maximizing "Flow". Escaping stagnation, boredom, and negative feelings may represent an equally great improvement in daily QoL for many psychiatric patients.

Finally, according to a daily QoL model formulated by Brandstätter (1994), an important determinant of well-being may be the adequacy of the fit between person and environment. Here, states of well-being are hypothesised to be dependent on the correspondence between an individual's goals, or motives, and the gratification provided by the environment in terms of specific behavioural settings.

In summary, we propose that the QoL approaches derived from the "happiness", "social indicators" and "health status" traditions may be operationalised within more dynamic models of daily life experience. New data and models that include the frequency of and variability in doing activities one likes, the experience of well-being that comes about when challenges and skills are in optimal balance, and the goodness of fit between an individual and his environment form a starting point for operationalising and further exploring QoL in real-life settings.

EXPERIENCE SAMPLING METHOD

Time-sampling methods offer a strategy for obtaining reliable, quantitative estimates of the frequencies and duration of various forms of behaviour or contexts. They have long been used in ethological studies of animal and human behaviour (Altmann, 1974; Whiting & Whiting, 1975; Wheeler & Reis, 1991). When self-assessments of emotional states are added, time-sampling methods allow us to investigate subjective as well as objective (behavioural) states in daily life.

The Experience Sampling Method (ESM) is a time-sampling approach in which subjects are signalled by an electronic device at random intervals throughout the day to complete a self-report form concerning aspects of their current situation, such as activity, physical location, social context, thoughts, motivation, and mood. Because data collection takes place in the context and time-frame of daily life, retrospective bias is reduced and ecological validity increased. Information concerning the reliability and validity of the ESM, as well as rates of compliance, has been reported elsewhere (Csikszentmihalyi & Larson, 1987; deVries, 1987; deVries & Delespaul, 1989; Delespaul, 1995). QoL theories were in fact a driving force behind the development of the ESM. Csikszentmihalyi and Csikszentmihalyi (1988) saw the advantage of using time-sampling methods to investigate optimal states or "Flow", while deVries (1987) believed that in individuals with a mental disorder, making repeated assessments in daily life might help to identify situations that are conducive to positive mental states, in addition to determinants of symptom variability.

Researchers have used ESM in studies of different psychiatric and (psycho)somatic disorders, using a wide range of hypotheses (deVries, 1992a). In Maastricht, data from a large number of studies have been combined in an archive that allows us to perform secondary analyses spanning a range of disorders. To get some basic insights into the effects of the illness on objective and subjective aspects of daily life functioning, the first study described below entails a comparison of time use and patterns of concurrent emotions in everyday activities. Next, we present an illustration of how aspects of daily QoL, measured with ESM, can be used to evaluate the effects of a pharmacological treatment. Finally, we present an example of the use of ESM data in planning interventions with the specific goal of improving an individual's QoL.

Time Use and Affective States in Illness and Health

What effects does illness have on time use and emotional experience during daily activities? Are these effects related to the diagnosis or severity of the disorder? As a first step toward answering these questions, we compared five groups of subjects selected from the Maastricht data archive: healthy controls ($n = 84$), patients with acute or chronic backpain ($n = 49$), anxiety disorders ($n = 77$), major unipolar depression ($n = 63$), and schizophrenia ($n = 55$). Subjects were signalled randomly, using a pre-programmed watch, to fill in ESM forms 10 times a day for six days. The forms included 7-point Likert scales for the evaluation of current thoughts, mood, motivation with respect to the current activity, physical well-being, and symptoms. The forms also contained open-ended questions assessing what the individual was doing and the social context when signalled. For this analysis, the 45 activity codes were combined into the categories of work, chores, social interactions, active leisure, passive leisure, and doing nothing. A small percentage of activities not fitting into one of the above categories (e.g. meals, transportation, personal hygiene) were excluded from subsequent analyses.

With respect to patterns of time use, differences between the diagnostic groups were statistically significant for the activities "work" and "doing nothing" only. As might be expected, control subjects spent the most time (22.1%) and schizophrenics the least time (4.9%) in work activities, with the other groups intermediate (pain: 10.5%; anxiety: 7.8%; depression: 8.6%). Time spent "doing nothing" mirrored work: it was lowest in controls (6.1%) and highest in schizophrenics, who spent 25% of their time in this context.

To gain further insight into the subjective experience of subjects in the five groups during different activities, mean ratings for the ESM item "happy" were computed first for each subject and then for each group, for each category of activity. There were both similarities and differences among the groups in how these common activities were experienced. Firstly, there were pronounced differences in mean ratings, with controls, pain patients, and schizophrenics reporting more positive emotional states (with means for "happy" of 4.98, 4.54, and 4.35, respectively), while anxiety and especially depressed patients reported lower happiness (means of 3.46 and 2.81, respectively). At the same time, the groups showed striking similarities both in the range of happiness ratings over different activities and in the ranking of activities according to how happy subjects were while doing them. Taking each subject's mean happiness level across all activities as a baseline, z-scores were computed for each ESM report. Figure 8.1 shows the mean deviations in happiness experienced in each activity context, by group. Happiness was lowest when "doing nothing" and was highest during active leisure. Passive leisure occupied a neutral position, with ratings close to individual mean levels. While social interactions were accompanied by positive mood in the control, pain, and depression groups, they were neutral in anxiety patients and even slightly negative in schizophrenics.

As mentioned earlier, QoL is thought to reflect both positive and negative emotional states. Repeating this analysis for the negative mood scale (including the items "angry", "anxious", and "lonely"), we found significant differences among the groups in mean levels, with schizophrenics reporting the most negative mood (2.61), followed by anxiety (2.26) and depression (2.11), with pain (1.29) and controls (1.32) scoring lowest. In contrast to happiness, however, negative mood was not highly dependent on the activity context. Only "doing nothing" was accompanied by worse than average negative mood in the control, anxiety, and depression groups, and negative mood tended to be slightly lower than average during social and active leisure activities in all groups except schizophrenia. Negative mood in schizophrenia and anxiety disorders tended to be lowest during work.

The implications of these results for daily QoL can be summarised as follows:

1. The finding that subjects experienced their least positive and most negative moods in the context of doing nothing suggests that this context, which was more frequent the more severe the disorder, may be a behavioural indicator of poor QoL at the daily level.
2. While subjects in all groups spent more time in passive leisure (such as watching television), active leisure (such as hobbies or sports) was associated with much more positive experience.
3. Time spent doing nothing was inversely correlated with time spent in productive activities. Work and household chores, although not highly preferred activities, were associated with average happiness and, especially in the psychiatric disorders, with relatively low negative mood. A shift in time use from inactivity to productive activity is likely to bring about improvements in mental state, and can be interpreted as a sign of improved QoL.

One of the limitations of aggregating data over diagnostic groups as well as over broad activity categories is that this may obscure clinically important individual differences. The following applications of ESM go beyond general patterns, in monitoring change and in evaluating daily QoL in individual patients.

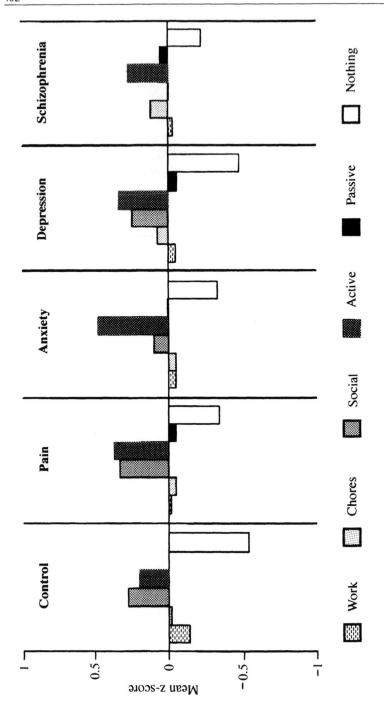

Figure 8.1 Within-subject variability in happiness, by current activity. Ratings for the ESM item "happy" were first standardised relative to each subject's mean level over all reports. Mean z-scores were then calculated for each diagnostic group. Since not every subject reported occurrences for all six categories of behaviour during ESM sampling, Ns for the activities vary

Monitoring the Effects of Treatment on Daily QoL

In general, mentally ill patients have a lower QoL, as compared with the general population (Franklin et al, 1986), and have been reported to be even less satisfied with life than patients with chronic somatic disorders (Huber et al, 1988). In particular, depressed patients have an impaired social functioning (Agosti et al, 1991; De Lisio et al, 1986; Gotlib, 1990) and pronounced work disabilities (De Lisio et al, 1986; Broadhead et al, 1990). Impairments in the performance of household roles and leisure activities have also been noted (De Lisio et al, 1986). Although several studies have evaluated the effects of antidepressants on QoL (Kocsis et al, 1988; Revicki et al, 1992; Rost et al, 1992; Turner et al, 1994; Lonnqvist et al, 1994), little is known about the effects of such interventions on daily QoL.

We have been using ESM to assess changes in the quality of daily life associated with pharmacological treatment for depression. A pilot study (Barge-Schaapveld et al, 1995) was carried out in five primary care practices in South Limburg, the Netherlands. Twenty-one patients completed the study. They ranged in age from 18 to 65 years, met DSM-III-R criteria for major depressive disorder and scored at least 18 on the 17-item version of the Hamilton depression rating scale. Patients were randomised to either fluvoxamine (100 mg) or amitriptyline (150 mg), which they received for six weeks. Subjects were sampled 10 times each day for two periods of six days, pre- and again post-treatment.

The ESM measures of subjective experience in daily contexts changed following six weeks of antidepressant treatment, especially in responders (post-treatment HAM-D $\leq$ 7; $n = 12$) as compared to non-responders ($n = 9$). Treatment responders increased their time spent doing household chores and reduced their passive leisure time. They also experienced greater increases in average positive mood and greater decreases in average negative mood during chores, passive leisure, and social activities than non-responders.

This study illustrates the sensitivity of ESM for evaluating the effects of pharmacological interventions at the daily life level, including some changes that were not picked up by a QoL questionnaire. It is premature to say whether changes in subjective experience preceded behavioural changes or whether patients' feelings improved as a result of increased productive time and decreased leisure time.

Using ESM Assessments to Optimise Individual QoL

Quality of life is a subjective assessment of an individual's condition of living and is directly influenced by the manifestations of illness. Since suffering is a personal appraisal, strategies to alleviate this suffering should take into account the specific daily life conditions and experiences of the individual. Differences in daily experience reflect the multitude of possible living situations and developmental histories. As a result, universal intervention strategies that disregard individual circumstances will have only marginal effects on QoL.

Several authors have used more personalised assessments and applied ESM in clinical situations such as: (1) a self-help strategy (Donner, 1992); (2) evaluating responses to therapeutic interventions for use in individualized case management (van der Poel & Delespaul, 1992); (3) examining the role of self-awareness in psychopathology and therapy (Figurski, 1992); (4) increasing the opportunities for optimal experience (Massimini et al, 1987); or (5) facilitating activities that promote optimal experience (Delle Fave & Massimini, 1992). Personalised QoL enhancement strategies should be seen as optimisation tasks. However, can we determine when the patient feels best and select the general parameters that describe those situations? Is it opportune for the patient to pursue those situations? For instance, although someone may like to fish and enjoys it, increasing the frequency of this activity could result in marital discord or neglect of work, leading to emotional and financial problems that will subsequently reduce QoL. In this paradigm, the person (and his or her relatives) may be taught to evaluate trade-offs in daily activities, with the aim of reducing the occurrence of symptoms and optimising the general level of well-being. In this personalised strategy, ESM can be incorporated in a dynamic process of recurrent assessment periods, intervention, and evaluation so as to further optimise QoL over time.

Sampling daily life experience using ESM generates useful treatment-related information that is not available to mental health professionals when only traditional assessment instruments such as clinical interviews, observations, and standardised questionnaires are used. Since in real life neither mental states nor salient aspects of the environment are well defined and their impact cannot be easily determined in the continuous flow of experience, patients are generally unable to formulate a strategy for behavioural change. Some individuals may be able to assess their mental state in one situation and contrast it to all other ones; for example, "I am unhappier when I am alone", but for most people, aggregating a picture of their experience over contexts yields poor results. Indeed, if the behavioural changes needed to optimise well-being were so obvious, patients would often be able to find solutions to their problems themselves and professional intervention would not be required.

In therapy, ESM data may function like a videotape of daily life, which the therapist and patient can view together. The new information may break through the high level of dependency between client and therapist. The process of reconstructing the week together fosters mutual respect and partnership. The detailed dimensions of a person's experience, visualised from the plots and frequency counts, averaged data, situational correlations, time-budgets, variability, stability, and patterns in their self-reports, provide the material for a script immediately available for clinical use (deVries, 1992b). One such use of ESM is in directive therapy or case management approaches, where the specific information provided by time-sampling may be used to guide changes in behaviour and activities in patients' lives. The case of Peter provides an example:

CASE STUDY

Peter is a 36-year-old man diagnosed as having chronic disorganised schizophrenia, with acute exacerbations. Psychopathology is severe, as shown by a mean BPRS item score of 2.83. BPRS items such as anxiety, guilt, hostility, distrust, aberrant thought content, and hallucinations were rated high (score > 3). Clinically, he appeared tense and hyperactive. Social functioning was reasonably high: 4.6 on a scale from 1 to 7. Ambulatory supervision was carried out weekly by a psychiatrist from the Social Psychiatric Service. Peter lives together with his 28-year-old wife, a schizophrenic woman showing primarily negative symptoms. She had refused to participate in the ESM study. They have a 5-month-old son and were living in a one-room studio, too small for a family of three. Given that both parents want to raise the child themselves, how can we improve their QoL and help to create the best possible environment for the baby?

The ESM time–budget assessments, clinical evaluations, and observation convinced us that the baby was being taken care of adequately. The parents shared responsibility for household chores and devoted much time to playing with the baby. Emotional states measured in different social contexts demonstrated that Peter experienced optimal states when he was alone with his son. Unfortunately, this situation was infrequent, occurring only 3% of the time. In contrast, in the company of his wife (26% of the time), he experienced the worst mental states, a situation that appeared to be neutralised if the child happened to be present (an additional 24% of the time). These data led to the conclusion that a more optimal experience could be reached if the couple reallocated the household chores, giving Peter more time alone with his son. Peter was also encouraged to spend more time with his friends (also a positive state) and less time with his wife. Since the need was clear for living quarters with more room for individual privacy, an attempt was made to get them a larger apartment. We decided not to try to influence Peter's "alone" time, assuming that he needed that time to compensate for social stress in the living situation (see Figure 8.2).

A reassessment in their new apartment, three months later, showed that although the parents had not been successful in reallocating household chores, Peter had been able to reduce the amount of time spent alone and with his wife (the contexts in which negative mental states had been the worst). Peter's overall mental state improved accordingly and the living conditions stabilised, giving the couple a better environment in which to raise their son (Delespaul et al, 1995).

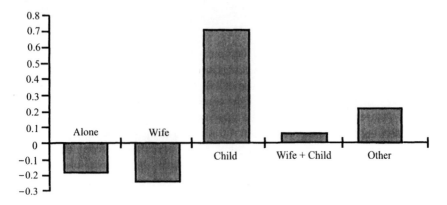

Figure 8.2   The breakdown of "feeling happy" (z-scores) by "persons present" shows clear differences in emotional state according to the social context. These patterns were used to plan interventions to optimise Peter's QoL

DISCUSSION

In contrast to standardised questionnaire and clinical interview measures of QoL, ESM shifts the assessment strategy from a one-time retrospective measure towards an aggregation of subjective and objective ratings of well-being, sampled repeatedly in the subject's normal daily environment. We have presented three applications of ESM in QoL research. In the first example, we have seen that ESM measures of behaviour and affect in daily life are able to discriminate between different diagnostic groups. Such measures are also sensitive to longitudinal clinical change, as illustrated by changes in daily activities and emotions in responders to treatment with an antidepressant, and by the results of a personalised intervention to change the amount of time spent in specific social contexts by a schizophrenic man.

In the future, ESM could be used to gain insight into a variety of treatment-related processes, such as decreases in daily QoL due to side-effects of long-term neuroleptic treatment. We have proposed that ESM assessments of QoL in daily life will enhance the reliability, validity, and sensitivity of the overall measure; additional studies will be necessary, however, to evaluate this claim and to clarify the areas in which this approach will be the most fruitful. Such studies can be expected to add to QoL research a deeper understanding of the dimensions that make up the concept, possibly leading to innovative assessment instruments for use in medical outcome research. ESM is proving to be a valuable tool in clinical practice, yielding information that can be used to design intervention strategies for optimising QoL in individual patients. ESM can provide new insights into the effects of mental disorders and their treatments, and should be added to the armoury of methods in this new area of medical research, which ultimately aims to improve the quality of life in both sickness and health.

ACKNOWLEDGEMENTS

ESM research on quality of life in mental disorders has been supported by research grants from Solvay Duphar (the Netherlands), the L.F. Saugstad Foundation, and the University of Limburg. We thank the patients and treatment staff of the Vijverdal Regional Psychiatric Hospital, the Maastricht Community Mental Health Center (RIAGG), and collaborating primary care practices in Hoensbroek, Heerlen and Maastricht. We gratefully acknowledge the assistance of T. Driesen, C. Dijkman and F. Van Goethem in various logistical aspects of the research, and the generosity of colleagues who contributed data to the ESM data archive. Some of the unpublished results were presented by the co-authors in separate papers at the Association of European Psychiatrists Symposium "Quality of Life and Disablities in Mental Disorders", Vienna, Austria, 4–7 April 1994.

CHAPTER NINE

Quality of Life and Comprehensive Clinical Diagnosis

Juan E. Mezzich, Margit M. Schmolke

A promising approach to articulate and potentiate the consideration of quality of life in clinical care is to insert it within an expanded or comprehensive diagnostic model. In this way, the assessment of quality of life might become an integral part of clinical evaluation, and thus be more readily incorporated in the regular health care process.

Interest in broader conceptualisations of clinical diagnosis can be found in ancient notions of disease and classification, yet it has been only in recent decades that extended and world-wide models of comprehensive diagnosis have emerged. Such models encompass a number of elements and structures (e.g. disease categories, levels of disability, idiographic or personalised statements) which are relevant to several aspects of a multi-dimensional concept of quality of life. It should be helpful to elucidate specific structural levels within a comprehensive diagnostic model, where aspects of quality of life and approaches to their assessment could be incorporated. The content and form of the instruments for such incorporation would also need to be determined.

The process of this discourse may illuminate our understanding of the concepts of comprehensive diagnosis and quality of life; it may also envision useful perspectives for their joint contribution to the advancement of effective clinical care.

COMPREHENSIVE CLINICAL DIAGNOSIS

Feinstein (1967) has noted that the basic role of diagnosis is to establish the patterns according to which clinicians observe, think, remember, and act. This points out the critical importance of diagnosis for defining the field and articulating clinical care.

From a formal viewpoint, diagnosis can be conceptualised as a synoptic representation of the clinical condition that is efficient, informative, and useful for care. These key attitudes are as follows:

1. Efficiency is a requirement of the summarising nature of a diagnostic statement. It is necessary for agility in a clinician's cognitive processing and for its effective handling (storage, processing, and retrieval) through modern informational technologies.
2. Informativeness refers to the need for sufficient grounds to understand the patient's condition as profoundly and thoroughly as possible.
3. The third requirement, usefulness for care, refers to the central role of diagnosis for treatment planning, in terms both of interventional techniques and of the professionals involved.

From a measuring viewpoint, while diagnosis has traditionally been framed typologically, in principle both typological and dimensional instruments can be used to describe the domains of interest.

From a content or domain point of view, several contrasting concepts of diagnosis have been offered. Most traditionally, although not without current endorsers, diagnosis has been equated with disorder or disease. Various levels of discourse for analysing a disease concept have led to corresponding forms of diagnosis, for example, physico-chemical or clinical. Some other concepts, such as Seguin's (1946), posit that disease represents a response of the whole person to both external and internal stimuli and as such, they argue for the need to contextualise the concept of disease and to articulate a number of domains beyond a biomedical formulation.

Broader concepts of diagnosis transcend the description or identification of a disease in order to consider elements of the patient's whole clinical condition. These include the psychosocial environment where the patient lives and illness emerges, as well as the consequences or impact of illness on the ability of the individual to perform basic social roles. For example, Adolph Meyer (1907) argued that psychiatrists should be concerned with understanding the sick person in terms of life experiences, rather than with fitting his/her symptoms into a classificatory schema. The historian and philosopher of medicine, Lain-Entralgo (1982) pointed out that the purpose of diagnosis, more than identifying disorders (nosological) or distinguishing one disorder from another (differential), is to understand what happens in the mind and body of the person who presents for care.

The contrast outlined above between restricted and contextualised concepts of diagnosis can be illustrated further through etymological analyses. The two principal meanings of the New Latin and Greek term *dia-gignoskein* which are discernible from several American dictionaries (Random House, 1971; Webster, 1976; Dorland's, 1974), are: (1) to identify and differentiate; and (2) to know thoroughly. It can be argued that the first meaning corresponds to the medical concept of nosological and differential diagnosis, and that the second involves understanding deeply the nature and context of a problem or situation. The latter appears to correspond to the concept of comprehensive diagnosis.

THE EVOLUTION OF DIAGNOSTIC SYSTEMS

Further light can be shed on the bases and clinical meaning of diagnosis by an examination of those traditions that have informed the historical evolution of diagnostic systems. An illuminating starting point is furnished by Nietzsche's (1872) Apollonian vs Dionysian dichotomy, originally applied to music and theatre, but also relevant to many other fields. He characterised the Apollonian dimension as harmonious, serene, disciplined, and well-balanced, and the Dionysian (critically complementary to the first one) as vital, ecstatic, unrestrained, and irrational.

Approaching diagnostic systems more directly, Nietzsche's dichotomy can be unfolded heuristically in terms of three philosophical traditions. The first one, Platonic, is characteristically universalistic, clear, ideal/rationalistic, and abstract. The second, Aristotelian, can be characterised as observational, naturalistic, thorough, and logical. The third, Hippocratic, is experiential, empathetic, contextual, and biographical. It can be suggested that the Platonic tradition overlaps with Nietzsche's Apollonian dimension and that the Hippocratic tradition is close to his Dionysian dimension, while the Aristotelian tradition has some similarities to both dimensions (i.e. its methodical logic approaches the Apollonian concept, and its naturalistic concern resonates with the Dionysian thrust).

Standard psychiatric nosologies (such as the various editions of the International Classification of Diseases and of the American Psychiatric Association's Diagnostic and Statistical Manual of Mental Disorders) appear to be firmly in line with the universalistic and clarity attributes of the Platonic tradition and, more recently, with the empiricism of the Aristotelian tradition. The multi-axial diagnostic approach (which attempts to portray the patient's whole clinical condition through a systematic assessment of its key aspects such as disorders, psychosocial context, and impact on functioning) appears to be informed by all three philosophical traditions. It is largely universalistic (in line with the Platonic tradition), contextualised in part (reflecting Hippocratic concerns), and, most prominently, Aristotelian in terms of thoroughness and naturalistic emphasis. The multi-axial approach is internationally considered as a major advance in diagnostic methodology (Maser & Kaelber, 1991; Mezzich et al, 1985) and is incorporated into both ICD-10 (Sartorius, 1994; WHO, 1997) and DSM-IV (American Psychiatric Association, 1994).

More recently emerging as an important component of a comprehensive diagnostic model is an idiographic formulation (Mezzich & Schmolke, 1995;

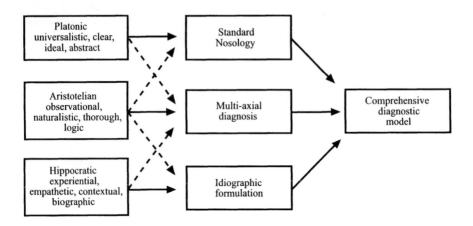

Figure 9.1   A Comprehensive diagnostic model and its philosophical roots

Mezzich, 1995). This involves a non-standardised presentation of clinicians' explanatory models and patients' perspectives. Such an idiographic formulation has roots primarily in the Hippocratic philosophical tradition (including its experiential, empathetic, contextual, and biographical concerns), and to a lesser extent in Aristotelian emphases on observation and thoroughness.

A nosological classification, a standardised multi-axial diagnosis, and an idiographic formulation are the key components of an emerging comprehensive diagnostic model. Figure 9.1 depicts the philosophical traditions mentioned above, the diagnostic systems they inform, and their interrelationships.

ON STRUCTURALLY ADVANCING DIAGNOSTIC SYSTEMS

One of the major recent advances in diagnostic methodology (Maser & Kaelber, 1991; Mezzich & Jorge, 1993) has been the systematisation of psychiatric nosology. This thrust has principally encompassed a syndromic, minimally aetiological organisation of the nosological classification, and the use of explicit or specific definitions of diagnostic categories. Both developments appear to have contributed to the achievement of higher levels of diagnostic reliability.

Advances in diagnostic validity (i.e. greater fulfilment of the purposes of diagnosis in regard to communication, understanding of the case, treatment planning and prognosis) would require work in the following directions:

1. One area for advancing diagnostic validity would be the refinement of pathological descriptions. For this, attentiveness to the results of empirical

research (biological, psychological, and social) would be important. The instruments for the description of pathology may be categorical – not only classical, but also prototypical (Cantor et al, 1980) – as well as dimensional, as has been experimented with for describing personality and schizophrenic pathology during the development of DSM-IV.

2. The further development of standardised multi-axial formulations offers another opportunity for upgrading diagnostic validity. Important here would be refining the concepts underlying the axial description of the patient's whole clinical condition and of the categorical and dimensional standardised instruments for appraising each of the axes.

3. The inclusion of an idiographic formulation as an important component of a comprehensive diagnostic model (complementary, rather than a confrontational alternative to standardised diagnosis) is another promising approach to advancing diagnostic validity. A major challenge in this development is the determination of the key elements of the clinician's explanatory models (e.g. biological, psychodynamic, cognitive-behavioural, socio-cultural) and the principal thrusts to organise the patient's perspectives (e.g. biographical, quality of life). Another challenge would be to develop efficient assessment procedures and recording formats, to minimise cumbersomeness and to facilitate the use of an idiographic formulation in regular clinical care.

Conceptually supportive of the comprehensive diagnostic model outlined above is the ongoing development of health status assessment instruments, characterised by a broad outlook and an emphasis on the positive aspects of health. The definition of health embodied in the constitution of the World Health Organization (1948) is paradigmatic of this approach. It proclaims that health is a state of complete physical, mental, and social well-being and not merely the absence of disease. To illustrate efforts at operationalising the assessment of health status, one can mention the broad health inventories designed as part of the Medical Outcomes Study (Stewart et al, 1988). The 20 items of the MOS Short-Form General Health Survey were selected to represent six health concepts: physical functioning (limitations of physical activities); role or occupational functioning; social functioning (interpersonal contacts); mental health (psychological distress and well-being); health perceptions (patients' own ratings of current general health); and pain (as distinguished from physical discomfort) (Stewart et al, 1994).

INCORPORATING QUALITY OF LIFE IN COMPREHENSIVE DIAGNOSTIC MODELS

Quality of life has been accorded a special place in health care (e.g. Spilker, 1990, 1996; Orley & Kuyken, 1994), as it is becoming clear that the purpose of such care cannot be only to eliminate symptoms or restore functioning, but also to help the individual to achieve fuller levels of health and the satisfaction of personal life aspirations.

A number of facets have been proposed to delineate the range of domains relevant to quality of life. Among the most frequently endorsed are: physical, psychological, independent functioning, social relationships, environmental factors, and higher personal aspirations. The Quality of Life Instrument (Kuyken & Orley, 1994), currently under development by the World Health Organization, has adopted these particular facets as constituent domains.

In order to assess all or even a fraction of these facets of quality of life a number of distinct instruments have been proposed. They vary in terms of the aspects they actually cover, as well as in regard to the scaling or measurement approach they use, which range from typological to dimensional procedures and from extensive instruments to one-item scales.

Considered next are different levels and structures in diagnostic systems where quality of life concepts can be incorporated. They are briefly described below.

1. *Disorder-specific scales as ad hoc assessment.* Considered here are quality of life instruments specifically developed for individuals afflicted by a particular illness or condition. Examples include the AIDS Health Assessment Questionnaire (Lubeck & Fries, 1991), the Arthritis Impact Measurement Scales (Meenan, Gertman & Mason, 1980), and the Diabetes Quality of Life instrument (Diabetes Control & Complications Trial Research Group, 1985). Here, quality of life is assessed not as an intrinsic part of a diagnostic system, but as a further evaluative study of individuals classified with a standard diagnostic schema (e.g. the International Classification of Diseases) as being affected by a particular disorder or condition.

2. *Generic instruments as specific axes.* Quality of life can also be assessed in a way generalisable to all patients or subjects, regardless of the specific diseases they may be experiencing. Examples include the World Health Organization Quality of Life Instrument WHOQOL (Kuyken & Orley, 1994), the Quality of Well-being Scale (Bush, 1984), and the Sickness Impact Profile (Bergner et al, 1981). Such generic instruments could be organised as special axes within a multi-axial diagnostic schema. In this way, generic measures of quality of life may have the place that social and occupational functioning scales have as optional axes in DSM-IV.

3. *Health status and quality of life assessments as multi-axial schemas.* Health status is a complex subject, as pointed out by a consensus conference (Walker and Ascher, 1986), which identified physical, cognitive, affective, social, and economic as its key aspects. Quality of life is also a pluralistic concept. The WHO Quality of Life Instrument encompasses the following six domains: physical, psychological, level of independence, social relationships, environment, and spirituality/religion/personal beliefs. Joyce (1987) pointed

out the significant thematic similarities between complex health status and quality of life concepts; in both cases, the assessment of thematic complexity may be profitably approached through a multi-axial procedure. Such a procedure provides coherence to the protean and heterogeneous content of these concepts, and ensures their systematic assessment.

4. *Complementary idiographic formulation.* The intricate, subjective, and not always standardisable information pertinent to quality of life makes it appropriate to consider an idiographic or personalised formulation as one vehicle for the inclusion of quality of life in comprehensive diagnostic systems. Qualitative research methods are very relevant here (World Health Organization, 1994). The relevance of idiographic formulations is predicated on the grounds of both the flexibility of such formulation and its prominent concern with the perspectives of the patient. Assessment of a subject in an idiographic formulation typically involves the use of flexible guidelines or suggested questions, rather than standardised or rigidly scheduled procedures.

The analysis presented above on the possible ways of incorporating quality of life concepts in comprehensive diagnostic models has been largely "architectural", in order to understand pertinent thematic relationships more clearly and heuristically. In line with this strategy, it should be illuminating to compare structurally two major assessment instruments developed by the World Health Organization. One, the ICD-10 multi-axial schema (Sartorius, 1994; Mezzich, 1994; WHO, 1997), is focused on pathology and clinical concerns, while the other, the WHO Quality of Life Instrument (WHOQOL), has a broader field of interest. As Table 9.1 shows, the first axis (Clinical Diagnoses, encompassing mental and non-mental disorders) of the ICD-10 multi-axial schema corresponds to the first two domains (Physical and Psychological) of the WHOQOL. The second ICD-10 axis (Disablements in four areas: personal care, occupational functioning, functioning with family, and broader social functioning) roughly corresponds to the third WHOQOL domain (Level of Independence). The third and final ICD-10 axis (Contextual Problems, including psychosocial environmental and personal lifestyle and management difficulties) overlaps thematically to some extent with the fourth and fifth WHOQOL domains (Social Relationships and Environment). The sixth WHOQOL domain (Spirituality, Religion and Personal Beliefs) is the only one without correspondence within the ICD-10 multi-axial schema.

These are also some important differential characteristics of quality of life assessment, as compared to standard multi-axial diagnosis. These characteristics are:

1. *Focus on the person.* While multi-axial diagnosis attempts to do greater justice to the complexity of the patient's clinical condition by considering not only illnesses but also their context, quality of life assessment is even more directly focused on the person of the individual examined.

Table 9.1   Structural comparison of WHO's encompassing Assessment schemes

ICD-10 multi-axial schema	WHO Quality of Life Instrument	
I. Clinical Diagnoses	I.	Physical Domain
	II.	Psychological Domain
II. Disablements	III.	Level of Independence
III. Contextual Problems	IV.	Social Relationships
	V.	Environment
	VI.	Spirituality/Religion/Personal Beliefs

2. *Subjective perspective.* Multiaxial diagnosis represents the clinician's judgement on the patient's condition. In contrast, quality of life assessment fundamentally displays the subjective viewpoint of the individual involved.
3. *Emphasis on positive health.* While multi-axial diagnosis is focused on disease and problems, quality of life assessment preferentially looks for assets and strengths, i.e. the more positive polarity of the health dimension.
4. *Greater cultural sensitivity.* While substantial attention is being paid to cultural factors influencing the multi-axial assessment of illness, its context and consequences, there is an even greater need to frame the assessment of quality of life culturally, given the culture-boundedness of many quality of life perceptions.
5. *Holistic approach.* Multi-axial diagnosis constitutes a reasonably comprehensive appraisal of the patient's condition. Quality of life assessment is even more encompassing of the totality of the individual involved. As shown in Table 9.1, it includes a domain involving spirituality and personal values and beliefs that is not covered in multi-axial diagnosis.

CONCLUSION

A historical and philosophical analysis of the roots and evolution of diagnostic systems suggests some promising points of convergence. An emerging comprehensive diagnostic model, involving a standardised multi-axial formulation of illnesses, their context and consequences, together with a complementary idiographic formulation, offers an opportunity to upgrade the validity and usefulness of diagnosis. Furthermore, such a model furnishes structures which can accommodate quality of life concepts and measures. In effect, disorder-specific scales may be helpful for additional post-diagnostic evaluation, generic scales may be used as additional or optional axes, the set of domains underlying quality of life may be arranged as a whole multi-axial schema, and finally, quality of life may be assessed as part of a complementary idiographic formulation.

By incorporating quality of life assessment within the structures of a comprehensive diagnostic model, opportunities are maximised for bringing such assessment to the mainstream of diagnostic evaluation and of the process of clinical care. Enriching diagnosis with quality of life concepts may advance deeper understanding of the patient's condition, designing a more adequate treatment strategy, fostering effective communication between clinician and patient, and the active engagement of the patient in the process of treatment and of achieving higher levels of health.

CHAPTER TEN

New Developments in Quality of Life Measurement in Schizophrenia

Marion Becker and Ronald Diamond

INTRODUCTION

Over the past two decades, there has been a growing interest in the quality of life of people with schizophrenia. The goals for treating persons with schizophrenia have changed radically as treatment has shifted from a hospital-based system of care to a community-based system. In traditional hospital-based systems, symptom reduction was considered the primary goal. While this objective remains important in community-based systems, the ability to live a stable life in the community has become a primary goal. Furthermore, improving quality of life has achieved a second role, as an indicator of outcome. One challenge in developing a system for routinely monitoring the outcomes of mental health treatment is finding ways of incorporating outcome measurement into routine clinical practice. There is a need to go beyond quality of life measurement to develop ways of using quality of life outcome information effectively to improve mental health treatment and to strengthen the working alliance between patients and their mental health service providers. There is a need to develop standards and criteria for quality of life and to rethink how we gather and use the information to improve service system quality and expand consumer choice. The standards for quality of life measurement and the outcome management systems developed in the next few years are critical, because they will influence the architecture of outcome management into the twenty-first century.

This chapter will present a new approach to defining and measuring quality of life in persons with schizophrenia. It will start with a brief overview of schizophrenia and provide a conceptual summary of quality of life measurement in persons with this disorder. Data on quality of life in schizophrenia from different responders' points of view are presented, along with suggestions for future research.

SCHIZOPHRENIA

Current research demonstrates that the eventual course and outcome of schizophrenia are much more heterogeneous than previously thought. The traditional view was that schizophrenia led to a persistent downhill course of increasing disability. We now know that the course is often erratic, with periods of relatively good functioning mixed with relapses and decreased function; often the pattern is unpredictable. Long-term outcome studies show that up to two-thirds of people with schizophrenia have a good long-term prognosis. Research suggests that some people eventually recover, becoming symptom-free and no longer needing medication or other treatment, although we know little about what promotes this recovery (Ciompi, 1980; Warner, 1985).

The unparalleled advances in the basic science of schizophrenia over the past 20 years bring general acceptance that it is a brain disorder (Knable et al, 1995). However, despite recent research and despite new pharmacological and psychosocial treatments, cure is not now a realistic treatment goal for most patients (Hegarty et al, 1994). Despite the newfound optimism engendered by recent long-term outcome studies and even with our best treatment, most people continue to suffer with schizophrenia for many years, or for the rest of their lives. As with many other chronic illnesses, the treatment goals are to maintain function, promote rehabilitation, and maximise quality of life.

Given the chronic nature of the illness, the complexity of treatment, and its cost to society, it is critical to use measurements to determine which patients are improving and which are not. To develop better treatment programmes, we must determine which programmes are most effective. This is not just true for research programmes with large budgets for outcome evaluation, but also for clinical services trying to improve their effectiveness, measure their impact, and defend their budgets in a period of increasing austerity (Tantam, 1988).

QUALITY OF LIFE AND DEINSTITUTIONALISATION

In the United States, interest in quality of life and the social disabilities associated with schizophrenia intensified in the wake of the deinstitutionalisation of the late 1960s and early 1970s with the wholesale transfer of psychiatric patients into the community, where they are increasingly visible.

A number of research projects demonstrated that appropriate community-based treatment and support could increase quality of life (Lehman et al, 1991; Levitt et al, 1990; Stein & Test, 1987; Sullivan et al, 1991). Too often, however, appropriate supports were not provided and people with schizophrenia were ejected from hospitals and abandoned in communities (Mechanic, 1986; Shadish &

Bootzin,1981). Although this transfer to the community was initially justified as improving the lives of people with schizophrenia, over time, it became apparent that it did not automatically improve anyone's life.

Research shows that community-living persons with schizophrenia are among the psychiatric patients with the lowest overall life satisfaction scores in the general population (Lehman et al 1986; Rosenfield, 1992). Quality of life, at least for some schizophrenics, was worse in the community than in long-stay hospitals (Lamb, 1979a, 1981; Schmidt et al, 1977). Empirical evidence shows that deinstitutionalized patients often live in substandard housing (Bachrach, 1982; Uehara, 1994), are dissatisfied with their finances, employment, social relationships, and personal safety (Lehman, 1992), and are overrepresented in the homeless population (Bassuk & Lamb, 1986; Drake et al, 1989; Rossi & Wright, 1987).

During the early phase of deinstitutionalisation, the primary concern was hospital recidivism. Could patients live in the community without returning to hospital? How could their tenure in the community be extended and stabilised? Over time, it became evident that just being out of the hospital was not enough (Bachrach, 1982, 1987; Solomon, 1992). Living situations and levels of despair that had been tolerated in hospitals became less acceptable to patients when comparisons with other populations in the community were possible. The patients' poor quality of life and their social disabilities caused growing concern, which in turn increased interest in targeting treatment toward these issues (Hadorn, 1993; Stein & Test, 1985). Concerns about the effects of deinstitutionalisation generated a substantial body of research on the correlates of successful adaptation and psychiatric rehabilitation (Anthony et al, 1978; Anthony & Farkas, 1982; Avison & Speechley, 1987; Carpenter & Strauss, 1991; Strauss & Carpenter, 1974, 1977).

As clinicians have continued working with patients in the community, they have gained a better understanding of the centrality of quality of life concerns for these patients, and have begun recognising that a patient's subjective experience of quality of life affects the motivation to seek treatment and continue with medication and rehabilitation (Diamond, 1985; Hogan et al, 1983). Some have even speculated that a patient's perception of quality of life may influence the phases and course of the illness (Strauss, 1989).

As a consequence of a profound shift in thinking about the abilities, needs, and aspirations of community-living persons with schizophrenia, improving their quality of life has emerged as *the* major goal of community treatment (Baker & Intagliata, 1982). Fuelled by the rise of the consumer movement and the growing importance of giving patients a voice in their treatment, quality of life assessments have also gained a place in processes of quality assurance and the difficult task of improving services for persons with schizophrenia (Becker, 1995; Bigelow et al, 1982; Ellwood, 1988; Geigle & Jones, 1990; Lehman & Burns, 1990; Levine, 1987; Llewellyn-Thomas et al, 1982).

QUALITY OF LIFE AS AN OUTCOME MEASURE IN MENTAL HEALTH

In the wake of deinstitutionalisation, clinicians working in the community began questioning the value of such traditional, common outcome measures as hospital recidivism rates and symptomatology (Lamb, 1979; Schmidt et al, 1977), seeing these as inadequate and simplistic. Hospital recidivism, for example, may reveal more about the mental health system and economic conditions than about the clinical status of the patient. Many admissions are precipitated by a concrete need, such as housing, that has little relationship to the patient's illness. The same patient who is admitted in one treatment system might be treated as an out-patient in another, where effective community-based crisis services and treatment services can meet the patient's clinical needs (Stein et al, 1990).

Likewise, positive symptoms of psychosis, such as delusions, hallucinations, and disorganization, were another traditional measure of severity of illness, and change in symptoms has been considered the primary indication of improvement (Revicki & Murray, 1994). While reliance on symptoms appeals to common sense, these are actually important only as markers for the severity of the underlying disease process or if they directly interfere with the person's life. On these criteria, symptoms are a poor measure for schizophrenia, since recent research shows that they have a relatively low correlation with ability to function or self-reported quality of life (Anthony & Rogers, 1995; Becker et al, 1993). Symptoms indicate little about treatment outcome from the patient's viewpoint. Furthermore, because symptoms are a poor predictor of function, they can be a misleading outcome indicator: two persons whose symptoms suggest similarly severe illness may actually have quite a different capacity to function in the community.

The main advantage of symptoms as an outcome measure is that they can be measured easily and with reasonable reliability (Patrick & Erickson, 1993; Revicki & Murray, 1994); without a practical alternative, these measures continue as the primary tool for assessing improvement. A recent review of therapeutic response in schizophrenia found that most clinical trials evaluated psychopathology and positive symptoms (Collins et al, 1991). While more recent studies have expanded their outcome focus to include negative symptoms, the patient's perspective about their experience of the disease or the outcome of treatment is not routinely collected. As quality of life gains importance as a focus of treatment and outcome research, the development of instruments to measure changes in this area easily and reliably gains urgency (Feinstein, 1992; Gill & Feinstein, 1994; Lehman, 1992; Patrick, 1992; Revicki, 1989). The publication of several large clinical trials showing that quality of life measures are responsive to important changes in clients' health status has further encouraged their use (Wilson & Cleary, 1995).

The emphasis on using quality of life (especially as perceived by patients themselves) as a goal of treatment has gained currency from the interest in consumer empowerment. Indeed, modern treatment of schizophrenia gives increased weight to the patients' values and goals, since all of us, schizophrenic or not, have the right to set, as much as possible, the direction and goals for our lives. There is also a growing belief that involving patients in their treatment produces better outcomes. Measuring the patient's subjective evaluation of various life domains is one approach to assessing how mental health services are meeting patient's goals (Becker et al, 1994; Sainfort et al, 1996).

Concern for the welfare of psychiatric patients in the community has also enlivened the debate over defining and measuring treatment effectiveness. This concern has challenged mental health professionals to learn to accurately measure quality of life in schizophrenia and tease out factors and remedies associated with its improvement. Doubtless, future research on quality of life as a concept, and as an indicator of outcome, will fundamentally change policies and programmes from a governmental perspective. Quality of life has replaced deinstitutionalisation and community adjustment as the mental health issue of the 1990s (Schalock et al, 1989).

QUALITY OF LIFE DEFINITION

Defining and measuring quality of life in the context of schizophrenia is extremely complex. Disagreements about the definition of quality of life abound, despite a growing body of medical research (Deyo, 1991; Mor & Guadogli, 1988; Spilker, 1992). As noted by Gill and Feinstein (1994), "Despite the proliferation of instruments and the burgeoning theoretical literature devoted to the measurement of quality of life, no unified approach has yet been devised for its measurement, and little agreement has been attained on what it means" (p. 619). Granted that the field lacks a consistent definition and measurement approach, consistent trends, ideas, and propositions unite the diversity of opinion about quality of life measurement. For example, there is general agreement about the essentially subjective nature of quality of life and an emerging consensus regarding its major component domains (Becker, 1995; Bergner, 1985, 1989; Diener, 1984, Spilker, 1996; Delespaul, 1995).

Most definitions of quality of life consider: (1) physical health status; (2) functional ability; (3) psychological status and well-being; (4) social interactions; and (5) economic status (Spilker, 1990). Quality of life instruments used in mental health generally include one or more of these aspects, often using Lehman's structured interview as the model for collecting data. However, there is little discussion let alone agreement in the literature, about a standard decision rule for criteria on which domains are essential for validly assessing a clinical programme. These limitations extend to the problem of weighting and scoring domains, which has been done arbitrarily. This lack of conceptual clarity and the absence of standardisation have exacerbated the problem of developing instruments, prevented generalisation between studies, and added to conceptual confusion (Guyatt et al, 1989; Mike, 1992; Mor & Guadogoli, 1988).

MEASUREMENT STRATEGIES FOR QUALITY OF LIFE

While there is no *gold standard* for measuring quality of life for persons with schizophrenia, many methods and instruments have been developed. For example, Van Dam et al (1981) estimated that more than 250 methods were used to assess quality of life in medicine; in 1990, Spilker et al reviewed more than 300 quality of life indices, with a diversity of measurement strategies and scaling approaches, ranging from disease-specific to generic. The instruments cover differing domains, use differing methods of aggregation, and ascribe various "weights" to different items and domains (Deyo, 1991; Berzon et al, 1995). A diversity of quality of life instruments and measurement methods have been developed for schizophrenia (see e.g. Becker et al, 1993; Bigelow et al, 1991b; Heinrichs et al, 1984; Lehman, 1988; Malm et al, 1981). Many of these instruments and measurement methods have limitations in general strategy and application. Disagreement about measuring methods in schizophrenia is generally attributed to differing views about patients' preferences and goals, the goals of researchers and clinicians, and different views of the appropriate roles of patients and their families (Baker & Intagliata, 1982; Becker, 1995).

Much discussion has focused on the role of patients' preferences in evaluating and scoring quality of life data (Pickney et al, 1991; Thepa & Rowland, 1995). Subjective and objective assessments of quality of life domains do not necessarily coincide, further complicating the process (Costa & McCrae, 1980; Delongis et al, 1982; Heady & Wearing, 1989; Rosen et al, 1995). Furthermore, some studies show that biological and psychosocial factors influence each other and that measures of subjective quality of life are affected by the clinical status of the patient (Becker et al, 1994; Lehman, 1992). Although a few studies have looked at the correlations between distinct domains of quality of life, researchers have not studied their interaction and no one knows how outcomes in these domains are related to treatments received.

Nevertheless, the importance of patients' perceptions is underscored by evidence that these perceptions of their quality of life (which include how they see their own health) reliably predict loss of function, morbidity, mortality, and functioning in physical, psychological, and social terms (Gill & Feinstein, 1994). The interrelatedness of different aspects of patients' lives is illustrated by data showing that psychopathology affects quality of life, although the exact nature of this interaction is undetermined (Becker et al, 1994; Lehman, 1992; Meltzer et al, 1990).

Until the complex relationship between subjective and objective dimensions of quality of life is better understood, global assessment will not be a useful or sufficient outcome measure for clinical trials or for evaluating mental health services. New instruments to measure patients' perceptions and specific elements that affect quality of life in schizophrenia must be developed; so that important interactions between objective and subjective factors can be understood. While several conceptual models for relationships among quality of life domains have been proposed, these models usually exclude some important aspects. Typically, proposed models have not been empirically tested (Wilson & Cleary, 1995). The chief goal of existing studies has been describing and measuring quality of life outcomes. Relatively unstudied are the relationship between them and other outcome measures, and links between domains in the quality of life construct.

SELECTING AN INSTRUMENT FOR MENTAL HEALTH SETTINGS

To be useful, an instrument for measuring quality of life in schizophrenia must be appropriate for the setting and reflect the aims of the researcher or practitioner using it. Any instrument designed for use in (typically overburdened) mental health treatment settings must be quick to administer and easy to understand and score. Its questions must fit categories which the clinicians feel are important. And since clinical records are often incomplete, disorganised, or illegible, the instrument (to minimise the clinician's time investment) must seek a minimum of information – from records or elsewhere. All information sought must be directly relevant to the clinical work. If an instrument will be completed by clinicians and patients, the information must be relevant and useful to both. Ideally, the information will also be directly useful to the planning, implementation, and evaluation of care. Along with Feinstein (1992), we believe that in clinical practice, the most important domains of quality of life are those that the patient wants to improve in the clinical setting.

The mental health field is witnessing an ongoing debate about the value of self-report and interview methods of quality of life measurement. Because of an untested assumption that persons with schizophrenia cannot reliably complete self-reporting questionnaires, most investigators have used interviews, which are expensive and have limited the use of quality of life as a routine outcome measure for clinical practice. However, there is growing empirical support for using shorter, self-administered instruments (Greenley & Greenberg, 1994). Data suggest that a brief, self-administered quality of life measure can yield results consistent with in-depth interviews (Greenley & Greenberg, 1994). Furthermore, evidence from research with physically ill persons suggests that self-administered instruments might suffer less contamination from social desirability concerns, which are stronger in interviews. In some studies, self-administered questionnaires have shown lower subjective quality of life rating than interviews (Bremer & McCauley, 1986). Because patients may be more honest about their feelings without the pressures of the face-to-face interview, self-administered assessments of quality of life could be more valid than interview assessments. Finally, self-report data collection is cost-effective; research consistently shows that personal interviews cost 3 to 10 times as much as self-report paper and pencil approaches (Anderson et al, 1986).

NEW DIRECTIONS IN QUALITY OF LIFE MEASUREMENT

In the United States, there has been a dramatic change in recent decades in the culture of the mental health delivery system and the roles of its participants. For example, the patient–doctor relationship has undergone rapid change away from a relationship based on paternalism towards one of patient autonomy. Along with this shift towards patient autonomy has come a rising consumer demand for a more participatory approach to outcome measurement and psychiatric research. A confluence of forces, including changes in disability policy from dependence to independence, and the work of the mental health consumer movement raised awareness of the centrality of patients' and families' point of view. This has sparked new, more patient- and family-centred approaches to quality of life measurement. This new participatory, patented approach to measurement is exemplified by the development of the Wisconsin Quality of Life Index (W-QLI).

Development of the W-QLI (initially called the Quality of Life Index for Mental Health, QLIMH), began in 1991 when a state Medicaid agency approached Becker to help with a cost-benefit assessment for clozapine, a new and very expensive antipsychotic. Medicaid wanted to develop authorisation criteria and assess which patients showed enough improvement with the medication to justify its continued use at high cost. It quickly became apparent that there was no easy way to assess "improvement" in a largely community-based sample of patients treated throughout the state. A significant number of patients did not seem to have improved using the required Brief Psychiatric Rating Scale (BPRS) scores, yet they were reported by treating clinicians as improved enough to warrant staying on clozapine, despite its high cost, risks, and need for weekly blood tests. We required an outcome measure that would capture the complexity of "improvement" from the patients' and clinicians' (and later the families') perspectives. It was also important to consider the complexity of change: one person may have significant improvement in one area, while someone else might improve very differently. A consensus developed that quality of life, with all its complexity, was the best outcome for measuring meaningful change in persons with treatment-resistant schizophrenia.

Since the literature did not reveal an instrument that would be easy to use, reflect client values and preferences, and include provider, client and family perspectives, we undertook to develop a new instrument. An advisory committee composed of psychiatric professionals, persons with schizophrenia, and family members guided the development.

Our measurement approach was influenced by the need for a practical index that clinicians would willingly use, and that would encompass what both clinicians and patients considered most important in their common-sense notion of "improvement". Our definition of quality of life was derived from many other definitions, including the work of Andrews and Withey (1976), Campbell et al (1976) and Ferrans and Powers (1992). Along with Ferrans (1990), we defined quality of life as "a person's sense of well-being that stems from satisfaction or dissatisfaction with the areas of life that are important to him/her". Since, according to our definition, quality of life is determined by the patient's values and perceptions of what's important, it followed that the instrument would have to allow for individual preference weighting.

Decisions on scoring are an integral part of instrument development. For example, there is no obvious way to decide whether the domain of health status is more or less important than that of interpersonal relationships. Allowing clinicians and family to rate the importance of different areas allows investigators to analyse whether the clinician, family, and patient agree on the relative importance of different areas of the patient's life. Developing the new instrument was complicated by the complexity of the construct, and by the number of possible methods of aggregation and scoring of each domain. The most common scoring approach has been the multi-faceted approach which provides a single score of quality of life by aggregating across items and domains. But in quality of life measurement for schizophrenia, important information about specific domains is lost in aggregation, which (1) decreases the clinical utility of the instrument; and (2) limits information about causation, which operates on specific outcomes, not on aggregations of domains.

While aggregated or single-score measures of quality of life may be adequate for economic decision-making, which simply looks at cost and outcome, they are not very helpful for clinical work. The mental-health objective of improving quality of life requires knowledge of which treatments improve overall quality of life, and about the processes which bring about that improvement. Domain-specific information will allow clinicians and researchers to understand the process by which patients judge their overall quality of life, and how different components are perceived and valued. Such data also help to discriminate between the long-term effects of competing therapies and in making resource-allocation decisions.

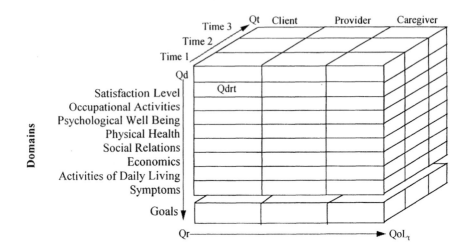

Qdrt = Evalutaion of a particular domain with respect to a particular responder at a certain point in time.
Qt   = Evaluation of Quality of Life across time.
Qd   = Evaluation across domains.
Qr   = Evaluation across responders.
QoL_t = Evaluation of Quality of Life as a whole (perceived QoL) at any point in time.

Figure 10.1   Measurement model for evaluating quality of life

The conceptual framework for the W-QLI includes eight semi-independent domains: life satisfaction, occupational activities, psychological well-being, physical health, social relations, economics, activities of daily living, and symptoms. Each domain is independently assessed by the patient, the primary clinician, and a family member or some other significant person (if available). Goal attainment is included as a ninth domain, with its own scoring strategy (see Figure 10.1). The instrument represents a new and unique approach to measurement. Although intended for people with schizophrenia, it can be used for other community-living people with serious, persistent mental illness.

MULTI-DIMENSIONALITY OF THE CONSTRUCT

In developing the Wisconsin Quality of Life Index, we conceptualised quality of life as a complex, multi-dimensional construct that includes subjective or perceived (patient-rated) as well as objective assessment of each domain. In this conceptual model, the greater the discrepancy between desired and achieved outcomes, the poorer the quality. Quality of life is a reflection of how patients perceive and react to important aspects of their lives, including health status. We argue that an individually preference-weighted measurement will be more accurate in reflecting the patients' evaluations, rather than clinicians' or researchers' evaluations. If, as suggested by Strauss (1989) and Diamond (1985) patients' subjective experiences influence the phases, course and outcome of schizophrenia, then it becomes particularly important that instruments reflect their experience.

Since the domains on W-QLI are all facets of a person's underlying quality of life, in our initial study we expected (and found) moderate correlations between and among them. Yet the observed correlations between domain scores were not strong enough to raise the possibility that the domains were not empirically distinct from one another. For example, in keeping with clinical descriptions and our experience, we found that activity of daily living (ADL) functioning was only weakly associated (0.33) with psychiatric symptoms. Our data show that patients with similar levels of ADL functioning can experience mild or severe psychiatric symptoms. Psychiatric symptoms and patients' global ratings of their QoL were only modestly correlated, suggesting that patient-perceived quality of life is not well predicted by their psychopathology. In the validation study of the W-QLI, the domain most strongly correlated with global quality of life was social relations (0.58) (Becker et al, 1993; Sainfort et al, 1996).

ISSUES OF SENSITIVITY IN QUALITY OF LIFE MEASUREMENT

Although most quality of life instruments give equal weight to the various domains, it is unlikely that each domain would have the same significance to persons of different ages, genders and ethnicity. Despite concern expressed about the cultural sensitivity of quality of life instruments, few have attempted to validate existing measures for diverse populations. Since subjective assessment of quality of life is inherently based on one's values, attitudes, and conceptual framework, it is very likely that significant differences in culture will affect the measurement of quality of life. Few of the commonly used instruments allow patients to speak for themselves, to evaluate separately the importance of different domains, or to add topics they might be particularly concerned about.

It is likely that different cultural groups will weight the domains differently. Unfortunately, initial data from the W-QLI did not include enough of a culturally diverse subject group to analyse this issue; preliminary data suggest that men and women with schizophrenia use different importance weighting. These gender differences are in the same direction as would be expected in the general population: for example, women rank interpersonal relationships as more important to their quality of life than men do, while men rank the importance of occupational activities higher than women do (Becker et al, 1994). As anticipated, we found differences between clinicians and patients in their weighting of domains: clinicians placed more importance on symptoms than patients did, while patients rated social relations more important than clinicians did (Sainfort et al, 1996).

ACHIEVING INDIVIDUAL GOALS AS PART OF QUALITY OF LIFE

Despite evidence about the importance of psychiatric patients' individual goals for treatment, quality of life instruments rarely ask about them or the degree to which patients believe they are being achieved. While one person may stress ability to work, another may stress absence of side-effects or improved personal relationships. Diamond (1985) suggests that these personal goals and aspirations affect compliance with medication and can therefore be important to outcome. Attention to patients' treatment goals can help to plan rehabilitation approaches and decide on vocational or residential placements (Anthony et al, 1990). Collaborative work on treatment goals also has the potential to improve the client–clinician working alliance, which is predictive of improved outcomes of care. The W-QLI index does ask about personal goals: patients state their goals for improvement with treatment, they rank the importance of the goals, and rate the degree to which they feel they have achieved their goal. Documenting patients' important and unmet needs may help clinicians to target their interventions to areas of greatest need (Figure 10.2). Information from the goals domain can be used to create a matrix of clients' needs; it also allows patients and providers to track progress toward goals that have been selected by the patient as most important.

A taxonomy of treatment goals for improvement with treatment proposed by clients, clinicians, and families was developed by Becker and Feinstein (1994) from the verbatim data provided by the W-QLI (Table 10.1). The outline of categories proposed by responders indicates that clients desire the very things that make up a good quality of life for the general population. The dimensions of the taxonomy of responders' goals for improvement with treatment bears a striking resemblance to the conceptual model of quality of life used to develop the W-QLI. This finding supports the sensibility of our conceptual model, which views quality of life in the context of patients' values and in relation to their goals and

Importance

	Not important	Important
Satisfaction domain Satisfied	Not important and satisfied	Important and satisfied
Not satisfied	Not important and not satisfied	Important and not satisfied

Figure 10.2 Needs matrix

expectations. The W-QLI model, with its individualised importance weighting, incorporates the individual's perspective, instead of imposing a socially prescriptive definition. Preliminary data collected with the W-QLI indicate that families and clients more frequently stress the importance of goals related to desires for improved social relations and interpersonal functioning, while

Table 10.1 Taxonomy of treatment goals for persons with schizophrenia proposed by clients, clinicians and families

1. Control of disease
   - 1.1   Features/Symptoms of disease
   - 1.2   Compliance
   - 1.3   Control of side-effects of treatments

2. Control of personal status
   - 2.1   Independence
   - 2.2   Occupation
   - 2.3   Self-care
   - 2.4   Quality of life

3. Interpersonal status
   - 3.1   Family relationships
   - 3.2   Relationships with others
   - 3.3   Social functioning

4. Caregiver relief
   - 4.1   Reduce family burden

5. Miscellaneous

clinicians more frequently stress goals related to symptom reduction and patients' compliance with treatment.

DIRECTIONS FOR FUTURE RESEARCH

Despite extensive investigation in medicine, we still know relatively little about the causal sequence of quality of life or the important interaction between objective and subjective quality of life factors. The situation is complicated by empirical evidence showing that positive quality of life evaluations represent different causal processes from negative evaluations (Costa & McCrae, 1980; Heady & Wearing, 1989) and that subjective and objective evaluations do not necessarily coincide. For example, depending on the study, patient mood can account for up to 40% of the variance in quality of life outcomes (Becker et al, 1994; Moum, 1988). While it is clear that quality of life is not independent of morbidity, the exact nature of the connection is unclear. Research has not examined the interaction of symptoms with occupational and functional outcomes in schizophrenia, so that we are uncertain about the relative importance of these factors to the course and outcome of the disease. Although most of the studies dealing with chronic mental illness have focused on schizophrenia, as noted earlier, they have mostly considered psychopathology and have been focused on positive and negative symptoms, rather than on functional or subjective outcomes (Fenton & McGlashan, 1991; Lehman & Burns, 1990; Pogue-Geile & Harrow, 1984). Thus, future research is needed on the relationship among domains, but until the necessary theoretical work is accomplished, the definitional confusions for quality of life are likely to continue.

Additional work needs to be done to validate the applicability of the numerous measures to diverse social–cultural groups and across the developmental and chronological age span. Further, we need studies to understand the psychological reaction of patients to their illness and to examine quality of life as several different causal sequences rather than a single outcome. Comparative studies are needed to determine which instruments or combinations of instruments and measurement approaches are most useful, reliable, and valid, for measuring quality of life in patients with schizophrenia.

To understand the complex dynamics of quality of life in schizophrenia, the interrelationship of important factors such as patients' coping style, mood, hopefulness, and quality of life evaluations needs to be studied. These factors have been shown to have an important influence on quality of life (Evans, 1981, 1991; Moum, 1988; Farran et al, 1994). For example, one possible way of coping with schizophrenia is for patients to substantially reduce their goals and expectations. While an avoidant style of coping may reduce negative quality of life, it also reduces positive events and therefore may reduce life quality. We propose that future research concentrate on investigating the causal sequence of quality of life and important interactions between psychiatric morbidity and other quality factors. Future studies with the W-QLI will include investigation of the links and interactions between domains, and the importance of culture, gender, economics, and treatment setting to quality of life outcomes in schizophrenia. Finally, an important new direction for quality of life research is the use of quality measurement as a means to structure and improve the working alliance between patients and service providers. In an era of health care reform, it will be increasingly important to link outcome measurement with outcome improvement and to use the process of measurement itself to improve quality of care.

CONCLUSION

Results from the validation studies of instruments document that quality of life measures can be sensitive to population differences and treatment effects (Bigelow et al, 1991b; Lehman, 1988; Levitt et al, 1990; Malm et al, 1981; Revicki et al, 1992; Lehman et al, 1991). Hence, they can be used to evaluate the effect of drug therapy on patients' lives, and measure the cost–benefits of mental health service (Hogan et al, 1983; Patrick, 1992; Revicki & Murray, 1994). Due to the variety of definitions and approaches used in existing research, interpreting and generalizing from existing research is difficult.

It is premature to make recommendations about specific instruments or to define a "gold standard". The challenge is to level the playing field by developing consistent definitions, scoring and concepts. Standardised approaches and instruments would allow meta-analysis of divergent studies and increase our understanding of quality of life as a treatment outcome and causal sequence in schizophrenia. A comprehensive and coherent theoretical model of quality of life is needed to inform the research methodology, to guide the construction of new instruments, and to help develop clinical practices to improve patients' quality of life.

QUALITY OF LIFE IN SPECIFIC MENTAL DISORDERS

CHAPTER ELEVEN

Quality of Life in Depression

Heinz Katschnig and Matthias C. Angermeyer

INTRODUCTION

Suppose you have experienced depressed mood most of the day for the last two weeks, have markedly diminished interest or pleasure in all or almost all activities, feel worthless and tired all the time and have recurrent thoughts of death (i.e. you suffer from Major Depression according to DSM-IV) – how would you evaluate your quality of life? Your evaluation would, of course, depend on how quality of life is defined. If it is equated with subjective well-being, happiness and life satisfaction – as is the case in most quality of life studies in medicine – it is obvious that you would judge your quality of life as reduced. If a judgement about satisfaction with various life domains is added, it would most probably reflect the typically bleak way in which depressed persons look at themselves, the world and the future (Beck, 1976).

As defined by operational criteria, depression is a highly prevalent disorder in the general population. At least one in six Americans suffers from a major depressive episode at some stage during his/her life, and the lifetime prevalence for the less severe but longer lasting form of depression – dysthymia – is over 6% (Kessler et al, 1994). Comorbidity with other psychiatric disorders, especially substance abuse and anxiety disorders is high (Weissman et al, 1996). Depression is also highly prevalent among medical patients, especially in those suffering from chronic conditions (Friedman & Booth-Kewley, 1987; Katon et al, 1990; von Korff et al, 1992), a fact that is seemingly not yet well understood in quality of life research on somatic disorders (Jacobson et al, 1997, see below).

Today's quality of life research has been decisively shaped both by the long-standing neglect of the patient's subjective experience of his/her disease in medicine and by consumer dissatisfaction with medical services (Albrecht & Fitzpatrick, 1994). The rising awareness of this neglect has – over the last two decades – led to two developments. Firstly, the application of *well-being scales* in medicine. Examples are the "Affect Balance Scale" (ABS) by Bradburn (1969), the "Quality of Well-Being Scale" (QWBS) by Kaplan et al (1976) and the "Psychological General Well-Being Index" (PGWB) by Dupuy (1984). Secondly, disease-specific instruments for measuring quality of life in somatically ill patients, which focus on the *subjective* view of the patient, were developed.

Of the literally hundreds of quality of life instruments developed in this period, virtually all put the emphasis on psychological well-being and subjective life satisfaction. Certainly, with a more and more technically determined medicine, assessing "quality of life" in terms of psychological well-being and satisfaction provides the basis for a more humanistic and holistic approach to the somatically ill patient. Today, it seems to be generally agreed that health-related quality of life (HRQOL) refers to the ways in which health, illness, and medical treatment influence an *individual's perception of functioning and well-being* (Jacobson et al, 1997, italics by the present authors). In a recent article, Gill and Feinstein (1994) emphatically supported this subjectivity approach in quality of life research.

In consequence, most quality of life instruments used today in medicine: (1) measure *subjective* well-being; (2) elicit the patient's *subjective* satisfaction with various aspects of life; and (3) are *self-rating* instruments. However, it will be argued below that relying on this "subjectivity" approach in assessing quality of life in depression is tautological. This is because of the overlap of the concepts of well-being and satisfaction with depression, and because of the negative influence of depressed mood on the perception of oneself and the environment. The following section of this chapter will discuss these problems, before we go on to advocate a broader and multi-dimensional concept of quality of life which includes social functioning and environmental living conditions.

DEPRESSION AND PSYCHOLOGICAL WELL-BEING: THE INDIVIDUAL'S PERSPECTIVE

In their frequently quoted paper "The Functioning and Well-being of Depressed Patients: Results from the Medical Outcomes Study" Wells et al (1989) report that a group of 2476 depressed patients (defined by a specific cut-off score on an eight-item depression symptom scale) scored below patients with chronic medical conditions on a well-being measure, defined as "perception of current health, such as feeling well or ill" and measured by five items. They used an earlier version of the now well known SF-36 (Ware & Sherbourne, 1992). Pyne et al (1997) applied the Quality of Well-Being (QWB) scale by Kaplan et al (1976) to assess the quality of life of patients with major depression. The *"quality of well-being index"* includes four subscales: symptom or problem complex, mobility, physical activity, and social activity, but produces a single figure between 0 ("death") and 1 ("asymptomatic optimal functioning"). Measured with this index, the reduction in quality of life associated with psychiatric symptoms of depression was found comparable to that observed among physically ill patients – a finding which is similar to that reported by Wells et al (1989).

Both studies use the term "well-being" and report that it is reduced in depressed persons, but it is doubtful whether they measured the same phenomenon. What does "well-being" mean? The literature on the meaning and measurement of psychological well-being – especially on the numbers and kinds of its subdimensions – is controversial. For instance, Ryff (1995) argues that "well-being" should be assessed on the following six theory-derived dimensions: personal growth and purpose in life, environmental mastery and autonomy, positive relations with others and self-acceptance. She criticises the issue often being simplified just to distinguishing two dimensions: happiness (the affective component of well-being) and satisfaction (the cognitive component), and says the theoretical foundation of this distinction is weak.

The discussion whether positive affect ("joy, happiness") and negative affect ("joylessness", "unhappiness") should be regarded as independent dimensions or just as opposite ends of one single dimension, is complex (see Ryff & Keyes, 1995; Bech, 1996). While it is justifiably argued by psychologists that "to be well psychologically is more than to be free of distress or other mental problems" (Ryff, 1995), i.e. that a person who is free of distress may or may not experience positive well-being in several domains, it is quite evident that depression excludes the experience of positive well-being. If joy and happiness are a component of psychological well-being, then "joylessness" in a depressive state means, by definition, that well-being is reduced. The old term "anhedonia" captures this characteristic feature of depression in a telling way.

Given this relationship, it is only logical that depression items, as representing negative affect, were included in virtually all of the several hundreds of quality of life instruments published to date. Examples are the QLQ-C30 (Aaronson et al, 1993) developed by the EORTC (European Organization for Research and Treatment of Cancer), the EUROQOL (EuroQol group, 1990), and the FACT (Functional Assessment of Cancer Therapy) developed by Cella et al (1993b). In many quality of life studies on somatic disorders explicit psychopathological rating scales such as the Hospital Anxiety and Depression Scale (HADS; Zigmond & Snaith, 1983) are overtly used as measures for "quality of life" (e.g. Hopwood et al, 1994).

Following the general trend of developing disease-specific quality of life instruments, two depression-specific quality of life inventories were also published a few years ago, the "Quality of Life in Depression Scale" (QLDS) by McKenna and Hunt (1992) and the "SmithKline Beecham Quality of Life Scale" (SBQOL) by Stoker et al (1992a,b). Both were primarily developed for measuring change in clinical trials of antidepressants and are self-rating instruments. A closer look at the items of these inventories suggests that the resulting measure for quality of life should be closely correlated with the severity of depression, since many items correspond to depression items in the usual rating scales for depression (e.g.: I have lost all pleasure in life; It is difficult for me to make even simple decisions; I feel useless; I do not enjoy life). A study by Katschnig et al (1996) confirmed this assumption. In 100 depressed and anxious patients, the total score of the Beck Depression Inventory, a self-rating instrument for assessing the severity of depression (BDI; Beck et al, 1961), correlated significantly both with the total scores of the QLDS (0.69) and with that of the SBQOL (0.70).

In addition to affective psychological well-being, subjective satisfaction with various life domains is usually separately assessed in health-related quality of life research. The Quality of Life Enjoyment and Satisfaction Questionnaire (Q-LES-Q) by Endicott et al (1993) already captures this distinction in its titles. But how independent are such satisfaction judgements from a state of depression? Cognitive theories of depression suggest that they are not (Beck, 1976). Similar evidence comes from psychological research, which indicates that people use their momentary affective state as information in making judgements of how happy and satisfied they are with their lives (Schwarz & Clore, 1983). In order to check whether this assumption is correct in a clinically depressed population, we also used the Quality of Life Enjoyment and Satisfaction Questionnaire (Q-LES-Q) in the above-mentioned sample (Katschnig et al, 1996). We not only found a high correlation between the BDI score and the "enjoyment dimension" of this questionnaire (0.62), but also with the aggregate satisfaction rating (0.62).

Finally, the use of the above-mentioned and most other quality of life inventories as self-rating instruments is highly problematic. It is difficult to know what a patient means when making the rating (Williams & Wilkinson, 1995), and the influence of negative affect and cognition on ratings is even less controllable than it is in an interview (Atkinson et al, 1997).

Thus, subjective assessment of one's well-being, ratings of subjective satisfaction with different life domains, and the application of self-rating scales are all of doubtful value when assessing the quality of life of depressed patients. Evidence is accumulating that the scores obtained in this way are closely correlated with the severity of depression and do not provide any useful additional information – especially if quality of life is to be assessed in a clinical setting where therapeutic action is the aim of the assessment (Atkinson et al, 1997). It seems that depression and reduced quality of life – as measured by the inventories discussed above – are tautological concepts, and measuring both with similar instruments is a clear case of measurement redundancy leading to spurious correlations (Monroe & Steiner, 1986). It is not much more than sticking the new label "quality of life" on the old bottle "depression". Thus, the finding that psychological well-being is impaired in depression must be regarded as at least trivial – if not problematic – since concentrating on assessing quality of life instead of on depression might lead to overlooking the presence of a treatable comorbid depression in somatically ill patients (Jacobson et al, 1997).

DEPRESSION, FUNCTIONING IN EVERYDAY LIFE AND LIVING CONDITIONS: THE CONTEXTUAL PERSPECTIVE

We contend that there is no way around a multi-dimensional concept of quality of life for depressed persons. In this connection, it is useful to stress the sociological perspective coming from the tradition of social indicators and health status research, which is a multi-dimensional one (Siegrist & Junge, 1989; Albrecht & Fitzpatrick, 1994).

In a recent study on the relocation of chronic psychiatric patients into the community, Barry and Crosby (1996) found a dissociation between the patients' subjective assessment of life satisfaction – which had not improved – and objective indices, for example improved living conditions, higher levels of social contact, and increased leisure activities. In chronic depression, such a dissociation might be observed the other way round: patients might be subjectively dissatisfied and complain about reduced well-being, while their objective functioning and/or actual living conditions, including social support, might be appropriate. Kay et al (1964) observed that complaints of loneliness in elderly depressed patients proved to have little association with actual isolation, while Morgado et al (1991) found that depressed patients unwittingly over-report poor social adjustment, which they reappraise when recovered.

Albrecht and Fitzpatrick (1994) have criticised the fact that such conceptual issues as the multi-dimensional nature of quality of life, as opposed to a uni-dimensional assessment of well-being, have been neglected so far in relevant research, and that psychometric considerations have unduly dominated conceptual thinking. Similarly, Romney and Evans (1996) have argued for a multi-dimensional model of quality of life and have demonstrated the usefulness of including other domains than psychological well-being and life satisfaction.

At least two additional domains – functioning in daily life or disability on the one hand, and environmental living conditions, both material and social, on the other – should be included in a broader quality of life concept. This approach is being pursued in psychiatry, both by new multi-axial diagnostic systems (e.g. the multiaxial version of the ICD-10; Janca et al, 1996; WHO, 1997) and by more complex assessment instruments which have been available for some time (e.g. the Standardised Interview to Assess Social Maladjustment and Dysfunction by Clare & Cairns, 1978; Katschnig, 1983). They are so far not used extensively in quality of life research, although social functioning is often assessed (but mostly as a self-report measure), while environmental living conditions are rarely included. Bech (1994) has stressed this multi-dimensional perspective by introducing the "PCASEE" model, where P stands for physical indicators, C for cognitive indicators, A for affective indicators, S for social indicators, E for economic-social stressors, and the second E for ego functions.

There is abundant evidence that both acute and chronic depression are associated with social dysfunction. Depression seems to impair the ability to interact appropriately with the social environment, in terms both of the fulfilment of more formal roles and of interacting with the immediate environment. Depressed persons thereby undermine positive feedback from others (Lewinsohn, 1974), which in turn prevents them from interacting properly, and so on. In psychological research, rejection of depressed persons by others is a consistent finding (Coyne, 1976; Gurtman, 1986).

One of the earliest methods used for assessing functioning in social roles is the "Social Adjustment Scale" (SAS) by Weissman and Paykel (1974). These authors demonstrated reduced functioning in social roles (such as parental, housewife, leisure) in depressed women; later, the same findings were reported for men (Weissman et al, 1978). Wells et al (1989) found that the extent to which depression interfered with work, housework, or schoolwork on the one hand and with social activities such as visiting friends or relatives on the other, was significantly higher than for chronic medical conditions. Also, the number of days in bed due to depression in the last 30 days was higher than in most other chronic conditions. Similarly, a large number of studies have documented that depression is accompanied by impairment and disabilities in role functioning (Blumenthal & Dielman, 1975; Fredrichs et al, 1982; Craig & Van Natta, 1983; Puig-Antick et al, 1985a; Klerman, 1989; Broadhead et al, 1990; Dew et al, 1991; Mintz et al, 1992; Tweed, 1993; Rogers et al, 1993; Lyness et al, 1993; Goethe & Fischer, 1995; Alexopoulos et al, 1996; Mauskopf et al, 1996; Lépine et al, 1997). It is beyond the scope of this chapter to analyse factors which affect the impairment associated with a depressive episode. Akiskal (1988) and Hirschfeld et al (1989) have suggested that pre-morbid personality factors may be important mediators of such impairment.

The extent of impairment of social functioning seems to be not so much dependent on the severity of depression, but on its duration. Several studies have found that dysthymia, a milder but longer lasting form of a depressive disorder, is associated with greater impairment in both social and occupational functioning than is episodic major depression (Stewart et al, 1988; Cassano et al, 1989; Wells et al, 1989; Johnson et al, 1992; Spitzer et al, 1995; Leader & Klein, 1996).

Both Bothwell and Weissman (1977) and Paykel et al (1978) found evidence of persisting social maladjustment after the ending of depression. Similar effects on social functioning have been reported by Goering et al (1983) and Puig-Antick et al (1985b), though some studies have failed to find persisting effects (Carson & Carson, 1984; Zeiss & Lewinson, 1988; Rhode et al, 1990). More recently, Tweed (1993) confirmed persisting effects, identifying certain symptoms (mood, an extended dysphoric period, fatigue, sexual disinterest, cognitive problems and suicidal ideation/behaviour) as being associated with both concurrent and lingering impairment. Why social disabilities persist even after the remission of depression is not quite clear. It might be that unrecognised subdepressive residual symptoms are responsible for this ongoing malfunctioning. Ormel et al (1993a) observed among depressed general practice attenders that 38% of patients were still at least mildly impaired in social role functioning three and a half years after baseline, while most other disabilities (self-care, family role, occupational role) had practically disappeared. In that study, improvements in symptoms and disabilities were largely synchronous, and patients with unimproved or residual symptoms continued to be dysfunctional (Ormel et al, 1993b). Wells et al (1992) carried out a longitudinal follow-up study on a subsample of their depressed patients of the "Medical Outcomes Study" (MOS) (Wells et al, 1989) and found that social functioning had only partially improved after two years.

In order to appreciate more fully the implications of the quality of life of depressed patients, one further step seems to be necessary: the assessment of the depressed patient's living conditions, which may influence his or her well-being and functioning and may contribute to chronicity or relapse. By impairing functioning in social roles and at work, depression may eventually lead to depriving the depressed person of both material and social support. (See also Ch. 5 this volume.)

Several epidemiological studies show that depressed persons are disadvantaged in many respects. In the OPCS Surveys of Psychiatric Morbidity in Great Britain, Meltzer et al (1996) reported that persons with depressive episodes have a significantly increased risk of living as a "lone person with child(ren)" or in a "one person only" household, and being unemployed or economically inactive. Men with a depressive episode had the highest percentage (25%) of all neurotic disorders for "permanently unable to work", as opposed to only 3% of those without neurotic disorders. In the US National Comorbidity Survey, Blazer et al (1994) found that major depression was significantly correlated with "separated/ widowed/divorced and never married" status and with employment classification as a homemaker. In the Epidemiological Catchment Area (ECA) study, men and women with a history of affective disorders were found to have greater difficulty obtaining and maintaining employment; those with a major depressive disorder in the last year were significantly more often financially dependent on other persons than were non-depressed subjects (Robins & Regier, 1991).

As a rule, it is impossible to distinguish between cause and effect in such cross-sectional studies; it is remarkable that, nevertheless, the social factors described above are usually discussed only under the topic of causative and not outcome aspects of depression (e.g. Smith & Weissman, 1992). Prospective longitudinal studies would be necessary to clarify this relationship. There are only a few such studies about the effect of depression on environmental living conditions. Merikangas (1984) reported the divorce rate among previously depressed patients to be nine times that of the general population, two years after discharge, while Coyne et al (1987; 1988) and Hammen (1990) stressed that depression leads to life disruptions (relational disruption, career setbacks, etc.). Wittchen and von Zerssen (1987) found an increased proportion of divorced persons among depressed patients, seven years after intake into their follow-up study, and nearly 10% prematurely in receipt of pensions. In an ECA panel study, Coryell et al (1993) demonstrated a decline in job status and income in a five-year follow-up study of patients with bipolar and unipolar affective disorder. In contrast, Catalano et al (1994) did not find an effect of clinical depression on unemployment.

As a whole these results suggest that the relationship between depression and disadvantaged social and material status might be a circular one. Depression may lead to disadvantage and disadvantage may lead to depression. Future studies should consider both possibilities (Katschnig & Nutzinger, 1988).

AN ACTION-ORIENTATED MULTI-DIMENSIONAL FRAMEWORK FOR ASSESSING QUALITY OF LIFE IN DEPRESSION

We have argued so far that – at least for depression, if not for all psychiatric and somatic disorders – a broad multi-dimensional concept of quality of life should be employed. Even if "quality of life" in the narrow sense of psychological well-being and satisfaction with one's life is the focus of interest, both functioning in everyday life and social and material environmental living conditions have to be considered, since they may influence both psychological well-being and satisfaction in various life domains. A further reason for going beyond well-being and satisfaction is the high correlation of these concepts with depression, which implies that quality of life information which relies on psychological well-being and satisfaction measures is redundant. Finally, if assessment of quality of life is to have management implications, the functioning and environmental living conditions of individuals should be assessed as possible targets of therapeutic action.

While the number of variables and dimensions to be considered in a multi-dimensional model of quality of life in depression is arbitrary, we would like to suggest a framework including four dimensions, two psychological and two sociological ones (Figure 11.1). Our main motive for this choice is the theoretical importance of these dimensions (at least in some contemporary thinking), the possibility of measuring at least some aspects of these dimensions in a valid and reliable way and – the main motive – the availability of therapeutic and management strategies which can be conceived as acting specifically on each of these dimensions.

The psychological dimensions comprise a cognitive (self-esteem, satisfaction) and an affective one (well-being). If disturbed the specific corresponding treatments are cognitive therapy (for negative cognitions) and pharmacotherapy or non-cognitive psychotherapy (for negative affect). Of course, many different concepts can be subsumed under "cognitive" and "affective". Since cognitive and

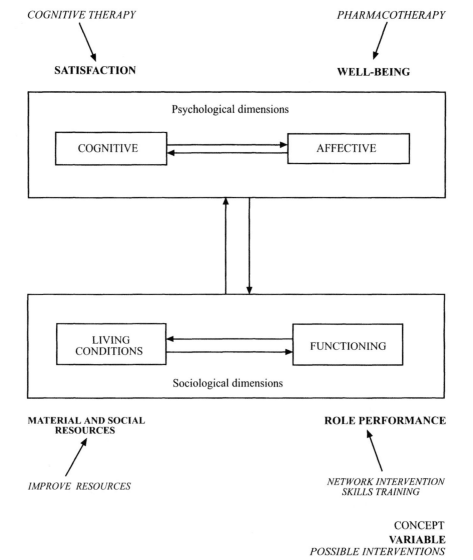

COGNITIVE THERAPY

PHARMACOTHERAPY

SATISFACTION

WELL-BEING

Psychological dimensions

COGNITIVE

AFFECTIVE

LIVING CONDITIONS

FUNCTIONING

Sociological dimensions

MATERIAL AND SOCIAL RESOURCES

ROLE PERFORMANCE

IMPROVE RESOURCES

NETWORK INTERVENTION SKILLS TRAINING

CONCEPT
VARIABLE
POSSIBLE INTERVENTIONS

Figure 11.1 An action-orientated multi-dimensional framework for assessing quality of life

affective factors are closely interrelated – according to cognitive theory cognitions influence emotions, whereas according to psychodynamic theories it is the other way round – they are subsumed here under the common heading "psychological dimensions".

The two sociological dimensions are "functioning in daily life" and "environmental living conditions", each with many possible subdimensions according to the life domains concerned, and differentiated according to both material and social aspects. Again, since both dimensions are closely interrelated (e.g. malfunctioning in social roles may lead to a break-up of relationships, with ensuing loneliness; lack of social support may lead to dysfunction in work roles), they are subsumed under one broad sociological heading. Management actions would comprise network intervention, skills training or role play for social dysfunction, and intervention aimed at the improvement of environmental resources (housing, jobs, social support).

In addition to the interrelations within each category, the psychological and sociological domains may influence each other. In this framework, it is assumed that practically all depicted causal relationships are possible. Thus, social disadvantage may be the cause of psychological ill-health ("depression"), as well as its consequence. The same is true for therapeutic intervention. Cognitive therapy, like pharmacotherapy, may eventually lead to better role functioning, while correcting social disadvantage (e.g. unemployment) might lead to the improvement of depression.

The main purpose of providing this framework is to demonstrate possible pathways for the origin of depression, its consequences, and possible interventions. These pathways have, to a large extent, still to be explored by empirical research, both descriptive and interventional. What is urgently needed are longitudinal studies which test such different pathways as the possible vicious circles "negative cognitions → depression → social malfunctioning → social disadvantage → negative cognitions", or "social disadvantage → social dysfunction → negative cognitions → depression" and so on. In addition, intervention studies would have to show at which points these circles can be interrupted. An example is a recently published study by Kocsis et al (1997) where it was shown that antidepressant pharmacotherapy can improve social functioning in dysthymic patients.

However, such research requires that the relevant variables are measurable in a valid and reliable way. Here, substantial work remains to be done. It is at least as difficult to assess a person's satisfaction with a specific aspect of life or the social support available to him/her as it is to elicit the presence of a specific psychopathological phenomenon; the traps in collecting these data are manifold. Self-rating procedures have no control over how a patient understands a specific item; self-reports (obtained either by self-rating or by interview) about functioning and living conditions may be heavily influenced by the emotional state of the respondent. Different measurement inventories may contain identical or very similar items, but nevertheless be labelled differently (in one instance a "depression rating scale" in the other a "well-being scale").

Measurement redundancy is one of the main problems in this field, that is, inventories or measures purporting to measure a specific phenomenon unwittingly also measure a different phenomenon (Monroe & Steiner, 1986). If a study aims at checking the relationship between such phenomena and uses redundant measurements, an identified correlation might be spurious.

For instance, many measures used in the quality of life field contain symptoms. This is obvious for the psychological well-being scales, but also for most of the more complex quality of life measures, which contain depression items. Also, the well-known Social Adjustment Scale (Weissman, 1975) contains symptoms, which has led Stewart et al (1988) to remove these symptoms from the scale, in order to assess properly the improvement of social functioning in a clinical trial of antidepressants. The most notable example of such a symptom-contaminated measure is the GAF (Global Assessment of Functioning), contained as Axis V in DSM-IV (American Psychiatric Association, 1994).

A more indirect kind of measurement redundancy takes place if the affective state of the respondent is not controlled for. Thus, depressed or manic patients might underestimate or overestimate their social support (Kay et al, 1964), and it is well known that satisfaction judgements are clearly influenced by actual mood state (Schwarz & Clore, 1983). One way out of this dilemma would be the use of third-party ratings (professionals or relatives), but few quality of life instruments (e.g. Spitzer et al, 1981; Becker et al, 1993) provide this possibility in addition to the usual self-reports. If such additional assessments by external observers are carried out, the results might be quite discrepant (Sainfort et al, 1996). An in-between strategy which at least reduces the influence of emotions on recall is the "experience sampling method" (ESM), whereby patients are prompted by a wrist-watch beep several times a day to report their thoughts, current activity, physical and social context (Barge-Schaapveld et al, 1995; Barge-Schaapveld et al, Ch. 8 this volume). A special case of measurement redundancy is the use of global indices, which is quite popular in quality of life research. Such global indices might be convenient for statistical purposes, but they are not useful either for planning clinical intervention or for correlational research, since they may contain unknown portions of other variables that they are finally correlated with.

In conclusion, there is no way around a multi-dimensional and differentiated assessment of quality of life in psychiatric, especially in emotional, disorders. As far as quality of life in depression is concerned, many questions remain open. Easy to use self-rating measures might be deceptive, especially when employed in clinical trials. Life is complicated, and there is no reason why one should not invest as much into properly assessing quality of life as into brain imaging.

CHAPTER TWELVE

Quality of Life in Anxiety Disorders

Franklin R. Schneier

INTRODUCTION

Anxiety disorders are among the most common mental disorders, and their familiarity may contribute to the perception that they are relatively mild forms of psychopathology. Yet these sufferers and the clinicians who treat them recognise that anxiety disorders have enormous effects on quality of life. While the impairment of this kind experienced by millions of people cannot be summarised by any single statistic, it is reflected in a recent estimate that the monetary costs of anxiety disorders account for 31.5% of the total costs of psychiatric disorder in the United States (DuPont et al, 1996).

Systematic assessment of quality of life in persons with anxiety disorders has been long neglected, but clinical experience suggests that specific forms of these disorders may affect it in different ways. Sufferers may be distracted from work, relationships, and recreation by cognitive symptoms of fear, worry, and obsession; they may be distressed by the physiological arousal symptoms which are prominent in panic disorders (PD), social phobia, post-traumatic stress disorder (PTSD), and generalised anxiety disorder (GAD); they may be limited by the avoidance which is intrinsic to the phobias and PTSD; and may be burdened by the secondary shame and demoralisation which sufferers of each of these disorders share. Comorbid conditions, often occurring secondary to the anxiety disorders, add to the strain.

Recently, however, researchers have begun to examine this question in a more sophisticated and comprehensive way, using a variety of approaches in different samples. The subjects include both persons in the community and patients in primary care or psychiatric treatment settings. Some studies have examined specific disorders, whereas others have studied anxiety symptoms or anxiety disorders as a single broad category. Many other studies have incidentally assessed aspects of quality of life in the context of other reports. This chapter will review the growing body of research specifically focused on quality of life in adults with anxiety disorders.

PANIC DISORDER AND AGORAPHOBIA

COMMUNITY SETTINGS

In the United States, systematic descriptions of impaired quality of life of persons with PD or panic attacks in the general population have emerged in reports from the Epidemiologic Catchment Area (ECA) study (Markowitz et al, 1989; Klerman et al, 1991). Researchers collected data from a random sample of over 18 000 adults living in five US communities. Klerman et al (1991) compared cases of lifetime DSM-III (American Psychiatric Association, 1980) PD ($n = 254$) and subsyndromal panic attacks ($n = 667$) with cases who had any other psychiatric disorder ($n = 4,857$) and persons with no such disorder ($n = 12,233$). Markowitz et al (1989) compared the same PD subjects ($n = 254$) to subjects with lifetime major depression without PD ($n = 738$) and subjects with neither panic nor major depression ($n = 17 113$). Demographic differences, comorbid mental disorders, and site differences were all controlled for in the following analyses.

Klerman et al (1991) reported that panic disorder (PD) subjects self-reported high rates of fair or poor physical health (35%) and fair or poor emotional health (38%). In comparison to subjects with no disorder, PD subjects were 5.7 times more likely to report fair or poor physical health, and 6.9 times more likely to report fair or poor emotional health. The rates among PD subjects did not differ from those among persons with subsyndromal panic, with major depression, or with any other psychiatric disorder.

Treatment-seeking may be another indicator of dissatisfaction with quality of life. Persons with PD or subsyndromal panic attacks had elevated rates of emergency department use, general medical professional care, and psychiatric professional care; of the use of minor tranquillisers, sleeping pills, or antidepressants; and of admission to psychiatric or general hospital for emotional problems. Of PD subjects 86% had sought at least some professional treatment, versus 67% of subsyndromal panic attack subjects, 66% of major depression subjects, and 31% of subjects with any other psychiatric disorder.

Economic limitations were assessed by the rate of receiving either welfare or disability payments. More persons with PD (27%) or subsyndromal panic attacks (19%) received public assistance, in comparison to persons with no psychiatric disorder (10%). The rate among persons with PD was also significantly greater than that among those with major depression (27% vs 16%). Periods of extended unemployment, with inability to look for work due to emotional problems, were reported by 9% of persons with PD and 3% of those with subsyndromal panic attacks.

Markowitz et al (1989) examined some other quality of life measures. In regard to social functioning, PD subjects did not differ from persons with major depression or with neither panic nor major depression in their likelihood of having spent time with relatives, friends, or in social activities in the prior two weeks. However, both panic subjects and depressed subjects were more likely to report having spent no time on hobbies in the prior two weeks. Both panic subjects and major depression subjects reported higher rates of not getting along well with their spouses, and of seldom or never confiding in their spouses. Suicide attempts were reported by 20% of PD subjects, which was a significantly greater rate than the 2% among persons with neither panic nor depression, but did not differ from the 15% rate among depressed persons.

More recently, data from the National Comorbidity Survey (NCS), a study of 8098 respondents in civilian household populations of the United States, using DSM-III-R diagnoses (American Psychiatric Association, 1987), have largely supported the ECA study results (Eaton et al, 1994). It is notable that the NCS yielded substantially higher prevalences of anxiety disorders than the ECA study, probably due to several methodological differences (Kessler et al, 1994). The NCS's larger anxiety disorder sample may include many milder cases, which would not have been identified in the ECA study.

Among 274 persons with panic disorder in the NCS, 106 (39%) also met criteria for agoraphobia. PD was associated with having had fewer than 12 years of education, but unlike the reports of the ECA data, it was not significantly associated with income. People who were not working, were unmarried, and those who were living alone tended to have a higher prevalence of PD than others.

In the NCS study, 86% of persons with a lifetime diagnosis of agoraphobia had any comorbid lifetime diagnosis, and 22% had a lifetime diagnosis of PD (Magee et al, 1996). Agoraphobia was more common among persons who were not working, not receiving education, and not being a homemaker. Serious interference with life and activities was reported by 27% of agoraphobics, but by only 3% of agoraphobics without comorbid disorders. Similarly, professional help for their phobias was sought by 41% of agoraphobics, and by 22% of agoraphobics without comorbid disorders. Employed persons who had had agoraphobia in the past 30 days reported missing a mean of 1.1 days of work per month. Agoraphobia was not associated with low social support, and agoraphobics were significantly less likely than others to live alone.

CLINICAL SETTINGS

Edlund and Swann (1987) studied economic and social disability in 30 out-patients attending a clinic for a biological study of PD. At the time of interview, 53% of patients were unemployed, 23% were working part-time, and 24% were working full time. It was reported by 83% that the quality of their work had declined at some time due to panic attacks or phobias. Also 67% lost jobs or income from jobs, and 50% were unable to drive beyond a 3-mile radius or on the freeway.

Siegel et al (1990) administered a questionnaire to 65 individuals attending a free informational seminar on panic, who either reported having been given a diagnosis of PD by a professional or confirmed DSM-III-R (American Psychiatric Association, 1987) criteria for panic disorder. These subjects reported a mean of 3.1 medical visits during the past month, with 47% of these visits to mental health professionals. Work missed due to illness averaged one day per month. Frequent life events which subjects attributed to their panic attacks were: losing a job (5%), leaving a job (17%), marital conflicts (9%), and depressed mood (27%). Subjects rated overall life satisfaction on a 7-point scale at a mean of 4.25 – lower than means for historical control studies of the general population (5.55) and of a group of patients with end-stage renal disease (5.0).

Perugi et al (1994) compared 48 Italian patients with PD, agoraphobia, and concomitant secondary chronic major depression to 35 patients with chronic major depression alone. They found that the group with chronic major depression alone had significantly more impairment in four of the nine areas of social adjustment examined: work, sexual adjustment, leisure activities, and interpersonal contacts. However, there were no differences in impairment in relationships with household members, parental role, household concerns, or personal well-being. The researchers suggest a number of explanations for the discrepancy of their findings with those of Markowitz et al (1989) described above, including differences between epidemiological and clinical samples, and the possibility that Italians place less value than Americans on "independence", resulting in less impairment in quality of life from agoraphobic dependency.

A World Health Organization study of 25 916 primary care facility patients in 14 countries examined impairment in functioning in persons with any of eight current psychiatric disorders, after controlling for physical disease severity (Ormel et al, 1994). Among 116 patients with ICD-10 PD, 58% were rated as having moderate or severe occupational role dysfunction, 55% had self-reported moderate or severe physical disability, and the mean number of disability days in the past month was 10.0. Among 159 patients with agoraphobia, 41% were rated as having moderate or severe occupational role dysfunction, 60% had self-reported moderate or severe physical disability, and the mean number of disability days in the past month was 7.3. When the analysis was limited to persons with a single psychiatric diagnosis, the severity of disability changed little for PD ($n = 28$), but decreased substantially for agoraphobia ($n = 38$).

Sherbourne et al (1996) assessed health-related quality of life in 433 out-patients with current PD from several sites. These patients were compared to more than 2400 out-patients with hypertension, diabetes, heart disease, arthritis, asthma, or major depression, participating in the Medical Outcomes Study (MOS). Health-related quality of life was assessed for each disease condition, controlling for other conditions, demographics, and study site.

Panic disorder patients had levels of mental health, role functioning, and social functioning which were substantially worse than those of patients with other major chronic medical illnesses, but better than or comparable to those of patients with depression. Their physical functioning, and perceptions of current health, however, were similar to general population norms.

In a study focusing on quality of marital life, Arrindell and Emmelkamp (1986) found that 30 female agoraphobic patients and their partners did not rate their marriages as more maladjusted or unpleasant than 11 non-phobic psychiatric patients and their partners. The agoraphobic patients and their partners were more similar to another control group of 38 happily married couples than to a control group of 14 maritally distressed couples.

EFFECTS OF TREATMENT

Arrindell et al (1986) assessed marital quality and general life adjustment in 25 married female agoraphobics who were treated with group exposure therapy and followed-up with their husbands for one year. The study sought to examine the idea that marital dysfunction may cause, perpetuate, or interfere with the treatment of agoraphobia. Clinically significant improvement was shown by 65% of the patients after treatment, and this improvement was generally maintained over a year of follow-up. On a standardised measure of marital quality, only 20% of patients and 24% of partners had scores comparable to a group of maritally distressed couples. Baseline marital quality was not correlated with severity of agoraphobia, and it did not predict response to exposure-based treatment. Whilst successful treatment did not have a negative effect on marital quality, unsuccessful treatment was associated with a deterioriation. Better initial work and social adjustment predicted better outcome on many measures.

Few other treatment studies in PD have focused on quality of life, although a recent consensus conference on the methodology of panic disorder research suggested that ratings of functional impairment, including social, work, and family impairment and use of medical care is essential (Shear & Maser, 1994). Many studies of both the behavioural and pharmacological treatment of PD, however, have demonstrated improvement in global ratings of social and work impairment, during and after treatment. One of the more widely used quality of life measures in studies of the pharmacological treatment of panic is the Sheehan Disability Scale (Sheehan, 1986), a self-rated measure with three items. Impairment in each of three areas of functioning (work, social, and family/home) is rated on an 11-point scale. Leon et al (1992) studied the scale's psychometric properties from two large multi-centre medication trials. He found that the scale demonstrated internal consistency, sensitivity to change with treatment, and validity in relation to severity of PD symptoms.

Economic measures may also reflect the toll of panic disorder on quality of life. Salvador-Carulla et al (1995) studied clinical and health care utilisation data on 61 patients with PD who completed a 12-month naturalistic treatment, during which two-thirds achieved remission of panic attacks. He compared various costs for the year prior to psychiatric treatment with the year of that treatment. The number of visits to non-psychiatric doctors was reduced from 313 in the year prior to treatment to 15 in the year of psychiatric treatment. Visits to emergency services decreased from 75 to 7. (Psychiatric visits, however, grew from 40 to 793.) There were dramatic decreases in the numbers of hospital admissions and diagnostic tests performed. Although all but two patients were treated with medication during the treatment phase, pharmaceutical costs actually decreased in the treatment year. Among patients who worked ($n = 29$), days of registered sick leave fell from 1050 to 190.

SUMMARY

Although PD with agoraphobia is the most studied anxiety disorder in regard to quality of life, existing studies only scratch the surface of the complex effects of this psychopathology on well-being. The available data, however, are highly consistent with clinical experience of substantial impairment, which is largely reversible through treatment.

Most striking from the community studies is the high rate of treatment-seeking among persons with panic disorder, which reflects the intensity of physical and psychological symptoms of acute panic. Evidence of the more chronic problems of this illness is present in global self-ratings of poor physical and emotional health in community, primary care, and psychiatric clinic samples. Both community and clinical samples rate important aspects of their quality of life worse than do persons with such severe conditions as end-stage renal disease or heart disease. In regard to physical health, however, more fine-grained measures show that physical functioning is less severely impaired, compared with some chronic general medical illnesses.

From the community data alone, it is not possible to determine whether the high frequency of unemployment and need for public financial assistance are cause or effect of PD. In clinical samples of patients, the even higher frequencies of employment problems and their frequent attribution to PD suggests that employment problems often occur secondary to the illness. Beyond these gross measures of quality of life in work, it is also clear that PD patients report frequent absence from work and a decline in their quality of work.

Again consistent with clinical experience, there is some evidence that social relationships are relatively spared in PD and agoraphobia. Panic subjects report less social than work impairment, and agoraphobics in the community are less likely to be living alone, perhaps reflecting their need for companionship to manage their fears. However, the same need for a companion to protect the sufferer may strain a relationship or cause the sufferer to put up with an otherwise unsatisfactory relationship. These conflicting pulls may explain the somewhat mixed findings on the quality of these persons' relationships and marriages.

The findings for agoraphobia are notable for the relatively low rates of impairment and treatment-seeking among those without comorbidity. This is consistent with the infrequent presentation of pure agoraphobia in clinical settings. The discrepancies in quality of life between persons with pure vs comorbid disorders demonstrate the importance of clearly defining the samples under study, if comparisons are to be meaningful. On the other hand, subsyndromal variants of full disorders may also detract seriously from quality of life, as has been shown for subsyndromal panic attacks.

Data on the effects of treatment of PD and agoraphobia on quality of life are limited, but they are consistent with clinical findings of frequent dramatic symptomatic improvement and corresponding improvement in quality of life. These reports are supported by economic analyses of the treatment of PD, demonstrating a decline in treatment-seeking behaviour and improvement in work function.

SOCIAL PHOBIA

COMMUNITY SETTINGS

The ECA study examined persons with social phobia (SP) whose fears were limited to any of three situations: eating in front of others, speaking in front of a small group of familiar people, or speaking to strangers/meeting new people. The fears had to interfere with life or activities "a lot" (Schneier et al, 1992). Persons with lifetime SP ($n = 361$) were significantly less likely to be married than other subjects. Social phobia was associated with significantly elevated rates of suicidal ideation, even when it occurred without any other lifetime disorder ($n = 112$), in comparison to persons with no disorder ($n = 9953$). The rate of suicide attempts was elevated among social phobics with comorbid disorders, even after controlling for comorbidity. Pure social phobics were also more likely to be financially dependent on welfare or disability benefits. There were increased rates of some measures of seeking out-patient treatment in SP, although not to the extent seen in PD.

At one site, Davidson et al (1993, 1994) further examined a subgroup of ECA subjects who either had lifetime social phobia ($n = 123$) or reported a social fear but denied interference with life or activities (subsyndromal social phobia, $n = 248$). Despite denying interference on the screening questions, the subsyndromal group resembled the SP group on many measures, including those related to impairment in functioning. In comparison to persons with no disorder ($n = 1,117$), persons with subsyndromal SP and no other disorders ($n = 135$) earned less income, were less educated, were less likely to be married or to have at least one close friend, and were more likely to report "no confidence in handling problems". They also reported higher numbers of total and negative life events during the preceding year, and higher rates of hypnotic or minor tranquilliser use. Persons in the subsyndromal SP group were also more likely to report higher rates of having had poor grades or having had to repeat a grade in school.

In the National Comorbidity Survey (Magee et al, 1996), current (30-day prevalence) SP was significantly elevated among persons with low education and low family income, the never-married, students, persons who are neither working, nor students, nor homemakers, and among those who live with their parents. Self-reported serious interference with life and activities, as assessed by a single question, was reported by 34% of (lifetime prevalence) social phobics, and by 14% of social phobics without comorbid disorders. Professional help for their phobias was sought by 44% of social phobics, and by 17% of social phobics without comorbid disorders. Social phobia was also associated with low social support. Employed persons who had had SP in the past 30 days reported missing a mean of 0.5 days of work per month, which did not differ significantly from the general population. Social phobia was also found to be unrelated to financial adversity, as defined by either low family income in the total sample or low earning in the subsample of respondents who were employed.

The somewhat milder impairment in quality of life among persons with anxiety disorders in the National Comorbidity Study, compared to the ECA study, seems particularly notable in regard to SP. The National Comorbidity Survey used twice as many probe questions in the diagnosis of SP as did the ECA study, and it yielded a much higher lifetime prevalence of social phobia (13% vs 3%). The higher prevalence may reflect the inclusion of milder cases. This highlights an issue of great importance in comparing quality of life between diagnostic groups which are not purely homogeneous: measures of severity of impairment in quality of life are highly dependent on the scope of symptoms and severity thresholds used to define the diagnostic group.

This conclusion is supported by Stein et al (1994), who conducted a telephone survey of social anxiety in 526 randomly selected adults. In this 19% reported that their most anxiety-provoking situation resulted in either "a moderate amount" or "a great deal" of either (1) "negative effect" on life at home, work or school; or (2) personal distress. However, the rates of negative effects/personal distress varied by situation feared: among the 80 respondents who feared only public speaking in front of a large audience (a situation queried by the NCS, but not the ECA study) only 22.5% reported substantial negative effects/distress; among the 238 respondents who had social fears not limited to public speaking, 34% reported substantial negative effects/distress. Thus, persons with public speaking fears alone reported less impairment than those with more generalised social fears.

CLINICAL SETTINGS

Liebowitz et al (1985) reported a case series of 11 clinic patients with DSM-III-R social phobia. Of these 2 were unable to work, and 6 were blocked from work advancement; 2 had dropped out of school; 4 had abused alcohol; and 5 avoided almost all social interaction outside their immediate family. Turner et al (1986), reported that 85% of DSM-III social phobic patients felt impaired in academic or school functioning, 92% felt their occupational performance was significantly impaired, 69% felt their general social functioning was impaired, and half of the unmarried social phobics felt that their heterosocial functioning was limited.

Schneier et al (1994) systematically described impairment in functioning in a sample of 32 patients with a principal DSM-III-R diagnosis of SP who were attending an anxiety disorders clinic. Patients were either currently or previously in treatment for social phobia ($n = 23$), or were entering treatment ($n = 9$), so that they represent a partially treated sample. This study used two new scales for the assessment of impairment in functioning. The Disability Profile is a clinician-rated instrument with items assessing current and most severe lifetime impairment due to mental disorder in eight domains of functioning. Each item is rated on a 5-point descriptively anchored scale ranging from 0 (no impairment) to 4 (severe impairment). The Liebowitz Self-Rated Disability Scale is a patient-rated instrument which assesses similar domains of functioning.

On each scale, more than half of all patients reported at least moderate impairment at some time in their lives, due to SP, in areas of school/education, work/employment, family relationships, marriage/dating/romantic relationships, friendships/social network, and other interests. At least moderate impairment was less common in areas of activities of daily living and suicidal behaviour/desire to live. Mean scores suggested the following typical level of impairment due to social phobia: these patients were able to work at a job appropriate to their abilities, but clearly performed beneath their abilities; they had clear impairment in dating activities or minor marital problems; they were able to have a few close friends, but friendships were fewer than desired; and they were able to participate in some non-work interests (e.g. religious activities, clubs, hobbies), but avoided some activities due to social phobic symptoms. Total scores for current disability correlated with most measures of the severity of SP symptoms. Clinicians' ratings of current impairment in family, marriage/dating, friendships, other interests, and activities of daily living were most highly correlated with measures of symptom severity. A normal control group reported virtually no impairment in functioning due to social anxiety on the rating instruments.

SUMMARY

The data on quality of life for persons with social phobia offer a stark contrast between community samples, in which only a minority of subjects report gross impairment, and clinical samples, in which most patients suffer major impairment. This is consistent with reports of only a small percentage of persons with SP seeking treatment. The level of major impairment of quality of life may vary substantially with the severity of this condition. It is notable, however, that when quality of life is assessed in greater detail, as was done by Davidson et al (1993), even "subsyndromal" social phobics, who initially deny impairment, turn out to be significantly impaired. The true severity of impairment in quality of life may be underestimated by casual surveys.

This tendency to underestimate impairment in quality of life may be particularly likely in SP. Because of its early age of onset, typically in the early teens, social phobia becomes a way of life for many sufferers, since they avoid jobs which require public speaking and limit socialisation to small groups of familiar friends. In this context, persons with SP may not readily identify chronic deficits in their own quality of life.

Persons whose fears are limited to one or a few performance situations, such as public speaking, usually experience less impairment than those with generalised social fears. Even pure public speaking phobics, however, report a substantial rate of serious impairment or distress. The amount of impairment may depend heavily on job requirements for performance activities: a public speaking phobia which is career-ending for a musical performer might be trivial for a homemaker.

Persons with generalised SP appear more likely to be impaired via secondary depression, alcohol abuse, or other comorbid disorders than those with non-generalised social phobia. Social phobics as a group have also been consistently shown to be less likely to be married and to have problems in areas of education, work function, and social life, though basic self-care and activities of daily living appear less likely to be impaired. More subtle forms of impairment, such as failing to achieve one's potential in work, or settling for less-satisfying social relationships due to social fears, are surely present, although more difficult to measure.

SPECIFIC PHOBIAS

Magee et al (1996) reported on quality of life in the National Comorbidity Survey for persons with simple phobias, now termed "specific phobias" by DSM-IV (American Psychiatric Association, 1994). In this community sample, 83% of persons with a simple phobia had comorbid psychiatric disorders. Simple phobia was more common among adults with low education (but not low income), those who were not working, not receiving education, and not being a homemaker, and among those who live with their parents. Self-reported serious interference with life and activities, as assessed by a single question, was reported by 34% of lifetime simple phobics, and by 25% of simple phobics without comorbid disorders. Professional help for their phobias was sought by 30% of simple phobics, and by 30% of simple phobics without comorbid disorders. Employed persons who had simple phobia in the past 30 days reported missing a mean of 0.7 days of work per month. Simple phobia was also associated with low social support.

Contrary to clinical suggestions that specific phobias rarely result in marked impairment (American Psychiatric Association, 1987), in this community survey, simple phobias appeared to impair quality of life to at least as great an extent as agoraphobia and social phobia. This was true even for cases with no comorbidity. This surprising finding suggests a need for more detailed investigation of simple phobia in community and clinical samples.

A recent clinical study (Roy-Byrne et al, 1994) supports the idea that specific phobias occurring with comorbid disorders are more impairing than those which occur alone. In a clinical sample of 73 subjects attending a dental fears research clinic, 40% of the specific phobia subjects were found to have another current DSM Axis I diagnosis. Subjects with a comorbid diagnosis self-reported more severe impairment in role function, social function, mental health, and health perceptions than persons with a dental phobia alone. They also reported a more unstable early home life, more trouble with peer relationships, more school refusal and sleep difficulties, and more childhood separation anxiety.

In summary, while there are limited data on quality of life in persons with specific phobias, it appears that the impact of this disorder has been underestimated. As with social phobia, the nature of the particular specific phobia may greatly influence the impairment it causes. Dental or blood/injection/injury phobias may lead to avoidance of preventive treatment or failure to deal with serious medical conditions early, when treatment may be most effective. Situational phobias of public transport, flying, driving or enclosed spaces may lead to life constrictions similar to those seen in agoraphobia.

OBSESSIVE-COMPULSIVE DISORDER

While obsessive-compulsive disorder (OCD) is generally believed to be one of the most impairing of anxiety disorders, there are surprisingly few data on this subject. The Munich Follow-Up Study (Wittchen et al, 1992) assessed the lifetime and six-month prevalence rates of DIS/DSM-III mental disorders in 483 adults from the general population. On a measure of objective quality of social relationships and subjective satisfaction in a variety of social areas, persons with OCD ($n = 12$) and persons with panic disorder ($n = 14$) were significantly more impaired than persons with no disorder, unlike ratings for PD or combined simple/social phobias. The small number of cases limits the generalisability of this finding, however.

In the ECA study (Karno et al, 1988), OCD was found to be more prevalent among divorced or separated and unemployed persons. There was also a significant association with lower socio-economic status. Subjects with lifetime OCD ($n = 468$) made significantly more use both of general medical practitioners for mental health care and of mental health specialists than did subjects with phobic or non-anxiety disorders, but less use than those with PD.

Zapotoczky (1994) has suggested that there are several aspects to the impairment of quality of life among persons with OCD. These include direct impairment by such means as loss of time to compulsive behaviour, impairment related to the social isolation that may accompany OCD, and that related to comorbid depression.

An additional source of impairment is the disruption in family relationships due to patients' demands for family members to accommodate to OCD rituals. Calvocoressi et al (1995) assessed a spouse or parent of 34 patients with obsessive-compulsive disorder; 88% of the relatives reported accommodating the patient's demands in this way. At least moderate modification of family routine because of the patient's symptoms was reported by 35%, modification of work schedule by 22%, and modification of leisure activities by 53%. Helping the patient by such accommodation caused at least moderate distress in 59% of relatives interviewed.

More difficult to measure is the subjective toll caused to OCD sufferers through feeling enslaved to unwanted obsessions and rituals. Some persons with OCD are able to suppress their rituals in public, but continue to be distracted by frequent obsessive thoughts. The bizarre quality of some compulsive behaviour also results in a deep sense of shame for many patients, which may lead to social isolation and depression. In clinical samples, many patients are severely limited in their social relationships and ability to work. Further study of the quality of life in OCD is much needed.

POST-TRAUMATIC STRESS DISORDER

Quality of life in persons with post-traumatic stress disorder (PTSD) has also been little studied. In an out-patient sample derived from a variety of clinical sites, Warshaw et al (1993) compared anxiety disorder patients with DSM-III-R PTSD ($n = 63$) to patients with trauma, but without PTSD ($n = 122$), and to patients with no history of trauma ($n = 503$). The groups did not differ significantly on most socio-demographic measures, but subjects with PTSD were significantly more likely to be receiving some form of public assistance, in particular, disability payments. PTSD subjects reported worse health, role functioning, and emotional health, but the groups did not differ significantly in regard to social functioning. Significantly more of the PTSD patients reported having made a suicide attempt (30%) or having been hospitalised (48%). PTSD patients also had higher rates of depression and alcohol abuse. The non-PTSD trauma group was intermediate on most measures.

PTSD may affect quality of life via persistent arousal symptoms, avoidance of stimuli associated with the traumatic event, or general numbing of emotional responsiveness. It differs from other anxiety disorders in the required presence of a precipitating traumatic event, and it is not clear how the identification of persons with PTSD as victims may impact on their quality of life. It is also likely that the nature and timing of the traumatic event (e.g. military trauma vs childhood sexual abuse) may yield different sequelae in respect to quality of life.

GENERALISED ANXIETY DISORDER

Massion et al (1993) examined 357 out-patients currently in an episode of either: (1) PD with agoraphobia ($n = 186$); (2) PD without agoraphobia ($n = 48$); (3) generalised anxiety disorder (GAD) without PD ($n = 63$); or (4) both GAD and PD ($n = 60$). Their findings must be considered in the light of the considerable comorbidity which was present, and which has plagued the more general validation of the diagnostic category of GAD: 78% of GAD subjects were in episodes of either another anxiety disorder or major depressive disorder, and only 2% had no lifetime history of another anxiety disorder or major depressive disorder. The three groups did not differ in ratings of overall satisfaction and functioning, or in self-ratings of emotional health, which was rated as fair or poor by 71% of the group as a whole. Subjects with both panic and GAD reported significantly lower levels of overall functioning and satisfaction and lower levels of emotional health. GAD (without PD) subjects reported a 13% rate of suicide attempts, which did not differ from the other groups. One-quarter of the GAD (without PD) subjects received disability payments, which did not differ from the other groups. There were no group differences in work missed during the past year, or in measures of marital functioning or social functioning.

Lee et al (1994) used the Short Form-36, a health-related quality of life instrument, to compare 156 patients meeting modified DSM-III-R criteria for GAD with persons who had diabetes, congestive heart failure, or no chronic condition. Results were adjusted by age, gender, race, and medical (but not psychiatric) comorbidities. The GAD patients generally reported less physical impairment than those with diabetes or heart disease, but were the most impaired of the groups on subscales of vitality, social function, role function, and mental health.

These studies suggest that persons with GAD do suffer impairment. However, further study is needed to determine the extent to which GAD itself contributes to impairment, beyond that attributable to comorbid disorders.

ANXIETY SYMPTOMS AND UNSPECIFIED ANXIETY DISORDERS

Some other studies have examined the influence of unspecified anxiety disorders or symptoms on quality of life. Ormel et al (1993a) studied social disability, depression, and anxiety in a cohort of 285 primary care patients over three and a half years. The level of disability was mildly elevated among patients with anxiety, and more elevated among patients with depression. Change in the severity of psychiatric illness was concordant with change in the level of disability. However, the findings were limited by the few cases with major anxiety disorders.

Wohlfarth et al (1993) assessed primary care patients for their extent of social dysfunctioning and its relationship to categories of anxiety and depressive disorders. They found that depressed patients suffered more social disability, regardless of whether their depression was accompanied by anxiety. In particular, depressed patients were more disabled occupationally, which was consistent with some earlier studies. "Borderline" severity anxiety disorder and "borderline" depression showed little interaction in regard to disability, but full depression was associated with more disability when it co-occurred with an anxiety disorder.

Bronisch and Hecht (1990) found that 20 in-patients with major depression and a comorbid anxiety disorder differed from 22 in-patients with major depression alone, in having a tendency towards social isolation, fewer confidants, and greater likelihood of living alone. There were no differences in social dysfunction, suggesting that such dysfunction is mainly related to depression, which adds to prior conflicting results on this issue. However, cases with severe depression and severe anxious symptoms *were* more impaired. The social dysfunction of comorbid cases may be more likely to persist and get worse over time.

CONCLUSIONS

While systematic study of this subject in persons with anxiety disorders has only recently begun, there is growing evidence of substantial impairment in subjective quality of life, objective functioning, and environmental circumstances in this population. All of the anxiety disorders seem to impair quality of life through the distress of the anxiety experience itself, the avoidance behaviour which often accompanies the anxiety, and the stigma attached to having emotional problems. The nature of the impairment in quality of life, however, shows some variation depending on the particular disorder. For example, social functioning may be relatively spared in PD, whereas persons with social phobia may be less impaired in respect to ability to travel. Different disorders may differ in the hierarchies of disability which accompany increasing severity of symptoms.

Existing data have focused on simple measures of severe functional impairment (e.g. unemployment) and global subjective reports of quality of life. One area that remains lacking is a fuller description of the ways that quality of life is impaired in these disorders. Within disorders, are some symptoms particularly disabling or protective? Across disorders, is age of onset or absence of social support a crucial factor in its effect on quality of life? The mechanisms leading to impairment remain unclear. To what extent are associated economic deficits causes of anxiety disorders or effects of anxiety disorders? The impact of treatment on improving quality of life, which is already apparent to clinicians, also needs to be clarified.

The study of quality of life across anxiety disorders should take into account several methodological problems. Accurate definition of the sample of persons studied is essential for determining the generalisability of results. Because of the high rates of psychiatric comorbidity in persons with anxiety disorders, it is essential that both current and lifetime comorbid disorders be considered, before effects on quality of life can be attributed to a particular syndrome.

CHAPTER THIRTEEN

Quality of Life in Schizophrenia

Julio Bobes and Maria P. González

INTRODUCTION

In the last 30 years, there has been increased interest in the field of quality of life in medicine in general and more recently in relation to mental disorders. What in our opinion are the most important events in this area are collected in chronological order in the box below.

Historical milestones in quality of life in mental health

1970s.	Deinstitutionalisation and development of community mental health programmes
1978.	Psychological General Well-Being Index (Dupuy)
1982.	First evaluations of community mental health programmes in terms of quality of life (Baker & Intagliata, Bigelow, Lehman)
1984.	Quality of Life Scale (Heinrichs, Hanlon and Carpenter)
1985.	New antidepressants: SSRIs, NSRIs, . . .
1988.	Quality of Life Interview (Lehman)
1988.	Disability Assessment Schedule (WHO)
1989.	Approval of the "Patient Outcome Research Act" by the US Congress
1990s.	Atypical antipsychotics
1992.	*Quality of Life Research*, vol. 1, no. 1
1992.	Quality of Life in Depression Scale (Hunt and McKenna)
1992.	Short Form-36 (Ware and Sherbourne)
1993.	World Health Organization Quality of Life Instrument (WHO)
1994.	7th Congress of the AEP (Vienna): "Quality of Life and Disabilities in Mental Disorders"
1995.	Seville Quality of Life Questionnaire (Giner et al)

Initial interest in quality of life in clinical psychiatry began with the change of care policy toward the severely mentally ill, resulting from the introduction and growing use of antipsychotic drugs and other factors. The development and stimulation of the American Community Support Systems funded by NIMH to promote life in the community for the chronically mentally ill, required the conceptualisation of new outcome measures for the evaluation of the effectiveness of such programmes. In relation to this, May (1979) (cited by Skantze et al, 1990) said "it is fairly easy to get patients out of the hospitals. The problem is keeping them out; preventing relapse, relieving their distress and improving their quality of life – which is a more difficult task."

In 1982, Baker and Intagliata, the authors responsible for the evaluation project in New York State, gave five reasons for focusing on quality of life as a desired outcome for programmes for the chronically mentally ill: comfort rather than cure, complex programmes require complex outcome measures, keeping the customer happy, re-emergence of the holistic perspective, and finally, quality of life is a good policy. Simultaneously, in Oregon, Bigelow et al (1982) developed and applied a concept and measure of quality of life as an outcome of mental health services. Since then, quality of life has been considered an important goal of mental health services, to the extent that the NIMH in its plan "Caring for Persons with Severe Mental Illness" selected quality of life as one of the major outcome variables to be assessed (Attkisson et al, 1992). Another important event related to the development of the concept of quality of life was the passing of the Patient Outcome Research Act by the US Congress in 1989. This Act obliged those conducting clinical trials to include quality of life as a basic outcome measure.

From this point on, different authors began to develop instruments to measure the quality of life of severe mentally ill patients. Various instruments have since been created, but only a few of them possess a conceptual model, published psychometric properties, and cultural and language adaptations. In 1996, Lehman and Burns presented an excellent review of the characteristics of the quality of life instruments more frequently employed in the evaluation of severe mental patients and they discuss the same subject in this volume (see Chapter 7). Furthermore, McKenna (1997) specifies, from his revision of quality of life instruments used in schizophrenia, the need for the development of a specific responsive quality of life outcome measure for schizophrenia.

Furthermore, the appearance of new antipsychotic drugs (clozapine, risperidone, olanzapine, sertindol, seroquel, and ziprasidone) with different therapeutic and side-effect profiles promoted further studies and a greater interest in assessing the quality of life of schizophrenic patients.

An expression of the growing interest in this field was shown in the organisation by the Association of European Psychiatrists (AEP) of a meeting in Vienna (1994) dedicated to quality of life and disabilities in mental disorders. A further development was the appearance in Spain (1995) of a new instrument for measuring quality of life in these patients.

MODELS OF QUALITY OF LIFE IN SCHIZOPHRENIA

Bigelow: Quality of Life as a Mental Health Service Outcome

The Bigelow et al model of quality of life was drawn from the need and role theories of Maslow and of Sarbin and Allen respectively (Bigelow et al, 1982, 1991b). In this model, quality of life is the result of the interaction between the fulfilment of needs and coping with the demands which society places upon its members. These two factors include, on the one hand, the society, with the opportunities it brings for the fulfilment of the patients' needs, and on the other hand, the patients themselves, with their psychological abilities for meeting the demands of society.

In this model, mental health services would try to compensate for the deficit in the abilities of psychiatric patients, and the consequently impaired participation in the normal opportunity structure, through moderating social demands, supplementing opportunities, and restoring abilities.

On the basis of this model, these authors developed their Quality of Life Questionnaire (Bigelow et al, 1990), which focuses on satisfaction and performance in important life domains.

Lehman: A General Model of Quality of Life

Based upon the data from two national surveys carried out in the 1970s on quality of life in the American population, Lehman developed a general model for chronic mental patients, in which he considers quality of life as a subjective concept which depends on the following three factors (Lehman, 1988):

- personal characteristics
- objective QoL indicators in several domains of life
- subjective QoL indicators in these same life domains

Objective and subjective indicators are two complementary measures of the patients' life experiences. While objective indicators reflect norms of function and lifestyle, subjective indicators show how patients feel about their lives, and are influenced by expectations, prior experiences and perceptions of current conditions.

Skantze and Malm: The Vulnerability–Stress–Coping–Quality of Life Model

According to a Vulnerability–Stress–Coping Quality of Life Model, Skantze and Malm (1994) described quality of life as a dynamic concept influenced by the

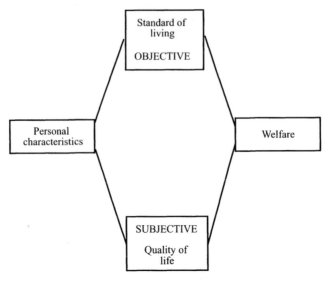

Figure 13.1   Model for the evaluation of quality of life. Reproduced with permission from Skantze et al, 1990.

difference between personal expectations and hopes on the one hand, and perceived reality on the other.

The model for the evaluation of quality of life in schizophrenic patients employed by Skantze et al (1990) implies that it is necessary to consider quality of life in its physical, social, and cultural context – that is, the person's standard of living.

Quality of life is a person's own subjective evaluation of her or his life situation, and thus can only be defined by a subjective index. Based on the results of their studies (1990, 1992), Skantze, Malm and their colleagues suggest that the patients' subjective evaluation of their lives depends more upon their 'inner world' than on the 'outer world'.

In contrast, "standard of living" implies an observer's evaluation of the patient's life situation, and is therefore assessed from an objective point of view. It is not in itself a goal, but a means for achieving personal quality of life goals (Skantze & Malm, 1994).

Awad: An Integrative Model of Quality of Life for Schizophrenic Patients Receiving Antipsychotic Treatment

In this multi-dimensional circular model, Awad (1995; Awad et al, 1997) defines quality of life as the patient's subjective perception of the outcome of an interaction between three major determinants:

- severity of psychotic symptoms
- side-effects (including subjective responses to antipsychotic drugs)
- level of psychosocial performance

This interaction may be modulated by many other factors such as resources, social network, personality, or values and attitudes. (See also Ch. 8 this volume.)

ARE SCHIZOPHRENIC PATIENTS ABLE TO EVALUATE THEIR OWN QUALITY OF LIFE?

Some authors are still concerned with the question of whether schizophrenic patients, due to their lack of insight into their illness and cognitive deficiencies, are capable of self-assessing their quality of life. In this sense, Lehman et al (1993), although having demonstrated convergent validity in the perception of quality of life between patients and clinicians, recommend caution and do not minimise their concern about the validity of quality of life assessments made by severely mentally ill patients.

Browne et al (1996) emphasised the view of several authors that a clinical evaluation of psychiatric patients' reports of quality of life would be desirable, due to the fact that self-reports could be influenced by persistent psychotic symptoms or by the idiosyncratic views and values of these patients and by adaptation to adverse circumstances (Lehman et al, 1993). In contrast, Skantze et al showed that schizophrenic patients feel, experience, and are able to report their social deficits, thus supporting the thesis that quality of life can only be assessed subjectively (Skantze et al, 1992).

From a methodological point of view, Lehman (1983a,b) demonstrated that it is feasible to collect statistically reliable quality of life data from chronic mental patients, and concluded that subjective quality of life assessments can be applied to such patients. None the less, from a clinical point of view, he asked whether one can really trust these patients' judgements of their well-being, and what would have to be done in the case of any discrepancy between them and clinicians. These discrepancies have also been reported by Sainfort et al (1996), using the Wisconsin Quality of Life Questionnaire – W-QOL – (Becker et al, 1993) in a sample of 40 schizophrenic patients from Wisconsin. The W-QOL represents an effort to solve this concern of validity by means of requiring information from the patient, and in some areas also from the clinician and family. Sainfort et al (1996) demonstrated little agreement between well-being ratings made by service providers and patients, in all domains except symptoms.

Independent of their position with reference to the validity of the schizophrenic patients' assessments, the majority of authors highlight the need for negotiating treatment and service goals between patients on the one hand, and professionals and politicians on the other.

CLINICAL STUDIES OF QUALITY OF LIFE IN SCHIZOPHRENIC PATIENTS

Reviewing the various studies in the literature concerning the quality of life of schizophrenic patients, we have found considerable differences in the methodology employed, thus making it difficult to establish comparisons.

Nevertheless, it can be concluded that, in general, the quality of life of schizophrenic patients is characterised by the following aspects:

■ It is worse than that of the general population and that of other physically ill patients
■ Young people, women, married persons, and those with a low level of education report a better quality of life
■ The longer the length of the illness, the worse the quality of life
■ Psychopathology, especially the negative syndrome, correlates negatively with quality of life

Table 13.1   Quality of life studies in schizophrenia

Authors, year	Country	n	Instrument
Baker and Intagliata (1982)	USA	118	SLDS
Bigelow et al (1982, 1990, 1991b)	USA	2.642	OQOL
Lehman et al (1982), Lehman (1983a), Lehman et al (1986), Lehman (1988), Lehman et al (1991, 1993)	USA	469	QOLI
Lauer and Stegmüller (1989)	Germany	30	QOLI
Simpson et al (1989)	UK	34	QOLI
Mercier et al (1990), Mercier and King (1994)	Canada	244	SLDS
Skantze et al (1990, 1992), Skantze and Malm (1994)	Sweden	61	QLS-100
Sullivan et al (1991, 1992)	USA	101	QOLI
Shtasel et al (1992)	USA	107	QLS
Jarema et al (1994)	Poland	41	SF-36
Barcia et al (1995), Morcillo et al (1995)	Spain	100	QLS
Kemmler et al (1995)	Austria	48	LQOL
Bobes et al (1996a,b)	Spain	78	QOLI, SF-36, WHOQOL
Sainfort et al (1996)	USA	40	WQOL
Shepherd et al (1996)	UK	–	LQOL
Awad et al (1997)	Canada	63	Gurin's global QoL question
Kentros (1997)	USA	21	QOLI
Scott et al (1997)	USA	719	QOLI

■ Lower side-effects and the combination of psychopharmacological and psychotherapeutic treatment improve quality of life

■ Patients integrated in community support programmes show a better quality of life than those who are institutionalised

In Table 13.1, we show some of the most representative studies concerning the quality of life of schizophrenic patients.

The Level of Quality of Life of Schizophrenic Patients

Several studies have confirmed the intuitive idea that patients with severe chronic mental illness have an impoverished quality of life, compared with that of the general population and other physically ill patients.

In this sense, Lehman et al (1982) evaluated the quality of life of a sample of residents in board-and-care homes in Los Angeles County, using the QOLI. They found that 56% of the patients felt mostly satisfied or delighted with their life in general, compared to the 91% of the general American population who reported satisfaction with their lives (Andrews & Withey, 1976). Lower levels of satisfaction were reported by Bobes et al (1996a,b), using the QOLI in a sample of 78 private schizophrenic outpatients from Oviedo (northern Spain), who found that only 35% of their patients were mostly satisfied–delighted. However, it is necessary to bear in mind the methodological difficulties, when comparing Spanish and American populations. In contrast, Larsen and Gerlach (1996) in Roskilde (Denmark) found that 53 schizophrenic out-patients being treated with depot neuroleptics reported a relatively high quality of life level, using the Psychological General Well-Being Index – PGWB – (Dupuy, 1978, 1984). The level was almost as high as that of the normal American population.

The mean general life satisfaction score reported by Lehman et al in their community residents from Los Angeles was 4.4, while the mean score for the national population was 5.5. This discrepancy decreased when compared with the scores from a sample of state hospital patients and community residents from Maryland (5.2) (Lehman et al, 1986), and with that from a sample of seriously mentally ill patients living in the community in Mississippi (5.3) (Sullivan et al, 1991).

When Lehman et al (1982) compared the quality of life reported by psychiatric patients with that reported by the socially disadvantaged groups from the general population (low socio-economic status, blacks, and unmarried parents), the differences decreased, although psychiatric patients still tended to be less satisfied. Unmarried parents showed levels of quality of life more similar to those of patients. Sullivan et al (1991), on the other hand, found that their patients differed strongly from the black subsample and were more similar to the low socio-economic group. Bobes et al (1997a) compared their private schizophrenic outpatients with climacteric and haemodialysis patients from general hospitals. All groups from Oviedo were assessed using the SF-36 (Ware & Sherbourne, 1992). They found that schizophrenic out-patients showed greater impairment in emotional role and social functioning, when compared to climacteric patients, and in mental health, emotional role, and vitality when compared to haemodialysis patients.

Skantze et al (1990), in a sample of schizophrenic out-patients from Gothenburg (Sweden) undergoing treatment with depot neuroleptics, reported that 84% of their out-patients could be considered to have a low quality of life, when assessed with the Quality of Life Self-report – QLS-100 – even though they had good physical and social standards of living. Later, Skantze et al (1992) confirmed that quality of life and standard of living are independent for schizophrenic patients. In 1983, Lehman had already concluded that subjective quality of life indicators were much better predictors of global well-being than the objective ones.

Browne et al (1996) also reported poor-to-moderate quality of life, using the Quality of Life Scale – QLS – (Heinrichs et al, 1984) in a representative sample of schizophrenic patients attending a catchment area rehabilitation centre in Dublin (Ireland).

The areas of life with the greatest level of dissatisfaction vary among studies. Thus, Lehman et al (1982), in community residents from Los Angeles, identified finance and personal safety as those areas in which patients were more dissatisfied. Finance was also found to be the area with greatest level of dissatisfaction in state hospital patients and community residents from Maryland (Lehman et al, 1986), and in seriously mentally ill patients living in the community in Mississippi (Sullivan et al, 1991). Skantze et al (1990) identified the following areas as being those more frequently reported as unsatisfactory: work and activities, inner experiences and mental health, contacts with others, and money. Kemmler et al (1995), employing the Lancashire Quality of Life Profile – LQOL – (Oliver, 1991b) in a sample of 48 schizophrenic out-patients from south Tyrol (northern Italy), also found finance to be the area with the greatest level of dissatisfaction. Shepherd et al (1996) obtained similar results using the LQOL in a subsample of patients from private community residential homes in London. In contrast, Bobes et al (1996a) in private out-patients from Oviedo, identified daily activities and health as the areas with the greatest level of dissatisfaction. This is of interest because health is one of the areas with the greatest level of satisfaction reported by several authors (Simpson et al, 1989; Sullivan et al, 1991; Kemmler et al, 1995; Shepherd et al, 1996), as well as one of the areas with the greatest weight in the perception of the global quality of life (Mercier et al, 1990).

Sociodemographic Factors and Quality of Life in Schizophrenic Patients

In 1983, Lehman, investigating board-and-care residents from Los Angeles County, found that socio-demographic and clinical characteristics did not have a major influence on the patients' global well-being. Women, married patients, and those with lower educational level were more satisfied with their lives as a whole, compared with other residents. However, Baker and Intagliata (1982), in a sample of 118 community support system clients, did not find a significant association between quality of life on the one hand, and age and sex on the other. Similar results were reported by Sullivan et al (1992) in a seriously mentally ill population living in the community in Mississippi and by Bobes et al (1996a) in private out-patients, who found that neither age, gender, nor marital status influenced satisfaction with life in general (QOLI). However, women significantly reported more satisfaction with daily activities and with family relationships than men.

Meltzer et al (1990), in a sample of treatment-resistant schizophrenic patients from Cleveland, failed to find relationships between age and gender and quality of life, when they were evaluated with the QLS. However, Browne et al (1996), in a sample of schizophrenic out-patients attending a rehabilitation centre in Dublin (Ireland), found that age was negatively correlated with the total QLS score, this being contrary to the data from the general American population survey, in which the elderly expressed greater satisfaction with life. On the other hand, Shtasel et al (1992), using the same scale in unmedicated patients, found that women revealed a better quality of life than men, and specifically showed better functioning in the social and engagement factors.

Skantze et al (1990), using the QLS-100 in out-patients undergoing maintenance treatment with depot neuroleptics, found no significant differences in the level of quality of life related to age, gender, standard of living, or having a modern house, but quality of life was significantly positively correlated with long survival time (> 2 yrs) in the community. However, in 1992, they reported that older patients and those with a higher level of education presented a significantly lower quality of life, while those in employment showed a significantly better quality of life. In contrast, Browne et al (1996) stated that in their sample, quality of life was not influenced by the length of full-time education or by the time since last employment.

The lack of association between gender and quality of life, found in a considerable proportion of studies, is qualified by Browne et al (1996) as somewhat surprising, since it is generally accepted that on the whole, women have a benign form of illness and a better long-term outcome.

Clinical and Psychopathological Factors and Quality of Life in Schizophrenic Patients

There is considerable concern in quality of life research in determining the influence of clinical variables upon the quality of life of schizophrenic patients. Thus, different studies have focused on variables such as diagnostic subtype, age of onset, length of illness, previous psychiatric hospitalisation, functional level, and so on. Even though the results are not conclusive, the majority of authors agree that a worse quality of life is associated with residual type, longer length of illness, and previous hospitalisation.

Barcia et al (1995), in a sample of 100 schizophrenic out-patients from Murcia (Spain), found a significant association between diagnostic subtype and quality of life assessed, using the QLS. The residual type was that with a worse quality of life level and cycloid psychosis that with a better level.

Meltzer et al (1990) failed to find relationships between age at onset of schizophrenia and length of illness on the one hand, and quality of life according to the QLS on the other, in treatment-resistant schizophrenic patients. In contrast, Morcillo et al (1995), in schizophrenic out-patients from Murcia (Spain), found a significant impairment in the quality of life, as measured by the QLS, according to length of illness, viz. – the longer the duration of illness, the worse the quality of life. Similar results were obtained by Browne et al (1996), who demonstrated a negative correlation between length of illness and quality of life scores (QLS). In contrast, Bobes et al (1996b), in private patients, did not find any significant correlation between length of illness and quality of life (QOLI).

On the other hand, while Meltzer et al (1990) found an inverse correlation between the number of previous hospitalisations and quality of life scores (QLS), and Browne et al (1996) found a negative correlation between cumulative length of previous hospitalisation and quality of life scores (QLS), Sullivan et al (1992) and Morcillo et al (1995) failed to find a significant association between the number of hospitalisations and quality of life, and Bobes et al (1996b) failed to find one between presence or absence of hospitalisation and quality of life.

Some studies have demonstrated the existence of a correlation between level of functioning and quality of life. Thus, Baker and Intagliata (1982), in community support system clients, obtained a positive correlation between level of functioning as measured by the GAS and the patients' self-reported quality of life (SLDS), although the coefficient was low in magnitude (0.29). Similarly, Mercier et al (1990) in Canada also found a moderate positive correlation (0.34) between GAS and SLDS scores, and in 1994 found that high GAS scores form part of the autonomy construct, which appeared to be the most influential factor in promoting patients' quality of life. Sullivan et al (1992) also reported a significant positive correlation between GAS scores and quality of life scores (QOLI). Bobes et al (1996b) also found a moderate relationship (−0.43) between disability, as measured by the DDS (WHO), and quality of life, that is the lower the disability, the higher the quality of life.

With reference to the psychopathology, a large number of studies agree with its influence upon quality of life, and particularly emphasise the relevance of negative symptoms in determining this in schizophrenic patients.

Thus, Meltzer et al (1990), studying treatment-resistant patients undergoing treatment with clozapine, reported that both positive and negative symptoms, as measured by the BPRS, influenced quality of life and that negative symptoms are more important than positive ones in determining their quality of life (QLS). In the same way, Lauer (1994) reported the results from a pilot study conducted in 1989 (Lauer & Stegmüller) in Germany in 30 schizophrenic patients. Using the QOLI, a significant negative correlation was found between subjective quality of life and acute psychopathology (BPRS). Similarly, Bobes et al (1996b) in schizophrenic out-patients, found significant negative correlations between psychopathology, as measured by the PANSS, and quality of life scores (QOLI), although the coefficients were low, the negative syndrome being the most important influence on the patients' quality of life. Browne et al (Dublin, 1996) also found a negative correlation between negative symptomatology (SANS) and quality of life (QLS).

In contrast, Larsen and Gerlach (1996), while finding a negative correlation between PGWB and the patients' rating of severity of illness, did not find correlation between the patients' subjective assessment of their quality of life and the PANSS scores.

Treatment and Quality of Life in Schizophrenic Patients

Meltzer et al, with their studies on clozapine, may be regarded as the pioneers in this field. Although they had previously reported (1989) data on the quality of life of 31 patients, it was in 1990 that they described 38 treatment-resistant schizophrenics from Cleveland who had been started on clozapine. Using the QLS, they found a significant improvement in the total score between baseline and after 6 months of treatment. There was an increase of 59.9% in the mean score, and in all four subscales, the interpersonal role and intrapsychic aspects being those with the largest mean increase (72.2% and 70.8% respectively). In 1992, having studied 25 of these 38 patients over a 12-month period, Meltzer reported the same results, i.e. a significant improvement in the total score and all subscales and, furthermore, a greater improvement in the instrumental role function, which reached similar levels to those of interpersonal and intrapsychic aspects. In 1993, the group reported results from all 96 patients who were admitted to an open trial of clozapine for treatment-resistant schizophrenia at the University Hospital of Cleveland, and demonstrated that quality of life scores only improved in patients who continued clozapine treatment for at least two years, this being an improvement of 242%.

Naber (1994), studying a sample of 250 schizophrenic patients from Germany, found that those on clozapine reported significantly greater well-being, as measured by means of his scale (SWN), than those on classic neuroleptics.

Another new antipsychotic that has been studied from a quality of life perspective is risperidone. Barcia et al (1996), in a nation-wide Spanish study using the QLS in 980 chronic schizophrenic out-patients, demonstrated significant

Table 13.2   Quality of life studies and psychopharmacological treatment in schizophrenia

Author, year	Country	Antipsychotic	Instrument
Meltzer et al (1989, 1990), Meltzer (1992), Meltzer et al (1993)	USA	Clozapine	QLS
Naber (1994)	Germany	Clozapine	SWN
Barcia et al (1996)	Spain	Risperidone	QLS
Browne et al (1996)	Ireland	Depot	QLS
Larsen and Gerlach (1996)	Denmark	Depot	PGWB
Bobes et al (1997b,c)	Spain	Risperidone	SF-36
Dernovsek (1997)	Slovenia	Depot	QLS

improvement after one, three, and six months on risperidone. Similarly, Bobes et al (1997b), using the SF-36 in 274 schizophrenic out-patients undergoing maintenance treatment with risperidone from all over Spain, observed significant improvements in five of the eight scales of the SF-36 after two and four months of treatment (Table 13.2).

With reference to the relationship between side-effects and quality of life, Larsen and Gerlach (1996), in their study on depot neuroleptics, did not find any correlation between the total UKU score and patients' quality of life measured by the PGWB. In contrast, Sullivan et al (1992) found a significant negative correlation between level of quality of life (QOLI) and the number of medication side-effects. Similarly, Browne et al (1996) found that those patients with tardive dyskinesia had a poorer quality of life (QLS), compared to patients without tardive dyskinesia.

In relation to treatment settings, the majority of studies (Lehman, et al, 1986, 1988, 1991; Browne et al, 1996; Shepherd et al, 1996) agree in demonstrating that a quality of life gradient exists among the different settings. Thus, the less restrictive the setting, the higher the feelings of well-being.

QUALITY OF LIFE IN CLINICAL TRIALS IN SCHIZOPHRENIC PATIENTS

Reviewing clinical trials of antipsychotics, we became aware that only a small number included the patients' own subjective opinions in the evaluation of their efficacy and side-effects. Awad and Hogan (1994) stated that this can be due to the fact that the concept of "subjective response to neuroleptics" and its implication for treatment outcome has escaped the attention of researchers and clinicians.

Fortunately, an increasing recognition now exists of the importance of assessing quality of life in clinical trials of new neuroleptics (Awad, 1992). One possible

Table 13.3 Quality of life in clinical trials of new antipsychotics

Author, year	Country	Antipsychotic	Instrument
ESTO (Zeneca Study GR.3B) (1996)	Europe	Seroquel	SF-36
Martin et al (1996)	17 countries	Olanzapine	QLS
Taminga (1996)	USA	Sertindol	QOLI
USA (Zeneca Study 3B) (1996)	USA	Seroquel	QOLI

explanation for this concerns the fact that in the United States, it is mandatory to include quality of life as a basic outcome measure in clinical trials. Another factor that may contribute to this is the development of new antipsychotics with better side-effect profiles and better tolerance, which are both important aspects of quality of life in schizophrenia (Bech & Hjortso, 1990).

Table 13.3 shows quality of life studies undertaken in clinical trials with new antipsychotics such as olanzapine, sertindol, and seroquel.

The results from a study on olanzapine (Martin et al, 1996) demonstrated that this new antipsychotic (doses 5–20 mg/day) had a greater positive impact on the quality of life of schizophrenic and other psychotic patients than haloperidol (doses 5–20 mg/day). Thus, significant differences were seen in the QLS total score and in two subscales: the intrapsychic aspects and the interpersonal relations after six weeks on treatment.

In this area, interest is progressively shifting towards the comparative quality of life profile under different antipsychotic drugs and two significant studies on the quality of life of patients under treatment with haloperidol versus olanzapine (Lehman and Scott) and olanzapine versus risperidone are currently under way.

FINAL CONSIDERATIONS

It is useful here to emphasise the necessity of including the assessment of quality of life within the standard evaluation (clinical, disability, socio-familial, etc.) of schizophrenic patients in everyday practice. The reasons for doing so are as follows:

■ Firstly, the currently available clinical scales do not evaluate the patient's situation globally. Various studies have unanimously demonstrated a low correlation between psychopathology and quality of life – which confirms the theory that the evaluation of quality of life measures is something clearly different from psychopathological evaluation.

■ Secondly, since "perfect" specific quality of life instruments do not currently exist there is a need for a generic instrument complemented by one of the available specific ones to be used.

■ Thirdly, a positive feedback exists between quality of life and therapeutic results, in such a way that in general, good results determine a better quality of life and vice versa.

■ Fourthly, both patients and their families are increasingly demanding that quality of life should be an essential aspect of the management and planning of care.

■ Fifthly, the evaluation of patients' quality of life forms part of the medical audit. At the present time, data on quality of life are required by different organisations, amongst which are included the Food and Drug Administration of the United States, insurance companies, health managers, clinicians, patients, and the general population itself.

CHAPTER FOURTEEN

Quality of Life and Child Psychiatric Disorders

Klaus Schmeck and Fritz Poustka

INTRODUCTION

In the last decade, health-related quality of life has become an increasingly important issue in somatic medicine. In former times, the quality of treatment has been equated with removing disorders or symptoms; mortality was used as the only important measure of outcome in life-threatening illnesses such as cancer. However, starting in the 1970s, the focus of attention changed to a more global view of outcome, which included quality of life of survivors as a matter of concern. Moreover, since many diseases have a chronic course, the aim of treatment cannot be cure, but rather the improvement of everyday life.

Although psychiatric disorders are often of a chronic nature and accompanied by a great variety of problems in daily life, health-related quality of life was not a matter of interest in this area until recently. Unfortunately, this is still the case for child and adolescent psychiatry. In a recent search of the literature (Medline) in the field of quality of life in child and adolescent psychiatry, no papers could be found. In important textbooks of child and adolescent psychiatry in Great Britain, USA, and Germany (Rutter et al, 1994; Wiener, 1991; Remschmidt & Schmidt, 1988), the acronym QoL cannot be found. However, in the psychosomatic medicine of childhood, quality of life has been recognised as an important issue. In allergy research with adolescents, for example (Juniper et al, 1994), or in clinical studies on childhood and adolescent asthma (Volmer, 1994), it is assessed via specially developed questionnaires. Similarly, outcome measures of cancer research often include assessment of patients' quality of life (Diehl et al, 1990). Up to now, about 800 measures of quality of life have been developed (Weber, 1995). Yet in spite of this remarkable effort, there is still no well-established measure of quality of life in child psychiatry. A WHO Working Party concluded in 1993 that existing measures are inadequate and that there is a need to develop and establish quality of life measures for children (Graham et al, 1995, unpublished).

In times of shortage of financial resources, quality assurance becomes more important; the shorter the money, the more medical institutions have to prove the quality of their work. With the knowledge of 20 years of quality of life research, we have to make the decision to use a specific treatment not only with regard to curing symptoms, but also with regard to how the patient's quality of life is likely to be affected during and after treatment.

GENERAL ASPECTS OF QUALITY OF LIFE IN CHILD AND ADOLESCENT PSYCHIATRY

The use of quality of life as a relevant measure of outcome marks a paradigmatic change in the medical view of disorders and their treatment, since the patient's subjective ratings of his/her living conditions are considered as well as such objective criteria as mortality or morbidity. Up to now, no generally accepted definition of quality of life exists, but, as Bullinger points out, there is a widely accepted consensus of aspects that are necessary for an operational definition: "Health-related quality of life can be understood as a psychological construct that describes the physical, mental, social and functional aspects of the patients' state of health and functioning in their own view" (Bullinger, 1994, translated by the authors). According to Ivan and Glazer (1994), quality of life can be seen as a "novel construct designed to capture essential aspects of psychosocial outcome in chronic pediatric illness that fail to be measured by traditional instruments, which are strictly disease-focused". This definition can equally be used in child psychiatric disorders.

Five aspects seem to be crucial for the description of health-related quality of life (Figure 14.1): (1) the disease with its impairing symptoms, (2) the treatment, (3) personal characteristics of the patient and (4) his or her living/upbringing conditions in the closer psychosocial and (5) the broader social and ecological environment (see Bullinger, 1994, who identifies disease/treatment, personal characteristics and living conditions as influencing factors for quality of life). These five aspects will be discussed in their special relation to child and adolescent psychiatry. We will also consider the question of how quality of life can be measured in this area.

INFLUENCE OF CHILD PSYCHIATRIC DISORDERS ON CHILDREN'S WELL-BEING

For psychiatrically disturbed children and adolescents, as for adult psychiatric patients, quality of life does not mean the search for an optimum level of happiness

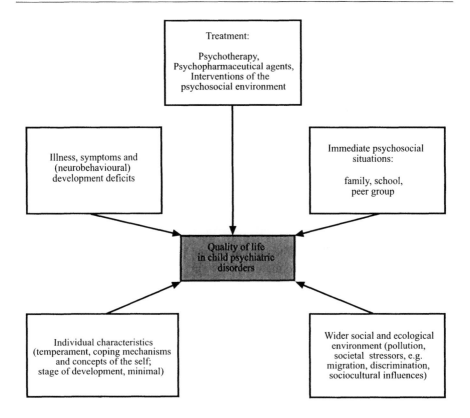

Figure 14.1 Influences on quality of life in child psychiatric disorders

but rather reduction of the impairment that is associated with their disorder (Katschnig, 1994). Schizophrenia with an onset in childhood or adolescence has a poorer prognosis than the adult psychosis: more than 50% run a chronic course, about 25% achieve partial remission, and only less than 25% complete remission (Schulz et al, 1994). Schmidt et al (1995) have confirmed the poor outcome of patients with a first episode of schizophrenia during adolescence. When followed-up 4 to 18 years after their first episode, 73% had experienced at least one further schizophrenic episode, 72% still required psychiatric treatment, 44% were impaired educationally and 58% with regard to social functions.

Schizoaffective psychoses in adolescence also have a poorer prognosis than those with onset in adult life (Schmidt et al, 1994). Schizophrenic symptoms which begin early may reveal an increased vulnerability or higher genetic burden (Schmidt et al, 1994), indicating greater severity of illness and a long-lasting impairment. Quality of life decreases sharply for psychotic adolescents: they show a failure to achieve the expected level of social development, with severe deterioration in functioning (e.g. in school) and at times require psychiatric hospitalisation. All indicators of quality of life (Bullinger, 1994) are impaired: (1) physical status through cenesthetic hallucinations and the adverse side-effects of neuroleptic medication; (2) mental status by distinct lack of concentration; (3) emotional status by paranoid anxieties and depressed mood; (4) behavioural status by the expression of bizarre behaviour; (5) social status by withdrawal and lack of satisfying relationships. Longitudinal comparisons between psychotic and non-psychotic adolescent patients showed significantly lower scores on the Global Assessment Scale for the psychotic group at all assessment times (Erlenmeyer-Kimling et al, 1990). In 73%, the disorder started with negative or non-specific symptoms and in 41%, the first signs of the disorder appeared before age 20. This strongly suggests that the most frequent initial symptoms – poor concentration, subjective thought disorder, lack of energy, suspiciousness, social withdrawal, slowing down, and anxiety – influence the neurodevelopmental process of maturation (Häfner, 1995; Häfner & Nowotny, 1995). This could have several implications, from reduced information-processing capacity (Arsanow et al, 1995) to heightened negative responses from their caregivers (Schmidt et al, 1995).

In child psychiatric conditions with disturbed behaviour, quality of life is more impaired by conflicts in social relations (with family members and peers) than by the symptomatology itself, so that in disruptive behaviour disorders, there is often more desire to change in significant others than in the patient himself. On the other hand, poor quality of social relations and comorbidity with mild neurological impairment and learning disabilities often leads to low self-esteem, which reinforces the externalising symptomatology; in addition, conduct disorders are quite often associated with depression. Distractibility, impulsiveness and aggression are common symptoms that disturb others like parents, teachers, or schoolmates, resulting in failure at school or chronic conflicts at home. Objective impairment is often more serious than the subjective appraisal of the patients themselves.

This is often very similar in chronic and severe eating disorders such as anorexia nervosa. Denial of symptoms and good functioning in school and peer groups over a long period can be associated with severe and sometimes even life-threatening somatic changes. Especially at the beginning of the disorder, losing weight leads to appreciation by friends and family members, so that quality of life seems to be stable or even increased. Thus, it is doubtful whether subjective ratings of quality of life by adolescent anorectic patients can lead to reliable and valid statements. There is a great variety of anxiety disorders in childhood and adolescence, with different levels of quality of life reduction. For example, in severe conditions of separation anxiety, everyday life is completely disturbed. Three main clinical features can be found: subjective distress, social dysfunction, and symptomatic inflexibility (Klein, 1994). These children are not able to participate in expected, age-appropriate social and academic activities, and they complain of somatic problems which have no medical cause. In extreme cases, school attendance is no longer possible because the patients refuse to leave their mothers. Even in milder cases, the quality of life of children with anxiety disorders is impaired by constant subjective distress, even in "normal" social situations.

TREATMENT

The association of quality of life and psychiatric treatment involves two main issues: (1) In which way does psychiatric treatment influence quality of life positively or negatively? (2) If complete remission cannot be reached, how can psychiatric treatment help the patients to live in an acceptable state?

Psychiatric disorders of childhood and adolescence such as psychoses, autism, obsessive-compulsive disorders, anxiety or eating disorders, depression, severe hyperkinetic syndromes or severe conduct disorders often have to be treated in an in-patient setting for weeks or months. Most patients feel released in the protection of the clinical surrounding, but, especially in the long run, it would be a major improvement of the patients' quality of life if they could be treated in day-care settings. The aim of treatment should be maximum help with minimum restriction. After the first days or weeks of crisis-intervention, many of the patients would be able to return to their familiar surroundings during nights and weekends, whilst still receiving sufficient psychiatric care during the day. If there is not a constant atmosphere of rejection or conflict in the family, this change of treatment setting could increase the quality of life of many child and adolescent psychiatric patients, who are at a difficult stage of their life. The gradual release of young patients from in-patient to out-patient status (Poustka, 1982) has rarely been a focus of research. Up to now, this kind of treatment has not been provided on an adequate scale and quality of life is still not a main issue in outcome research.

Psychopharmacological treatment in childhood and adolescence is associated with substantial benefits, but also with distinct complications. For example, acute dystonic reactions are very common in the neuroleptic therapy of children and adolescents (Taylor, 1994). Especially during the first days of neuroleptic treatment, the young patients should be carefully observed and treated with antiparkinson medication if necessary. Such adverse side-effects of drugs in adolescence can severely influence later compliance in adult life. Problems of compliance also arise in the case of relapse-prevention in adolescent bipolar disorder. These adolescents, who do not have a long history of psychiatric disorder, find it hard to understand that they should bear an acute impairment of quality of life caused by the side-effects of lithium (e.g. weight gain) to prevent greater impairment of quality of life (i.e. rehospitalisation) in the future (for the relation of pharmacotherapy, compliance, and quality of life see Weber, 1990). Angermeyer (1994) postulates that non-compliance with neuroleptic maintenance therapy is caused by its consequences for the patient's quality of life. More than in adult psychiatry, the compliance of child and adolescent psychiatric patients depends to a large extent on the compliance of their parents.

Quite often, clinical psychiatric treatment cannot lead to a full remission of symptoms (e.g. in psychoses or severe obsessive-compulsive and eating disorders), or else the family environment is so noxious that a return to it would destroy the therapeutic effect that had been gained. In these cases, an out-of-home placement is necessary but – especially for older adolescents and young adults – is very difficult to find in an adequate form. For instance, it is out of the question that an 18-year-old schizophrenic patient should be forced to live in a residence together with chronic schizophrenic patients of 40, 50 or 60 years of age. Therefore, a very important aspect of the long-term quality of life of young psychiatric patients is for them to be placed in surroundings that are sufficiently sheltered, but at the same time provide adequate stimulation and social support, so that both rehabilitation and relapse-prevention are possible. At the moment, such facilities are so rare in Germany that the quality of life of young psychiatric patients with chronic disorders is often diminished by their actual living conditions.

PERSONAL CHARACTERISTICS OF THE PATIENT

In chronic diseases, there is often a dissociation between symptoms and quality of life, especially in conditions of mild to moderate severity (Katschnig, 1994). This is due to patients' varying premorbid personality traits and actual coping strategies (as well as to different living conditions, which are discussed below).

Personality traits such as temperamental factors are viewed as having a constitutional biological basis that influences the style of behaviour. According to Thomas and Chess (1977), temperament is "a general term referring to the *how* of behaviour. It differs from ability, which is concerned with the *what* and *how well* of behaving, and from motivation, which accounts for *why* a person does what he is doing. Temperament by contrast concerns the *way* in which an individual behaves" (p. 9). A central concept of temperamental research is "goodness of fit", which is seen as a protective factor for healthy development. "Poorness of fit, on the other hand, exists when demands and expectations are excessive and not compatible with the child's temperament, abilities, and other characteristics. With such a fit, the child is likely to experience excessive stress and vulnerability, and healthy development is jeopardised" (Chess & Thomas, 1992, p. 73). Whilst it is very difficult or even impossible for a child to change his/her temperamental style of behaviour (which is postulated as having a biological or genetic basis), goodness of fit between child and environment can most often be achieved by changes in the child's psychosocial environment. For example, parents could try to change their educational style in order to increase goodness of fit. On the other hand, a long-lasting poorness of fit will constantly produce trouble both for children and for their environment.

A different point of view is that of how children are able to cope with the effects of their chronic illness. Lazarus and Folkman (1984) define "coping with illness" as the processes used to register, compensate for or overcome emotionally, cognitively or behaviourally existing or expected stresses that are connected with illness. Thus, the coping mechanisms reveal a concept of how to handle and diminish the negative impacts of chronic illness (Voll & Poustka, 1994). Like children and adolescents with handicaps or chronic somatic diseases, the child psychiatric patient's "relatively harmonious daily functioning and necessary equilibrium between person and environment is fundamentally shaken over an extended period of time (since, as a rule, the person does not have the psychic means to cope with the serious changes in her/his individual life situation immediately and without complications) and, therefore, the irrevocable losses that have occurred mean that the affected person has to make a complete adaptation" (Voll & Poustka, 1994). Coping with illness should lead to the recovery of control and maintenance of the optimum level of quality of life that is possible after the threatening experience of a psychiatric disorder.

PSYCHOSOCIAL ENVIRONMENT

In comparison with adult psychiatry, it is much more necessary in child and adolescent psychiatry to get information about family functioning in order to understand a child's psychiatric problem. During childhood and adolescence, it is possible to watch the development of disturbance and to recognise the effects of psychosocial stresses. The younger the child, the more important are parents and other family members for the child's well-being. Adverse life events in the early psychosocial environment can affect later adult psychiatric symptoms (Cadoret et al, 1990). According to the work of Rutter and coworkers (Rutter & Quinton, 1977), six factors have been repeatedly identified (Voll et al, 1982) that are significantly associated with child psychiatric disorder: severe marital discord, low social status, overcrowding or large family size, paternal criminality, maternal psychiatric disorder, and the placement of a child in the local authority's care (Garmezy & Masten, 1994). Because knowledge of a child's psychosocial situation is so essential for understanding his/her general situation, the Multi-axial Classification System (MAS, Rutter et al, 1975; WHO, 1991b) includes on its fifth axis the assessment of this area (van Goor-Lambo et al, 1990). Rated items are: abnormal intrafamilial relations, parental psychiatric disturbance, inadequate or distorted intrafamilial communication, abnormal conditions of upbringing, abnormal direct environment, acute adverse life events, social stressors (such as migration or discrimination), chronic stressors associated with school or job, and adverse life events or situations due to the child's behavioural problems or impairment (WHO, 1988b, van Goor-Lambo et al, 1990, 1994; Table 14.1).

Table 14.1   Outline of Axis Five: associated abnormal psychosocial situations of the multiaxial classification of child psychiatric disorders

1   Abnormal Intrafamilial Relationships
1.0 Lack of Warmth in Parent–Child Relationship
1.1 Intrafamilial Discord Among Adults
1.2 Hostility towards or Scapegoating of the Child
1.3 Physical Child Abuse
1.4 Sexual Abuse (Within the Family)
1.8 Other

2   Mental Disorder, Deviance or Handicap in the Child's Primary Support Group
2.0 Parental Mental Disorder /Deviance
2.1 Parental Handicap /Disability
2.2 Disability in Sibling
2.8 Other

3   Inadequate or Distorted Intrafamilial Communication

4   Abnormal Qualities of Upbringing
4.0 Parental Overprotection
4.1 Inadequate Parental Supervision /Control
4.2 Experiential Privation
4.3 Inappropriate Parental Pressures
4.8 Other

5   Abnormal Immediate Environment
5.0 Institutional Upbringing
5.1 Anomalous Parenting Situation
5.2 Isolated Family
5.3 Living Conditions that Create a Potentially Hazardous Psychosocial Situation
5.8 Other

6   Acute Life Events
6.0 Loss of a Love Relationship
6.1 Removals from Home Carrying Significant Contextual Threat
6.2 Negatively Altered Pattern of Family Relationships
6.3 Events Resulting in Loss of Self-Esteem
6.4 Sexual Abuse (Extrafamilial)
6.5 Personal Frightening Experience
6.8 Other

7   Societal Stressors
7.0 Persecution or Adverse Discrimination
7.1 Migration of Social Transplantation
7.8 Other

8   Chronic Interpersonal Stress Associated With School / Work
8.0 Discordant Relationships with Peers
8.1 Scapegoating of Child by Teachers / Work Supervisors
8.2 General Unrest at School / Work
8.8 Other

9   Stressful Events / Situations Resulting From Child's Disorder / Disability
9.0 Institutional Upbringing
9.1 Removal from Home Carrying Significant Contextual Threat
9.2 Events Resulting in Loss of Self-Esteem
9.8 Other

Source: WHO (1988b)

According to the concept of vulnerability (Zubin & Spring, 1977; Nüchterlein, 1987), the interaction of biological factors and early psychosocial stressors leads to a disposition towards a certain kind of particular psychiatric disturbance, while acute psychosocial stressors trigger the onset of the disorder. Corresponding to this widely accepted theory, there is no disease without a specific form of vulnerability, and adverse psychosocial events alone rarely cause illness. Nevertheless, subjects without any specific form of vulnerability also suffer from the effects of these acute psychosocial adversities. Marital discord, overcrowding, paternal criminality, or maternal psychiatric disorder, for example, have a distinct impact on children's and adolescents' well-being, and lead to a substantial impairment of their quality of life.

Opposite to the concept of vulnerability is that of resilience to stress, which helps the understanding of healthy development under bad conditions (Rutter, 1987). Wyman et al (1992) were able to demonstrate that caregiver–child relationships play a key role in moderating children's developmental outcomes under conditions of high stress. Stress-resilient children who had been exposed to major life-stress reported more positive relationships with primary caregivers, stable family environments, inductive and consistent family discipline practices, and positive expectations for their futures.

From another point of view, the child's psychiatric disturbance itself has an influence on family climate and leads to a burden being placed on caregivers (Cook & Pickett, 1987). For example, the behaviour of a boy with hyperactivity and oppositional-defiant disorder can be so annoying that it leads to negative parental reactions and rejection, which again reinforces the child's symptoms. Usually, if the parents' quality of life is affected (and this is definitely the case when their children have severe mental disorders), this also affects the children's quality of life, since they are not able to escape from the negative parental reactions. Therefore, the assessment of family relationships is a crucial aspect of the assessment of quality of life in children (see Graham et al, unpublished).

ECOLOGICAL AND SOCIAL ENVIRONMENT

The actual somatic and psychological condition of an individual cannot be understood without taking into account the effects of constant interactions with both the ecological and social environment. Quality of life of children, adolescents and adults is strongly influenced by these factors.

In the discipline of environmental psychology (Ittelson et al, 1974), the dynamic interactions between environmental influences (i.e. architecture, urban noise, crowding, etc.) and subjective living conditions are investigated. Environmental medicine (Blumenthal, 1985) adds further important influences on human well-being with regard to the effects of pollution, allergens, infectious agents, mutagens or physical agents. Noise is one of the most comprehensively studied physical agents in the environmental sciences. There is no doubt that human functioning is affected by high noise, and that noise has to be regarded as an environmental stressor which can produce stress reactions (Spreng, 1984; de Jong, 1993). However, up to now, there are no satisfactory answers to the question whether exposure to noise leads to long-term damage or even disease (Ising & Kruppa, 1993; Griefahn, 1982).

In a field study in northern Germany (Poustka et al, 1992; Schmeck & Poustka, 1993), we examined the effects of low-altitude flight noise on children and adolescents. In order to disentangle the complexity of influences on children's health, this investigation included measurement of the objective noise burden, subjective impairment by noise, amount of psychosocial stressors in children's environment, and the children's traits such as intelligence, neurological impairment, or noise sensitivity.

In a multi-level analysis, we used analysis of covariance to evaluate the relative importance of noise in comparison to other influential parameters. Global psychiatric disturbance of children and adolescents was not different between the two areas, and the number of DSM-III diagnoses was similar. The most important variable to explain the variance of global psychiatric disturbance was "psychosocial stress" (Poustka, 1991). Searching for a possible influence of noise on different psychiatric syndromes, we were able to demonstrate a highly significant influence of noise on anxiety syndromes such as separation anxiety or agoraphobia, especially in younger children. Psychophysiological activity was also significantly higher in the high-noise area, where children showed an elevated level of heart rate, skin conductance and spontaneous fluctuations, and reduced adaptation of systolic blood pressure. In spite of raised levels of autonomic activity, we did not find any significant difference in somatic or psychosomatic complaints or disorders between the two areas with different noise burdens. Parents in the high-noise area did not report more symptoms like "headaches", "dizziness", "pains", "skin problems", "allergies", "asthma" or "nervousness" in their children (for further details see Schmeck, 1992). However, a significant positive correlation was found between psychosocial stress and medical problems: 31.8% of children with high psychosocial stress had some kind of medical problem in comparison to 20.6% of low-stressed children.

Summarising the above results, we were able to demonstrate that the noise of military jetfighters has a significant influence on the level of psychophysiological arousal in children. However, this higher level of autonomous activity is not associated with greater medical problems or global psychiatric disturbance, with the exception of higher levels of anxiety in young children who live in the area with frequent low-altitude flight noise.

Nevertheless, it would be misleading to come to the conclusion that military aircraft noise does not substantially affect children's lives. Beneath the clinical threshold of somatic or psychiatric disorders, we found a distinct impact of military aircraft noise on children's quality of life. Most of the children and their families (more than 70%) felt constantly annoyed by the noise and threatened (more than

55%) by the jets themselves (e.g. fear of an aircraft crash in their living area). If we compare the living conditions of these children with WHO's definition of health, a substantial difference can be found. The results of this study support the view that quality of life is an issue that should be included, if the effects of pollution or other environmental stressors are being investigated. Though definite somatic effects are often hard to prove, we still have to take into account the impairment of quality of life which sometimes has an even greater impact on the subjective well-being of the affected population (Aurand et al, 1993).

Besides the important influence of the ecological environment, we should not forget the effects of society on the individual. In the 1970s, "anti-psychiatrists" such as Szasz (1970) postulated in their "labelling-theory" that it is not biological or genetic influences which lead to psychiatric illness, but rather sociological influences that lead to a stigmatisation of deviant behaviour and subsequent labelling of it as "mad". Although this extreme point of view can no longer be maintained in the face of a huge amount of scientific data which reveal important biological and genetic influences on the development of most psychiatric disorders (see Baumann, 1993), the stigmatisation of psychiatric illness in childhood and adolescence (as in adulthood) is still a daily experience. One of the greatest worries of child and adolescent psychiatric patients in both in-patient or out-patient treatment is how to explain to friends, teachers, or schoolmates that they suffer from a psychiatric disturbance and have had contact with child psychiatry. In the same way, many parents try to deny as long as possible the existence of such "shameful" problems. Frequently, teachers put up with the deviant and annoying behaviour of disturbed pupils for too long (which leads to a delay of adequate treatment) because they are afraid of the possible negative consequences if the child or adolescent gets in contact with child psychiatry. Therefore, official certificates with the words "Child Psychiatry" on them are sometimes problematic for patients and parents. Child psychiatric patients are aware of these prejudices in society; they not only have to cope with their disturbance but also with the problem that it is difficult to talk about it. Thus, a self-assertive way of dealing with their problems is rendered more difficult, and subjective well-being is reduced. If we define quality of life as "aspects of the patients' state of health and functioning in their own view" (see above), then this "own view" can be changed by social influences.

MEASUREMENT OF QUALITY OF LIFE IN CHILD PSYCHIATRIC PATIENTS

In somatic or psychosomatic medicine, there are already several measures of children's quality of life. In Germany for example, Bullinger et al (1994) developed the KINDL-questionnaire, which consists of four components: (1) physical status,

(2) mental status, (3) social integration and (4) functioning in everyday life. Petermann (1991) developed a questionnaire to check the quality of life of young asthma patients. (For a survey of the issue "asthma and quality of life" see Petermann & Bergmann, 1994.)

As mentioned above, no such instrument to assess health-related quality of life exists in child and adolescent psychiatry. Certain aspects such as global psychological, social, and occupational (for children: school) functioning can be assessed with the Global Assessment of Functioning (GAF) Scale of DSM-IV (American Psychiatric Association, 1994). Functioning can be assessed on an operationalised scale from "1" ("Persistent danger of severely hurting self or others [e.g., recurrent violence] OR persistent inability to maintain minimal personal hygiene OR serious suicidal act with clear expectation of death") to "100" ("Superior functioning in a wide range of activities, life's problems never seem to get out of hand, is sought out by others because of his or her many positive qualities. No symptoms"). Intermediate codes can be used when appropriate. With the Social & Occupational Functioning Assessment Scale (SOFAS), any impairment in social and occupational functioning that is due to general medical conditions is considered (DSM-IV).

In Europe, child psychiatrists mostly use the ICD-10-based Multi-axial Classification System (MAS), which in its last revision consists of six independent axes (WHO, 1991b). On the sixth axis of MAS, global aspects of psychosocial adaptation are assessed. Included are: relations to family members, peers or adults out of the home, mastering of social situations (global independence, personal hygiene and order), school or job adaptation, interests and leisure activities. The rating is operationalised on a scale from "0" (excellent social adaptation) to "8" (needs permanent care). Both DSM-IV Axis V and MAS Axis 6 are based on clinical judgments of functioning. The patient's subjective point of view, that is essential for the assessment of quality of life, is not included. Graham et al (1995, unpublished) have started the development of a new instrument for the assessment of health-related quality of life in childhood (CQOL). Such measures designed to assess children and adolescents should be developmentally appropriate, so that children are able to understand the questions, which should reflect the changing features of quality of life with age (Graham et al, 1995, unpublished). According to these authors, a WHO Child Psychology & Psychiatry Working Party proposed in 1993 "that new measures should be child-centered, employ subjective self-report where possible, be age-related or at least developmentally appropriate, have a generic core and specific modules, and put an emphasis on health-enhancing aspects of quality of life" (p. 6).

In the Graham et al questionnaire, 15 main domains of children's lives are covered:

1. Getting about and using hands.
2. Doing things for self.

3. Soiling or wetting.
4. School.
5. Out-of-school activities.
6. Friends.
7. Family relationships.
8. Discomfort due to bodily symptoms.
9. Worries.
10. Depression.
11. Seeing.
12. Communication.
13. Eating.
14. Sleep.
15. Appearance.

First analyses showed reasonable reliability and validity, but further investigation is necessary if this questionnaire is to be established as a standard measure of childhood quality of life.

CONCLUSIONS

Many aspects of intervention in child psychiatry are mediated and reflected by the immediate or wider social environment of the child. Thus, monitoring the outcome of intervention in this special situation of developmental dimensions is influenced by much reactive response, which itself has an impact on maturation, probably biasing educational pathways. Longitudinal observations are lacking on the feedback of developmental delays and of changes in life quality dimensions. Proposals for a new form of measurement are on the way, but no data exist for changes in the functioning of the child, the impact of different abnormal psychosocial situations, or subclinical changes in behaviour with long-standing effects on outcome (as discussed above in relation to different clinical syndromes). Research on quality of life in child psychiatry in this respect is in its infancy.

CHAPTER FIFTEEN

Quality of Life and Mental Disorders of Elders

Barry Gurland and Sydney Katz

INTRODUCTION

As a prologue to the main issues addressed in this chapter, there is an account of (1) the quality of life context for mental disorders occurring among elders, as determined by the biological, psychological, and social changes of ageing, and (2) the structure and content of a language which can be applied to description and exploration of the quality of life of elders with mental disorder. In the main body of this chapter, there follows consideration of (3) the quality of life impacts of mental disorders which are concentrated in late life, namely, Alzheimer's disease and related dementias.

QUALITY OF LIFE CONTEXT FOR MENTAL DISORDERS AMONG ELDERS

While mental symptoms are integral to psychiatric disorders, such symptoms – for example, distress, helplessness, depression, pain, and mood or sleep disturbances – also accompany physical disorders and occur among elders who seem well. This overlap makes it difficult to distinguish age-related patterns of quality of life from quality patterns attributable to mental disorders and, consequently, to determine how specific mental disorders affect the quality of living. A shortage of population-based information about age-related mental signs and symptoms adds to these difficulties. As a context for later statements about the place of specific mental disorders in the quality of elders' lives, we begin by reviewing the background of attention to elders' quality of life, available population-based information, and pertinent issues.

Increased attention to quality of life can be traced back to the late nineteenth century, when a series of scientific, educational, and social advances spawned control of infections in developed countries – mainly among children (Katz, 1987). Life expectancy increased, as did the numbers of elders and the volume of chronic diseases – burdensome conditions that are today's leading causes of death. Despite continued advances in treatment, life expectancy has not kept pace, probably because human populations are nearing the biological limits of the life-span, and society asks whether treatments lead to better, if longer lives.

Technological and social changes add attention to the broad effects covered by the term "quality of life". Exposed to improved methods of communication, people are more sensitive to threats to their quality of living. They know that new products can harm as well as benefit: they worry, for example, about harmful effects from radiation, pesticides, organ transplants, and gene manipulation. Better informed, they actively seek quality in life through good care, safe environments, economic security, and ethical conduct by medicine, business, law, and government.

The language used to describe the needs and challenges faced by elders expresses key aspects of quality of life and shows what information is needed (Katz & Gurland, 1991). Witnessed by those who serve elders, that language covers subsistence and safety, distresses of dependence and dislocation from home, and losses in self-esteem, affection, decision-making roles, and social position. It recognises family conflicts and how deeply elders' well-being affects those near and dear. This language also depicts material and moral dilemmas involved in weighty decisions, for example, about moves into nursing homes or assent to high-risk treatments. Regarding services, it embraces costs and comprehensive effects (e.g. overall well-being, adaptiveness, and long-term social, economic, and ethical consequences).

The foregoing description portrays quality of life as an entity explained by objective and subjective features of body, mind, values, life experiences, and environment (Katz & Gurland, 1991). Relatedly, ecological principles of past and present scholars support the idea that quality of life is only explained in terms of the interconnected whole of its parts (Bateson, 1979).

These principles assert that determinant factors in living nature are irreducible wholes, and that dynamic functions and powers of living nature are interwoven arrangements of all parts of the whole. In real life, these principles operate through decisions and actions that influence elders' quality of life. For example, choosing a nursing home for Mother requires comprehensive awareness of her bodily needs, mental needs, values, life experiences, environmental predilections, and material resources.

Clearly, psycho-geriatric decisions and actions require information about the intricate links between specific mental disorders and quality of living – beginning with information that allows one to separate quality of life patterns specific to mental disorders from normative age-related patterns of quality of life. Recognising the need for this knowledge, we now examine the availability of age-related normative information about factors that bear upon the quality of living.

In the US, life expectancy increased from 47 to 76 years in the twentieth century. The fraction of people aged 65 or more tripled, and more now live beyond age 85 (Furner, 1993). In parallel, heart disease, stroke, and cancer have become the leading causes of death. Although age-adjusted rates of death from cancer have increased, death rates for heart disease and stroke are declining. Some 5 to 10% of US elders have moderate to severe dementia (Mortimer et al, 1981; Gurland et al, 1993).

Recent surveys report that 95% of US elders live in the community, and the rest in nursing homes (Fulton & Katz, 1986). Of those who live in the community, one-half live with spouses and one-third live alone (Fulton & Katz, 1986; Prochaska et al, 1993). A total of 70% claim good or excellent health (Furner, 1993: Benson & Marano, 1994). About one-third are hearing-impaired; one-tenth have impaired sight; and less than two in a hundred are speech-impaired (Benson & Marano, 1994). Most report no health-related troubles with daily home management or self-care tasks (Fulton et al, 1989; Furner, 1993; Prochaska et al, 1993). About one in four have difficulty in shopping, using phones, managing money, preparing meals, or doing housework (2–15% for individual home management tasks). About one in ten report difficulty in walking, going out, getting in and out of a bed or chair, bathing, dressing, toileting, or eating (1–6% for individual self-care tasks).

Selected population-based information is available. For example, reasoning that physical independence is necessary for active life, Katz and his colleagues used life table methodologies to examine physical changes in a probability sample of Massachusetts elders (Katz et al, 1983; Fulton & Katz, 1986). They projected that poor older Americans can expect fewer years of physically independent life than advantaged elders. In a longitudinal study of US elders, Mor and his colleagues analysed the relation between active lifestyles and changes in physical function. They concluded, "those who did not report regular exercising or walking a mile were 1.5 times more likely to decline than those who did, controlling for reported medical conditions and demographic factors" (Mor et al, 1989).

Gurland, in a cross-national US/UK survey, found that the prevalence rate of pervasive or clinical depression among elders in New York City and London was similar – about one in eight (Gurland et al, 1983). However, among those who lived at home, ill disabled New Yorkers were more often depressed than their London counterparts; while the reverse was true for ill, disabled elders in nursing homes or other long-term care facilities. Differences in access to personal services seemed to explain these subjective variances, suggesting interrelationships among objective and subjective events.

In sum, surveys have provided normative, health-related information of importance to elders' quality of life. Typically, facts cover objective events, for example, diseases, mental conditions, disabilities, and death. Although information is available about certain subjective events (e.g. perceived health, mood, and depression), little is known about such key matters as beliefs, values, and fears. As to composite objective–subjective functions that enable quality living, useful population-based information has been collected about mobility, self-care, and home management, but facts about other composite functions are yet to be produced. Although related information has been collected in several developed countries, prevailing methodological differences prevent clear, generalisable comparisons (Feinleib, 1991; Myers, 1993). Overall, a serious shortage of population-based explanatory and predictive information prevails.

Lacking information, practitioners do not now cover the full range of features that favour quality living. Physicians, well trained in anatomy, biochemistry, pathology, and physiology, emphasise the objective causes and consequences of diseases. They stress diagnosis and treatment of diseases, rather than quality living: they know less about psychiatric problems, chronic conditions, and health than about physical problems, acute conditions, and disease. Conjointly, psychiatrists who are expected to deal with life's quality (an holistic entity) need holistic information about the web of parts that explain quality living – qualitative and quantitative information that (1) clarifies ubiquitous, vague mental manifestations, and (2) describes cause–effect interactions between specific mental disorders and quality of life.

Regarding much-needed information about relationships between mental disorders and quality living, we highlight research's limited abilities to fill the gaps. Limited by ambiguous language, incomplete concepts, and scarce measures, research has provided meagre information about subjectivity and about the intricate web of biological, psychological, social, and environmental features that make up quality of life. To make headway, integrated concepts must be developed, as well as meaningful, reproducible languages and measures that enable cumulative studies and syntheses to be carried out. In this way, production of the required information will be furthered.

Having described how interest in the quality of elders' lives emerged, and the nature of available relevant information, we will proceed to discuss a language for the quality of life of elders with mental disorders. Following that, we will consider the place of quality of life in specific mental disorders.

A LANGUAGE FOR QUALITY OF LIFE OF ELDERS WITH MENTAL DISORDER

A repository of terms referencing quality of life is found in measuring instruments commonly used in clinical and research work in ageing. These terms usually emerge from social and clinical concerns, and form a consensually defined language of quality of life, which tends to be increasingly widely shared as it proves useful in resolving treatment, administrative and policy matters, or serves a research agenda.

We have arranged these terms under 19 *domains* as shown in Table 15.1 on the following pages. The 19 domains group together distinctive *challenges to adaptation* and the sets of *responses* that reflect the elder's efforts to meet each challenge. A method of evaluating the elder's success or failure in adaptational responses is given in Table 15.1, pointing to signs of failure, inefficiency, reduced margin, or faulty mechanisms. Intact quality of life is regarded as emanating from adaptive responses, while impaired quality of life emanates from maladaptive responses. As a means of making full use of the table for organising the paper and making the text more readable, we have adopted a convention of cross-referencing discussion of domains between text and Table: the numerical designation for a domain is shown in the table and placed appropriately in the text, within brackets and with the prefix "D".

Further discussion will refer mainly to impaired qualities of life. Nevertheless, in principle, it is the profile of impaired, intact, and positive qualities of life that is most useful in understanding the outcomes of mental disorders in elders, the need for relief and help by the patient and involved others, and the efficacy or effectiveness of treatment.

The degree to which adaptation (hence quality of life) is impaired, that is the *severity* of maladaptation, is described by *intensity* and *extensity* terms. Intensity conveys the level of impairment at a stated point in time, usually the present; for example, such terms as "very, completely, partially, trivially, moderately, agonisingly, unbearably, or desperately impaired". Extensity refers to the degree to which impairment pervades the elder's daily and extended life: frequency and duration of impaired states and periods of relief, number and frequency of encounters with precipitating circumstances, perceptions of brevity or endlessness; and numbers and proportions of thoughts or activities which are intruded upon by impairments (for example relationships, routines of sleep or appetite, movements, tasks).

Objective viewpoints employ descriptors such as "unable, dependent, slow, inefficient, clumsy, dangerous, weak" dealing with observable qualities. *Subjective viewpoints* represent internal states, such as "distress, pain, discomfort, dissatisfaction, frustration". Certain domains seem to warrant terms that lean towards the objective, and others to subjective descriptors. Performance of tasks in the basic and instrumental activities of daily living (D 2,3) evokes a relatively objective language, while in the domains (D 10,15) of comfort preservation and gratification the terms more naturally refer to subjective content. Nevertheless, almost all the domains allow either an objective or a subjective viewpoint to be injected into the content of language. For example, basic tasks may be objectively completed but with a reported sense of discomfort, or may be poorly performed but to the satisfaction of the patient. Conversely, feelings may be manifested by observable behaviour. Quality of life language can also be phrased to represent the *perspectives* of various parties who have a legitimate involvement in the elder's life: family, formal caregivers, therapists, administrators, planners, and policy-makers.

Table 15.1   Provisional Structure and Contents of Domains of Quality of Life

Domain label	Challenge to adaptation	Issue in judging adaptation / maladaptation

Evaluating responses (to adaptive challenges): In every domain, review *failures or inability* (dependence on personal assistance, omissions, infrequency): *inefficiency or difficulty* (errors, repetition, slowness, limited endurance, strain, use of devices); *breakdown under stress* (exceptionally trying conditions, under pressure, paced, against resistance, in novel situations); *deficits in enabling mechanisms* (abilities that facilitate the achievement of adaptive goals).

1 Useful Mobility	Move field of operations to optimal site	Can this person physically get to where they need or want to be, so that they can do what they need or want to do?

Responses: controlling head, turning body, sitting up in bed, transferring from bed, sitting in a chair, (crawling), rising from sitting, standing, moving around room, moving room-to-room, up and down stairs, moving into street, distances outside. To operational fields: bedside table, tray on bed, seat with a view, seat at writing desk or dining table, bookshelves, chest of drawers, fireplace, wall switch, kitchen, toilet, television set, computer, side-walk for recreation, shops, cinema, club, place of worship, friend's house, vehicle, workplace.

2 Basic Activities of Daily Living	Routinely maintain self as operator	Can this person keep their body in working order? (taking in food and water, conserving heat, eliminating, cleaning).

Responses: feeding (swallowing, using fingers, with cutlery, cutting, dentures), dressing (choosing, sequencing, donning), continence, use of toilet (requesting, locating, arranging clothes, squatting, aiming, wiping, flushing), hygienic grooming (cleaning teeth, bathing, showering).

3 Instrumental Activities of Daily Living	Manipulate immediate environment by low technology	Can this person keep their living and working areas maintained, properly supplied and producing?

Responses: cooking; preparing snacks, fluids, a meal; working stove, switches, faucets, locks; cleaning, tidying, doing laundry, shopping, following lists, paying bills, handling cash, making simple repairs, placing and moving furniture, performing basic routines at usual work and place of employment.

4 Technological Activities of Daily Living	Manipulate immediate environment by higher technology	Can this person manage technical apparatus (household appliances) requiring up-to-date instruction?

Responses: telephoning (touch-tone, directories), operating a coffee machine, regulating the fridge, television, radio; mailing procedures, spectacles, hearing aid, hair drier; video, camera, microwave, home computers, fax; electric wheelchairs, bicycles, cars; opening bottles, using household chemicals, taking medication.

| 5 Navigational Skills | Find way around operational sphere | Can this person find their way around the areas in which they customarily live, work and play? |

Responses: finding way in-house and outside, by familiarity, by directions, road signs, maps; keeping to right side of road, staying within appropriate territory (e.g. not invading other's private areas). *Employing:* range of perceptions.

| 6 Orientational Skills | Keep track of momentum in time space and personal landmarks of operational sphere | Can this person keep track of what is remaining the same and what is changing in themselves and the world around them? |

Responses: keeping track of time, identifying self and others, recognising location, remaining aware of shifts in location (bearings), remembering placement of objects.

| 7 Receptive Communication | Gather information about the operational sphere | Can this person pick up useful information about the world around them and the objects and persons in it? |

Responses: reading instructions, learning, communicating (receptive, aural, visual, by restricted mode); simple facts, complex facts, observations, oral instructions; anticipation of events, understanding situations. (May be limited by access to information.)

| 8 Expressive Communication | Shape the operational sphere with information | Can this person impart information to others so as to obtain needed or desired responses, services, or other changes? |

Responses: communicating (expressive, aural, visual, restricted mode) basic needs, wishes, interests, simple instructions, complex instructions, writing and mailing letters, advising, teaching, conveying messages.

| 9 Preserve Health | Keep healthy | Can this person's *body* defend itself and can the *person* take the necessary steps to preserve their health? |

Responses: avoiding dangers and accidents (burning pots, gas, shock, overflowing water, falling, cutting, attack by others), minimising harmful practices (alcohol, drugs, smoking, poor nutrition, toxins), promoting health (exercise, early consultation), managing treatment (medical visits, following health and medication regimes, avoiding overdose or neglect, reporting side-effects), medical help-seeking.

| 10 Symptoms and Mood | Preserve physical and mental comfort | Can this person's body keep them mentally and physically comfortable and can the person take the necessary steps to aid this process? |

Responses: balancing emotions and attitudes, relieving pain, monitoring and adjusting comfort, containing or modulating anxiety, fear, regrets, stresses (e.g. caused by losses, threats of illness or dying, family tensions, humiliations, rejections, physical conditions or operations and injuries). *Specifically avoiding:* *Affective suffering* (feelings of being depressed, unhappy, blue, sad, miserable, empty, tearful, guilty, torn by doubts, tormented by scruples, lonely, self-depreciatory and low self-esteem, regrets about lost opportunities, intruding on every thought, and relationship); *Emotional instability* (up and down, roller-coaster) emotions, overreactive (e.g. prolonged mourning, shame associated with illness, guilt over contributing to illness by habits); *Somatic distress* (interference with sleep, restlessness at night, poor appetite, unplanned loss of weight, constipation, vague aches and pains, bad taste in the mouth; pain, irritation, breathlessness, weakness, difficulty swallowing, constipation, nausea, strain, drowsiness and faintness; symptoms preventing movement and activity).

11 Social and Interpersonal Relations	Preserve social contracts and options	Can this person meet the standards of behaviour of their group, manage their ordinary civic duties, and protect their property and rights?

Responses: keeping and nurturing relationships (taking an interest in others, engaging in social activities, exchanging services, stabilising identity); protecting, claiming and exercising rights, making judgements about the donation of property, maintaining appearances; using community resources, helping others, being cooperative, obeying the law, not being a menace or nuisance to society; desisting from objectionable acts (noise, soiling, poor hygiene, inappropriate dress, disorderly appearance, hoarding, making false accusations, other disturbing behaviour), fitting into normative patterns (sleeping at night, keeping appointments), not making false accusations, avoiding reclusiveness, resisting indignities (e.g. loss of privacy).

12 Autonomy	Retain and exercise choice	Can this person make their own choices in personal matters?

Responses: freedom or control with respect to what, when and how one uses existing capacities to conduct one's life, including interests and activities, socialising, clothes, routines, sleeping, food, following prescribed treatments, alternatives in treatment, leaving service setting; understanding options, motivation to use options.

13 Financial Management	Preserve and wield material resources	Can this person handle their ordinary business and bureaucratic affairs?

Responses: balancing chequebook, safekeeping, depositing and withdrawing cash, keeping track of cash and belongings, earning money, maintaining a job, saving, investing, claiming entitlements and benefits, keeping financial records, assembling tax records, filling out business and insurance forms, avoiding exploitation, remaining solvent.

14 Environmental Fit	Select and shape the operational sphere	Can this person find or make a suitable place to live, work and receive services?

Responses: analysing potential of place for satisfactions and dissatisfactions, efforts at transformations to improve potential, searching for better match, matching expectations with needs, comparison with alternatives, with respect to non-medical influences on quality of life (housing, safety, crime, local facilities; opportunities for gratifications, and for preserving and increasing material, economic and intellectual resources; climate, maintenance of environment; social potential); and medical influences (treatment and services, improvements and side-effects attributed to treatment, extent and frequency of set-backs; treatment available elsewhere). Achieving satisfaction with environment, being aware of alternatives, not feeling stuck in wrong place, reconciling current health service benefits with long-term prognosis, budget planning to achieve goals for changing environment, not afraid to try alternatives.

15 Obtain Gratification	Extract pleasure from life	Can this person obtain pleasure, pride, and personal fulfilment?

Responses: act according to own values, follow interests, engage in religious and aesthetic experience; take pleasure in sexual, tactile and gustatory and other sensory stimulation, get excitement from motor activity (e.g. sports), games, passive entertainment (e.g. reading and TV); relaxing in leisure time; feeling productive, useful, appreciated and respected; reach personal goals, maintain leisure interests; incentives to live (enjoy usual interests), sense of mastery, value life despite pain and troubles.

16 Self-Perceived Health	Integrate information on health	Can this person realistically sum up their health status and use the information to serve their needs?

Responses: viewing of health image: compared to others of same age, other patients, previous state; interpreting symptoms as indicating disease, having a diagnosed condition; evaluating physical appearance, ability to get around, ability to take care of self, manage own life; feeling a new person, feeling great, periods of feeling vulnerable, assessing risk for dying, keeping views concordant with facts; awareness of health problems without exaggeration of deficits and threats, views of health are neither uniformly positive nor uniformly negative.

17 Future Image	Integrate information on future	Can this person realistically take into consideration the future and go forward with plan for it?

Responses: reconciling chances for survival, recovery, relief, and for re-establishing relationships and activities of the past; anticipation of limitations and discomforts as well as incentives; projecting from the progression of illness and response to therapy; general expectation (e.g. optimism) and reservations; accepting irreducible uncertainties, anticipating discontinuities in style of life, loss of cherished traditions; keeping anticipation concordant with best information; keeping up hope for the future despite lack of objective guarantees, keeping plans keyed to expectations.

18 General Well-Being	Integrate information on quality of life	Can this person realistically take into consideration their current life and make decisions in that context?

Responses: balancing and reconciling objective and subjective, adaptive and maladaptive responses and consequences within and across all domains; over past, concurrent and future time; attuned and modulated by preference and value weightings; imbued with empathy for other's quality of life; trading benefits against costs, in the light of expectations for duration and change; actions are predictable on basis of integrated evaluation, awareness of status of each domain; actions are not dominated by narrow window in time; consistent and relatively stable evaluation.

| 19 Effective Coordination | Use abilities to best advantage | Can this person carry out initiatives, obligations or commands? |

Responses: motivate responses to challenges in all domains, reconcile any conflicts between responses across domains, integrate responses in an adaptive manner across domains; balance the demands of short- and long-range challenges; coordinate objective and subjective responses for reciprocal support in meeting those respective challenges; maintain strong motivations and steady goals, pointed planning; consider immediate adaptive challenge with regard for other domains; attend to both emotional and pragmatic goals; skills and capacities are well used; can express or demonstrate goals beyond immediate needs.

Grades of severity of impairment in quality of life can sometimes be ranked in *hierarchical order.* The order may replicate the sequences of impairments during the course of a disorder. Predictions can be based on knowledge of the hierarchical sequences, thus guiding planning and evaluation of treatment.

ALZHEIMER'S DISEASE AND RELATED DEMENTIAS

Because of restraints on space, this chapter deals with the application of quality of life language only to the dementias. We have elsewhere addressed geriatric depression and other mental disorders of elders (Gurland & Katz, 1992; Gurland et al, 1997).

WORKING DEFINITION OF DEMENTIA-SPECIFIC QUALITY OF LIFE

Quality of life is deemed to be *impaired* by Alzheimer's disease or one of the related dementias ("dementia" for short) when, as a result of the dementia, a person: (1) *objectively fails* to adapt to those demands of daily living which rely on cognitive skills, or (2) has an *inadequate margin* of reserve capacity for adaptation, or (3) *subjectively* has a feeling of discomfort during the exercise of cognitively driven processes, or is dissatisfied with the effects of cognitively driven task performance, or (4) has *declined* from a best level of these aspects of performance. Although the definition emphasises impaired quality of life, it can be readily translated into terms that refer to *intact* or even *positive* quality of life.

OBJECTIVE EVIDENCE OF IMPAIRED QUALITY OF LIFE DUE TO DEMENTIA

Failure of adaptation as an effect of dementia will be most prominently evident in the patient's dislocation from the accustomed environment (D 14) through admission to a nursing home or transfer to a caregiver's home; or neglect, injury, or mortality (D 9) from poor performance of cognitive tasks. More immediate evidence is found in the dependence of the patient on another person for the completion of specific tasks; particularly the basic (D 2) and instrumental activities of daily living (D 3). The type of assistance given to elders with dependent needs may range from encouragement, reminders, and advice, to hands-on help in completing a task, or to full displacement, by a surrogate, of the patient's initiatives or activities in executing the task.

SUBJECTIVE EVIDENCE OF IMPAIRED QUALITY OF LIFE DUE TO DEMENTIA

Feelings of difficulty, anxiety, frustration, or slowness in finding objects (D 6), remembering names (D 6,7,11) socialising (D 11), dressing (D 2), and so on, or being bothered or embarrassed or feeling handicapped by errors or inability in everyday tasks (D 2,3,4). Where these subjective views are restricted to concrete problems, they fall under the umbrella of memory complaints by elders; if more diffuse, they raise the spectre of depression.

Memory complaints by elders, although subjective, are increased in incipient dementia, and for that reason must be taken seriously (O'Brien et al, 1992), especially if the complaints are of recent decline (Christensen, 1991). However, the relationship is not strong and most complainers will remain normal over the next several years (O'Brien et al, 1992). Discrepancies occur between self-perceived and objectively measured memory performance (Hanninen et al, 1994). There are influences other than dementia leading to such complaints: a general tendency towards somatic complaints (Hanninen et al, 1994), and depressed mood (O'Connor et al, 1990; Feehan et al, 1991; Grut et al, 1993), as well as cognitive deficits not reaching levels warranting a diagnosis of dementia (McGlone et al, 1990; Grut et al, 1993). Relative to an informant's report, the patient's complaints are exaggerated in the early stages of dementia and minimised in the late stages (Feehan et al, 1991; Grut et al, 1993).

Depression in dementia: Rates of depressed mood increase with the onset of dementia (Alexopoulos et al, 1993b; Skoog, 1993), symptoms of depression being among the most frequent initial symptoms of the dementia patient as reported by caregivers (la Rue et al, 1993). Depression in patients with dementia tends to recover within a few years (Forsell et al, 1994). Anxiety levels also appear to be lowered in the later and severe stages of dementia (Koenders et al, 1993).

CONTEXT

Adaptation is modified by context, especially motivation and the environment. An elder is typically highly motivated to perform tasks independently and well; this is a premise for evaluating the tasks of basic activities of daily living (D 2), where privacy and initiatives about timing, frequency, pace, and style are usually highly valued. It can be assumed that if an elder cannot meet these adaptive challenges independently, then it is not for lack of trying. However, caregivers may be motivated to intrude into the patient's prerogatives and usurp initiatives in even the most personal tasks, because it may be easier and quicker for the caregiver to take over the task than to fit into the patient's limits of competence. It has been noted that the giving of supervisory guidance by the caregiver to a patient with dementia is a less common form of help than doing the task for the patient (Fulmer et al, personal communication). In other cases, restructuring the home or provision of assistive devices can extend or restore the patient's adaptation and independence. Therefore, either evaluations of an elder's adaptive capacity must be qualified by the context, or the context must be optimised to determine potential performance, or kept standard for purposes of comparisons with other elders or over time.

STANDARDS

There is no single standard against which to weigh decline, maintenance, or improvement of adaptation (see also under *Evaluating responses to adaptive challenges* in Table 15.1). Full independence in a task meets a standard that minimises demand for personal care services and maximises the probability of retaining residence in the community. Degrees of failure in independence include assistance in the shape of devices, a restructured or sheltered environment, advice and stand-by supervision, intervention only at difficult steps in the task, and joint efforts on the part of caregiver and patient. Erosion of the margin of reserve for performance of tasks in a domain may be indicated by changes in efficiency (e.g. speed, errors, repetitions, awkwardness), or by a sense of laboured and fatiguing execution of the tasks, or by degradation of performance under specially challenging conditions.

MECHANISMS

Functional impairment in everyday activities (D 2,3,4) is highly related to cognitive status (Warren et al, 1989; Nadler et al, 1993; Zanetti et al, 1993), but cannot be accurately predicted from knowledge of the cognitive status and therefore should be independently assessed (Inouye et al, 1993). Alzheimer cases have been distinguished from multi-infarct dementias by having better motor function for equal levels of cognitive impairment (DeBettignies et al, 1993). Early dementias may show deficits in constructional skills (Edwards et al, 1991). Visuo-spatial deficits and apraxias have been noted to account for some errors in performing the activities of daily living (Van Deusen, 1992). Functional deterioration in dementia is postponed in skills that have been highly practised (Loewenstein et al, 1992).

Certain tasks draw disproportionately and mainly upon cognitive skills, which therefore can act as specific indicators of cognitively driven performance (Barberger et al, 1992): examples are using the telephone (D 4), managing personal financial and business matters (e.g. paying bills, balancing bank balances, obtaining due credit) (D 13), managing cash transactions (e.g. paying for purchases and receiving correct change) (involved in D 3), going out and returning home alone (D 5); remembering shopping lists, messages, chores (D 7); self-administering medication (D 4), selecting appropriate clothes and dressing in the right order (D 2), or recognising family and friends (D 6).

Some *behavioural problems* (D 11) of dementia, such as suspiciousness, appear less related to the level of cognitive impairment and can perhaps be better understood in terms of the patient's individual psychological status (Teri et al, 1988). Underlying neurotransmitter systems are not known and neuroleptics are not definitively proven to be useful in controlling behavioural problems of dementia such as psychotic symptoms, agitation, and aggressiveness (Devanand et al, 1988).

Depression in dementia (D 10) as emotional response to the advent of dementia is to be expected (Kim & Rovner, 1994), but the pathology of Alzheimer's disease has also been directly implicated (Skoog, 1993; O'Brien et al, 1993). Severity of depression has been related to communication problems (D 7,8) and impairment (D 2,3,4) of instrumental (in mild dementias) and (in severe dementias) basic activities of daily living (Fitz & Teri, 1994), though Agbayewa et al (1991) reported depression to be a weak correlate of disability in dementia. Recovery from depression in dementia (Forsell et al, 1994) may be reinforced in some cases by loss of insight and communication ability, or by changes in neurotransmitter balance, psychological adaptation (Foster & Cataldo, 1994), or treatment. Insight into functional deficits is lost in advanced dementias, especially in those elders with paranoid delusions (Mangone et al, 1991).

TYPES OF MEASURES

Inventories and questionnaires: an extensive review of scales useful for the assessment of dementia, including staging, function, and behavioural problems is provided by Kluger and Ferris (1991). The contents of these measures cover the domains previously listed to a varying extent.

The Daily Activities Questionnaire is aimed at measuring the functional problems of Alzheimer's disease (Oakle et al, 1991). The Clifton Assessment Procedures for the Elderly (Pattie & Gilleard, 1979) provide a behaviour rating scale covering D 1,2,3,5,6,11,13; this is based on a staff member's report, though it could also be completed by an informal caregiver. Indicators of impairment parallel to those listed range over the degrees of maladaptation given above under "standards". Other behavioural rating scales include the NM scale for mental states, by Nishimura et al (1993), NOSGER (Nurses' Observation Scale for Geriatric Patients) (Tremmel & Spiegel, 1993) which has a multi-dimensional coverage of behavioural changes in D 2,3,6,10,11. The Gottfries–Brane–Steen (GBS) scale includes identifiable areas of content in D 2,5,6,10,19 (Nyth & Brane, 1992).

Structured tests of function: keeping constant the degree of challenge offered by tasks of daily living, standard tests have been constructed. These are generally simulations of familiar tasks, often set up in a laboratory, and sometimes capable of portability. One example is the Activities of Daily Living Situational Test (Skurla et al, 1988). Materials are arranged in a research site for simulating adaptive capacity in certain domains (indicated in brackets): (D 2) dressing involving an appropriate selection of clothing for particular weather conditions, sequencing order of dressing, correctly matching shoes to feet, and managing buttons and snaps; (D 3) purchasing goods, including use of cash to buy a snack; and (D 4) telephoning and making coffee. The Direct Assessment of Functional Status (Loewenstein et al, 1989) has a similar style, but covers somewhat different tasks, including (D 1) use of transportation, (D 2) grooming and eating, (D 3) remembering shopping lists, (D 7) telling time, (D 8) addressing a letter (stuffing the envelope, addressing, stamping, sealing), (D 13) handling change and balancing a chequebook. The Kitchen Task Assessment (KTA) (Baum & Edwards, 1993) allows an evaluation of the degree to which a person requires help in preparing a meal. The Structured Assessment of Independent Living Skills (SAILS) assesses functioning in (D 2) motor skills, dressing, eating, (D 3,4) instrumental tasks, (D 5,6) orientation, (D 7,8) communication, (D 11) social activities, and (D 13) handling money (Mahurin et al, 1991). The Scale of Competence in Independent Living Skills (SCILS) is discussed in a paper by Searight et al (1989).

Measures of stages of deterioration have been developed through statistical techniques, producing about six distinctive stages (Overall et al, 1990), though clinical development has produced as many as 16 discernible levels (stages and substages) in the progression of dementia (Reisberg, 1990). The earliest and latest stages of dementia are the least well documented in terms of their impact on quality of life. Cases in the "borderzone" between (1) dementias meeting diagnostic criteria and (2) normals without cognitive impairment are particularly difficult to characterise and distinguish (Forsell et al, 1992). Deficits in switching of selective attention, such as occur early in dementia, may impair driving skills and increase the risk of accidents before diagnosis is certain (Parasuraman & Nestor, 1991), especially since Alzheimer cases in the earlier stages of the illness may be active motor car drivers (Carr et al, 1990). Efforts are being made to explore the perceptions and experiences of persons with advanced dementia, for example through application of attachment theory to the false belief these patients may develop that their parents are still alive (Miesen, 1993). Sensorimotor development, described by Piaget and proved useful for the study of early development, has been found to be also useful for yielding information about the last stages of deterioration in dementia (Sclan et al, 1990). The ADL functions comprise vegetative-like capacities which are essential for survival, such as feeding, and culturally learned skills, such as dressing; rehabilitation appears to be more successful with the cultural than with the vegetative functions (Caradoc-Davies & Dixon, 1991).

Even the end-stages of dementia, where the standard cognitive scales have bottomed out, can be discriminated by motor and verbal signs elicited by the Glasgow Coma Scale, and neurological features such as myoclonus and primitive reflexes (Benesch et al, 1993). The ethical and cultural aspects of social death, when the dementia eclipses the person's personality, have been explored by Sweeting and Gilhooly (1991–2).

As an alternative to setting standards for adaptation which rely on norms from a demographically matched general population, or the previous (premorbid) performance of the individual, the reference framework can be a position on a hierarchy of functioning. Severity of impairment in quality of life induced by dementia often, some claim always, follows an orderly progression through well-defined stages. This pattern is captured by the Global Deterioration Scale for Primary Degenerative Dementia (Reisberg et al, 1982), which defines seven stages of severity, based on symptoms and signs and associated neuropsychological test scores. Behavioural indicators range from complaints of difficulty in finding objects or remembering names, in the very mild stages, through intermediate stages with problems in concentrating, failing at a job or losing the way, to forgetting recent general and personal events and showing inability to do complex tasks, to dependence on assistance and difficulty in choosing clothes, to severe stages of forgetting name of spouse and events of past life, requiring assistance with basic activities, and being incontinent; and in the most severe stage, loss of verbal ability and advent of the need for assistance with toilet and eating. Pfeffer et al (1982) constructed a comparable measure, the Scale of Functional Capacity, also with seven levels of severity arranged in a hierarchy, and including a distinction between questionable and mildly affected dementias, relying on standards of degrees of maladaptation. In a systematic manner, Hughes et al (1982) offer in the Clinical Dementia Rating, five levels of severity of dementia, with a category for "questionable dementia" intervening between a healthy state and mild dementia. Levels are defined by profiles of performance in D 2,3,5,6, resulting from impaired memory, judgement (e.g. in complex problems), community affairs (D 13,3,11), home and hobbies (D 15), and personal care (D 2).

PERSPECTIVES

Sources: information on functioning is conventionally gathered from the person by self-report. However, in the instance of dementia, because of doubts about the accuracy of a patient's reports, it is often the practice to interview an informant who knows the person well. The informant is typically a spouse or daughter who is also a caregiver, but may be a nurse or personal attendant. The third party is not only able to report on the patient's status, but also has a legitimate view of their own problems as caregivers; being possibly harassed, burdened, alienated (e.g. the patient forgets caregiver's name, shared experiences), concerned, distressed (by noisiness of patient, soiling, interference with caregiver's social life, being kept awake at night).

The clinical importance of the perspective of the caregiver, and related consideration of the latter's well-being, has been emphasised by several investigators (Brodaty & Hadzi, 1990; O'Connor et al, 1991; Rubin et al, 1987). The dementia patient's task impairments most affecting the quality of the caregiver's life were examined by Teri et al (1989). The problems mentioned in descending order of frequency were: disorientation (64%), underactivity (43%), no interest in others, poor hygiene, inappropriate dress, muteness, sleep reversal, trouble getting out of bed, and incontinence of urine, between 10% and 20%; and, less than 10%, inability to dress, soiling of faeces, wandering, needing assistance in walking, and feeding. Behavioural problems of dementia are the most stressful to caregivers according to Kluger and Ferris (1991). Inability to manage feeding routines was found in 10% of nursing home residents, and carried the heaviest demands on staff time (Sandman et al, 1990). This behaviour impairs the quality of both the patient's and the caregiver's lives (Forstl et al, 1993), being often more troubling to the caregiver than to the patient.

Disturbing behaviour affects a substantial proportion of dementia of all types (Teri, 1986), with rates being highest in the more advanced stages of dementia (Drachman et al, 1992; Teri et al, 1988). It includes suspiciousness, hallucinations, delusions, misidentifications, disorientation, forgetfulness, dependence, wakeful activity at night, wandering, incontinence, emotional liability, aggressiveness, damaging or injurious acts, and inappropriate public behaviour (Drachman et al, 1992; Forstl et al,1993; Devanand et al, 1988; Haley et al, 1987; Teri et al, 1988). Agitated behaviour induced by dementia includes aggression, non-aggressive behaviour (e.g. pacing, undressing in public), and verbal types (e.g. perseveration) (Cohen-Mansfield et al, 1990). The Caretaker Obstreperous-Behavior Rating Assessment (COBRA) Scale (Drachman et al, 1992), and the Revised Memory and Behavior Problems Checklist (RMBPC) (Teri et al, 1992), are designed to record behavioural disturbance in dementia. The Demented patients Functioning in Daily Living Scale (DFDL) inventories abnormal behaviour in nursing home residents with dementia (Aoki et al, 1990).

Suspiciousness (Teri et al, 1988) may be found in as many as 18% of nursing home admissions (Gray et al, 1992). The speed of deterioration in dementia is accelerated in the presence of certain behavioural problems such as agitation (Teri et al, 1990).

INTEGRATIVE APPROACHES

Full assessment of the impact of dementia on the quality of life of a patient and caregivers produces a large amount of information. Further processing of this information is necessary for purposes of summary, and for unifying disparate data to represent the whole person. Several alternatives have been attempted: multidimensional profiles, placement on a global scale, and classification by diagnostic criteria or by thresholds of severity. An innovative method of integrating data for groups of persons has been introduced through the concept and measurement of Active Mind Expectancy, defined as the period of time that a characterised group is likely (at a designated level of actuarial probability) to remain in a good enough state of cognitive health to be independent and active in selected cognitively driven functions. Analogous to the model of Active Life Expectancy (Katz et al, 1983), estimates have been calculated of the duration of dementia-free life expected at various ages. For example, at age 65, a person might expect on average 16.9 years of dementia-free life, according to Ritchie et al (1994).

LONGITUDINAL COURSE AND OUTCOME

A complete description of qualities of life in dementia should incorporate the full course of the disorder. Measures must be sensitive to changes induced by natural history or intervention. Changes around the levels of the borderzone of cognitive health are of special point for establishing whether impairments in quality of life preceded or followed the diagnosis of dementia, and which qualities are preserved in the earlier stages of dementia.

Research within and around the borderzone of cognitive health, i.e. the range of cognitive impairment in which both cases and non-cases of dementia occur with comparable frequency (Gurland et al, 1995), can sharpen many issues. One such issue is whether the dichotomy of normal and disease states embodied in diagnosis is more clinically useful than a transitional continuum of cognitive and quality of life changes. Another is the interactions between objective and subjective viewpoints on transitional states of quality of life; labelling effects on patient and family are included in this consideration. Borderzone states are likely to be more vulnerable to cultural bias in assessment and diagnosis than states of clear-cut normality or advanced dementia; culture-fair methods can be best developed and tested in these borderzone cases. Appropriately sensitive indicators of links between cognitive and quality of life changes in the borderzone states open up new avenues for early intervention in order to prevent unnecessary declines in maintenance of quality of life, despite the advent and progression of dementia.

COGNITIVE HEALTH

Chronic diseases such as dementia are particularly illuminated by going beyond diagnosis to connections between disease and impairment in quality of life (Katz & Gurland, 1991; Gurland & Katz, 1992). This approach gives prominence to dementia as a state of cognitive ill-health. Descriptors of cognitive health can be found in the language of the domains of adaptational challenges: the most salient for cognitive health are subjective and objective aspects of D 2,3,4,5,6; also D 10 (mental comfort); D 7,8 (communication); and D 11,12,13,15.

Profiles of cognitive health can also serve to judge the value of competing diagnostic concepts of dementia and the corresponding alternatives for operational criteria. A choice among these concepts may be governed by the purpose intended for the use of diagnosis. For many purposes, the most salient diagnostic concept is one which is clearly related to consequences for impairment of quality of life. This frame of reference can circumvent doubts about the extent of culture-bias in diagnosis: criteria for diagnosis can be adapted to each culture so as to achieve consistent effects on quality of life. In that case, readily interpretable cross-cultural comparisons can be made of diagnostic frequencies, determinants, course and outcomes, family involvement, and service utilisation (Gurland et al, 1997).

FUTURE DIRECTIONS – USEFULNESS OF THE PROVISIONAL LANGUAGE STRUCTURE

There is yet to emerge a comprehensive language of quality of life for research and clinical applications to mental disorders of elders. A provisional outline of the structure and content elements for a suitable language was presented here. Its potential usefulness was illustrated by demonstrating its relevance to the impairment of quality of life that is found in Alzheimer's disease and related dementias.

Revising and fleshing out the proposed structure for a language of quality of life will occur as further applications are attempted. Even on an interim basis, the outlined language can assist in the selection and construction of assessment instruments for particular clinical and research purposes. Concepts imbedded in this prototype language structure can be examined and modified, as data and insights accumulate: with respect to the nature, number, and designation of domains; clustering of adaptive and maladaptive responses; subjective and objective viewpoints, perspectives of concerned parties; the relationship between intensity, extensity, and severity; the mechanisms of causation and consequence; and the integrating relationships among domains.

Traditional approaches to classification of mental disorder need to be reconciled with the language of quality of life. This is especially germane to the mental disorders of elders, where multiple health and social conditions combine to affect quality of life in ways that defy simple attribution to a given mental disorder. Setting diagnosis in the context of quality of life language can guide the development and monitoring of intervention to the benefit of the patient.

TREATMENT AND MANAGEMENT ISSUES

Psychotropic Medication and Quality of Life: A Conceptual Framework for Assessing Their Relationship

Matthias C. Angermeyer and Heinz Katschnig

INTRODUCTION

Looking back at the development of the pharmacological treatment of psychiatric disorders, it is clear that in the beginning, its primary aim was the reduction of psychopathological symptoms or, ideally, their complete elimination. However, an additional therapeutic objective soon came into being: preventing the recurrence of the acute symptomatology. In the case of schizophrenia, this meant prevention of relapse, whereas for affective disorders, the aim was long-term prophylaxis. Improvement of patients' quality of life as a therapeutic aim only appeared on the scene in recent years (Angermeyer, 1994). It was in 1990 that, for the first time, the results of a study on the effect of psychotropic drugs on quality of life were published (Meltzer et al, 1990).

Since then, interest in quality of life has increased markedly. In the main, this was stimulated by the development of psychotropic drugs of the "second generation" (i.e. atypical neuroleptics, serotonin reuptake inhibitors) which display fewer side-effects and hence raised hopes that their effect on the subjective well-being of patients might be less severe. Since then, quality of life has increasingly been applied as an outcome measure in clinical trials of psychotropic drugs, although few results of those studies have been published to date. Hence it appears still too early to give an overview of the current state of affairs of empirical research in this field. Rather, we will attempt to develop a conceptual framework for the assessment of the impact of pharmacotherapy on quality of life, which could

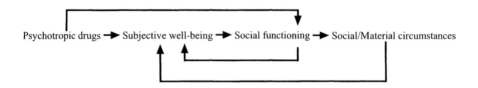

Figure 16.1   Effect of psychotropic drugs on the three components of quality of life

be of benefit for further studies. (Another attempt in this direction has recently been presented by Awad, 1992.)

It is useful to distinguish three components of quality of life: firstly, subjective well-being, secondly, functioning in social roles, and thirdly, social and material living conditions (Katschnig, Ch. 1 this volume). All three components can be affected by psychopharmacotherapy. First of all, psychotropic drugs exert a direct influence on subjective well-being, but beyond that, they can have an effect on the level of social functioning – either directly or indirectly through influencing subjective well-being. Social functioning, then, can have consequences for the social and material circumstances of living. Finally, changes in both level of social functioning and living conditions can have repercussions for subjective well-being (Figure 16.1). Before discussing the relationship between psychotropic medication and the various components of quality of life in more detail, we will briefly describe the wanted and unwanted effects of these drugs.

DESIRED AND UNDESIRED EFFECTS OF PSYCHOTROPIC DRUGS

The main aim of treatment with psychotropic drugs is the *reduction or elimination of symptoms*. Conventional neuroleptics produce mainly a reduction of productive psychotic symptoms, in particular of delusions and hallucinations. Antidepressants – as suggested by their name – lead to the lifting of depressive mood, help to restore interest in one's environment and the ability to enjoy life, and reduce the lack of motivation as well as the somatic symptoms associated with depression. In addition, they are suitable for the treatment of anxiety disorders, obsessive-compulsive disorders, and eating disorders. Lithium and the anticonvulsants carbamazepine and valproic acid are used in the treatment of mania. Benzodiazepines lead to the reduction of anxiety.

Long-term treatment with neuroleptics aims at the *maintenance of an achieved remission* or the *prevention of a relapse* of the schizophrenic psychosis. Antidepressants serve the same aims with unipolar depression. Lithium and the anticonvulsants are used for *prophylaxis* against the recurrence of affective disorders.

Unfortunately, though, the effects of psychopharmacotherapy are not only of a positive nature; these drugs also have numerous *side-effects* which are unpleasant for the patient. The most important side-effects of the various drugs with a potential impact on patients' subjective well-being are summarised in Table 16.1. They range from psychological and neurological symptoms through disturbances of the autonomic nervous system (particularly anticholinergic effects and orthostatic dysregulation), gastrointestinal complaints, metabolic disorders (weight gain), and disturbances of sexual function to dermatological side-effects (e.g. allergic rashes).

Looking at this overview, two things are particularly striking. Among the psychotropic drugs of the first generation, benzodiazepines seem to have the least side-effects, at least at first glance. The side-effects of conventional neuroleptics, tricyclic antidepressants, lithium, and anticonvulsants appear to be more significant. Further, it becomes apparent that psychotropic drugs of the second generation display a more favourable profile of side-effects, and thus should have a less severe impact on subjective well-being. This is true for atypical neuroleptics, for which fewer extrapyramidal side-effects are observed, and for selective serotonin reuptake inhibitors (SSRIs) due to the absence of anticholinergic effects.

Benzodiazepines have a further advantage in comparison with other psychotropic drugs: the short duration of the latency period before the *onset of the desired effect*. While the anxiolytic action of benzodiazepines starts after approximately 30 minutes, neuroleptics may take several days until the beginning of their antipsychotic effect. With lithium treatment, it takes at least 10 to 14 days until the onset of the antimanic effect, and valproic acid requires a similarly long period to cause a reduction of manic symptoms. The antidepressant effect of both tricyclic antidepressants and SSRIs may take as long as two to three weeks to occur. As far as panic attacks are concerned, their frequency and intensity only eases off after SSRIs have been taken for at least a two-week period, while full protection is only achieved after six to eight weeks.

However, with the *onset of unwanted effects*, the situation is quite different. Frequently, they begin prior to the onset of the desired effects. The anticholinergic effect of tricyclic antidepressants, for example, occurs immediately after the start of treatment, the agitation and gastrointestinal complaints quite often caused by SSRIs arrive at their maximum between the fourth and the seventh day. The sedating effect of many neuroleptics (which in certain cases might be desired from the therapeutic point of view) occurs before the onset of their antipsychotic effect. Here too, benzodiazepines are an exception; their unwanted effects (fatigue, drowsiness) begin concurrently with the anxiolytic effect. Low-dose dependency, which poses a major pharmacological problem with benzodiazepines, only occurs after prolonged use over several weeks or months.

Table 16.1 Some side-effects of different classes of psychotropic drugs which may have implications for quality of life. (Note that (1) there may be variations within a class of drugs for specific compounds; (2) many side-effects are dose-dependent; (3) some side-effects are only present initially; (4) some side effects are age dependent)

	Typical NLs		Atypical NLs	TCAs	MAOIs	SSRIs	Lithium	Anti-convulsants	Benzo-diazepines
	low potent	high potent							
Cognitive impairment (impaired memory and recall, poor concentration, impaired attention)	+	+	(+)				(+)		+
Jitteriness (inner restlessness, irritability)				+	+	+			(+)
Anxiety						(+)			
Sedation	+		+[a]	+	+			(+)	+
Insomnia					+	+			
Extrapyramidal side-effects (acute dystonia, parkinsonism, akathisia, tardive dyskinesia)	(+)	+							
Tremor							+	+	
Ataxia								+	
Anticholinergic side-effects (dry mouth, blurred vision, difficulty in micturition, constipation)	(+)		+[c]	+					
Orthostatic hypotension (dizziness, fainting, falls)	+			+	(+)				
Headache					(+)	(+)			(+)

Table 16.1 ctnd

	Typical NLs		Atypical NLs	TCAs	MAOIs	SSRIs	Lithium	Anti-convulsants	Benzo-diazepines
	low potent	high potent							
Sweating	(+)		(+)	(+)	(+)				
Hypersalivation			+a						
Polyuria, polydipsia							+		
Gastrointestinal disturbances (nausea, vomiting, diarrhoea)					(+)	+	+	+	
Anorexia						(+)		(+)	
Weight gain	+	(+)	+	(+)	(+)	+	+	+b	
Anorgasmia, failure of ejaculation					+	+	+		
Reduced libido, erectile dysfunction	+	+	+	(+)	(+)				
Galactorrhoea, gynaecomastia	(+)	(+)							
Dermatological disorders (e.g. photosensitivity, skin rash)	(+)			(+)		(+)	(+)	(+)	

NLs, Neuroleptics; TCAs, Tricyclic antidepressants; MAOIs, Monoamine oxidase inhibitors; SSRIs, Selective serotonin reuptake; a clozapine; b valproic acid; c only tricyclic compounds.

PSYCHOTROPIC DRUGS AND SUBJECTIVE WELL-BEING

Both psychiatrists and patients would agree that the aim of psychiatric treatment is to improve the subjective well-being of patients. In some cases, though, there might be disagreement about the best way to achieve this objective. Psychiatrists, for example, generally consider the reduction of psychopathological symptoms by means of psychopharmacotherapy as desirable, since in their view, symptom reduction automatically means an increase in the patients' well-being. The patients, however, might take a different view. Van Putten et al (1975) reported that some schizophrenic patients stopped taking their medication so as to be able to re-experience their well-loved delusions of grandeur, as well as pleasant auditory hallucinations. Patients with bipolar affective disorders who undergo long-term prophylaxis not uncommonly miss their "highs" and find it hard to get used to the new "middle-of-the-road" state.

The prevention of relapse of schizophrenic psychosis plays a central part in the clinical reasoning of psychiatrists. Not least, this is motivated by the long-term negative consequences for the patients' social situation (and hence for their quality of life) that are almost inevitable with a relapse. Thus, psychiatrists will tolerate the undesired effects of drug treatment more readily than patients, who frequently directly experience the medication's negative effect on their subjective well-being. That the risk of recurrence of a psychotic episode in the future could be reduced might appear a rather intangible variable, in comparison with the treatment's short-term negative consequences. The issue becomes further complicated by the fact that neuroleptics do not provide 100% protection, and that without psycho-pharmacological treatment, relapse will not necessarily occur, although the risk of this is greatly increased.

The way in which the effect of drug treatment on subjective well-being is evaluated depends greatly on the importance assumed by the various aspects of quality of life which are positively or negatively influenced by the treatment. Young men, for example, might consider sexual dysfunction in the wake of neuroleptic treatment as a particularly grave reduction of their quality of life. On the other hand, the weight gain occurring with many psychotropic drugs might represent a serious problem for many women. The meaning of these side-effects and their consequences for patients' compliance with treatment has long been underestimated by psychiatrists (Amering & Katschnig, 1993a).

In addition to these direct pharmacological effects, indirect psychosocial effects of psychopharmacological treatment are important. First, there are the *practical implications* of this type of treatment, which can have a negative impact on subjective well-being. The simple fact of having to take drugs several times a day, or the regular blood tests necessary during treatment with clozapine, can themselves be perceived as a nuisance. In addition, the limitations on everyday life required with most psychotropic drugs may impose a strain on subjective well-being, as, for example, abstinence from alcohol. Regardless of the fact that it can represent a limitation of quality of life in itself, this can also lead to embarrassing social situations in which patients have to justify themselves for not drinking alcohol. This involves the risk that they have to "disclose" their psychiatric disorder. Another practical implication is keeping to a particular diet (with irreversible monoamine oxydase inhibitors), or unfitness to drive or operate machinery when taking drugs that may cause a prolonged reaction time (particularly benzodiazepines, sedating tricyclic antidepressants, and low-potency neuroleptics).

Beyond these practical concomitants, the *symbolic implications* of psychopharmacological treatment play an important part in subjective well-being. On the one hand, the awareness that one is taking a drug which has been proved to reduce the risk of relapse in a perceivable manner can give patients a sense of security. No longer do they need to feel at the mercy of the illness. Rather, they have gained – to a certain extent – control over the disorder. On the other hand, "dependence" on the drug can represent a problem in so far as it is not the patient him/herself who crucially influences the mental state, but an external agent. In addition, taking the drug painfully reminds patients that they suffer from a disease that frequently takes a chronic course. Again and again, patients draw the wrong conclusion – that in order to recover, they simply have to discontinue their drug treatment (Diamond, 1985). The fact that patients have to take medication, then, puts them firmly in the role of the "mentally ill", with all its negative social implications.

PSYCHOTROPIC DRUGS AND SOCIAL FUNCTIONING

In addition to its effect on subjective well-being, psychopharmacological treatment can affect a patient's level of social functioning. Again, this has both positive and negative dimensions. It may be expected that the reduction of symptoms will create the prerequisite for patients to regain their ability to fulfil the role expectations directed at them by others. However, one problem with treating schizophrenic disorders by means of traditional neuroleptics is the fact that, while being generally successful in suppressing the "positive" symptoms, these drugs do not (or only marginally) lead to an improvement of negative symptoms such as affect flattening, lack of motivation, anhedonia, or concentration deficits. On the contrary, not uncommonly, they may even intensify them (see above). Yet it is precisely these negative symptoms which have a considerable effect on the level of social functioning after an acute psychotic episode has subsided. Here, some of the newly developed atypical neuroleptics point to progress, as they seem to permit more effective treatment of certain negative symptoms. Antidepressants, besides reducing depressive symptoms, may also have a positive effect on social functioning in general (Stewart et al, 1988) or on specific domains like work performance (Agosti et al 1991; Mintz et al, 1992), functioning in the home, or social relationships (Agosti et al, 1991).

In most cases, however, psychosocial programmes seem to be necessary in addition to pharmacotherapy in order to achieve an improvement of social functioning, as has become most evident in the treatment of schizophrenia. With regard to panic attacks, the use of antidepressants may often be sufficient to reduce their frequency or to prevent their occurrence altogether. Nevertheless, behavioural therapy might be required for patients to give up their agoraphobic behaviour, induced by the fear of attacks, and learn to actively engage in their social roles again.

Psychotropic drugs do not only positively influence the level of social adaptation, but can also affect the latter in a negative manner. This is rooted in their numerous side-effects, discussed above. The negative impact on social adaptation may be illustrated by using a few examples from the area of work. Parkinsonism caused by neuroleptics and a lithium-induced tremor can be a severe impairment in performing tasks that require manual skills. Disturbances of visual accommodation due to the anticholinergic effect of tricyclic antidepressants will represent a grave hindrance for all who have to do a lot of reading. Dryness of mouth caused by the same pharmacological mechanism can be a severe nuisance for those whose occupation requires much speaking (e.g. teachers). The cognitive impairments observed in connection with neuroleptic treatment (concentration deficits in particular) can be an impediment for all intellectual activities. Artists may experience the reduction of creativity reported for lithium treatment as a serious problem.

Furthermore, the social relationships of a patient can be affected negatively through the side-effects of psychotropic drugs. This is particularly true for the extrapyramidal symptoms occurring during treatment with traditional neuroleptics, as the latter visibly stigmatise those affected. While schizophrenic patients normally are, to a certain degree, in a position to decide whether they want to reveal themselves to be schizophrenic or would rather have their disorder undetected, people suffering from extrapyramidal symptoms are clearly recognisable as being mentally ill, whether they want this or not. So the "discreditable" turn into the "discredited" (Goffman, 1963).

Further, extrapyramidal symptoms, especially hypomimia, as well as motivational, cognitive and affective impairments caused by conventional neuroleptic drugs, aggravate the difficulties in interpersonal interaction and social contact that people with schizophrenia encounter anyway. Also, the weight gain produced by a number of psychotropic drugs can, due to the reduction of the attractiveness of a person's physical appearance, adversely influence his/her chances of making friends and finding a partner. Sexual side-effects must also be mentioned here.

PSYCHOTROPIC DRUGS AND SOCIAL/ MATERIAL CIRCUMSTANCES

Thanks to their effect on social functioning described above, psychotropic drugs can influence patients' social and material living conditions both directly and indirectly. Here too, both positive and negative effects may occur. An example is the capacity to work: an improvement with the aid of psychotropic medication can have a positive influence on the patients' financial situation. As a result, they can afford a higher standard of living, which might involve renting a more expensive flat, spending more money on leisure pursuits, travelling, and so on. In addition, having an income of their own enables the patients to live more independently and to become more autonomous, as they are no longer dependent on the support of others. Beyond its economic effect, the ability to fulfil the requirements of a job successfully also opens up new fields of social interaction for patients. The workplace being a central source of social contact in our society, having a job is a crucial means for those affected by mental illness to step out of their isolation or to prevent it from happening in the first place. Further, occupational roles can be an important part of social identity. The experience of being "useful", then, is likely to stimulate patients' self-confidence, which in turn, might encourage them to establish social contacts outside the occupational setting. All that should be beneficial in enhancing their subjective well-being. However, the opposite would be true if patients, due to the severe side-effects of their medication, were eventually no longer able to perform their accustomed tasks – in the workplace and beyond. Hence the "second generation" drugs, with their less pronounced side-effects, promise to be a step forward in relation to patients' quality of life.

ATTITUDE TOWARDS PSYCHOTROPIC DRUGS AND QUALITY OF LIFE

People with mental disorders not only suffer from "an inferior health, but also from an inferior disease", as the Austrian writer Robert Musil remarked in his famous novel *Man Without Qualities*. By being given psychotropic drugs, they also receive a type of treatment which is inferior in the eyes of the public. A representative survey conducted in the Federal Republic of Germany showed that while psychotherapy was generally held in high esteem by the lay public, psychopharmacotherapy was rejected by the vast majority. People were even more ready to endorse alternative methods such as natural remedies or meditation and yoga than to recommend psychotropic drugs for the treatment of severe disorders such as schizophrenia or major depression (Angermeyer & Matschinger, 1996; Angermeyer et al, 1993). In a national survey of the risk perception of prescription drugs undertaken in Sweden in 1988, cigarette smoking, pesticides, and alcohol stood out highest in perceived risk, immediately followed by antidepressants – which were judged the most risky prescription drug of all, and even more risky than nuclear power (Slovic et al, 1989).

Thus, the public image of psychotropic drugs seems to be characterised by a "pharmacophobia" (Amering & Katschnig, 1993b), though of late there appears to be a change in attitude, at least as far as the United States are concerned. In keeping with previous experience, we may expect the same development to take place in Europe after the usual lag of time. At the centre of attention are the modern antidepressants, in particular the first SSRI fluoxetine, which is marketed in the United States and many other countries under the brand name Prozac. This drug has managed to gain social acceptance in very little time – and, most interestingly, especially within those social circles which, until then, had been part of the "friends and supporters of psychotherapy" (as the American sociologist Kadushin (1969) called it) and for which the use of medication had been politically incorrect. According to the *New York Times*, no other drug since the great Valium hype has been consumed so eagerly as Prozac.

Much of this is being attributed to the messianic heraldry of the book *Listening to Prozac* by the American psychiatrist Peter Kramer (1993). In his paean to this drug, Kramer claims that Prozac has transformative powers, that it goes beyond treating illness to changing personality – turning self-doubt into confidence, increasing sex appeal and energy, even improving one's business acumen. According to Kramer, after taking Prozac, his patients not only felt well again, but even better than before. Thus, this drug promises not only to eliminate disorder-induced reductions in quality of life, but also the gain of a level of quality of life unknown and not experienced until then. However, there is no scientific support for this view and Kramer's observations were uncontrolled.

CONCLUSION

As mentioned at the start, research on the issue of psychotropic drugs and quality of life is only beginning to appear on the scene. Major efforts are still required with regard to the conceptualisation of the relationship between the two. This chapter represents an attempt in this direction. A further, yet largely unresolved problem is the development of suitable instruments for the assessment of the effect of drug treatment on quality of life.

The impact of psychotropic drugs on quality of life seems to be of considerable importance for compliance by patients; there are preliminary data on this association (e.g. Naber, 1995). Detailed studies investigating the relative importance of the various positive and negative effects of psychotropic drugs on the various domains of quality of life, however, remain to be done. Considering the dimensions of non-compliance – e.g. that only 30–40% of chronic schizophrenic patients regularly take neuroleptic drugs (Naber, 1995) – the need for further research is evident.

ACKNOWLEDGEMENTS

The authors wish to thank B. Schulze, R. Kilian and J. Tegeler for helpful comments.

CHAPTER SEVENTEEN

Psychotherapy and Quality of Life

Gerhard Lenz and Ulrike Demal

In the last 20 years, the concept of quality of life (QoL) has gained importance in the assessment of therapeutic interventions in chronic diseases (e.g. cancer) and measurement of it is becoming increasingly relevant to controlled clinical trials (Guyatt et al, 1989). Though QoL is influenced by many factors other than health, health researchers are mainly interested in what is described as "health-related" quality of life.

Quality of life has both a subjective component (well-being, life satisfaction), and an objective component (functioning, social roles), as well as including external circumstances (e.g. standard of living). It is still a matter of discussion how much of each of these components should be included in QoL measurements. The usual criteria for quality of life are strongly orientated to standard concepts of normal life without illness. But illness may change people in different ways and there is great variation between patients in what they consider as priorities in their life, in what they want to achieve, and in what can increase their life satisfaction. In his discussion of compliance problems, Linden (1981) has focused on the necessity of evaluating illness concepts and the patient's subjective values and goals, if therapeutic interventions of any type are to be applied appropriately.

Bullinger et al (1993) have stressed the necessity of anthropological and sociological studies to identify cultural variations in the indicators used to define health and well-being and people's expectations concerning physical and emotional functioning. International collaboration in medical research needs instruments which are applicable cross-culturally for the assessment of health-related quality of life (HRQL) in clinical trials.

Gill and Feinstein (1994) evaluated how well quality of life is being measured in the medical literature. They randomly selected 75 articles from three data-sources; 159 different "Quality of Life" instruments were used in those studies. The instruments most commonly employed were the Sickness Impact Profile (Bergner et al, 1981), the Functional Living Index – Cancer (Schipper et al, 1984) and the Karnovsky Performance Index (Karnovsky & Burchenal, 1949). Of the 159 instruments, 136 were used only once. Investigators had conceptually defined QoL in only 11 (15%) of the 75 articles, identified the targeted domains in only 35 (47%), given reasons for selecting the chosen QoL instruments in only 27 (36%), and aggregated their results into a composite QoL-score in only 27 (38%) of 71 eligible articles. No article distinguished "overall" from health-related quality of life. Therapeutic interventions in these studies were rare and did not include psychotherapy.

PSYCHOTHERAPY RESEARCH

The overarching goal of psychotherapy research is to understand the mechanisms through which such treatment operates and to assess the impact of moderating influences on both maladaptive and adaptive functioning (Akhtar & Samuel, 1995). Outcome-orientated research (Smith et al, 1980; Grawe et al, 1994) concerns itself with the scientific evaluation of the effectiveness of psychotherapy. Process-orientated psychotherapy research (Orlinsky et al, 1994) investigates the extent to which outcome is determined by the interaction of the patient's psychopathological characteristics and personality on the one hand and the therapists' skills, personality, and particularly their technique on the other (Akhtar & Samuel, 1995).

In psychotherapy research, much emphasis has been put on research issues, ethical issues, the nature of control groups, statistical issues, issues of effectiveness and, in the case of outcome research, on therapy modality and diagnosis (APA Commission on Psychotherapies, 1982). In the measurement of therapeutic outcome, importance has mostly been put on symptoms and personality factors, less often on impairment in functioning or subjective distress. The concept of quality of life seems to be without importance in major reviews of psychotherapy research (Luborsky et al, 1975; Smith et al, 1980; APA Commission on Psychotherapies, 1982; Bachrach et al, 1991; Baumann & Reinecker-Hecht, 1986; Grawe et al, 1994; Bergin & Garfield, 1994). Interestingly, the QoL of psychotherapists was a matter of concern in one paper (Reimer, 1994), which focuses on the lack of life satisfaction and on health risks (alcoholism, suicide, marital problems) which seem to be increased among doctors in general and psychotherapists in particular.

One of the most important and recent reviews on the outcome of psychotherapy is that by Grawe et al (1994), who reviewed 897 controlled studies of various psychotherapeutic treatments. Each study was evaluated with an extensive assessment instrument containing more than 1000 items in seven major areas:

1. General descriptive information about study and investigation.
2. Design and methodology of study.

3. Information about patients, therapists, and therapy method.
4. Information about assessment of validity of the study.
5. Measures (global rating), main symptoms, personality factors, interpersonal relations, leisure-time behaviour, job performance, sexual behaviour, and psychophysiological measurements.
6. Evaluation.
7. Results (effect size).

For *client-centred psychotherapy* (mainly for patients with neurotic disorders), significant effects of therapy could be observed on main symptoms and mood. Improvements were also reported in the area of personality and in interpersonal relations (especially in those who had out-patient treatment in groups). The effects of psychotherapy on leisure-time activity were investigated in only one study, in which there was a positive effect; effects on job performance were not investigated. Effects on sexual behaviour were investigated in one study, but proved to be without influence. In none of the cited studies were specific instruments for assessment of QoL used. Grawe et al (1994) also reported that for *psychoanalytically-orientated psychotherapy* and *short-term psychoanalytic therapies*, improvement was found in symptoms, but there was less in the areas of personality or interpersonal relationships. In one study, improvement in job performance was reported.

The methods of weighting in the meta-analytic approach of Grawe et al (1994) have been mainly criticised by psychoanalysts (Tschuschke et al, 1994). Bachrach et al (1991) reviewed findings by psychoanalysts on the efficacy of *psychoanalysis*: these studies varied in meeting outcome research criteria, but QoL was not used as an outcome measure in any of them. The concept of "quality of life" is mainly seen as a slogan by psychoanalysts (Hau, 1977), and although some aspects of life satisfaction (wishes for instinctual satisfaction and for protection, acceptance, and love) are seen as very important, they are not primary outcome measures.

In contrast to psychoanalytic treatment studies, those on *cognitive and behavioural treatment* are more orientated to the assessment of objective psychosocial functioning and subjective well-being; here again, assessments are not carried out with specific instruments for QoL.

In their review of 74 studies on *assertiveness-training*, Grawe et al (1994) report the effects of therapy not only on assertiveness but also on interpersonal relations, personality, and general well-being.

In 62 studies on *confrontation therapy* (mostly for phobic and obsessive-compulsive patients), the same authors found a significant reduction in symptoms in 90% of patients who had gradual *in vivo* confrontation, improvement in subjective well-being in 50%, improvement in interpersonal relationships in 30%, as well as improvement in job performance and leisure-time activity (reduction of avoidance behaviour). No improvement was found in sexual behaviour or personality factors.

Cognitive therapy (Beck et al, 1979) was initially developed for the treatment of depressive patients, and later for anxiety disorders and a wide variety of other conditions, including personality disorder. Grawe et al (1994) list 16 studies which reported impressive efficacy not only on main symptoms but also in the areas of interpersonal relations, personality, and leisure-time activity. The "National Institute of Mental Health Treatment of Depression Collaborative Research Program" (Elkin et al, 1989; Shea et al, 1992) was the first coordinated multi-site study initiated by the US NIMH in the field of psychotherapy research. The treatment phase consisted of 16 weeks of randomly assigned treatment with either *cognitive behavioural therapy* (CBT) or *interpersonal therapy (IPT)*, or imipramine hydrochloride plus clinical management, or placebo plus clinical management. Follow-up assessments were carried out 6, 12, and 18 months after treatment. Of all patients entering treatment for which there were follow-up data, the proportion who recovered and remained well during follow-up (no relapse of Major Depressive Disorder) did not differ significantly among the four treatments. In cross-sectional analyses of social functioning for the total sample, no significant differences were found among any of the treatment conditions at 6 or 12 months. At 18 months, IPT was significantly superior to imipramine plus clinical management; it differed at a trend level from CBT in global social functioning, but not significantly from placebo plus clinical management. Although some instruments in this study measured aspects of QoL, no specific instruments for its assessment were used. Interpersonal therapy, amitryptiline and the combination of both were investigated in an acute treatment study by Weissman et al (1979). IPT proved to be highly effective, especially in combination with the drug. In their one-year follow-up, Weissman et al (1981a) found no difference for IPT on clinical symptoms of depression, but it did have a main effect on measures of social functioning.

For *marital therapy,* Grawe et al (1994) list 35 controlled studies. In 29 of these, Behavioural Marital Therapy (BMT) was applied, mainly for marital problems, sexual problems, or depression of one partner. In many studies, measurements were only on the main problems or symptoms, but in some, they were also on relationships, general well-being, personality, or job performance. These studies show an impressive effect of BMT, with significant improvement in the main problems; however, in two-thirds of the measurements, positive effects of the therapy could also be found in other areas (interpersonal relationships, sexual relationship, job performance). Improvement in general well-being occurred only when treatment was given for other than marital problems.

Only a few studies have examined the relationship between QoL and psychotherapy more specifically, and these were uncontrolled. One of them was a mainly retrospective investigation of 74 patients with neurotic disorder diagnosed by ICD-9 (WHO, 1978) (Anxiety Disorder $n = 34$, Conversion Disorder $n = 9$, Obsessive Compulsive Disorder $n = 6$, Neurotic Depression $n = 14$, other $n = 11$). The effects of in-patient behaviour therapy were studied one year after discharge from hospital (Holub, 1990). One area studied was QoL, measured by the scale devised by Plog (1976), with subscales on housing, leisure time, social contacts, job, and general satisfaction with treatment. About half of patients were satisfied in most areas of QoL; the dissatisfaction reported by about 40% was mainly with close relationships and their use of leisure time. However, these two areas improved markedly after treatment, and scores remained stable at follow-up after one year. Significant correlations were found between successful treatment on a symptomatic level and the following subscales of quality of life: general satisfaction with living situation ($p < 0.01$), use of leisure time ($p < 0.01$), and social contacts ($p < 0.01$).

Another investigation (Rubin et al, 1995) measured the QoL in Panic Disorder patients. Using HRQL-ratings ("Quality of Well Being-QWB"), it was found that subjects with panic disorder had suffered a significant decrease in health-related quality of life compared to "healthy" controls. The disability in panic disorder approached that of illnesses like non-insulin-dependent diabetes. With Cognitive Behavioural treatment (CBT), the QoL in patients with panic disorder demonstrated delayed but sustained improvement, reaching levels which did not differ from controls.

Demal et al (1996) assessed QoL using the Longitudinal Interval Follow-Up Evaluation, LIFE (Keller et al, 1987) in a sample of 74 patients with Obsessive Compulsive Disorder (OCD) treated with CBT and a serotonin reuptake inhibitor. Patients were investigated three times: on the day of admission (baseline), 6 months later (follow-up I), and 12 months after follow-up I (follow-up II). The semi-structured interview format covered the following areas of psychosocial functioning: work, interpersonal relationships with family and friends, sex, recreation; a global social adjustment score (GSA-LIFE) was given, which represented an overall rating. At admission, 18% of the patients showed slight and 82% marked impairment in psychosocial functioning (GSA-LIFE). At follow-up I, after discontinuation of controlled treatment, improvement in symptoms was evident, as well as in psychosocial functioning (14% no pychosocial impairment; 44% slight impairment; 42% marked impairment). A further improvement was seen at follow-up II, where 40% of patients showed no impairment, 30% were slightly impaired, and 30% markedly impaired. Of the 40% "best functioning" patients none had clinical OCD according to the Yale–Brown Obsessive Compulsive Scale (Goodman et al, 1989). In sum, 44% of the patients had a significant improvement in QoL (GSA-LIFE), as well as in symptoms, from baseline to follow-up II.

In another study on patients with Panic Disorder and Agoraphobia, Scheibe et al (1993) found that one-year supportive group psychotherapy improved not only symptoms, but also psychosocial functioning (partner relationship, sex, social adjustment) as assessed with LIFE, and overall satisfaction with life as assessed with GSA-LIFE.

Our observation at the Behaviour Modification Ward at the University of Vienna, Department of Psychiatry, where we applied the "Berlin Quality of Life Profile", BLP (Priebe et al, 1995) prior to and three months after termination of in-patient behaviour therapy was that patients were still only fairly satisfied with their QoL after treatment, but QoL improved in some areas (e.g. getting along with others, leisure-time activities). With regard to QoL our sample was comparable with the sample of out-patients in a community service for the mentally ill, investigated by Priebe et al (1995).

PSYCHOSOCIAL INTERVENTIONS FOR CANCER PATIENTS

The effect of psychological therapy on the psychosocial adjustment of cancer patients has been evaluated in several systematic studies, but reported results are difficult to interpret, in view of some methodological deficiencies. One problem in comparing different studies is the lack of a consistent definition of "Quality of Life". In some studies QoL refers to physical and in others to emotional well-being of cancer patients, while in others, there is a mixture of both. Different scales and ratings have been used for assessing QoL, and most studies lack control groups. Another problem is that some authors have reported on the effects of "psycho-therapy" or "counselling" without describing the treatment more specifically, yet full descriptions are required to allow psychotherapy trials to be replicated and valid conclusions to be drawn from them. Review of the literature shows that psychosocial interventions are generally applied to decrease feelings of alienation by talking to others, to reduce anxiety about the treatments, to assist in clarifying misperceptions, and to lessen feelings of isolation, helplessness, and being neglected by others. These interventions have the added benefit of encouraging more responsibility to get well and enhancing compliance with medical regimes. Another goal of intervention is psychosocial adjustment and the ability to carry out daily activities. There are four major categories of intervention described most frequently. These are educational techniques, behavioural training (e.g. progressive muscular relaxation, hypnosis, deep breathing, meditation, biofeedback, passive relaxation, guided imagery, systematic desensitisation), individual psychotherapy, and group intervention. Here, we will focus particularly on those studies where quality of life was actually measured. To the best of our knowledge, no study has investigated the impact of educational techniques on quality of life. Studies using behavioural training, individual psychotherapy, or group intervention are presented in Table 17.1.

One scale used to assess QoL is the Karnovsky Performance Status Scale, KPS (Karnovsky & Burchenal, 1949). As Clark and Fallowfield (1986) point out, this scale is almost invariably used when assessment of QoL is actually made at all, but its frequency of usage is no indication of appropriateness and this scale, whilst useful as a measure of health performance status, is not a satisfactory estimation of QoL. Ratings from 0–100 are made by the clinicians, 100 being normal with no evidence of disease, and 0 being the terminal point of the scale, that is, death. There are several problems with this method, in particular the assumption that a patient with a low score due to immobility necessarily has a poorer QoL than a patient with a higher score and vice versa. To give an example, an incontinent, wheelchair-bound cancer patient might achieve only 40 on the scale, despite the fact that this patient might have a good social support and experience rich and happy relationships. A breast cancer patient with a score of possibly 80 might, on the other hand, be emotionally crippled by depression, which the scale does not attempt to address. Yet the concomitant loss of libido and self-esteem would give her an extremely poor QoL. Another major criticism is that the scale takes no account of pre-treatment levels of activity. This is potentially serious when comparing the effects of similar biological disease burdens in active, working extroverts with those in more passive, housebound patients.

The Functional Living Index – Cancer, FLIC (Schipper et al, 1984), measures the quality of cancer patients' day-to-day functioning including physical and psychological aspects as well as familial and social relations. It contains 22 items, each scored on a 7-point Likert scale. Considerable construct validity data are published (Schipper et al, 1984), but there is no information on the reliability of the measure. A major criticism is that the FLIC allows only a total score, which incorporates both psychological and physical factors.

The QL-Index (Spitzer et al, 1981) was specifically developed for use by doctors to measure the QoL in cancer patients. It is quick to complete (one minute on average), and simple to score, administer and analyse. The QL-index covers a comprehensive range of QoL dimensions. Five items – activity, living, health, support, and outlook on life – are rated on a 3-point scale from 0–2, giving a maximum score of 10. The test has a high interrater correlation and good correlations between self-rating of patients and those of their doctors. Like all QoL scales, it has some limitations, for example giving equal weighting to all items contained in the index.

The Psychological Adjustment to Illness Scale, PAIS (Morrow et al, 1978), examines a patient's global adjustment to illness with 45 questions in seven principal psychosocial domains (health care, vocational environment, domestic environment, sexual relationships, extended family relationships, social environment and psychological distress). Ratings for each question within each domain are made on a 4-point (0–3) scale; these generate a PAIS total score, which is a composite score of subjective well-being and objective disability and thus mixes subjective and objective aspects of quality of life.

Another scale used is the Cancer Inventory of Problem Situations, CIPS (Heinrich et al, 1984). It is self-administered, requires approximately 20 minutes to complete, and consists of 141 problem statements grouped into 21 categories, which are then subdivided under four main headings (personal care, medical situation, interpersonal interactions, miscellaneous). The patient indicates on a 5-point scale, ranging from "not at all" to "very much", how much of a problem each statement has been in the preceding month. The instrument appears to be more sensitive than a semi-structured interview, but there are two main criticisms of the test – that no normative data exist yet, and that it has only been validated on a small sample. However, the CIPS might be a useful instrument for assessing the psychosocial and physical impact of treatment programmes, with a view to tailoring therapy to cause minimal distress.

The results of the study by Lyles et al (1982) suggest that progressive muscular relaxation and guided imagery can be an effective adjunctive procedure for reducing the side-effects experienced by many cancer chemotherapy patients. Moreover, the relaxation procedure helped patients to function better not only in the clinic during chemotherapy treatments, but also at home during the days following these. It was clear from the home record forms and from communication with the patients that those practising progressive muscular relaxation daily "improved substantially in QoL", that is, they had less functional impairment at home.

Gruber et al (1988) studied the effect of behavioural training on the immune system. Over a period of one year, subjects who had no prior experience with either technique used imagery and relaxation. In addition to several elevated measures of immune system function, patients showed improvement in psychosocial functioning.

In the study by Linn et al (1982), counselling was found to be effective in reducing denial but maintaining hope, encouraging patients to participate in meaningful activities, helping them to complete any unfinished business, and providing increased self-esteem and life satisfaction. While it was not possible to improve physical functioning or survival in patients, counselling intervention "helped to enhance QoL".

Cella et al (1993a) found significant improvement in QoL, assessed with the FLIC, after an eight-week support group. This group was modelled on principles of wellness in the context of life-threatening illness (Cella, 1990) and group dynamics related to mutual and peer support. The authors point out that the improvement in overall FLIC score resulted from improvement in its psychological rather than its physical items, that is, improvement in QoL was primarily in social and emotional dimensions.

Heinrich and Schag (1985) studied the effects of a six-week structured small group programme. The major component of the group treatment included education and information (concerning cancer, cancer therapy, the psychosocial impact of cancer, stress, and adaptive coping), relaxation exercises, cognitive therapy, problem-solving training, and activity management. The latter included a walking exercise component as well as a contract in order to increase positively valued individual and couple activities. Improvement was found in the treatment group in respect of psychosocial adjustment (PAIS).

Berglund et al (1994) undertook a study with 98 cancer patients who took part in a rehabilitation programme, while 101 patients served as controls. The intervention

Table 17.1 Psychological interventions and quality of life (QoL) in cancer patients

Study, year	Patients	Treatment	Control group	Follow-up	Outcome QoL	Instruments assessing QoL
Lyles et al (1982)	50, mixed cancer	(1) Relaxation guided imagery (2) Talking	No treatment	75 days	QoL ↑	Simple questions about functional impairment at home
Gruber et al (1988)	10, metastatic cancer	Behavioural training on immune system (Relaxation and guided imagery)	—	1 yr	QoL ↑	Information from nurses about functional impairment Karnovsky Performance Status Scale (KPS)
Linn et al (1982)	120, late-stage cancer	Individual counselling	No treatment	1 yr	Life satisfaction ↑ QoL ↑	Questions regarding "Life Satisfaction", "Social Isolation" Nurse-rated functional status for daily activities
Cella et al (1993a)	77, mixed cancer	8-week support group	—	8 wks	QoL ↑	Self-report Functional living index (FLIC)
Heinrich & Schag (1985)	51, mixed cancer	Stress and activity management group treatment programme (relaxation, cognitive therapy, problem solving, activity management)	Current available care	8 wks	QoL ↑	6-point scale from "terrible" to "excellent" Karnovsky Performance Status Scale (KPS) Psychological Adjustment to Illness Scale (PAIS)
Berglund et al (1994)	199, mixed cancer	11-structured 2-hour group sessions (physical training, coping skills, information)	No treatment	12 wks	QoL ↑	Quality of Life Index Cancer Inventory of Problem Situations (CIPS)
Cunningham et al (1993)	402, mixed cancer	7 weekly 2-hour sessions (relaxation, mental imagery, discussion, role modelling, emotional ventilation)	—	5 mths	QoL ↑	Functional Living Index (FLIC)

consisted of 11 structured 2-hour group sessions. Physical training, coping skills, and information were the primary goals of the programme. Subjects in the experimental group improved significantly in physical training, "fighting spirit", information, psychosocial functioning, and satisfaction with life.

Cunningham et al (1993) investigated the effect of a brief group coping skills programme. Subgroups based on religious status, gender, educational level, marital status and previous experience with mental self-help techniques did not vary significantly, but the overall programme increased coping skills and enhanced psychosocial functioning. It appeared to benefit younger patients somewhat more than older ones. Improvements in quality of physical, psychological, familial, and social life were evidenced by the FLIC. Scores, and patients' sense of self-efficacy were also increased.

In summary, cancer patients may benefit from a variety of psychological interventions: a structured intervention consisting of health education, stress management, and behavioural training (coping including problem-solving techniques), together with psychosocial group support, seems to offer the greatest potential benefit (Fawzy et al, 1995).

THE EFFECT OF PSYCHOSOCIAL INTERVENTIONS ON QUALITY OF LIFE IN PATIENTS WITH CARDIOVASCULAR DISEASE

Psychiatrists and psychologists have for many years been interested in psychosocial factors contributing to cardiovascular disorder, and its psychosocial consequences, as well as its possible modification by treatment. However, not much emphasis has been put on the assessment of quality of life in treatment studies. As Mayou (1990) has emphasised, major problems in quality of life research are of two kinds. Firstly, unprecise concepts of quality of life with questionable objective criteria (e.g. the uncertain significance of rates of return to work) and very general subjective criteria (with neglect of the mental state and of the individual meaning of quality of life). Secondly, problems of measurement: in clinical trials, very simple ad hoc measures have often been used as an aspect of outcome (Fletcher et al, 1987; Wenger et al, 1984).

Main areas of research are "Type A" (coronary-prone) behaviour pattern, and hypertension. In a large-scale prospective study, Rosenmann et al (1975) showed that a certain pattern of behaviour – elicited during a structured interview – was an independent risk factor for the development of coronary heart disease (CHD) among white males. The presence of this pattern of behaviour, termed "Type A", was associated with twice as many eventual incidents of CHD as were found in those who were not positive for this behaviour pattern ("Type B"). The behaviour in this cluster included time urgency, hostility, unrewarded striving, and certain facial and motor behaviours as well as speech styles.

From reviews of the literature (Blanchard, 1994) it seems clear that, at least for males, "Type A" behaviour can be changed through cognitive behavioural treatment; that this change also leads to reduced non-fatal recurrences and cardiac deaths could be shown in a large-scale secondary prevention trial among male patients with myocardial infarction (Friedman et al, 1986). It would thus seem prudent to add an appropriate intervention for "Type A" behaviour to routine rehabilitation programmes for cardiac patients. While exercise-counselling, dietary management, and smoking cessation are routine parts of such rehabilitation programmes, wholesale inclusion of an "anti-Type-A" component has yet to occur. However, until now, there exists no primary prevention trial with "Type A" behaviour analogous to the multiple risk factor intervention trial (Rosenmann et al, 1975) to see whether changing "Type A" behaviour can reduce the incidence of initial morbidity from CHD. It seems that the main focus of research in this field has been more on "quantity" than on "quality" of life.

The effects of psychosocial interventions on quality of life have rarely been investigated with appropriate measures and control groups. Only studies of rehabilitation after myocardial infarction have shown that the majority of patients recover well without any special form of extra care (Blumenthal & Emery, 1988). In the study of Mayou et al (1981), few differences were found between three types of intervention (standard care, extra counselling-exercise classes, and a battery of specific measures). However, counselled patients reported longer working time and greater frequency of sexual activity, 18 months later.

Hypertension continues to be a major public health problem in many Western countries. In the USA, primarily through an aggressive public education programme, 85% of those affected are aware of their elevated blood pressure status (up from 50%), and the percentage of those affected whose blood pressure is under control has increased from 16 to 57% (Blanchard, 1994). Thus, while there has been some success, much remains to be done to control this well-documented risk factor for cardiovascular disease and stroke.

The advantages of drug treatment for severe hypertension are substantial, but there is still uncertainty about the best treatment for many people with mild hypertension (Williams, 1987). Many patients comply poorly with treatment, while many drugs cause depression and other side-effects which reduce quality of life. Three broad approaches of non-drug treatment for newly discovered cases of mild hypertension have been described: stress management, aerobic exercise, and dietary alterations (primarily weight loss or sodium restriction) (Blanchard et al, 1988). Stress management refers to various arousal reduction techniques such as relaxation training in its several varieties, biofeedback training and cognitive procedures that emphasise coping abilities with external events or inner reactions to such events. The effects of stress management approaches on hypertension are still a matter of controversy in the literature. Most direct comparisons of stress management approaches with antihypertensive medication have shown the medication to work more rapidly, as well as to have a greater antihypertensive effect (Blanchard, 1994). Some studies of relaxation and stress management in hypertension have shown a reduction of anxiety (Bali, 1979) and of anxiety and depression (Wadden, 1984), while increasing a sense of well-being (Patel, 1973; Peters et al, 1977).

In a randomised, controlled trial, Patel and Marmot (1987) showed that relaxation and stress-management training were associated with a reduction in blood pressure maintained over four years of observation. At a four-year follow-up, significantly more subjects in the relaxation group reported improvement in relationships at work, general health, enjoyment of life, and personal and family relationships compared to those in the control group. A similar but statistically insignificant trend was shown for the general level of physical energy, sexual life, concentration at work, mental well-being, and social life.

Comprehensive, multi-modal, non-drug approaches as an adjunct to drug therapy have been proposed by Rotering-Steinberg (1989). The treatment programme consists of information about hypertension, self-measurement of blood pressure, dietary education, stress management, and observation of compliance for medication as an adjunct to the usual drug therapy. In a controlled study, major parts of this programme have been evaluated by Lenz-Schmit (1987). This author not only found a reduction of systolic and diastolic blood pressure in the intervention group, but also an increase of knowledge about the disorder and treatment, a reduction in the amount of antihypertensive medication and a change in living habits.

One problem with such a comprehensive approach, of course, is that it needs a multi-professional team, which is only available in some institutions, or has to be specifically organised, for example by several general practitioners.

CONCLUSIONS

The concept of quality of life has been well known for long time in the social sciences focusing on the life satisfaction of the population (Bullinger, 1994). In medicine, the concept of "health related quality of life" is more orientated on subjective functioning in a somatic, psychological, and social perspective (according to the WHO definition of health). In psychotherapy research and treatment, this subjective view of the patient will be of increasing importance in the assessment of the outcome of treatment, although several limitations of this approach have to be taken into account: on the one hand, subjective well-being will increase during successful psychotherapy (relief from symptoms, reduction of avoidance behaviour, increase in social functioning, leisure-time activities, and general well-being, etc.). On the other hand, the increased reality-orientation might also reduce subjective well-being, at least in the short term. Patients entering psychotherapy are often unaware of problems, for example regarding their marital relationship, and during treatment, they may discover a variety of difficulties which may decrease their subjective well-being for some time. But in addition, many "objective criteria" in quality of life instruments are questionable: the significance of rates of return to work is uncertain, for example for those of late middle age at a time when unemployment is high and when early retirement is possible and increasingly attractive; in the case of a patient who moves out of the luxurious apartment of his parents to become independent and self-reliant, psychotherapy could be considered successful, although the QoL considering housing will decline; living alone can be a success after termination of an unhappy relationship, but it can also be a failure because of difficulties in maintaining contacts with other people. Poor QoL, independent of psychiatric disorder, such as unemployment due to the economic situation, may increase psychological problems and in this case psychotherapy will not increase QoL.

In some disorders, such as depression, QoL and depressive symptoms can hardly be separated, making it difficult to assess QoL. Some newly developed QoL instruments for depression, for example the "Quality of Life in Depression Scale", QLDS (Hunt & McKenna, 1992a,b) confuse QoL and subjective assessment of symptomatology. Advances have been made in developing assessment devices for QoL that might be integrated in the evaluation of clinical improvement (Frisch et al, 1992).

Despite these difficulties and although theories of quality of life have not so far been very conclusive, psychotherapy research can no longer neglect the concept. Health economic factors and the cost-effectiveness of treatment are important in discussions about the financial coverage of psychotherapy in many countries: the usual assessments of symptoms and personality factors no longer seem to be enough for the evaluation of health, while subjective well-being and objective components of QoL have also to be taken into account.

CHAPTER EIGHTEEN

Whose Life is it Anyway? Quality of Life for Long-stay Patients Discharged from Psychiatric Hospitals

Julian Leff

Each of us strives to achieve the highest quality of life possible within the constraints created by personal, economic, and societal factors. There have been many periods in history during which the quality of life for some or most of the people has been so abysmal that it has led to death: for example the Third Reich, the famine in Ethiopia, the Cultural Revolution in China. Under less extreme conditions, there are still large variations in the quality of life within populations, some of which stem from the unavoidable depredations of ill-health. A concern with the measurement of quality of life has developed in the past two decades, stimulated by the growth of the consumer movement (Nader, 1973) which led to advocacy organisations for patients and their relatives, and by the escalating costs of health care. The latter faces professionals with uncomfortable choices as to which patients to prioritise, given limited resources. This problem has been sharpened by the development of expensive techniques and apparatus which can keep alive people who would otherwise have faced almost certain death within a short period of time. The painful situation professionals can find themselves in was anticipated by Bernard Shaw (1911) in *The Doctor's Dilemma,* in which the doctors have to choose between saving the life of a dull, but worthy, colleague or that of an unscrupulous, but brilliant, artist. In this instance, the professional arbiters of life and death were required to judge the relative value of the contribution each of the two sick men was likely to make to society. Pragmatic considerations of this kind do not currently enter into our decisions about who should receive treatment, although recent suggestions that there should be an upper age limit for certain kinds of medical and surgical interventions presage such a development.

A major controversy in the assessment of quality of life centres on whether to include a professional view of the patients' situation as well as seeking the subjective experience of the patients themselves. The salient issues are whether patients are always capable of making a rational appraisal of their situation, and whether professionals are able to make a valid judgement of patients' quality of life. These issues merit some discussion.

In the past, patients' views about the quality of care they received were almost totally ignored: this was one facet of the paternalism that characterised custodial care. It was easy to dismiss the views of long-stay patients by asserting that they were psychotic and were likely to make irrational judgements. However, in the case of patients suffering from a functional psychosis, this argument is not supported by the evidence. Weinstein (1979) reviewed 25 studies undertaken between 1956 and 1977 which used questionnaires to measure patients' attitudes towards psychiatric hospitalisation. He concluded that in 13 out of 16 studies in which the appropriate measures were included, length of time in the institution was not related to patients' attitudes.

The study by the Team for the Assessment of Psychiatric Services (TAPS), examined the issue of the reliability of assessing the attitudes of long-stay patients. Thornicroft et al (1993) used the Patient Attitude Questionnaire (PAQ) to assess the attitude of psychiatric patients towards their treatment settings and staff. To measure test–retest reliability, the questionnaire was administered to 43 long-stay patients in two psychiatric hospitals, on two occasions, six months apart. Of the 13 items included in the reliability analysis, only one failed to show satisfactory reliability over time – patients' views on the helpfulness of occupation. It was notable that of all the attitude items retested on the second occasion, 66% of the responses were identical to those given initially. Hence, unreliability of responses cannot be used as a reason to avoid seeking long-stay patients' opinions about their quality of life.

The patient's view is obviously necessary, but is it sufficient? In order to answer this question, we need to consider some specific examples in which the patient's judgement is impaired by a psychiatric condition. The most obvious is Alzheimer's disease. Patients with advanced dementia cannot be expected to comment on their quality of life, yet this judgement is extremely important, particularly as such patients have been subject to abuse on occasions. We can, of course, use the relative, when one is available, as a proxy for the patient. Otherwise, an independent judge can be asked to assess the quality of the caring environment. This can be in terms of physical and architectural features of the care setting, for example using measures derived from the MEAP (Moos & Lemke, 1984). It is also possible to make naturalistic observations of day-to-day behaviour and social activity as well as staff activities. This approach was taken in the TAPS study of psychogeriatric services, and showed that there was more staff interaction with patients in the community homes than in the psychiatric hospital. Additionally, patients were noted to spend more time drinking tea in the community homes, which was in accord with the relatives' perception that there was greater opportunity to make drinks for the patients in the community settings. Thus, these two approaches, each of which is a substitute for the patient's expression of satisfaction, concur in indicating a better quality of life in the community homes (Wills & Leff, 1996).

Though the necessity for an independent judgement is obvious in the case of demented patients, the argument can be extended to patients with psychotic illnesses. Consider the paranoid patient who decides to withdraw from contact with other people and to live a solitary life. This patient may well express a high degree of satisfaction with his/her chosen life style. However the psychiatric professional, with the benefit of experience of similar patients, is able to predict that isolation leads to the accumulation of negative symptoms and an eventual deterioration in the quality of life, which may be imperceptible to the patient.

A failure to appreciate the ominous nature of some aspects of their life can also be a feature of non-psychotic patients. In a study of family therapy for marital disharmony and neurotic disorders, Asen et al (1991) found that the therapists were very effective in reducing both critical and over-involved attitudes expressed by parents. Subjects' satisfaction, measured at the end of treatment, correlated positively with reduction in criticism, indicating that they were pleased with the fact that they experienced less anger. However, their satisfaction correlated negatively with reduction in over-involvement. This suggests that they were displeased with the loss of closeness, even though the therapists and researchers knew that if it were not modified, it would lead to continuing problems in family functioning.

Most researchers in this area agree that both the patient's perspective and that of an independent judge are needed to provide a balanced view of the quality of life. Lehman's scale (Lehman et al, 1982), which is one of the most widely used, measures objective attributes of quality of life and life satisfaction in eight life domains: living situation, family, social relations, leisure activities, work, finances, personal safety, and health. Mukherjee (1989) emphasised the importance of including both subjective and objective measures within an assessment battery.

TAPS ASSESSMENT INSTRUMENTS

The choice of measuring instruments is obviously crucial in assessing patients' quality of life. For the TAPS study of long-stay patients, a batch of nine schedules was compiled. It was considered desirable, where possible, to use existing instruments with established reliability, for which data would be available for purposes of comparison. However, it proved necessary to adapt some schedules, while in certain areas there was no suitable instrument, so that new ones had to be developed. Each area will be considered in turn.

PERSONAL DATA AND PSYCHIATRIC HISTORY

We needed to collect information on the patients' gender, ethnicity, and marital status, as well as their living conditions before they were admitted to the psychiatric hospital. These data were abstracted from the case notes, as well as details of contacts with the psychiatric and forensic services and the diagnosis, currently and at time of first admission.

PHYSICAL HEALTH INDEX

Many of the patients were elderly and suffered from degenerative diseases of the pulmonary, cardiovascular, and musculoskeletal systems. Since poor health, whether mental or physical, reduces the quality of life, it was deemed important to assess the patients' physical health as well as their psychiatric state. There were not enough trained staff to examine all the patients physically, so the relevant information was obtained from medical and nursing staff and from the case notes.

MENTAL STATE EXAMINATION

As with physical health, a high level of mental health contributes to quality of life. However, there is often disagreement between patients and professionals over the issue of psychiatric symptoms and treatment with medication. Patients with partial or no insight often maintain that there is nothing the matter with them, when professionals are sure they are suffering from delusions and/or hallucinations. Under these circumstances, the prescription of neuroleptic drugs, which often have unpleasant side-effects, will usually be viewed by patients as reducing their quality of life. Professionals, by contrast, will judge the overall benefit of reducing the likelihood of relapse to outweigh the unpleasant effects of drugs. Hence, they will see the drugs as enhancing the patients' quality of life. To assess the patients' mental state, we used the Present State Examination (PSE; Wing et al, 1974), but it was not possible to conduct a full assessment of every patient. Up to one-third of the patients could not be interviewed because they were mute, incoherent, or uncooperative. In these cases, it was usually possible to make an assessment of the patients' non-verbal behaviour and mood.

PROBLEMS OF SOCIAL BEHAVIOUR

As with psychiatric symptoms, disturbed behaviour may affect the people who come into contact with the patients much more than the patients themselves. In the long run, this will reduce their quality of life by alienating friends and relatives who could provide emotional and other forms of support. We chose to use the Social Behaviour Schedule (SBS), which has been validated and found to be reliable by Sturt and Wykes (1986). The SBS covers behaviour stemming from positive symptoms, such as verbal and physical hostility, and from negative symptoms such as poor hygiene.

Once we began interviewing patients in the community, we realised that there were areas of activity in which the patients operated which were not covered by the SBS. Because it was developed on hospital populations, it was not designed to assess skills such as shopping, using public transport, and choosing clothing suitable for the weather. Consequently, we developed a supplementary instrument, the Basic Everyday Living Skills Schedule (BELS), which does cover these important community activities.

PATIENT SATISFACTION

One of the most salient areas of assessment for quality of life is the patients' views of the care they receive. These have often been unjustly neglected in the past, on the grounds that long-term psychotic patients were unreliable informants. In fact, as discussed above, we found the Patient Attitude Questionnaire (PAQ) that was developed to have an acceptable test–retest reliability (Thornicroft et al, 1993). From the results of this study, it was concluded that long-term psychiatric patients are able to give clear and consistent views about the care they receive and about the carers.

THE QUALITY OF THE ENVIRONMENT

A criticism often levelled at institutional care is that it deprives the patient of autonomy, imposing a host of rules and regulations which benefit the staff rather than their clients (Goffman, 1961). We extended the Hospital Hostel Practices Profile (Wing & Brown, 1970) to include questions about the wearing of uniforms by the staff and the availability of privacy, as well as adding a new section on the proximity of amenities such as shops, day centres, parks and cinemas. The latter obviously gains in importance when patients move out of a large institution, where most amenities are provided on site, into residences in the community. The extended schedule is named the Environmental Index (EI).

SOCIAL INTEGRATION

It is conceivable that long-stay patients discharged from psychiatric hospitals might remain socially isolated from the communities in which they have been relocated.

This isolation could be maintained by their neighbours' avoidance of contact with them and by the care staff in their homes overprotecting them from ordinary social interchange with the public. In order to investigate this possibility, it is necessary to define the extent of the patients' social networks, the people included in them, and the quality of relationships. Existing schedules were developed for use with healthy individuals and people suffering from neuroses, and were inappropriate for the socially impaired population to be studied. Therefore, an interview was developed which was specifically tailored to the long-stay patients. It is called the Social Network Schedule (SNS) and its validity and reliability have been established (Dunn et al, 1990; Leff et al, 1990).

ECONOMIC EVALUATION

Collaboration with health economists in the University of Kent Personal Social Services Research Unit was established at the beginning of the TAPS Project, and comprehensive costing of patients' care, both inside and outside psychiatric hospitals, is being pursued. In order to record all services received by patients living in the community, a Community Services Receipt Schedule has been developed. Economic data will not be presented in this chapter, but are available in other publications (Beecham et al, 1991; Knapp et al, 1990, 1993).

The series of schedules used provides a relatively comprehensive picture of patients' quality of life, which includes the perspective of the patients themselves as well as the more detached view of the research workers, none of whom were involved in providing services for the patients. The relatives have not been consulted in this study, because all the patients were long-stay initially and only a handful returned to their families on discharge.

DESIGN OF THE STUDY

TAPS was set up in response to a decision by the North East Thames Regional Health Authority (NETRHA) to close two large psychiatric hospitals over a ten-year period. Both hospitals were opened in the Victorian era, Friern in 1851 and Claybury in 1895. Both contained over 2400 patients at their peak in the early 1950s, and both had declined to between 800 and 900 patients each in 1983, the year the closure decision was announced. TAPS undertook to study the effects of closure on the three main patient populations: the long-stay non-demented, the psychogeriatric, and patients spending brief periods on the admission wards. Here, the findings for the first of those three groups will be presented.

The long-stay patients were defined as those spending more than one year in hospital, who, if aged over 65, did not suffer from dementia. A small group of patients under 65 with various organic brain conditions was included. A census of the two hospitals was carried out, and identified 770 patients who met these criteria. However, this was not the entire sample, because patients were being admitted to the acute wards until shortly before closure of the hospital, and some of them stayed for more than a year, hence satisfying our inclusion criteria. These new long-stay patients accumulated at a surprisingly high rate, so that the sample size grew to 1166, of whom the new long-stay constituted one-third.

The ideal scientific design would have been to randomise patients to be discharged or to remain in hospital for a further period of time, and to compare the outcomes of the two groups. This was not possible for a variety of reasons, both ethical and practical. Instead, a matched case-control design was adopted. Each patient due to be discharged was matched with a patient likely to stay some time longer on six criteria: age, gender, hospital, total time in hospital, diagnosis, and number of social behaviour problems. It was possible to match each discharged patient ("leaver") quite closely with a patient who stayed ("match") for the first four years of the study. In the fifth year, the pool of remaining patients had shrunk to the point where it was possible only to match every two leavers to one patient who stayed. Thereafter the matching procedure broke down, and each patient had to be used as his/her own control, in a "before and after" design.

The group of patients discharged in the course of a year is designated a cohort. Cohort 1 left the two hospitals between September 1985 and August 1986. Friern hospital was eventually closed, as planned, in March 1993, by which time eight cohorts had left. The closure programme for Claybury was delayed for various administrative reasons, and the hospital remains open at the time of writing. For this reason, TAPS ceased following-up Claybury patients after Cohort 5. A one-year follow-up study has been completed of the first five cohorts of leavers and their matches (Leff et al, 1996). A one-year follow-up has also been conducted of the total long-stay population of Friern Hospital (eight cohorts). A five-year follow-up has also been instituted, because of the importance of monitoring the outcome of these patients, 80% of whom suffer from schizophrenia, over a longer period; this study has been completed on the first two cohorts (Leff et al, 1994). An overview of the variety of follow-up data collected so far will be presented here. Before doing so, however, it is necessary to explain the policy for funding the reprovision of psychiatric care and the nature of the community placements.

"DOWRIES" AND STAFFED HOMES

The problem facing any programme of reprovision for a psychiatric hospital is how to mobilise the resources, both revenue and capital, which are tied up in the hospital. NETRHA's approach to this problem was to attach a "dowry" to each long-stay patient who was discharged to a newly provided placement in the community. The dowry was calculated by dividing the annual revenue cost of the hospital by the number of patients housed in it. This amounted to £14 000 per year in 1985, and was increased each year to keep pace with inflation. This amount of revenue was added to the budget of the district health authority taking responsibility for the patient, and remained in it for an unlimited period. This amount could not be saved from the hospital budget each time a patient was discharged, but only when it was possible to close a whole ward and redeploy the staff. NETRHA recognised this problem, and guaranteed to fund double running costs, maintaining the hospital budget as well as transferring revenue to the community, until the requisite savings could be made. They also advanced £20 million in capital for investment in community facilities for Friern patients, with the expectation that this sum could be recovered on sale of the Friern site which was prime development land. In the event, this has now happened. Thus NETRHA's financial support of the reprovision programme has been generous, but the health economics team have calculated that the revenue and capital required to develop the community services do not exceed the resources available in the psychiatric hospital.

The capital has been mainly used to buy ordinary houses in the community and to convert them for the patients' use; in most houses, each patient has his/her own bedroom. A high proportion (78%) of the homes have staff resident on the premises. Some of the houses are staffed day and night, and for the most disabled patients the staff:patient ratio is as high as 1:1. Some are staffed by nurses who used to work in the two psychiatric hospitals, and are owned by the district health authorities. Others are owned and run by voluntary agencies, while a relatively small proportion are privately run. The average number of residents per house is five. The staffed home, an ordinary house in an ordinary street, has turned out to be the standard form of accommodation for the ex-long-stay patient.

OUTCOME FOR THE PATIENTS

DEATH, CRIME AND VAGRANCY

The worst possible effect on the quality of life of discharging patients would, of course, be death. The stress of the move to a strikingly different environment could conceivably result in suicide or exacerbation of an existing physical illness. Alternatively, patients in the community, removed from close scrutiny by hospital staff, might suffer from neglect of physical illnesses which could progress to death. In fact, there was no evidence for any of these possibilities. In the first five cohorts, the death rate during the one-year follow-up was 2.6 for the leavers, compared with 5.2 for the matches – a non-significant difference. The rate in the last three unmatched cohorts was 4.1, which is not different from either the earlier leavers or their matches. There were two suicides among the eight cohorts of leavers, and one among the earlier matches.

The public and the media are particularly concerned about the level of violence shown by psychiatrically ill people in the community, especially unprovoked homicidal attacks on strangers. From the point of view of the patients' quality of life, however, they themselves are more exposed in the community to the risk of harassment, and of robbery by criminals who see them as easy targets. Thus it is important to consider crimes committed both *by* patients and *against* them.

During the first year in the community, of the 695 patients for whom we had information on criminal acts, 20 were either accused or convicted of offences. Some of these were relatively trivial, such as being drunk and disorderly and sending a threatening letter, but there were seven physical assaults on another person. Two patients were admitted involuntarily to psychiatric hospitals following assaults; in addition, one patient was involved in a pub brawl, while another attacked his father with a knife, neither of these being admitted. One patient abducted and assaulted a female patient. Only two patients were sent to prison. One stopped taking his medication, became increasingly paranoid, and threw a cup of tea over a stranger in a café. The police were called and he was found to be carrying a knife; he was put in prison briefly, soon being transferred to a psychiatric hospital. The second patient was a young man with a dependent personality. On the day of discharge from hospital, he touched the breasts of a woman in the street and was convicted of attempted rape; he was still in prison when interviewed at the one-year follow-up. Nine patients were the victims of crime or accidents: three of them being involved in road traffic accidents. Two patients were victimised at work, two were assaulted and robbed, and one was stolen from. One patient alleged that he had been robbed, but did not proceed with an investigation.

While all these incidents are regrettable, neither the rate of perpetration of crime nor of being victimised appears to be particularly high.

The public is naturally concerned about and alarmed by the growing presence on the streets of homeless mentally ill people; this escalating problem is regularly ascribed by the media to the closure of psychiatric hospitals. Certainly, homelessness and the necessity to sleep rough represent the bottom of the scale for quality of life. In the TAPS study, only seven out of the total group of 737 discharged patients could not be traced in the first year and are presumed to have become homeless. Of these, four had previously been vagrant before becoming long-stay and probably returned to this way of life. It is reassuring to note that during the first year in the community, no patient was lost from a staffed home.

A five-year follow-up has been completed on the first four cohorts, totalling 359 patients. Between the one-year and five-year follow-ups, no additional patients were lost from the study. Thus, the proportion of patients who probably became homeless in the five years after discharge amounts to 1%. This is not a figure to be complacent about, but it is not of a magnitude to account for the alarming rise in mentally ill homeless people, for which there are other probable causes (Leff, 1993).

PSYCHIATRIC SYMPTOMS

Patients' mental state was remarkably stable over the one-year follow-up period. The total score on the PSE was 14.76 in hospital and 14.80 in the community. Most of the subscores showed no change over time; in particular, delusions and hallucinations were unchanged. It is possible that there was a transient increase in symptoms in response to the move into the community, but if so, this had settled by the time of the follow-up. In one important area, however, there was a significant change, namely negative symptoms. Because the distribution of scores was markedly skewed, it was necessary to conduct a non-parametric analysis on the scores dichotomised into 0 and 1+. The proportion of patients with no negative symptoms increased from 39.6% to 44.8%. A further significant reduction in negative symptoms was observed in Cohorts 1 and 2 between the first and fifth year follow-up. This improvement is important since negative symptoms are a major obstacle to rehabilitation. These findings also have implications for the theory of institutionalisation. Wing and Brown (1970) demonstrated that the level of negative symptoms exhibited by long-stay patients in psychiatric hospitals varied with the amount of stimulation provided by the staff. These results from the TAPS study indicate that negative symptoms also respond to the increased stimulation consequent on discharge to community settings.

PROBLEMS OF SOCIAL BEHAVIOUR

For the total sample of patients, there was a small but significant reduction in the number of social behaviour problems, as recorded with the SBS at the one-year follow-up. However, the earlier matched comparison involving the first five cohorts of leavers revealed a reduction of the same magnitude for patients who remained in hospital. This suggests that rehabilitation has an equally effective impact on social behaviour, whether it is undertaken in the psychiatric hospital or in the community.

The BELS, used to supplement the SBS, revealed a significant reduction of 15% in the proportion of patients with severe problems of compliance with medication when they moved from hospital to the community. This seemed to be related to an alteration in patients' attitude to medication, which will be presented below.

PATIENTS' SATISFACTION

Major changes in patients' attitudes were found at the one-year follow-up; these were particularly dramatic with respect to satisfaction with the current care environment. Whereas 33.4% of patients questioned while in hospital wished to remain there, 82.5% wanted to stay in their community homes when seen one year after discharge. This proportion rose to 86% of the first two cohorts interviewed after five years in the community. The main benefit of life in the community, mentioned spontaneously by the patients, was their increased freedom. This aspect of the caring environment was specified by only 3.8% of patients when interviewed in hospital, but by 19.6% when seen in the community at one year, and double this proportion, 38%, after five years.

A more surprising area of attitudinal change that was detected was in relation to the helpfulness of medication. The proportion expressing a favourable view rose from 55.9% in hospital to 72.3% after one year in the community. Presumably, this contributed to the reduction in problems with compliance observed by the community staff.

THE QUALITY OF THE ENVIRONMENT

This was the area of measurement which showed the most dramatic change. The total score on the EI fell from an average of 26.2 to 9.9, indicating that there were far fewer rules and restrictions in the community homes than in the two hospitals. It is of interest that the fall in EI score was rather less for the later cohorts than the earlier ones, suggesting that the community care staff were applying more restrictions to the patients with the greatest degree of disability. Even so, the final cohort to be discharged experienced a drop in EI score of 9 points. As indicated above, patients responded very positively to their increased freedom. In fact, their satisfaction grew steadily over the five-year follow-up, even though there was little change in restrictiveness over this period, suggesting that they came to appreciate their freedom more and more with the passage of time.

PHYSICAL HEALTH

Over the one-year follow-up, there was an increase of 6% in patients with physical immobility, but this was of the same magnitude for both leavers and their matches, indicating that it was a consequence of ageing rather than of the move to the community. An increase of 8% in patients with incontinence also affected leavers and matches equally. Over the five-year follow-up, the total care received by the patients for physical ill-health increased significantly. Thus, there was no suggestion that patients' physical condition was being neglected.

SOCIAL INTEGRATION

The size of patients' social networks was no greater after five years in the community than it had been in hospital, but there were major changes in the quality of relationships. After one year in the community, patients had made more friends –

an average of two additional friends each. This has to be seen in the context of the total network size, which was only eight on average. Between the one- and five-year follow-ups, there was no change in the number of friends, but a significant increase in the number of confidants. Confidants represent the most intense form of relationship, which clearly took longer to establish than friendships.

It would have been possible for all the patients' meaningful social contacts to have been with other patients and with staff members. However, once they were living in the community, patients established social relationships outside the mental health network, with ordinary people including neighbours, members of church clubs, and local shopkeepers. Hence, true social integration was occurring, although not experienced by all the discharged patients.

CONCLUSIONS

The intensive study by TAPS of long-stay patients has shown considerable improvement in their quality of life consequent on discharge to homes in the community. In particular, they were living under much freer conditions and greatly appreciated the increased freedom. The great majority of patients wanted to stay in their community homes. Their social networks were enriched by friends and confidants, some of whom were ordinary folk living and working in the neighbourhood. Over the longer term, there was a decrease in negative symptoms, at least for the earlier cohorts to be discharged. The move into the community did not lead to an increase in deaths or suicides, and only a handful of patients were lost from the system. Even this could have been avoided if those particular patients had been placed in staffed homes: four of them had been vagrants before becoming long-stay, and this should be considered a strong indication that staffed accommodation is required. These improvements in patients' quality of life, evident both from subjective and objective appraisals, were not achieved by an unrealistic outlay of revenue and capital. Neither type of cost exceeded the resources available within the psychiatric hospitals (Knapp et al, 1993).

One warning note must be sounded. When Friern Hospital closed in March 1993, there were 72 patients who were judged to be too disturbed for the standard community homes, mostly on account of aggressive or violent behaviour. These "difficult to place" patients will be found in every psychiatric hospital and require specialised facilities (Trieman & Leff, 1996). The three health districts responsible for the Friern patients chose three different solutions: a locked ward in a general hospital, a locked house in the community, and three purpose-built open houses in the grounds of another psychiatric hospital. TAPS is conducting a follow-up study of these units to determine which solution is preferable. Whatever the outcome, this problem will have to be tackled by every organisation intending to close a psychiatric hospital. Creative solutions will need to be found, if the quality of life of the most disabled long-stay patients is to be improved.

CHAPTER NINETEEN

The Quality of Life of the Relatives of the Mentally Ill

Maria D. Simon

While patients' quality of life has received a good deal of attention in recent years, studies of their informal carers, such as family members and relatives, are rare. The few systematic studies of caregivers that have been done have tended to concentrate on carers of the aged, the chronically physically disabled, and to a lesser degree the mentally incapacitated (Herman et al, 1994).

Similarly, criteria have been established and instruments devised to measure the quality of life of persons suffering from mental illness, but no standardised device exists in respect of their carers.

In fact, a good deal is known about this subject, even though the data have generally been collected with other perspectives in mind. The sources of information are for the most part not academic researchers but the carers themselves. Family carers in many countries of the world have been quite articulate in assessing their situation, expressing their needs, and campaigning for improvements.

Questionnaire surveys on carers' burdens have been carried out by family associations in the United States (Johnson, 1990; Spaniol et al, 1985), in Great Britain (Atkinson, 1988) and several other European countries (e.g. France, Spain, Holland, Italy). Among the most recent are an Austrian questionnaire survey (Katschnig et al, 1993) and a comparative survey of ten European countries under the auspices of EUFAMI, the Federation of European Associations of Families of the Mentally Ill (Hogman, 1994). In considering the determinants of carers' quality of life, we shall freely draw on such cumulative evidence, in particular the Austrian and European surveys of relatives' burdens.

Quality of Life (QoL) is a composite concept as well as a subjective category. An individual's QoL is the result of an interplay between personality and situational variables, which no doubt carry different weights in different individuals.

No one factor by itself determines carers' life quality, yet, beyond the multiplicity of personalities and influences in different settings, commonalities can be seen. Caregivers all share a similar fate: their life is dominated by the fact that they take responsibility for their mentally ill family members. They all carry very similar psychological burdens and are exposed to similar situational stressors. Their radius of freedom to react to these pressures is limited by external (societal) forces.

The principal factors that interact to shape a carer's perception of his/her quality of life are:

- personal characteristics
- situational stressors
- societal stressors, and
- iatrogenic stressors

CHARACTERISTICS OF CARERS

The view that the majority of carers everywhere share a number of characteristics is confirmed by the EUFAMI survey (Hogman, 1994):

1. The carers' average age is rather high (60 years, some are in their eighties and nineties)
2. The percentage of females ranges from 72% (England and Germany) to 88% (Austria).
3. Approximately 70% of carers are mothers, more often alone than living in a functioning partnership.
4. One of the most striking consequences of carers' age and burden is impairment of their health, beyond what is usual for their years. The following figures from the European survey relate to the Austrian sample ($n = 200$): 91% report health problems, many of them psychological and psychosomatic ones. The leading complaints were brooding (70%), fatigue (62%), irritability (65%), insomnia (56%), and back pain (51%).
5. A significant minority of carers are partners, grandparents, friends, siblings, and adult children, the last of these being sometimes still adolescents. They too are prone to impairment in their normal functioning, development, and relationships through the vicissitudes of their carer role. Not enough attention is being paid to their problems.

SITUATIONAL STRESSORS

Sources of situational stress stem from the constant strain that goes with having to care for, or live with the presence of one or more mentally ill persons, together with the concomitant friction this causes within the nuclear family environment. Some of these immediate sources of strain are:

1. Existential aspects of living with mental illness in the family, such as constant nervous arousal. According to the EUFAMI Survey, nearly 8% of respondents are caring for two or more mentally ill relatives.
2. Coping with patients' rejection of treatment; according to the European Survey over 50% of carers take it upon themselves to ensure that the patient takes the prescribed medication.
3. Dealing with patients' aberrations, such as delusions, hallucinations, bizarre behaviour, and persecutory ideas (Katschnig et al, 1994; Simon, 1994). Also, in a high proportion of cases, mental illness exists in conjunction with other types of problem behaviour, such as excessive drug use, substance abuse, alcoholism, or sexual deviation (e.g. exhibitionism).
4. Coping with aggressive behaviour from patients. At least eight out of ten carers in Europe have experienced some form of violence from their relative: verbal abuse is very common, damage to property is reported in about 40%, and physical violence in 30–40% of cases (Hogman, 1994).
5. Living in the constant presence of fear and worry, with no relief in sight. There are two dominant fears uppermost in the carers' mind:

   (a) Fear of the future: in the Austrian study (Kramer et al, 1993) in answer to the question, "What is your greatest concern?", over 90% replied "The future – what will happen to my mentally ill family member when I am incapacitated or gone";
   (b) Fear of a relapse into acute psychosis. This fear is realistic, and carers' helplessness is compounded by the frequent refusal of treatment on the part of patients.

6. Excessive workload. Approximately one-third of the carers from ten countries report that they spend more than 30 hours per week caring for the patient. The highest proportion is reported from Spain (39%), and the lowest from Germany (13%) (Hogman, 1994). "Burn-out" is a common complaint, and can be accounted for by the sheer duration of caring; more than 50% of the respondents have been caring for the patient longer than 15 years (Katschnig et al, 1993). There is rarely a chance for respite: according to the European survey, 60–90% of the carers felt in need of respite care (Hogman, 1994).
7. Coping with negative symptoms, such as patients' inactivity, withdrawal, anxiety, and frustration. Carers often have to walk the tightrope between activating yet not overstimulating the patient.

8. Living in the presence of suicidal threats and attempts by the sufferer. In the Austrian survey, 61% of relatives reported threats of suicide and 39% suicidal attempts. These are not idle gestures, since it is known that 10% of persons with psychotic illness will end their own lives.
9. Family upheaval and break-up: coping with lack of understanding and support from family members, relatives, and acquaintances. Rejection of the patient by fathers and siblings is common.
10. Doing justice to the needs and expectations of other family members.
11. Staying "cool" in the face of overpowering unremitting strain; controlling one's own reactions, so as not to exhibit high Expressed Emotion.
12. Changing one's lifeplan. The care of a mentally ill family member often entails drastic changes in lifestyle. Many carers have to give up or curtail gainful employment, see their career shattered, or have to drastically revise their plans and hopes for the retirement years (Katschnig et al, 1993; Hogman, 1994). Ageing parents, as well as sibling and children, are denied their age-appropriate roles (Bühler, 1969; Erikson, 1959; Lefley, 1987).

SOCIETAL STRESSORS

The prime cause of societal stresses is indifference and neglect, which accounts for most of the other deficiencies and stigma that beset the carers and their families. This also applies to the lack of research interest in carers' burdens and societal role. The first of these stressors is the inadequacy of services. The families of the mentally ill bear the brunt of the deinstitutionalisation movement, since it is estimated that between 50 and 65% of persons with severe chronic mental illness are cared for by their relatives. Practically everywhere, savings from the reduction of hospital beds have not been redirected to set up an adequate network of community services for treatment, rehabilitation, and independent or sheltered living. One of the most glaring deficiencies is the inadequacy of crisis services.

Secondly, there is stigma and social exclusion. Mental illness still stigmatises both the sufferers and their relatives. Since sensationalism in the popular media about "mad criminals" is rarely counteracted by low-key factual information, the public at large is uninformed about and afraid of persons labelled as mentally ill, and this is generalised to their relatives. In consequence, the social network shrinks, not only for the sufferer but for his or her carers as well. In the European survey between 25% (England) and 61% (Belgium) of respondents reported having experienced stigma; and between 16% (Ireland) and 65% (Belgium) of the carers are reportedly shunned by their former friends (Hogman, 1994).

Thirdly, there is extra financial cost. Between 42% (Belgium) and 78% (Spain) of carers cite extra costs as one of their burdens; the European average is 50% (Hogman, 1994). The fact, mentioned above, that many carers have had to give up or reduce outside employment adds to the financial strain.

IATROGENIC STRESSORS

Lefley (1990) has pointed out that some of the most noxious stresses are caused by mental health professionals themselves, and by inappropriate psychiatric services. Among these are:

1. Attribution of familial causation: although this is less common now than in the past, parent-blaming still persists. According to the Austrian survey, approximately 45% of the carers have experienced blame. In those instances, blame came most often from the sufferer himself (34%), quite often reinforced by psychotherapists, 32% from relatives and friends, while 15% were blamed by psychiatrists, 7% by psychologists and 3% by social workers (Katschnig et al, 1996).

2. Failure of mental health professionals to provide information and support, or refusal to communicate: many professionals do not realise the crucial role that relatives play as the primary carers in community psychiatry. They do not understand relatives' need for information and support for the task that has befallen them as a consequence of deinstitutionalisation. In the Austrian survey, 93% of respondents wanted relatives to be given more information about the illness and treatment, and 84% wanted more frequent contact with the patient's doctors (Katschnig et al, 1994). While most professionals plead pressures of other work for their neglect of carers' wish for information, some refuse contact on principle, pleading confidentiality.

3. Ignorance of family burden: at the root of professionals' refusal to communicate with the carers is often the fact that they are not aware of what caring for a chronic mentally ill person entails. They are not acquainted with the problems of everyday living in these circumstances. Their advice, even if prompted by the best of intentions, often fails to meet the needs of the relatives. Professionals' refusal to communicate with carers and other evasive behaviour is quite likely to be due to their own feeling of helplessness and inadequacy, but this is not admitted; rather, it is glossed over or rationalised.

4. Difficulties of access to in-patient treatment: with the reduction of beds in psychiatric hospitals and legal limitations of involuntary psychiatric hospitalisation, it has become increasingly difficult in most countries to obtain psychiatric help. Yet emergency situations requiring involuntary hospitalisation occur frequently. The European survey showed that consistently in all ten countries under consideration, approximately 60% of patients have at one time or another been admitted to hospital against their will. The range is from 40% in Holland to 73% in Sweden (Hogman, 1994). Appropriate crisis services that could prevent an involuntary commitment in many cases are mostly lacking, and as a rule it is the carer, who is least qualified for this, who has to set the procedure for commitment in motion.

5. Difficulties of access to appropriate out-patient treatment: a significant source of support for carers is appropriate out-patient treatment facilities. In many countries or regions, out-patient community support of chronic patients is lacking or inadequate. Two omissions in particular are glaring:

   (a) Patients are released from hospital to their families without a plan for continued treatment or other follow-up. Often, patients will not receive follow-up treatment from the community mental health facility unless they present themselves there on their own initiative. Many, who are the most in need of treatment, are not able to do this.

   (b) With a few notable exceptions in Britain and the Netherlands, chronic patients are not provided with a key worker (e.g. case manager, community nurse) who will actively coordinate support and safeguard further treatment (Hogman, 1994).

THE CONSEQUENCES OF STRESS

What then is the result of all the stresses that are brought to bear on the carer? It is grief, confusion, anger, self-blaming, frustration, isolation, guilt-feeling, burn-out, desperation, and a breakdown of psychological defences. Normal reactions to the stress situations are unavailable: carers cannot run away and they must not act out their anger. Usually, they cannot even get a rest, and a holiday is an unheard of luxury. With normal outlets blocked, what follows are pathological stress reactions, such as unfocused anger, vague fears, resorting to quack remedies, chronic fatigue, and psychosomatic illness. If QoL has something to do with the fulfilment of basic human needs, and if these burdens of caregiving are all that life has to offer a carer, then his/her QoL is very low indeed.

But is there not another side to caring for a loved and valued family member? Is stress always distress? It is said that stress can be a welcome challenge, so are there any compensatory benefits from caring?

BENEFITS FROM CARING

In the Austrian study, carers were asked whether they had derived any benefits from caring. In the face of the evident burdens, the investigators had low expectations on this point, and were surprised to note that 45% of the respondents reported having benefited. These benefits were quite diverse: for example a more profound understanding of the human condition; greater tolerance for deviant behaviour; having found new friends among fellow-carers; satisfaction from being needed by someone; satisfaction from having a task in one's old age; meeting a challenge; greater family solidarity in the face of adversity; getting closer to one's partner; and finding solace in religion.

Even so, it is only a minority that can derive gain from adversity, and these persons have certain exceptional characteristics. They are basically resourceful personalities, are relatively privileged, have joined self-help organisations, enjoy a modicum of economic security, and they have been able to call on some support not generally available. In other words, they manage to cope. In contrast to them, the majority of carers are overwhelmed by their burdens and can see no mitigating circumstances.

CONCLUSION

Katschnig et al (1994) state that QoL has three dimensions: objective functioning in a socially defined role, material circumstances (standard of living) and subjective well-being, which I will discuss in turn.

Carers' socially assigned role is that of primary agents in the community care for the chronic severely mentally ill. This assigned role is implicit; it is not socially acknowledged and confirmed with the usual trappings of an office. In order to find satisfaction in a role, it is necessary to be able to muster the means to cope with it, and to be recognised, appreciated, and suitably rewarded. Yet, as has been amply illustrated above, carers are denied both means and rewards. The means denied to them are the requisite material and immaterial support, while the denied rewards include the withholding of recognition of their role as front-line mental health workers. Thus, their role as primary caregivers cannot be a source of much life satisfaction.

From the available data, it appears that families of the mentally ill are a cross-section of the general population, so that economic security is no doubt a problem, as it is with many other people. Yet carers, in answering the question about "the greatest worry" in the Austrian survey (Katschnig et al, 1993), mentioned financial hardships only infrequently as their most pressing problem. This may appear to confirm the finding of a Swedish study of QoL of sufferers (Skantze et al, 1992), that the standard of living is a weak indicator of quality of life. However, this no doubt applies only when the basic economic needs are met, which happens only for those who live in a welfare state.

When a carer is asked what his/her QoL depends on, he/she will almost certainly reply: "It depends on my ill family member's condition. If he/she is well, I am well; if he/she suffers, I suffer." This suggests that the carer's life satisfaction is a "dependent variable" of the patient's QoL. It does not mean that carers' and patients' needs and priorities are identical, but that all considerations other than the patient's state are subordinate in the carer's perception of his/her own QoL.

The factors that interact to determine carers' QoL are twofold. The importance that the carer attaches to the patient's condition can be described as the "general factor". The "specific factors" are the stresses and rewards of caring (individual, situational, societal), many of which have been discussed above. In most instances, the sufferer's and consequently the carer's QoL is low, but caregivers' QoL could be better, if some obvious remedies were applied. Carers should be supported in their own right and not be regarded just as appendages of the patient (Atkinson, 1991). They should be put in a position that enables them to cope, and should be given a voice in all measures that affect their life and well-being. The caregiver's role in community care should be made explicit. It should be understood that carers cannot fulfil their assigned task in society without appropriate support and recognition. Just as the QoL of sufferers determines to a large extent the QoL of carers, so an improved QoL for the family carers would lead to a better life for all concerned.

CHAPTER TWENTY

Integrating Consumer Perspectives on Quality of Life in Research and Service Planning

Peter Stastny and Michaela Amering

INTRODUCTION

The question of integrating a consumer perspective in the development of optimal services and in the assessment of their outcomes, particularly in the QoL domain, cannot be adequately addressed without an understanding of the recent changes in roles that psychiatric patients can assume *vis-à-vis* mental health and rehabilitation services. Indeed, the recent attention of researchers to the issue of quality of life may be a response to the growth of the "consumer/survivor movement" along with an increasing distrust of traditional medicine and the shift towards more consumer-orientated and "holistic" methods of treatment. The new roles and the accompanying changes in the perspectives of professional staff are likely to influence the nature of mental health practice and research. A variety of new relationships between researchers and subjects and between clinicians and patients will be the basis for a new understanding of the QoL concept. This chapter reviews the nature and impact of consumer empowerment and the resulting role changes on service implementation and QoL research. One main concern is to present a theoretical base for the recent developments in psychiatric and rehabilitation services that promote consumer empowerment. This development is manifested by the rapid growth of consumer-run initiatives, particularly in the USA (Emerick, 1991); by the considerable efforts made by the federal and local agencies in supporting consumer-run programmes (van Tosh, 1995); by the employment of consumers as service providers (Felton et al, 1995) and by the increasing number of research studies focusing on the effects of consumer-run programmes on their participants, their clients, and the system of care (McLean, 1995).

It is worth noting to what extent notions of increased consumer involvement have begun to permeate the literature on QoL and needs assessment. In a recent editorial in the *British Journal of Psychiatry* (1994), Slade discusses various factors which influence the perception of need and concludes that need is "a socially negotiated concept". Slade quotes Stevens and Gabbay (1991) with regard to the distinction between demand (what the user asks for) and need (what people can be expected to benefit from), and concludes that "it is wrong to assume that need equates with a professional's assessment". Furthermore, Slade asserts that "accurate needs assessment requires maximal user involvement". He underlines this by quoting the UK Department of Health and Social Services Inspectorate (1991) which stated that "All users ... should be encouraged to participate to the limit of their capacity. ... Where it is impossible to reconcile different perceptions, these differences should be acknowledged and recorded." In another recent editorial addressing the issue of patient satisfaction in evaluative studies, Williams and Wilkinson (1995) conclude: "The success or failure of satisfaction surveys must be measured against their contribution to getting mental health services 'closer to the public'. As we have pointed out, satisfaction surveys are an inefficient method to achieve this. If becoming closer to the public and being people-centred are to be integral objectives of mental health services, the patients' perspective must be understood in greater detail." This implies that a service satisfaction measure may be bypassing a more differentiated and profound perspective on service delivery and outcomes.

Another recent editorial in *The Lancet* (1995) criticises the use of quality of life instruments in clinical outcome studies. "The uncritical acceptance of 'expert'-driven questionnaires into clinical trial protocols will only diminish the importance of the patient's perspective." The editorial quotes Gill and Feinstein (1994), who evaluated the medical literature concerned with the assessment of quality of life. They found a "deplorable lack of conceptual and methodological concern". These authors view quality of life as "rather than being a mere rating of health status, ... actually a uniquely personal perception, representing the way that individual patients feel about their health status or non-medical aspects of their lives". They state that "The need to incorporate patients' values and preferences is what distinguishes quality of life from all other measurements of health."

These expert conclusions obviously reflect what consumers have been trying to tell us for quite a while, but what still seems to be difficult for researchers and clinicians to integrate in their work. While other branches of medicine have fewer problems with taking consumers' perspectives at face value, mental health practice still has a long way to go. Professional centrism may keep us from advancing in gaining knowledge on how to promote health and enhance quality of life in collaboration with consumers.

FROM TOTAL INSTITUTION TO GRADUAL EMPOWERMENT

Given our premise that valid assessments of QoL are intimately linked to the social context and the relative autonomy of the subjects in question, we want to outline a trajectory which demonstrates a gradual reduction of dependency on institutional structures. Consumer empowerment and the concomitant practical changes have occurred within the historical context of social interventions which were designed by mental health professionals to control, segregate, assist, treat and support persons with psychiatric illnesses and disabilities. Five paradigms underlying these interventions are discernible and have been applied over the course of this century to address the needs of this population and of their communities, which were often at odds with each other.

Architectural institutionalisation (1), the method of the asylum, is the first and most prominent structure, designed to segregate, administer, categorise, study and treat such individuals. Since long-term institutionalisation is virtually synonymous with low QoL and very limited autonomy, it is mentioned here only for its historical significance. A second, more insidious form of institutionalisation, is the *programmatic engagement in community-based structures (2)*, which often resemble hospital fragments, portable asylums so to speak. This issue of extramural institutionalisation has been addressed extensively and is applicable to the concept of "sheltered" environments, be they in the residential or vocational domains (Chamberlin & Rogers, 1990). In such settings, a complex web of medical and social interventions is woven to represent a prosthetic or supportive environment, with only limited options for achieving independence.

The third paradigm, favoured by practitioners of modern rehabilitative techniques such as Anthony et al (1984), can best be characterised as an *integrationist/normatising approach (3)*. It represents a more subtle, ostensibly individualized methodology, aimed at situating persons with psychiatric disabilities in environments of their choice, engaged in activities of their choosing. While these methods appear better suited to furthering recovery, empowerment and quality of life, it is still not proven whether such rehabilitative interventions can indeed achieve these outcomes. Clinical experience suggests that success in this area depends greatly on personal and contextual variables that are frequently not addressed by these rehabilitation methods. For example, family ties and friendships, long-term relationships with service providers, and personal perseveration may outweigh the effects of goal setting, learned skills, and problem-solving abilities.

The remaining two paradigms are of particular relevance to the issue of enhancing consumer empowerment and meaningful involvement in services. Thereby, they add additional dimensions to the QoL concept which are not taken into consideration in traditional research on the subject. The historically earlier one is a *network paradigm (4)*, which suggests that the enhancement of individual autonomy, QoL and treatment outcome is mediated by achieving membership in viable and supportive networks, with optimal proportions of peers, relatives, other friends and professional members. This paradigm is the guiding principle of the Fairweather Lodge model (Fairweather et al, 1969) and plays an important role in the affirmative business model (Granger & Baron, 1996), which together are possibly the most successful network interventions. While factors such as economic incentives, reasonable accommodation and meaningful work are clearly central, the element of support built into the emerging networks may be the most salient feature of these interventions. Unfortunately, neither of these two promising models has been evaluated with QoL as an outcome variable.

Consumer empowerment and associated role changes (5) is the most recent paradigm, and the one whose integration in the planning and evaluation of clinical and rehabilitative interventions appears as the most promising. It aims at the enhancement of individual empowerment through participation in self-help groups or autonomous organisations. The main principle underlying individual empowerment is a shift from an external to an internal locus of control; in other words, a shift from paternalistically administered methods to grassroots democracy and citizen-generated responses. It is astonishing that so little formal research on the effects of this shift on persons with psychiatric disabilities has occurred. To mention only one of its dramatic results, we cite a study by Rodin (1986) in which elderly residents of a nursing home were randomly assigned to two conditions: (1) control over daily activities, including menus, leisure activities, and time schedules; and (2) programme as usual, designed by administrators. The subjects in the experimental group demonstrated a significant difference in life expectancy compared to the control group. In addition to this rather powerful general effect on "health", there are scores of studies that try to demonstrate positive effects on specific physical conditions. Beyond such relatively mechanistic shifts in locus of control, empowerment must be viewed as a process: "the mechanism by which people, organisations, and communities gain mastery over their lives" (Zimmerman & Rappaport, 1988). These authors go on to say that "empowerment may lead to a sense of control; ... [or] it may lead to actual control, the practical power to effect their own lives." Rappaport stresses the many variations of empowerment, which seems easier to define in its absence: powerlessness, real or imagined; learned helplessness; alienation; loss of a sense of control over one's life. The concept of empowerment applies to virtually any group of individuals within our society who utilise self-generated or self-invested strategies to achieve greater participation and control in their communities.

The application of the empowerment concept to the lives of persons with psychiatric disabilities is one of its most striking manifestations. This should by no means minimise its role in the rehabilitation of other disability groups; suffice it to mention the self-advocacy movement of persons with developmental disabilities and the disability rights movement, spearheaded by persons with a variety of physical disabilities. On the individual level, there is growing evidence that self-management of symptoms decreases relapse, at least in schizophrenia, and improves overall outcome. Esso Leete, concurring with her diagnosis of schizophrenia, describes this process in *Schizophrenia Bulletin* (Leete, 1989). John Strauss (1989) and Marvin Herz et al (1982) are emphasising specific personal responses to aspects of illness as key in recovery and relapse prevention. Moving from the individual to the social organisational plane, we enter a rather complex area, boasting few empirical results. However, dramatic case studies provide evidence that individual empowerment may be engendered, amplified and maintained in the right environment and organisational context. The "Hearing Voices" movement publicised by Romme and Escher (1989) provides an excellent example wherein individual experiences of self-management are translated into a social movement which adopts empowerment as a major theme in its activities. These experiences lead to the theoretical assumption that consumer-controlled alternatives provide its participants with a fundamentally different experience from other, more traditional service organisations, one that is uniquely suited to maximise and maintain positive outcomes, including enhanced QoL, with the goal of enabling former full-time patients to live and work under their chosen terms.

Understanding these five paradigms is a precondition for developing a platform from which consumer perspectives can be articulated in a relatively unencumbered fashion, and where QoL assessments can occur which capture the essence of this concept – subjective views of life circumstances and health status.

PROGRAMMATIC EXAMPLES

Moving from the theoretical to the practical realm, we undertake a brief excursion into experimental programmes which offer to enhance QoL through promoting significant levels of individual autonomy and empowerment. A body of largely qualitative research has begun to emerge, which can help us to understand these unique organisations (McLean, 1995; van Tosh, 1995). Some of these programmes specifically aim to increase levels of functioning and independence among its participants. These may be called *self-help skills training programmes (1)*. They include, for example, "self-directed rehabilitation" (Knight, 1991), based on self-help principles and following a specific curriculum which teaches coping with symptoms as well as other recovery-orientated strategies. Another approach can be discerned in programmes aimed at training and placing former patients in human services jobs, *consumers-as-service-providers (2)*, for example consumer case management, peer counselling, and peer specialist services (Felton et al, 1995). A third kind of empowering programme are *consumer-run businesses (3)*. Such businesses have been successfully initiated in some European countries, aided by generous government subsidies, as well as in the United States. Examples include the

Italian Cooperative Movements, a consumer-run TV and video production company (White Light) in Vermont; the Wyman Way Coop in New Hampshire; and Incube, Inc., a technical assistance agency to assist consumers in starting businesses (Granger & Baron, 1996).

Most of these business enterprises do not specifically aim at achieving measurable outcomes in QoL or functional areas. They provide rehabilitative and supportive functions to their members. A free-standing programme run by and for consumers which employs their peers in meaningful work and remunerates them with significant salaries qualifies as a consumer-run business. The key issue in determining whether a particular programme is consumer-run or not is the type of management it utilizes. Most mental health and rehabilitation programmes are run by professionals *for* their clients. Some programmes employ a partnership model, by which both clients and staff share roles of responsibility. This can be a social firm in which skilled workers without mental health experience occupy key functions, but consult regularly with the client-staff, or an organisation run by former patients with a board of directors consisting of both ex-patients and professionals. The purest case of a consumer-run business is when all key positions are occupied by ex-patients, who may decide to employ professionals in subordinate staff positions. The two elements most relevant in such programmes are the level of control of individuals in their own rehabilitation and the level of organisational/managerial control exerted by current or former service recipients.

The type of consumer-run programme and its management structure are relevant in determining the level of consumer involvement. Individual choice, goal setting, and control over resources have been identified as a crucial condition for successful rehabilitation outcome (Anthony & Jansen, 1984). One of the conditions under which the latter becomes possible is the replacement of staff by empowered service recipients. That is to say, clients of rehabilitation programmes are being served by their peers, who may or may not have special training in this area.

These types of programmes not only increase consumer involvement, but actually lead to better outcomes. This can be explained by a number of factors. Role modelling, which is seeing a former patient succeed in a new and unexpected role, may increase optimism and motivation among peers. The absence of stigmatising and limiting attitudes, all too common among traditional service providers, may result in a more collaborative effort. Greater trust in the capacities and competence of peers may lead to better actual results, rather than the cautious stance commonly taken in traditional rehabilitation programmes. Greater solidarity and identification among clients may lead to more vigorous and effective advocacy efforts to achieve client goals and develop the necessary resources. In addition, other principles of self-help apply: a premium is put on the value of personal experience; on sharing and disclosure; strategies for coping; peer support and peer counselling.

CONSEQUENCES FOR QoL RESEARCH: FROM OUTCOME TO PROCESS; FROM OBSERVATION TO PARTICIPATION

These changes in the provision of services, aimed at enhancing personal empowerment and real options for former clients, have significant consequences in the research arena. On the conceptual level, new and empowered roles of "subjects" imply a new relationship between subjectivity and scientific objectivity. The goal of research and evaluation can no longer simply be the generation of group-level data composed of individual ratings and observations. Neither is the method of "single-case studies", collecting behavioural observations of a single individual over time and abstracting them from their source, appropriate for this new level of inquiry. Instead, a composite data picture has to be created which allows an integration of subjective expressions of meaning and aspiration with the traditional depersonalised quantitative approach.

This leads to a reconceptualisation of the relationship between subjects and researchers. Researchers are beginning to enter a collaborative discourse, wherein subjects can assume authorship over portions of the research and participate in its development. Such participation, the details of which remain elusive at this time, raises many thorny issues, in particular about questions of validity and generalisability. More specifically, to open bi-directional channels of communication between researchers and subjects in the course of carrying out an evaluation requires a thorough understanding of the impact of such open feedback cycles on the outcome of the project. This leads to a revision of outcome and its associated variables from the perspective of the subjects. External criteria of "good" versus "bad" outcome will have to be supplemented with or replaced by internal criteria, which may contradict the validity of the external ones. For example, "relapse", "rehospitalisation" and "functional adjustment" are terms frequently used by researchers to determine the success or failure of rehabilitative interventions. In its stead, "quality of life", "satisfaction", "recovery" and "empowerment" have been proposed by persons diagnosed as mentally ill. In addition, the cross-sectional, pre-and-post methods of assessing outcome dimensions have to be replaced by a longitudinal approach, focusing on "trajectories" and the "process of recovery/healing". Cumulative statistical methods may not do justice to the experiences of longitudinal change and might have to be complemented by frequent probes of "subjective" inputs utilising new data collection methods (e.g. "experience sampling", deVries, 1987).

Another complex issue in the evaluation of programmes with significant levels of consumer involvement is the impact of simultaneously occurring dissemination and implementation activities. Many participants in consumer-run initiatives place a premium on outreach and system change. This strikes a balance with internal operations dedicated to accomplishing the more narrowly defined tasks of the project. The changes in operation that result from this practice must be carefully monitored by internal and external observers to assure a fidelity to contextual and internal developments that may not have been predictable.

On a practical level this creates the need for new methods of research development. Early partnerships and collaborations have to be established between researchers, consumers, and consumers who are researchers. In open discussions about the aims and methods of the proposed study, such partnerships can result in substantial changes in design as well as generating new questions and hypotheses. In general, researchers must begin to search for field-generated research questions utilising a variety of methods such as focus groups, to increase the relevance of their research to consumers of services. At times this will necessitate policy decisions in order to prioritise research questions given a finite research budget. The example of "cost" might illustrate this process best, often constituting an overriding research interest among service planners and administrators, while concerns such as "quality of life" are much more central to consumers.

These developments will necessitate a new emphasis on variables reflecting the concept of personal empowerment in the context of organisational development. On the individual level, the construct of "psychological empowerment" (Zimmermann & Rappaport, 1988) has been derived and validated from a series of pre-existing constructs. It focuses on individual strengths and competencies as well as on the resulting proactive behaviour. The constructs that contribute in unique and separate ways to psychological empowerment include: (1) goal achievement; (2) mastery; (3) self-efficacy; (4) perceived competence; (5) internal/external locus of control; (6) a desire for control; and (7) a desire to affiliate. The validation of such new constructs leads to the development of new instruments that measure them. A number of groups are currently working on developing and field-testing an "empowerment measure". Other efforts are based on factor analyses of a number of the above listed variables and constructs.

New measurements will also need to be introduced to reflect variables of the organisational level. This includes the quality of management and leadership; the group's basic values and ideology; their internal relations and ties to outside entities (i.e. mental health and rehabilitation services and self-help/consumer organisations); and organisational development (personnel, production, evolving structures, etc.). While some of these concepts were proposed over 30 years ago by researchers such as Bales and Moos, their dry sociological apparatus, which limited their applications, is being replaced by dynamic organisations composed of current and former patients in a variety of unconventional roles.

In addition, areas that have received little attention in traditional outcome studies will need to be understood better and reflected in new variables and instruments. This may include the meaningfulness of work and other activities, the level of cooperation and cohesion among group members, role perceptions and relations, hierarchies and other organisational structures, the phenomena of burn-out and transitions – to cite but a few.

CONCLUSIONS

There can be no doubt that the emergence of consumer involvement and empowerment poses a formidable challenge to current practices in mental health programme development and evaluation. This has been pointed out in a number of recent publications by ex-patients who have become researchers or service planners (McCabe & Unzicker, 1995; Campbell & Schraiber, 1989). One possible response is an attempt to establish a new programmatic category for services derived from empowerment principles, that is, "self-help and empowerment services" (OMH, 1996). While such a response might allow an impact assessment of distinct "self-help" interventions on QoL and other outcome variables, it falls short of providing an understanding whether these new concepts can reframe and invigorate all clinical and rehabilitative services, rather than being yet another marginal programme among others such as creative art therapies.

Beginning efforts in this area are being made in studies that assess differences in outcome between peer-run service models, partnership models and traditional services (Nikkel et al, 1992; Dumont, 1996). However, the jury is still out on these studies and no large-scale evaluation of consumer-run services is under way. If anything, the limited resources allotted to these consumer-run alternatives make it likely that the full potential of their impact on client outcomes cannot be realised. This is particularly lamentable considering that a vast proportion of mental health resources is still being expended on interventions, that is, state hospitals, which have at best a minimal, if not a negative impact on QoL and other community-based outcomes. It remains to be seen whether the new emphasis on cost-containment and outcome maximising in managed care approaches will generate a climate for more consumer involvement and empowerment-orientated interventions. On the face of it, such an approach would make sense, given that the "customer" is supposed to be driving these types of systems. However, at least in the USA, the initial experience of health maintenance organisations is beginning to show that curtailing certain services without introducing others can have a detrimental effect on outcome and on consumer satisfaction. Nevertheless, as pointed out by Mechanic et al (1995), there is a great potential for broad constructive changes driven by cost-containment practices. Consumer advocates have begun to seize this opportunity and to introduce self-help, empowerment and quality of life as key elements into some of the more progressive models. It remains to be seen whether the "fourth revolution in mental health", after deinstitutionalisation, community mental health and self-help, can really transcend the limitations of earlier efforts to redesign the mental health system.

CHAPTER TWENTY-ONE

Quality of Life of Staff Working in Psychiatric Services

Reinhold Kilian

INTRODUCTION

In 1978, Cherniss and Egnatios presented three main reasons for dealing with the quality of the working life of psychiatric staff which still seem significant today. First, given that satisfying, meaningful, and interesting working conditions are increasingly seen as a basic right for both blue-collar and white-collar workers, they should also be considered as a right for those working in the helping professions. Secondly, since there are strong indications for positive relationships between job satisfaction and work motivation or work performance, it must be suspected that quality of work life in psychiatric services is a crucial factor in relation to the quality of service delivery. Thirdly, because people who are better qualified usually have greater possibilities to choose between different job offers, it is likely that they will gravitate to those segments of the labour market where the working conditions are most favourable. As a consequence, segments with poor working conditions are in danger of becoming "employment slums" through processes of negative selection (Cherniss & Egnatios, 1978a, p. 309). Whereas the first reason concerns the ethical dimension of work in general, the two others are directly connected with the quality of life (QoL) of mentally ill patients, because psychiatric services will only be able to improve the QoL of their clients if they are able to offer working conditions which will be attractive to the more talented, creative, and compassionate professionals.

BURN-OUT AS A DIMENSION OF QUALITY OF WORK LIFE

Since it was first developed by Freudenberger in 1974, the concept of "staff-burn-out" has been increasingly used to describe and analyse a common phenomenon resulting from the particular working conditions in human services. Though the core of the burn-out concept consists of a state of emotional exhaustion related to work overload (Freudenberger, 1974), many authors who have studied working conditions in human services have extended the definition by including attitudinal, motivational, behavioural, and psychosocial aspects. The definition of burn-out used by Maslach (1976; 1978a; 1979), Maslach and Jackson (1978, 1979, 1981) and Pines and Maslach (1978; 1980) includes the development of cynical and dehumanising attitudes toward clients by service professionals. In contrast, both Perlman and Hartman (1982) and Cherniss (1980) focused more on a decrease in job motivation, performance, and productivity, whereas the definition used by the Berkeley Planning Associates (1977) stresses estrangement from job and clients. In a review of nearly 50 empirical studies on staff burn-out between 1974 and 1981, and a synthesis of the definitions of burn-out used in these, Perlman and Hartman (1982) came to the conclusion that the following three dimensions constitute the common core: (1) emotional/physical exhaustion; (2) lowered job productivity; and (3) overdepersonalisation. All other symptoms and components which have been discussed within the framework of burn-out (such as low morale, negative self-concept, anger, cynicism, negative attitudes toward clientele, increased emotionality, suspiciousness, overconfidence, depression, rigidity, absenteeism, more time spent on job, leaving job, or drug use) may be correlates, but do not seem to be part of its prime definition (Perlman & Hartman, 1982, p. 293).

Irrespective of whether these symptoms will be regarded as primary constituents or as secondary correlates of burn-out, they all refer to serious impairment of the QoL of individuals working in human services, as well as to the quality of the services provided. During the last two decades, different theoretical models of the aetiology of burn-out and of the factors influencing the aetiological process have been developed, and there have been many empirical studies within different health-care settings. The different theories on the process of burn-out will be discussed here, together with an assessment of the significance of these theories for the mental health sector, based on existing empirical studies.

THE AETIOLOGY OF BURN-OUT IN HUMAN SERVICES

In contrast to working in industry or trade, working in the mental health field or in other human services involves direct responsibility for the well-being of other people. "If a salesperson or factory worker makes a mistake, the consequences usually are not as grave. The Ford Motor Company recalled 500 000 automobiles because of errors in design or manufacture, and this action does not greatly disturb the public. But the recall of clients by a community mental health center because of errors in treatment is unthinkable. The public's reaction would not be so mild" (Cherniss, 1980, p. 49). Under favourable conditions, this particular characteristic of human service work can be a rich source of accomplishment and work satisfaction, and many people working in the sector of mental health feel, as stated by Florence Nightingale, that "the nursing of the sick is a vocation as well as a profession". But given less favourable conditions, permanent direct involvement with the problems and the misery of other people can also become a source of stress and frustration.

> In many health and social service organizations, professionals are required to work intensely and intimately with people on a large scale, continuous basis. They learn about these people's psychological, social, and/or physical problems, and they are expected to provide aid or treatment of some kind. Some aspects of this job involve "dirty work", which refers to tasks that are particularly upsetting or embarrassing to perform, even though necessary. This type of professional interaction arouses strong feelings of emotion and personal stress, which can often be disruptive and incapacitating. (Maslach & Pines, 1977, p. 100)

However, the development of staff burn-out is not regarded as a direct consequence of these particular characteristics of human service work, but rather as a result of either inadequate individual reactions or inadequate organisational frameworks, or both (Harrison, 1983). Within the theory of human stress (Lazarus, 1966; Lazarus & Launier, 1978; Lazarus & Folkman, 1984), human beings interact with their environment through both cognitive appraisal and behavioural activities. Through processes of *primary* cognitive appraisal an individual defines the meaning and the demands of the situation, for example whether a situation is a possible source of stress or not. How the individual actually deals with the perceived demands or threats of the situation depends on his *secondary* appraisal of his/her coping resources. Lazarus and his colleagues have shown that this two-part sequence of primary and secondary appraisal, which forms the core of the coping process, will be influenced by both personal and environmental factors (see Figure 21.1).

Within this general model of coping, staff burn-out is regarded as a negative outcome of the coping process due either to inadequate definitions of the situational demands or to inadequate reactions to these demands by the staff members, which again might be caused by either individual, organisational, or environmental factors. From the structure of relationships symbolised by the paths of the model, it becomes evident that organisational and individual factors of the coping process are widely interconnected and that burn-out should therefore not be traced back to one of these factors alone. For conceptual clarity, however, it seems useful to discuss the individual and organisational factors separately, before being concerned with the interdependencies between the two levels.

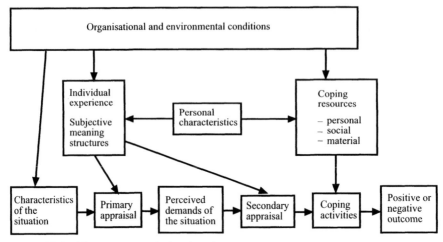

Figure 21.1   The stress-appraisal and coping process

THE INDIVIDUAL FACTORS OF COPING AND BURN-OUT

Discussing the individual factors of inadequate coping and burn-out, Farber (1983) starts with the empirically confirmed assumption that those human service workers who tend to burn out have particular personal characteristics and meaning structures, for they are "emphatic, sensitive, humane, dedicated, idealistic, and people-oriented, but at the same time anxious, introverted, obsessional, overenthusiastic, and susceptible to overidentification with others" (Farber, 1983, p. 4). What burn-out-prone people lack, in other words, and what Maslach and Pines (1977) saw as a primary precondition for efficient human service work, is the ability to defend themselves against the strong emotional involvement with the clients' problems, through techniques of detachment. This is because "by treating clients or patients in a more remote, objective way, it becomes easier to perform the necessary interviews, tests, or operations without suffering strong psychological discomfort" (Maslach & Pines, 1977, p. 100). As a paradoxical consequence of this lack of detachment, those affected not uncommonly react to the arising emotional exhaustion with a change to the opposite extreme of overdepersonalisation, which includes the loss of "any positive feelings, sympathy, or respect for clients or patients" and the development of "a very cynical and dehumanized perception of these people" (Maslach & Pines, 1977, p. 101). In the case of people who work with the long-term mentally ill, Lamb (1979b) has stated that idealism and overenthusiasm often lead to unrealistic expectations regarding rehabilitation which, for the most part, cannot be fulfilled by their clients. "Most of [these staff members] enter the field with enthusiasm and good intentions. But after perhaps a year or two, they get burned out: they lose their enthusiasm; they no longer like their contact with long-term patients; they get bored, frustrated, and resentful. Worst of all, they become ineffective" (Lamb, 1979b, p. 396).

In addition to these factors, which are of particular relevance for the process of coping with job stress and the development of burn-out within the human services, several others have been found to be relevant to coping with stress in general, but are also believed to influence the development of burn-out. Cherniss (1980) emphasises the importance of *learned helplessness* within the aetiological process of burn-out. Developed by Seligman (1975), this concept suggests that animate beings who are forced into situations in which they have no control over rewards and punishments for a prolonged time, will develop a generalised feeling of helplessness, which undermines their motivation to solve problems through active behaviour. Though Seligman developed his theory on the basis of experiments with dogs, the same phenomenon has also been found in humans, and its influence on human coping behaviour has been empirically confirmed (Cherniss, 1980). Similar to learned helplessness, the concept of *locus of control* developed by Rotter (1966) suggests that if, during their learning history, individuals repeatedly find that punishment and reward are not contingent upon their own behaviour, they will develop a generalised external locus of control. "In general, internal-external control refers to the degree to which the individual believes that what happens to him or her results from his or her own behaviour versus the degree to which the individual believes that what happens to her or him results from luck, chance, fate, or forces beyond his or her control" (Rotter, 1982, p. 313). Within the framework of stress theory, learned helplessness and locus of control have become two of the most important individual predictors of coping behaviour (Pearlin et al, 1981; Lazarus and Folkman, 1984). People who feel helpless or who hold an external locus of control have been found to cope with problems in a passive and emotion-focused manner, such as behavioural or mental disengagement, denial, avoidance, and drug use, whereas people who feel empowered and hold an internal locus of control tend to use more active and problem-focused coping strategies, such as active planning, problem-focused action, and seeking social support (Carver et al, 1989). Since passive and emotion-focused coping strategies are closely related to symptoms of burn-out, the concepts of learned helplessness and locus of control should also become part of every theoretical concept of the aetiology of burn-out (Cherniss, 1980).

Yet another important individual factor in this aetiology has been emphasised by Harrison (1983) within the framework of his *social competence model*. "Social competence refers to how one feels about one's capacity to interact with, and therefore to influence the social environment" (Harrison, 1983, p. 35). Like the concepts of learned helplessness and locus of control, that of social competence stems from social learning theory. In contrast to these former concepts, however, social competence focuses not on the controllability of the environment, but rather on the expectations concerning the efficacy of one's own actions. As formulated by the originator of the concept of *self-efficacy expectations,* Albert Bandura: "An outcome expectancy is defined as a person's estimate that a certain behaviour will lead to certain outcomes. An efficacy expectation is the conviction that one can successfully execute the behaviour required to produce the outcomes" (Bandura, 1977, p. 193). Though they are similar to the concepts of learned helplessness and locus of control, those of social competence and self-efficacy expectations enhance the clarity of the burn-out model. This is because they offer the possibility of differentiating between individuals who feel that they don't know how to cope with problems and those who know what has to be done, but feel that they lack the necessary skills and abilities to carry out the required activities. Both of these cognitive orientations can become sources of ineffective coping and burn-out, but for the prevention of burn-out, it makes a great difference whether learned helplessness or lack of self-efficacy expectations have been suspected as the main causes of staff burn-out in a particular work setting.

ORGANISATIONAL AND ENVIRONMENTAL FACTORS OF COPING AND BURN-OUT

On the organisational level, Cherniss (1980) sees three components that are particularly relevant for the aetiology of burn-out: "The role structure, the power structure, and the normative structure" (Cherniss, 1980, p. 79).

By means of the role structure, the various tasks and duties resulting from the aims of a particular organisation are allocated to different role patterns, which are commonly associated with the different occupational groups working in that organisation. For the individual worker, the patterns of his occupational role define in more or less detail what he/she has to do, in which way, and by which means. Role structures differ widely not only between particular types of organisations, such as industrial plants or psychiatric hospitals, but also between organisations of the same type and even between individual parts of the same organisation, such as the different wards of a psychiatric hospital. Through research on dysfunctional aspects of organisational role structures, Kahn et al (1964) found that role conflict and role ambiguity are the most important sources of job stress and burn-out.

Role overload, as the most overt form of role conflict, indicates that the demands associated with a particular occupational position exceed the abilities and the resources of the worker. In human services, role overload primarily results from exceedingly high client–staff ratios. "An example is the social worker in one program who was responsible for co-ordinating after-care services for over 200 ex-hospital patients. Responsibility for 20 such clients would begin to strain her capacity to perform adequately; a case load of 200 made it impossible to function effectively" (Cherniss, 1980, p. 81). Extreme role overload, such as in that example, not only leads to physical and mental exhaustion of the worker, but also leaves no opportunity for feelings of success and accomplishment. If the worker is forced to realise that despite all of his/her efforts, he/she has no chance of accomplishing any intended result, the development of burn-out seems to be an unavoidable consequence (Cherniss, 1980). As an empirical confirmation of the importance of role overload in the aetiology of burn-out, different studies in psychiatric institutions come to the conclusion that:

> the larger the ratio of patients to staff, the less staff members liked their jobs, and the more they tried to separate them from their lives. In settings with larger patient-to-staff ratios, staff said they would change their jobs if given a chance. They did not seek job-fulfillment or social interaction in their jobs; to them the best thing about their work was the job conditions – for example, salary. They limited their after-hours involvement with the institutions or the patients to handling emergency cases. (Pines & Maslach, 1978, p. 234 – see also Cherniss, 1980; Cherniss & Egnatios, 1978b; Sullivan, 1989; McCarthy, 1985)

Another form of role conflict which has been found to contribute to stress and burn-out in human services results from incompatible role demands. Psychiatric service workers sometimes feel obliged to act as rehabilitation counsellors and agents of social control at the same time, whereby the adequate fulfilment of the one role often contradicts the fulfilment of the other (Cherniss, 1980). Role conflicts of this type often result from the human service worker's perception that the bureaucratic demands of the organisation contradict the needs of the clients.

> Professionally oriented helpers tend to believe in and follow a particular set of norms regarding the helping relationship. These norms constitute the professional service ideal, and they are an important part of the culture of professionalism. Unfortunately, human service programs are public institutions that tend to be organized along bureaucratic lines, and there are situations in which the professional service ideal comes into conflict with organisational self interest and the bureaucratic mode of functioning. (Cherniss, 1980, p. 86)

In contrast to role overload and conflicting role demands, *role ambiguity* occurs when the worker lacks the information necessary for adequate performance of the task (Cherniss, 1980; Wise & Berlin, 1981). As summarised by Kahn et al (1964), role ambiguity includes the following dimensions:

1. Lack of information concerning the scopes and the responsibilities of the job.
2. Lack of information about the co-workers' expectations.
3. Lack of information required to perform the job adequately.
4. Lack of information about opportunities for advancement.
5. Lack of information about supervisors' evaluations.
6. Lack of information about what is happening in the organisation.

Different authors have stressed the high prevalence of these dimensions in human service work. For the field of psychiatric services, Cherniss (1980, p. 91) emphasised that "a lack of clear feedback concerning the results of one's work, ambiguous goals and criteria for work (such as the goal of psychological growth), the long and uncertain time perspective necessary for results to become visible, and the problem of authorship – that is, not knowing whether a helper's efforts were responsible for positive change in a client" seem to be the most important forms of role ambiguity experienced by the workers. The author sees the reasons for the concentration of these particular modes of role ambiguity in the fact that there is no general consensus of opinion about the right method of psychiatric work.

> For instance, despite hundreds of studies, controversy concerning the efficacy of psychotherapy still exists. There is no clear-cut evidence that psychotherapy is better than benign neglect. Similarly, the superiority of one therapeutic school over another cannot be established conclusively. Thus, the mental health practitioner inevitably must work in a dense cognitive fog. (Cherniss, 1980, p. 91)

This general problem of mental health services was aggravated by the community mental health movement during the 1970s, because the rapid development of new services which resulted entailed new forms of role demands, for which many of the mental health professionals had not received adequate training (Cherniss & Egnatios, 1978a). In addition to this lack of training, these authors found that many of the staff members of the new community mental health services expressed the feeling that the expectations and the objectives of these new services were less well defined.

Whereas role conflict and role ambiguity affect the aetiology of staff burn-out primarily by overtaxing the staff members' abilities to fulfil the demands associated with their occupational roles, there are some other aspects of the role structure which produce stress and burn-out by understimulation and lack of challenge. *Task variety, task identity,* and *learning opportunities* have been identified as very important factors of job design which affect the work satisfaction of human service staff members (Cherniss, 1980; Sarata, 1974; Sarata & Jeppesen, 1977). Task variety and task identity are aspects of the working conditions which are closely connected to the division of labour within a particular work setting. As we know from industrial work settings, high fragmentation of tasks, as in assembly-line work, leads to boredom and loss of meaning, and research suggests that despite its greater variety in relation to assembly-line work, human service work can also be overly fragmented (Sarata & Jeppesen, 1977). "Thus, a staff member who only teaches basket-weaving to after-care patients during a typical day would lack variety compared with another staff member who does various types of counseling with various types of clients, interspersed with supervision and program development activities" (Cherniss, 1980, p. 93). Task identity, in contrast to task variety, means that a worker gets an understanding of the whole process of work within his organisation as well as of his own contribution to the final product. In mental health services, there are great differences in the degree to which the different tasks resulting from a particular rehabilitation programme are assigned to different professionals, such as psychiatrists, social workers, occupational therapists and nursing staff. The more fragmented the rehabilitation process, the less the individual psychiatrist or social worker will be able to get a comprehensive understanding of the client's development (Cherniss, 1980). As a possible consequence, the individual staff members may be confronted with the experience that the success of their own efforts depends in great part on forces which they cannot comprehend and which are apparently out of their control. As with task variety and task identity, the *learning opportunities* offered by a particular occupational role have been identified as an important factor of job stimulation. "In human service work, helpers often feel that they are giving constantly and getting very little in return. This imbalance is a source of dissatisfaction which exacerbates job stress and burnout. However when helpers believe that they are learning and growing professionally in their work, they begin to perceive that they are getting as well as giving" (Cherniss, 1980, p. 94).

Considering the different aspects of the role structure and their impact on the process of coping and burn-out, it becomes obvious that the relationships between role conflict and role ambiguity on the one hand and task variety, task identity, and learning opportunities on the other, are quite complex. Because the enlarging of task variety can easily lead to greater role conflicts, and since the reduction of role ambiguity through task fragmentation can lead to decreased task identity, Cherniss (1980) suggests that the ideal strategy to prevent staff burn-out in human services will be the development of a role structure which minimises role conflict and ambiguity, while maximising task variety, task identity, and learning opportunities.

The possibility of developing such an ideal role structure depends in great part on the *power structure* and *normative structure* of the relevant organisation. The degree to which the process of decision-making within a human service organisation is hierarchically formalised and centralised seems to be a crucial factor in the aetiology of staff dissatisfaction and burn-out (Cherniss, 1980). The results of several empirical studies suggest that restricted autonomy and lack of influence on decision-making causes feelings of alienation and helplessness in these staff members (Pearlin, 1967; Aiken & Hage, 1966) and that staff members often suffer from arbitrary decisions by outside agencies which, in their opinion, are based more on bureaucratic and political needs than on the needs of their clients (Dehlinger & Perlman, 1978). Cherniss and Egnatios (1978c) found that the staff members of 22 community mental health programmes wanted more autonomy than they actually had on 11 aspects of decision-making that affected their work.

Whereas role conflict, task variety, and task identity are primarily associated with the power structure of a human service organisation, the normative structure, including the goals, norms, and ideologies of an organisation or a particular programme, greatly affect the degree of role ambiguity experienced by the staff members. Clarity of the programme contents and methods seems to be a basic precondition for effective and satisfying human service work, but, unfortunately, the definitions of programme goals are often too vague or too general for their transformation into practical daily activities. Supporting staff members in their effort of filling the gap between general goals and their daily practice therefore seems to be a crucial factor in reducing role ambiguity. Cherniss (1980) and Cherniss and Krantz (1983) suggest that the development of a *guiding philosophy of treatment* would be very helpful for that purpose. The term "guiding treatment philosophy" states that there are some common principles of daily work which are accepted by all members of the organisation. Such principles may be based on theoretical approaches, such as different therapeutic or educational schools, or on ideological principles such as religion. More importantly, they should be developed with extensive participation by staff members (Cherniss, 1980).

THE RELATIONSHIPS BETWEEN INDIVIDUAL AND ORGANISATIONAL FACTORS

Though staff burn-out is a consequence of inadequate coping with job stress, its causes cannot be traced back to the individual's behaviour alone. Some personality traits have been identified as rendering individuals more vulnerable to burn-out, but on the whole, the most important individual factors in the aetiology of burn-out, such as learned helplessness, external locus of control, lack of self-efficacy, or feelings of incompetence, are most likely to be related to organisational factors, such as work overload, conflicting and diffuse role expectations, and lack of influence and autonomy. Unfortunately, during the last decade, only a small number of empirical studies have tested the hypothesis of the relationships between organisational and individual factors of staff burn-out in psychiatric services (McCarthy, 1985; Cronin-Stubbs & Brophy, 1985; Cacciacarne et al, 1986; Lipson & Koehler, 1986; Sullivan, 1989; Vaccaro & Clark, 1987; Clark & Vaccaro, 1987; Hipwell et al, 1989; Handy, 1991a; 1991b), and these differ greatly in their methodological and theoretical background. Most of these studies focused on a particular setting, such as a psychiatric emergency room (Lipson & Koehler, 1986) or a forensic psychiatric ward (Cacciacarne et al, 1986), or on a particular occupational group, such as psychiatrists (Vaccaro & Clark, 1987; Clark & Vaccaro, 1987) or nursing staff (McCarthy, 1985; Cronin-Stubbs & Brophy; 1985; Hipwell et al, 1989; Handy, 1991a,b). This limited the possibilities for comparing the prevalence of burn-out in different settings, such as community mental health centres or psychiatric hospital wards, or for different occupations, such as nurses, psychiatrists, social workers, psychologists or occupational therapists. The problem with drawing comparisons on such a limited database can be demonstrated by the fact that one of the few studies which compared the burn-out prevalence of different occupational groups came to the conclusion that the level among psychiatrists is very low in relation to that among nursing staff (Cacciacarne et al, 1986). On the other hand, studies which focused on the prevalence in community mental health psychiatrists alone suggested that this occupational group has a very high risk of burning out (Vaccaro & Clark, 1987; Clark & Vaccaro, 1987).

Among the more recent studies on staff burn-out, however, are two noteworthy ones which, despite their very different methodological and theoretical conceptions, seem to represent comprehensive research on this topic. The first is the study of Kelloway and Barling (1991) on the relationships between job characteristics, symptoms of burn-out, and mental health of hospital staff, while the second is the combined qualitative and quantitative study of Handy (1991a,b) on the social context of occupational stress of hospital and community mental health nursing staff. Using the technique of confirmatory path analysis, Kelloway and Barling first tested the hypothesis that characteristics of the job (autonomy, task variety, task identity, feedback from the job, feedback from co-workers, role ambiguity, and role conflict) are positively related to symptoms of burn-out, and that symptoms of burn-out negatively affect workers' mental health status. Next, the alternative hypothesis – that a worker's mental health status affects the characteristics of his job and the experience of burn-out – was tested. From comparison of the statistical fit of both models, it was concluded that burn-out is a consequence of poor job characteristics, and that mental health problems are a consequence and not a cause of it (Kelloway & Barling, 1991, p. 299).

In contrast to Kelloway and Barling, Handy (1991a,b) widened the theoretical scope of the burn-out concept by including the broader socio-cultural and socio-structural context of mental health services into her model of job stress and burn-out. From sociological theory on the socio-cultural aspects of psychiatric institutions in modern societies, she concluded that there are three *key interlinked contradictions* between the psychiatric sector and society: first, that between the mandates to help and to control mentally ill people; secondly, the contradiction between releasing mentally ill people from conventional role demands because of their illness and connecting this release with the demand for medical compliance, as a central dimension of the sick role; and thirdly, the contradiction between the commitments of psychiatric professionals to the alleviation of mental illness and to the identification of subtle forms of behavioural deviation and personal distress as psychiatric problems (Handy, 1991b, pp. 820 f.). To explore the implications of this threefold contradiction for the working situation and for the experience of work-related stress by the staff members of psychiatric services, Handy observed the nursing staff within a mental hospital setting and within a community mental health setting by the methods of participant observation, activity diaries, in-depth interviews, and official statistical data. Interpreting these comprehensive data, the author comes to the conclusion that in both settings:

the structural contradictions of the psychiatric system were reflected in the equivocal motives and understandings which the various participants habitually brought to their everyday interactions. As a result of these ambiguities, the activities of all parties tended to take place within various unacknowledged conditions and to have a range of unintended and paradoxical consequences. These could be highly distressing for all involved and often reflected the emotionally charged and personality significant nature of psychiatry's subject matter. Unfortunately, the structural contradictions which created the initial conditions for these unintended outcomes often ensured that coping strategies which the various participants employed also rebounded upon them and had the unforeseen consequence of intensifying the initial tensions within the system. (Handy, 1991b, p. 829)

In spite of the known limitations of qualitative data, particularly with regard to the generalisation of results, this study seems to be of great practical relevance. After the completion of her study, the author conducted different workshops for staff members, with the purpose of providing them with feedback based on the results. The participating nursing staff members commented that their better understanding of the structural problems of the psychiatric system helped them to deal with their daily conflicts in a more comfortable way. These workshops also motivated staff members to institute a series of changes on the organisational level of their work.

CONCLUSIONS AND GENERAL OUTLOOK

For more than 20 years, job stress and burn-out have been identified as major negative aspects of the quality of work life in psychiatric services, and many strategies for the enhancement of coping behaviour and the prevention of burn-out were developed during the 1980s (Cherniss, 1980; Edelwich & Brodsky, 1982; Tubesing & Tubesing, 1982; Freudenberger, 1983; Pines, 1982, 1983; Shapiro, 1982; Golembiewsky, 1982; Cherniss & Krantz, 1983; Scully, 1983; Aber, 1983; Cronin-Stubbs & Brophy, 1985; Handy, 1991a). Unfortunately, no systematic research on the implementation and evaluation of such strategies within psychiatric services yet exists. On the other hand, more recent studies on the burn-out of psychiatric staff members suggest that the risk is still high. Because there are some groups of people working in psychiatric services for whom only few or even no burn-out studies exist, such as members of complementary services, semi- or non-professional helpers, or relatives of mentally ill people, it must be suspected that the level in this field is very high indeed. Furthermore, the rapid development of new psychiatric services may entail a change of the aetiological dynamics of burn-out for those professional groups which were extensively investigated.

Considering the negative consequences of inadequate coping and burn-out for people working in psychiatric services, and its importance for the effectiveness and quality of these services, additional theoretical work and empirical research are needed, at least on the following topics: (1) the development of a comprehensive theoretical model of the aetiology of burn-out which includes the individual, the organisational, and the macro-sociological level; (2) systematic research on the epidemiology of burn-out in different settings and for the different professional and semi-professional groups working in psychiatric care; (3) systematic research on the personal, institutional, and financial consequences of inadequate coping and burn-out, which also includes the consequences for the quality of life of the clients; and (4) systematic research on the implementation and evaluation of preventive strategies.

In addition to these research topics, prevention of staff burn-out and the enhancement of quality of working life should be included as explicit programme goals, when planning and implementing new psychiatric services.

POLICY AND PLANNING

Measuring Quality of Life in Cost Analysis: Controversies and Use in Mental Health

Luis Salvador-Carulla

INTRODUCTION

Over the last decade, the demand for economic analysis of health-care alternatives has risen for a wide range of reasons such as resource allocation, health planning, health priority setting, or drug approval and drug pricing. There is no question about the need for including quality of life (QoL) information in such studies. However, the methods of QoL assessment in cost analysis are controversial.

Health economists have introduced new concepts and novel methodologies to medical research. The flow of cost information is growing rapidly and it may be difficult to interpret for the lay psychiatrist, although good introductory reviews exist, both on general health economics (Drummond et al, 1987), and on their application to mental health (Netten & Beecham, 1993; Knapp, 1995). From a broad perspective, *cost* is defined as "the value of what is given up to provide care", and *benefit* as "the value of what is gained, in terms of improved health status" (Maynard, 1993). In the context of cost analysis, the definition of benefit is restricted to "those outcomes that are expressed in monetary rather than physical units". Whether years of life gained or intangibles such as quality of life and disability can be converted into monetary units is controversial, particularly in the mental health sector.

Economics is concerned with maximising the benefits we obtain from using scarce resources. Techniques are based on neoclassical microeconomic theory (Guerrien, 1992), and several forms of the Production of Welfare model (Shiell et al, 1990). Within welfare economics, the opportunity model is currently used in cost analysis. According to the *opportunity* approach, the costs of a programme or a treatment represent the benefits that could have been obtained had the same resources been allocated to other use. Therefore, the cost of using a resource in a particular service is the benefit forgone by losing its best alternative, which is used as a comparator (Knapp, 1993). The priority choice should be based on marginal costs, i.e. a new alternative will be preferred up to the point where the marginal benefit equals its marginal cost, but not beyond that point (Murray, 1994). In this context, cost studies are traditionally classified in four major groups according to the way outcomes are measured: cost-minimisation, cost-benefit, cost-effectiveness, and cost-utility (Drummond et al, 1987).

Cost-minimisation analysis: This approach is taken when the effects or outputs of the alternatives are the same. Thus, it may be assumed that two drugs with similar efficacy and similar adverse effects have identical output, so they can be compared by their costs. This assumption is difficult to prove in psychiatry, so this approach is seldom used in mental health economics.

Cost-benefit analysis: All inputs and outputs are converted into monetary units, choosing the alternative with a better cost/benefit ratio. This approach is considered best from the economic point of view, since it uses continuous data and allows perfect trade-off comparison among different alternatives. But this is not the case in the health-care sector, where it is questionable that clinical outcomes and intangible measures, such as quality of life, can be converted into monetary units. Cost-benefit is rather unrealistic in health economics, given the problems of obtaining meaningful monetary valuations of health gains, the lack of available cost-benefit information in the health sector, and the absence of data on opportunity costs (Mason, 1994).

Cost-effectiveness analysis: The alternative is proposed on the basis that it offers more of a given outcome per unit cost. This type of analysis can be performed when the alternatives' outcomes can be measured with the same units. Costs are measured here in monetary units, and outcomes are transformed into natural or physical units such as mortality rates, years of healthy life gained, or number of cases in remission. Incremental costs and marginal benefits have to be measured here. This approach allows comparison between different diseases and populations, and it uses units of morbidity and mortality closer to a clinician's perspective, but it does not capture intangible outcomes such as psychiatric symptoms, quality of life or disability.

Cost-utility analysis: This type of analysis presents health outcomes in a single measure that summarises the extension of life and a utility value or "quality of life" of that extension. Cost-utility analysis can be considered as a particular form of cost-effectiveness that allows cross-comparison and trade-offs among alternatives according to a global index. From a historical perspective, the cost-utility approach was based on the "expected utility theory", conceived by Daniel Bernouilli in 1738 and formalised by von Neumann and Morgenstern in the late 1940s. According to this theory, every result of a choice between two alternatives (preference) produces a certain degree of well-being or *utility*. Subjective utility (the satisfaction derived from the alternative chosen), differs from the objective expected monetary gains on several points, such as risk assumption, choice certainty, degree of probability, or previous experience and cognition. For example, choices concerning gains are associated with risk aversion, while those concerning losses are associated with risk assumption, even when the expected monetary changes are equal for both choices. When certainty is included as an alternative, the low-probability choices are overestimated and the high or intermediate probabilities are underestimated, producing a shift in the risk assumption (Kahneman & Tversky, 1982). The value function provides a description of the relationship between the subjective value and the objective amount that can be gained or lost. Weinstein and colleagues set out the facets of cost-utility analysis in the 1970s, describing Quality-Adjusted Life Years (QALYs) as the net effectiveness of the alternative in question expressed by the trade-offs between additional survival and quality of life. Williams (1985) pioneered the QALY studies in the UK, with a different model based on the Classification of Illness States (Rosser & Kind, 1978), and its associated matrix for weighting individual "value of life". Over the last decade, a growing number of studies have used several techniques for cost-utility analysis. (For a full review of these historical aspects see: Kahneman & Tversky,1982; Loomes & McKenzie, 1990; La Puma & Lawlor, 1990; Johannesson et al, 1994.)

STAGES OF HEALTH DECISION-MAKING ACCORDING TO THE COST-UTILITY APPROACH

Decision-makers who allocate resources should choose between the relative importance of different health outcomes, such as mortality reduction or disability prevention. In the absence of appropriate information, politicians tend to allocate resources inconsistently. Traditionally, this problem was overcome in the service area by indicators, such as characteristics of services, success in meeting previously established objectives and client engagement; or by health-care activities such as number of cases treated or number of consultations. However, these proxy measures are weak indicators of "efficiency" and are not useful for treatment choice. Health outcome assessment is a further step that deserves more credit (Shiell et al, 1990). According to the utility model, the usefulness of health status measures for priority setting is increased if they incorporate preference measurements, and when relevant components (mortality and morbidity) can be aggregated into a single measure. Spiegelhalter and colleagues (1992) have proposed an eight-stage process of decision-making based on health index utilisation. This process includes the gathering of relevant information (costs, quality of life, and survival data), converting the survival data to a single unit, turning the quality of life data into a 0–1 scale, and combining both of them into a single, global measure that might be comparable across patients or programmes. There are several alternative universal index measures. The most frequently used are different types of QALYs (Kind et al, 1990; La Puma & Lawlor, 1990; Johannesson et al, 1994), and the Disability Adjusted Life Years (DALY) (Murray, 1994). As the "Quality of Life" concept in health economics differs from the medical field, and some measures assess different health constructs, utility measures such as QALYs and DALYs are grouped here under a common name: Index Adjusted Life Years (IALYs).

Cost-utility analysis fully incorporates "quality of life" and related factors into economic analysis, being particularly relevant to psychiatry. Apart from the specific value choices, the major difference between global index measures and natural measures is the inclusion of the time lived with disability, psychological distress and related issues. The 1990 Global Burden of Disease study showed that 34% of all disease burden is attributable to disability. The use of a cost-utility approach allowed comparisons between over 100 conditions, showing that neuropsychiatric disorders are the second morbidity burden among non-infectious diseases in the world (World Bank Report, 1993). Furthermore, neuropsychiatric diseases appear as major problems when DALYs are used, but not employing natural measures such as the potential years of life lost (Murray, 1994). Therefore, cost-utility analysis may contribute to prioritising resource allocation in mental health in the future. On the other hand, cost-utility and cost-effectiveness studies are rapidly gaining credit in psychopharmacology. Cost-utility analysis has been recommended both in the Australian Guidelines (ACDHSH, 1995), and in the Canadian Guidelines for Economic Analysis of Pharmaceutical Products (Torrance et al, 1996). This technology has been used in recent studies in order to compare effectiveness of psychotropic drugs (Kamlet et al, 1992; Hatziandreu et al, 1994; Revicki et al, 1995). It has also been used for assessing cost-per-QALY in schizophrenia (Wilkinson et al, 1992).

Cost-per-QALY information is not being advocated as the only criterion for decision-making, but as an extra source of data to add to the information currently used (Gudex, 1990). Nevertheless, the development of a single, universal index for cost-utility analysis is controversial; studies may use different methods for calculating the same index, and conceptual, methodological and statistical issues arise regarding the reliability and validity of these complex techniques. These issues are reviewed here following a modified version of Spiegelhalter's approach (Spiegelhalter et al, 1992): (1) basic health measures used for constructing a universal index; (2) composite measures: global survival index and global health index (utility measures); (3) construction of the universal health index; (4) utilisation of the universal index in decision analysis; (5) alternatives to classical cost-utility analysis (Table 22.1).

Table 22.1   Stages in developing health decision analysis according to cost-per-IALY data[a]

1. Unaided intuitive judgement
2. Consideration of available data on costs and health benefits of each programme or treatment alternative
3. Collection of validated costing, quality of life, and survival data for each programme
4. Summary of survival benefits as single measure[b]
5. Use of common multi-dimensional quality of life measures across programmes
6. Collapse of quality of life measures to a single 0–1 scale
7. Combination of quality of life and survival data into single measure (e.g. QALY)
8. Decisions made by ranking programmes according to their return in QALYs per monetary unit and funding strictly according to rank order (e.g. QALY league tables)

[a] Index Adjusted Life Years (including QALY and DALY).
[b] Stage "4" was numbered "6" in the original paper.
Source: Adapted from Spiegelhalter et al (1992).

BASIC MEASURES FOR CONSTRUCTING A UNIVERSAL HEALTH INDEX

CARDINAL DATA (COSTS AND DEATH RATES)

There are different methods of collecting cost data that have been reviewed elsewhere (Drummond et al, 1987; Netten & Beecham, 1993). A study may consider only direct health core costs derived from health service utilisation, or it can include all direct costs related to the disease or the programme. This second alternative is preferred. The issue of indirect costs related to productivity loss is a subject of debate due to the conceptual problems and methodological difficulties involved (Drummond, 1992). A segregate analysis of these data is usually recommended, and some authors advocate for not including them in the final cost-per-index analysis.

In 1947, M. Dempsey introduced the concept of measuring time lost due to mortality rather than crude death rates. Since then, a wide number of methods for measuring years of life lost have been proposed (Murray, 1994).

ORDINAL DATA (HEALTH-FUNCTION STATUS)

Health status, functional status and quality of life are three concepts sometimes used interchangeably (Guyatt et al, 1993). Apart from in-depth conceptual analysis, health-related quality of life (HRQL) can be considered a value-laden, multi-dimensional and bipolar concept comprising three major domains: physical, psychological and social functioning. These can be broken down into multiple dimensions. Instruments for assessing HRQL can be classified as *specific* and *generic*. Generic *HRQL rating scales* (health profiles) are multi-dimensional instruments, such as the Sickness Impact Profile (SIP), the Quality of Well-Being Scale (QWBS), the Nottingham Health Profile (NHP) or the RAND Medical Outcomes Study (SF-36), which are designed for psychosocial health assessment. Economists criticise the use of these instruments for utility analysis since they do not adequately consider values and individual preferences. In fact, these instruments were not originally intended for economic analysis, though they could be used for gathering quality of life data and allow comparison across programmes. The simultaneous use of health profiles and utility measurements to complement QoL information has been recommended (Guyatt et al, 1993; Torrance et al, 1996); and some of the aforementioned instruments have been used in cost-utility studies in order to obtain preference weightings (see below).

The lack of a proper assessment of values and preferences in current HRQoL instruments has also been addressed from the medical perspective. Individual Quality of Life (IQoL) instruments, such as the Evaluation of Individual Quality of Life (SEIQoL) or the Repertory Grid for Measurement of individual Quality of Life, apply different techniques for identifying factors that are relevant to every particular subject and for calculating the weight that the individual attributes to each factor (Joyce, 1994). These recent instruments may be relevant for future developments in the cost-utility field, since the present techniques use average preferences from heterogeneous respondents (general population, experts, health staff, patients), and individual preferences cannot always be accurately assessed by others.

COMPOSITE MEASURES FOR CONSTRUCTING A UNIVERSAL INDEX

SURVIVAL MEASURES

At least four different methods for estimating the time lost due to premature death have been suggested for replacing age-standardised death rates: potential years of life lost, period expected years of life lost, cohort expected years of life lost and standard expected years of life lost. The pros and cons of these survival measures have been thoroughly reviewed by Murray (1994).

UTILITY MEASURES

The theoretical background for utility measure construction is heterogeneous (Gonzales et al, 1994), including classical "expected utility theory", "prospect (value) theory", and "multi-attribute utility theory", where conjoint analysis avoids the need to value every potential health state. Utility measures incorporate preference/value measurements and define quality of life as a single number or index along a continuum, generally from death (0.0) to full health (1.0). These measures reflect both the health status and the value of the health status to the individual (scores less than zero may reflect health states worse than death) (Becker, 1995; Guyatt et al, 1993). Values below "0" are not considered in some standards (e.g. Canadian guidelines), while suicidal patients may value their health status as "worse than death".

Factors Related to Utility Measure Construction

The main factors in constructing such measures focus on the empirical determination of preferences, the sources of data (people whose valuations are used), and the valuation method (ranking order and systems for aggregating preferences) (Megone, 1990).

Determination of Preferences

The psychology of preferences is an extremely complex field, which is generally outside the clinician's scientific background (for a review see Kahneman & Tversky, 1982).

Rosser and Kind (1978) did not find sociodemographic differences in respondents' choices, nor did Gonzales and colleagues (1994) in depressed patients. Nevertheless, individual diversity does influence election between health alternatives, since preferences are culturally laden, and differences by age group have been postulated (Murray, 1994). Apart from intergroup differences, there are also differences across individuals depending on previous experience, attitudes and baseline status. Thus, the same monetary gain could be considered wasteful or inappropriate depending on whether the individual's wage has grown or decreased lately; and the election may change dramatically with slight changes in the presentation of alternatives (Kahneman & Tversky, 1982). Other factors influencing health preferences include information level, personality and cognitive characteristics, or even the type of health insurance. There are various examples of health preference liability (e.g. choice of childbirth services changed over time both during pregnancy and post-natally) (Loomes & McKenzie, 1990). Better information may improve preference choices, but even a fully informed subject can derive objects which are simply not in his interest (Megone, 1990). Intraindividual differences over time have been described as well.

There is also a lengthy debate on whether individual patient preferences can adequately be assessed by others. The point of reference for the election may vary as the individual adapts to a new situation. Thus, ill people adjust to their lives in order to reduce real loss, and rate their health status better than healthy subjects. For example, chronically ill elderly rate themselves better than their physicians believe they are (La Puma & Lawlor, 1990; Loomes & McKenzie, 1990), and healthy people consider haemodialysis to be worse than renal patients submitted to these techniques think that it is (Sackett & Torrance, 1979). On the other hand, coping strategies such as denial may induce significant choice changes in some groups of patients (e.g. cancer).

Internal representations of some health states are more complex than those of others. A lay individual may figure out the suffering and consequences of a kidney transplant or a heart attack (although this needs further research), but people find it difficult to make choices concerning death. The Carr–Hill postulate states that the inclusion of death makes people formulate irrealistic health choices (Spiegelhalter et al, 1992).

Things are even more problematic when choices and risks are placed for conditions as far from lay people's experience as depression, severe personality disorder or psychosis. The importance of knowledge, information, attitudes and expectations in mental health preferences has been pointed out by some authors (Chisholm et al, 1995; Becker, 1995). Gonzales and colleagues (1994) found that, in depressed patients, preference ratings for depression were lower than those reported by the general public for the same condition, contrary to what happens in non-mental diseases, where preference choices are higher than in those expressed by the general public. On the other hand, people may not be the best judges of their own welfare, particularly in those patients with lack of insight or impaired cognitive function, such as mental retardation, dementia, and some severely ill psychiatric patients (e.g. mentally retarded individuals may try to please the interviewer by giving what they think is the correct answer) (Culyer, 1990; Shiell et al, 1990). A different type of distortion may arise when valuating health choices of people with comorbidities, particularly in the mental health sector.

Thus, the preferences of healthy people may be a questionable choice for constructing utility measures of mental health alternatives, and IALYs developed in the context of allocation of acute medical conditions may not be helpful in considering improvements in the outcomes of those with mental illness.

Sources of Data for Preference Choice

Preferences and values can be obtained from different populations such as healthy individuals, doctors, nurses or other health professionals, expert groups, relatives, patients or even policy-makers. For example, the Rosser matrix of health states was obtained from a heterogeneous sample of 70 subjects. The 10 doctors assigned a higher value to the subjective feelings of suffering, and resembled the healthy volunteer group in their choices, whereas nurses showed closer agreement to patients' choices (Kind et al, 1990). Such heterogeneity questions the overall validity of the results, particularly when major differences can be found in the appraisal of different subject groups. On the other hand, reliability may also be questioned. A reassessment of the Rosser–Kind matrix, obtained from nearly 300 subjects by Rosser and colleagues, revealed differences from the original matrix (e.g. the value assigned to "moderate distress and unable to work" changed from 0.9 to 0.35) (Spiegelhalter et al, 1992; Rosser et al, 1992). On the other hand,

Murray's DALYs were obtained exclusively from experts' choices over six classes of disabilities (Murray, 1994).

Methods for Assessing Preferences/Values

Several methods have been described (for a review see Kind, 1990; La Puma & Lawlor, 1990; Badia & Rovira, 1994; Murray, 1994).

Category Rating. This calls for subjects to classify states into one of a limited number of ordered categories. Subjects are expected to sort the states into categories according to their perceived seriousness between two extreme health states. Problems of category rating in depression have been put forward by Gonzales and colleagues (Gonzales et al, 1994). Several methods for category rating have been proposed including verbal analogue scaling (disease categories calibration) or linear-analogue thermometrical scales (e.g. Euroqol).

Paired Comparisons. Such methods require subjects to make judgements about pairs of states, essentially answering the question "Is state A worse than state B?" No estimate is made of the magnitude of the relationship.

Magnitude Estimation. This is designed to elicit valuations from subjects by asking direct questions about the relative value of the time spent in one state compared to another. A single health state might be designated as reference state and assigned a unit value. The subject is asked to indicate the magnitude of the ratio between that reference state and other health states and express this ratio as a number. Where the rank order of states has been established prior to magnitude estimation, it is permissible to work with successive pairs of states (Kind, 1990).

Person Trade-off. This asks individuals to choose between curing a certain number of patients in one illness state (or disability class) versus another number in a different class. For example, respondents are asked to make a choice between curing X patients in an A state, and Y in a B state. X and Y are changed until the respondent is indifferent to both choices. The $X:Y$ ratio expresses the relative utility of health states A and B. As an example, the final result can be that curing a single person in state A equals curing three in state B.

Time Trade-off. This elicits how much time an individual would exchange living in one state versus another particular health state (e.g. being healthy). For example, option 1 is being healthy (state A) for 2 years (t_a) and then dying; and option 2 is being 5 years (t_b) under treatment with a certain drug for breast cancer (state B) followed by death. Then t_a and t_b are changed until the respondent assigns an equal value to both choices. The "indifference" ratio t_a/t_b shows the respondent's utility (relative preference) for being treated with the known drug for breast cancer. A result can be that living 0.4 years healthy equals 1 year in state "A". This method may seem useful for acute conditions or those with clear-cut time limits, but the way it could be applied to psychiatry is a matter of debate (Shiell et al, 1990). The time trade-off mathematical function has been reviewed by Johannesson and colleagues (1994).

Standard Gambles. These ask individuals to choose between the certainty of living in a health state versus a chance of getting well at a probability p and dying at a probability $1-p$. The probability (p) is changed until the respondent is indifferent about the two choices. Here the utility is represented by the p value. According to their proposers standard gambles may allow decision-making under uncertainty conditions.

Instruments

In medicine, quality of life is a status function, while in health economics "quality of life" is a utility function. In the first case, a subjective rating scale can provide information about the patient's present status in several dimensions related to the QoL construct; while in health economics, the assessment will be based on the individual's preference between two health states or equivalent elections. The assessment of preferences has not been properly addressed in most of the available psychometric literature in mental health. In fact, the development of medical and health economic QoL instruments has followed separate paths, and they show major differences in their conceptual framework and psychometric properties.

Generic Health-status Profiles

Utility measures can be drawn directly from generic health profiles, although many problems are found in this process, since it is necessary to perform a careful review of the psychometric properties of the instrument being used: mainly consistency, reliability, validity, sensitivity to change, and transcultural standardisation (here consistency/homogeneity is considered independent of external reliability). There are relatively few generic quality of life scales with full analysis of their psychometric properties. However, the psychometric properties of health-status QoL scales are better known than those of the utility scales. The usefulness of generic health profiles (e.g. Nottingham Health Profile, SF-36) for economic evaluation has been reviewed by some authors (Brazier, 1993; Whynes & Neilson, 1993). Most health-status scales are not preference-orientated, and include few items concerning these issues.

Utility Instruments

The quality criteria of most of the available utility measures (e.g. Quality of Well-Being Scale, Torrance Health Utility Index, the Rosser–Kind Matrix, EuroQol, Murray's disability weightings), have not been sufficiently tested, particularly their consistency, sensitivity to change, validity and reliability (test–retest, inter-informant, and interrater reliability if the choices are made by external raters after an interview). Factors such as individual changes in health preferences over time raise serious doubts about the reliability of these measures. At its best, our present knowledge concerning this issue does not support the transferability of current utility measures. Most of them are considered by the authors to be in the development stage (Kind et al, 1990; Essink-Bot et al, 1993). Three utility measures are discussed below.

Rosser–Kind Matrix (Rosser & Kind, 1978). This two-dimensional scale, also known as the Charing Cross health indicator (CH-X), lists eight levels of disability and four levels of distress, allocating patients' QoL on an 8×4 matrix and providing 29 states of illness, where 6 are "marked states" (Tables 22.2 and 22.3). The ranking order of severity was deduced from magnitude estimation between certainty choices in 70 subjects with different current health experiences; weightings were improved in successive versions of the scale (Rosser & Kind, 1978; Kind et al, 1990). Williams applied the Rosser–Kind matrix to cost-per-QALY calculations. He also suggested alternative methods for obtaining Rosser-classified quality of life data, such as the use of a shortened version of the Health Measurement Questionnaire or direct professional judgement (Williams, 1985; Whynes & Neilson, 1993). Psychometric testing includes convergent validity, differences among methods for data collection (Whynes & Neilson, 1993), and sensitivity to change in schizophrenia. This indicator was insensitive to variations in the severity of mental disorders (Wilkinson et al, 1992). According to its content, the Rosser–Kind matrix is closer to Murray's DALY than to other QALY indices. Although the authors consider it a ratio scale, this is questionable (see below). Furthermore, the CH-X provides average values, contains a bias toward physical disability (mostly due to general mobility), does not adequately weigh disability and distress in psychiatric patients, neglects relevant factors in health choices such as risk attitudes and uncertainties, shows interindividual variability, may not be applicable to chronic conditions (particularly mental illness), and is not suitable for comparison between mental health and medical programmes (Kahneman & Tversky, 1982; Loomes & McKenzie, 1990; Wilkinson et al, 1992). The Index of Health-related Quality of Life (IHQL) is a new version of the CH-X which is currently being tested. It adds a third dimension (physical discomfort), subdivides the three dimensions into 44 scales and gives 107 descriptors of states (Rosser et al, 1992).

EuroQoL. This instrument uses thermometer visual analogue scaling (VAS) for assessing health status during the previous year. Section one assesses five dimensions: mobility, self-care, usual activities, pain/discomfort, and anxiety/depression, which theoretically allows 243 composite health status descriptions. Section two provides a self-rating of the general health status (Badia & Rovira, 1994). VAS rating is assumed to be a quasi-interval measure, although further research on its scaling process has been recommended. EuroQoL has been defined as an "internationally standardised,

Table 22.2   Descriptions of disability and distress in the Rosser–Kind matrix

Disability	Distress
1 No disability	1 None
2 Not in 3 but slight social disability	2 Mild
3 Not in 4 but severe social disability and /or performance at work. Able to do all housework except very heavy tasks	3 Moderate
4 Not in 5 but choice of work or performance at work severely limited. Housewives and old people able to do light housework only, but able to go out shopping	4 Severe
5 Not in 6 but unable to undertake any paid employment. Unable to continue any education. Old people confined to home except for escorted outing and short walks and unable to do shopping. Housewives only able to perform a few simple tasks	
6 Not in 7 but confined to chair or wheelchair or able to move around the home only with support from an assistant	
7 Not in 8 but confined to bed	
8 Unconscious	

feasible, valid and reliable method for the measurement of the general public's valuations of non-disease-specific health outcomes" (Essink-Bot et al, 1993). However, its psychometric properties have not yet been fully analysed. For example, EuroQoL mood dimension may be too vague for mental health assessment.

Murray's Disability Weighting. Murray (1994) developed a measure in order to assess all health outcomes that represent loss of welfare (morbidity burden) for calculating DALYs in the 1990 World Bank Report (1993). Six disability classes

Table 22.3   A Value/utility scale for QALY calculations according to the Rosser–Kind matrix

Disability	Distress			
	1	2	3	4
1	1.00	0.96	0.99	0.97
2	0.99	0.99	0.97	0.93
3	0.98	0.97	0.96	0.91
4	0.96	0.96	0.94	0.87
5	0.95	0.94	0.90	0.70
6	0.88	0.85	0.68	0.00
7	0.68	0.56	0.00	−1.49
8	−0.03			

Source: Adapted from Wilkinson et al (1992). Reproduced by permission of the University of Liverpool

Table 22.4 Definitions of disability weighting for DALYs calculation

Class 1	Limited ability to perform at least one activity in one of the following areas: recreation, education, procreation or occupation	0.096
Class 2	Limited ability to perform most activities in one of the following areas: recreation, education, procreation or occupation	0.220
Class 3	Limited ability to perform activities in two or more of the following areas: recreation, education, procreation or occupation	0.400
Class 4	Limited ability to perform most activities in all of the following areas: recreation, education, procreation or occupation	0.600
Class 5	Needs assistance with instrumental activities of daily living such as meal preparation, shopping or homework	0.810
Class 6	Needs assistance with activities of daily living such as eating, personal hygiene or toilet use	0.920

Source: Adapted from Murray (1994). Reproduced by permission.

were defined, between perfect health and death, according to the dimensions of the WHO Disability Assessment Scale. Every class was operationally defined and weights between 0 and 1 were assigned, based on expert opinions (Table 22.4). Time lived in each class was multiplied by the disability weight to make it comparable with the years lost due to premature mortality. Therefore, DALY is an indicator of the time lived with a disability and the time lost due to premature mortality, which is calculated using standard expected years lost. Here, as in all other cases, the final aim of the utility measure is to develop a universal index of health status in order to fully apply economic techniques to health decision-making.

CONSTRUCTION OF A UNIVERSAL INDEX: INDEX ADJUSTED LIFE YEARS

GENERAL DESCRIPTION

In the late 1960s, D. F. Sullivan proposed a global index of health status incorporating information on morbidity and mortality. The economic reasons for promoting such an approach have been analysed by Murray (Murray, 1994).

Klarman applied this index to the cost comparison of treatment alternatives in chronic renal failure (Klarman et al, 1968). The QALY is the arithmetic product of life expectancy and an adjustment for the quality of the remaining life-years gained (Kind, 1990). It combines effects on survival and morbidity in a single measure that reflects trade-offs between these two factors, providing a means by which health-care programmes with different ability to extend life and reduce morbidity can be compared. Cost-utility analysis incorporates utility measures in order to obtain a cost-per-Index Adjusted Life Years. The utility measure should be, at least, an interval scale, although a ratio scale is ideally preferred. IALYs are intended to be a macro tool. They use aggregate community preferences and trade-offs to determine what is best for an individual patient regardless of whether individual and societal preferences are the same. For that reason, using QALY as a "micro" clinical decision-making tool is considered inappropriate (La Puma & Lawlor, 1990; Wilkinson et al, 1992). It has been stated that IALYs allow a combination of different information, incorporate patient's preferences in clinical decision, weigh the presumed importance of various factors and produce a number which is comparable among diseases and population groups that allows decision-making under uncertainty (Becker, 1995). However, the advantages of this parameter are overwhelmed by its conceptual and methodological problems.

Whether quality of life can be measured in a way that facilitates its comparison with quantitative data (e.g. costs) is a key question in this debate. Most health economists, even those critical to the current available instruments (Loomes & McKenzie, 1990), think that this is possible; they consider present problems as those of a technique in the developmental stage, or regard cost-utility approach "as the worst technique with the exception of all the others" (Badia & Rovira, 1994). Some economists, biostatisticians and clinicians are more critical, questioning the overall appropriateness of such techniques for exploring values to be placed on quality of life measures that include death, the feasibility of explicit trade-offs between categories, and the possibility of misleading results that may lead to unwise or unfair decisions (Hirst, 1990; Spiegelhalter et al, 1992; Brazier, 1993).

CONCEPTUAL AND METHODOLOGICAL ISSUES RELATED TO THE UNIVERSAL INDEX POSTULATE

Critics of the Utility Approach

As it has been stated above, the so-called "universal index theory" is founded on a series of economic principles, postulates and models, some of which are called "theories", although they lack appropriate verification. Furthermore, the whole background of "neoclassical microeconomic theory" has been questioned (Guerrien, 1992). These critics are concerned with the model of perfect competition and the rationality principle that provide the basis for the utility function. The use of the neoclassical microeconomic approach for confronting macroeconomic issues is also controversial. While the neoclassical approach is suitable for working with individual preferences and for providing local descriptors, macroeconomic analysis works with aggregates and provides global descriptors. It is a contradiction that IALYs, developed as "macro" tools, are founded on the expected utility model, a simplification presumed to work only at local level (Guerrien, 1992).

The expected utility approach is based on a series of normative assumptions whose descriptive validity has been strongly criticised, questioning the overall validity of this model (Loomes & McKenzie, 1990; Megone, 1990; Seedhouse, 1995; Cohen, 1996):

1. *Constant proportional time trade-off.* This entails that an individual may sacrifice some constant proportion of his remaining years of life in order to achieve a given improvement in his health status. According to this assumption, duration and quality of life are not different from other commodities that can be purchased. It may be plausible to ask for the value of certainty of a particular sum of money, but it is less plausible to ask for the value of X years of life, since these are prospects that cannot be delivered or accurately imagined. Some studies suggest that certain later stages of life are valued higher than earlier stages, casting further doubts about the validity of this axiom (Johannesson et al, 1994). The stability of individuals' preferences over time has to be proved.

2. *Constant proportional risk attitude.* The feasibility of representing risk attitude as a constant value in the utility function is questioned by empirical findings on the experience of financial risks and experiments on the psychology of preferences.

3. *Independence assumption.* This implies that risks are independent of health preferences. Preferences of agents in delayed risk situations will not satisfy the independence axiom. Kahneman and Tversky (1982) provide several examples of the complex relationship between risk assumption and preferences. Cohen (1996) concludes that this axiom is not applicable to medical decision, particularly for those involving non-trivial risk of death.

Results may differ when certainty is included in the choice (gambling effect) and when alternatives are framed in different ways (framing effect), among other factors (Kahneman & Tversky, 1982; Loomes & McKenzie, 1990). Furthermore, the way to incorporate discounting into cost-utility analysis is not clear (Johannesson et al, 1994), and these measures do not consider externalities: Can environmental characteristics be considered distinct from final outcome? It could be argued that the provision of a comfortable, safe domestic environment is an important objective, particularly for people with mental handicap, in which case the IALY does not have a set of categories to measure this achievement (Shiell et al, 1990).

Critics of the Single Measure

According to some authors, preferences are multi-factorial in essence, depending on beliefs, attitudes, sympathy, desires or commitments (Megone, 1990). Therefore, it is impossible to reduce preference information to a single unit; being multi-dimensional, the measure should also be multi-dimensional (Hirst, 1990). This is extensible to several components of such aggregates. For example, disability and quality of life are multi-dimensional constructs whose aggregation is uncertain, unless basic dimensions are also considered. Problems found in the assessment of disability with the Rosser–Kind matrix may reflect this issue.

The possibility of aggregating cardinal and ordinal data into a single measure is also controversial. This aggregate is clearly inappropriate when category scaling has been used for constructing the IALY. Some experts argue that magnitude estimation and analogous techniques produce "true" ratio scales (interval scales that include a zero point such as measurement of pressure), justifying the use of IALYs as if they were cardinal numbers. Although magnitude estimation may improve ordinal rating, it is questionable that it may allow not only ratio scaling, but also full interval scaling. An interval scale is one in which numbers are assigned to the response of categories in such a way that a unit change in scale values represents a constant change across the range of the whole scale such as Celsius degrees (McDowell & Newell, 1987). Considering IALYs more than ordinal scales is uncertain due to the difficulties of preference assessment and the psychometric properties of such instruments.

Problems in aggregating direct and indirect costs led health economists to recommend a disaggregate display of such data in health economic studies. This is in clear contradiction to the use of a universal index of quality of life or disability, which implies an even more questionable way of aggregating multi-dimensional data with heterogeneous scaling properties.

UTILISATION OF IALYs IN HEALTH DECISION-MAKING: THE LEAGUE TABLES

In 1982, Kaplan and Bush summarised several cost-utility studies in a table that compared the cost-effectiveness of several screening programmes per well-year gained using the Quality of Well-Being Scale (Kaplan & Bush, 1982). In 1992, Laupacis and colleagues developed the league table approach, designing a grid that combined information on the quality of the studies being considered and the cost-per-QALY of interventions. The quality of every study was rated in three categories (effectiveness, quality of life and costs), and then the study was classified according to four levels of evidence (I: highest quality in the three categories, to IV: Highest quality in none). The alternatives were classified into five grades (from grade A: most effective and cost-saving, to grade E: least effective and most costly interventions)

(Laupacis et al, 1992). The more effective and less costly alternative *dominates* over the others. Mason (1994) has reviewed the pros and cons of such techniques, stressing the danger of presenting cost-utility ratios in a highly aggregated form, and the importance of including only direct costs or even descriptive outcome data. Current league tables, based on cost-utility data, may not be useful for decision-making. The enormous variability in the calculation techniques and data sources makes the comparison nearly impossible unless the same method is used across studies (Revicki, 1995).

Some practical applications of utility measures for policy decision-making in Oregon and in the North Western Health Authority in the UK, yield conflicting results (La Puma & Lawlor, 1990; Gudex, 1990; Spiegelhalter et al, 1992).

ALTERNATIVES TO CLASSICAL COST-UTILITY ANALYSIS

Alternatives to traditional CUA are being proposed at nearly all stages of the health decision process. The use of individual health-status measures, such as the Individual Quality of Life (IQoL) instruments have already been discussed. Alternatives to QALY include multi-dimensional representation of disablement (Hirst, 1990); or the use of other single measures such as HYEs, SAVE or Q-Twist. Healthy Years Equivalents (HYEs) is a measure based on scenarios of ill-health over a given time period, intended to overcome some problems of QALYs, such as the influence of duration of health condition and expected prognosis. It uses a two-stage standard gamble technique to perform preference measurements for each unique health path (Mehrez & Gafni, 1991). Canadian Guidelines do not favour this approach until more research is available (Torrance et al, 1996). The Saved Young Life Equivalents (SAVE) is another alternative to QALYs which yield social values from health improvements instead of valuing preferences for health states (Nord, 1992). Quality-adjusted Time Without Symptoms or Toxicity (Q-Twist) counts disease progression or severe adverse events as negative outcomes (Guyatt et al, 1993), introducing new elements that may be useful in the cost-analysis of certain psychotropic drugs, such as antipsychotics. However, all these alternatives are at their infancy and their properties cannot be fully analysed yet.

Cost-effectiveness analysis, including highly reliable, disaggregate data regarding health-status QoL and disability, may provide a cautious alternative to classical CUA, until better measures have been tested.

CONCLUSIONS

Health economists' perspective on quality of life differs greatly from that developed in the medical sector. Cost-utility analysis was designed as an economic tool for improving health decision-making by producing a common output index that would integrate costs and intangibles in order to allow cross-comparison. However, CUA is funded on a number of assumptions that are not well established, some of them without an adequate theoretical background. CUA uses a series of techniques, most of them at different stages of development, which provide heterogeneous results. These differences prevent any possibility of comparison among the available studies. Most instruments for measuring utility do not fulfil quality criteria regarding their reliability, validity and transferability, and the feasibility of constructing a universal health index (IALY) is hampered with serious doubts, as are its applications for decision-making using systems such as the QALY league tables.

These problems are even greater in the case of mental disorders. Nevertheless, reports such as the 1990 Global Burden of Disease study (World Bank Report, 1993) clarify the importance of mental diseases in comparison with other non-infectious diseases and highlight the underfunding of this group of disorders. Although flawed and imperfect, some economic information is better than none, as it may contribute to highlighting the importance of mental diseases within the health sector. On the other hand, the overall validity of cost-per-QALY studies in psychopharmacology is questionable, unless it is limited to the local level.

This review has been critical of current cost-utility information, although quality of life data must be included in cost analysis. At present, some alternatives to the available methodologies are being developed. Economists have furnished new technologies, concepts and paradigms to our field. Until now, results have been either confusing or relatively modest. In any case, these technologies have come to stay and they will eventually influence every aspect of psychiatric research.

ACKNOWLEDGEMENT

This paper was supported by the Spanish "Fondo de Investigaciones Sanitarias" (FIS Grant no. 95/1961).

CHAPTER TWENTY-THREE

Organisation of Care and Quality of Life of Persons with Serious and Persistent Mental Illness

David Mechanic

Quality of life (QoL) is a broad arena encompassing both objective and subjective components of performance and well-being as well as environmental aspects. Although effective medical and psychiatric care that improves affect and function typically improves quality of life also in many ways, other aspects are remote from what psychiatrists and other doctors do. Thus it is essential to distinguish carefully between what can reasonably be expected from high-quality medical interventions and what facets must depend on other social or community initiatives. In adopting QoL as a relevant outcome in evaluating mental health services more broadly, we must be realistic as to what can be expected from one or another intervention. Applying this concept inappropriately or too globally can lead us to underestimate the usefulness of specialised interventions.

This point can be illustrated by the perceived needs of persons with serious and persistent mental illness. We asked clients about the services they were receiving and their needs for more help in some 15 aspects and found that the highest priorities were in those remote from usual conceptions of psychiatric care (Uttaro & Mechanic, 1994). Putting it simply, what clients most wanted was to have the roles and opportunities that most people have: activities to keep oneself occupied and involved, intimate relationships with boyfriends or girlfriends, a job, a decent place to live, and money. Psychiatric care tends to focus on medication management, and most were receiving all such help they wanted: only 5% wanted more help with medication. In contrast, there was a high level of expressed need for social role restoration, and assistance for controlling symptoms and feelings of anger.

These data suggest that improving patients' quality of life in many high-priority areas is likely to depend on aspects substantially outside the control of mental health personnel. Such personnel could do a great deal to help the client locate suitable housing, attain disability and social security benefits, get a job and perform appropriately, and the like. But even in the best of circumstances, they have little control over the housing stock, the adequacy of disability entitlements, or the availability of jobs and what they pay. Moreover, their capacity to deal with disorganised families, community stigma, and threatening neighbourhoods that lead to victimisation is also quite limited. Yet many of these factors are central to patients' lives and how they perceive them.

As we proceed to examine organisational and financial arrangements that facilitate improved QoL, two other elements must be kept in mind. First, there is now abundant evidence that the association between objective and subjective indicators of quality of life is modest. Thus, while it is appropriate to set standards for decent minimal living conditions, these may not be correlated with subjective response. For example, most people in the community perceive shelter in supervised housing and in public shelters, however limited, as preferable to living on the streets, but some patients see the issue differently. This response can often be attributed to mental illness, but not always: there are many trade-offs in living conditions. Residence in a dilapidated and impoverished area may offer a patient more opportunities for activities and resources to reduce daily boredom than a more middle-class residence, but such residence also increases the probability of victimisation. Clients may prefer the risk because of the need to reduce the awful boredom they feel. Thus, comprehensive judgements of overall QoL are difficult to make without knowing their preferences.

Second, it is evident that while one can easily measure global QoL, different factors affect varying dimensions of it. Some general factors such as positive affect and sense of personal control and empowerment, relate to many different dimensions of QoL, but even these are related more strongly to some dimensions than to others (Rosenfield & Nease-Todd, 1993). Thus, in studying the impact of any specific intervention, whether in housing, employment, or anything else, it is essential to use the correct QoL outcome measure. Simply measuring global QoL may underestimate the value of the intervention.

THE ROLE OF CLIENT AFFECT IN EVALUATING QoL

Some studies measure objective aspects of the quality of the patient environment by having independent raters make the assessment; early important work on the assessment of hospital environments on patient function, for example, was of this kind. Raters assessed how much time patients spent doing nothing, whether they had a place to keep personal possessions, whether they had basic personal items, and so on (Wing, 1993). Most studies of QoL, however, focus on reports or ratings of clients about their lives and how they perceive them. It is well established that persons with negative affect not only provide more negative subjective responses, but also may report objective aspects differently, such as how many friends they have, the safety of their neighbourhoods, the quality of their housing, and recreational opportunities available to them.

In the case of "objective" QoL indicators, it is often possible to check the respondent's report against independent observations or reports by other informants about the same issues. Subjective QoL, however, cannot be validated in the same way. Depressive symptoms at the time of the interview represent perhaps the single best predictor of what people say about their lives, and particularly the subjective aspects (Mechanic et al, 1994). However, there are alternative ways in which this can be interpreted. To the extent that clients regard their lives as dismal, for whatever reason, it is still dismal and this is significant. From a practical standpoint, however, we often want to separate those factors affecting QoL which are associated directly with illness and comorbidities from those due to other factors. In this context, we might regard the effects of depression and other negative affects as artefacts. One corrective approach is to use multivariate statistical techniques that allow the predictors of QoL to be examined, independent of measures of negative affect. In my judgement, it is important to do so routinely in evaluating the wide assortment of factors that affect QoL.

ISSUES IN FINANCING AND ORGANISATION OF SERVICES

The foregoing should already make clear that protecting or enhancing the quality of life of persons with serious mental illness extends well beyond even the most excellent medical and psychiatric care. The problem is very much compounded outside of hospital, and especially in large urban areas, where mental health personnel have little control over the environment or the client. Hospital care has many disadvantages, but those responsible for the service have control over many aspects of the patient's life including housing, nutrition, supervision, and a programme of daily activity. In communities, and particularly in large densely populated urban areas, these responsibilities are dispersed among different levels of government and different sectoral bureaucracies, each with its own goals, culture, priorities, and reward structures. Bringing the necessary services together is a formidable endeavour. The primary challenge of community mental health is to direct the efforts of these various bureaucracies in the case of individual patients and to reduce fragmentation. The problematic areas often include social services, employment and vocational services, housing, social security and disability insurance, criminal justice, and even medical care.

Systems of services can only be as good as the quality of the specific interventions they incorporate. In many areas affecting quality of life, we lack sufficient information as to what modalities work best with patients who vary in diagnosis, psychiatric history, dangerousness, age, education, ethnicity and culture, and other characteristics. Attention to family structures and processes is important for all patients, but in some cultural groups, it is difficult even to begin without involving the family in organising treatment and care. Many mental health programmes include sheltered work and employment, but relatively few deal well with patients who have high levels of education and skill. Client groups are highly heterogeneous and do not respond uniformly to different forms of intervention.

Whatever the current state of psychiatric and social intervention, effectiveness will also depend on the organisational and financial arrangements for providing services. To address quality of life issues, the service package must be comprehensive, flexible, and accessible; continuity of responsibility and care to avoid fragmentation must be assured. Moreover, a clinical and financial structure must be in place to ensure that the necessary mix of services, needed at any point in time, can be accessed. The typical services approach directed to this task is case management.

CASE MANAGEMENT

Case management is a term that misleads more than it reveals: the term has now become politically correct and it is applied to models that have little in common (Spitz, 1978). Case managers vary in their professional education and skills, ranging in background from graduate nursing, social work, and psychology to having little training or experience. Case managers may perform a variety of functions; some provide therapy as well as brokering other needed services, while some others work entirely on the brokering principle. Some case managers may have considerable control over many of the resources needed, while others can do little more than exhort professionals and bureaucratic officials, who may have little regard for them and are not much influenced. Caseloads may vary from as few as 10 patients per case manager in intensive programmes to as many as 50 or even 100. Case managers often work within bureaucracies where they are faced with intense conflict between service needs and economics, and where the rewards are greater for withholding services than for meeting people's needs. Finally, case management may be organized around individuals or teams, be more or less assertive, and may be free-standing or organised within a well-planned system of services that assumes continuing clinical responsibility for patients, wherever they might be.

Given this diversity, it should be no surprise that the case management literature gives little guidance. Rarely does it report on the characteristics of patients, medication history and compliance, and many other crucial issues. Some studies find that case management is cost-beneficial, while others find that it increases costs without improving patient function or quality of life (Franklin et al, 1987). In many instances, case management is seen to reduce the use of in-patient care, but only occasionally is it convincingly demonstrated that patients' outcomes are also improved (Olfson, 1990). Most studies have serious selection biases and other methodological problems, and rarely is sufficient information provided on what works well with different subgroups of patients. It seems clear enough that a certain intensity of services is needed to achieve positive effects, but there is no linear relationship between cost and staff intensity on the one hand and the quality of the outcomes achieved on the other (Dietzen & Bond, 1993).

The model of assertive case management (PACT) developed in Wisconsin by Stein and Test (1980) stands out as one of the more successful approaches, supported by the results of reasonably good randomised trials in several countries (New South Wales Dept. of Health, 1983; Marks et al, 1994). Evaluation of this model showed that highly impaired patients could be cared for almost exclusively in the community. When compared to randomised controls, patients had higher earnings from work, involvement in more social activities, more contact with friends, greater life satisfaction, and also fewer symptoms. Economic evaluations of this and other PACT-like programmes suggest that they have higher cost-benefit outcomes than conventional care (Weisbrod et al, 1980; Knapp et al, 1994). Most efforts to replicate the programme show that in-patient care can be reduced, but many do not replicate the favourable findings on symptoms and function. Most studies of community care, in contrast to conventional in-patient/out-patient care, find higher patient satisfaction.

Some of these conflicting findings may be due to variations in the assertive case management, contrasting patient populations, varying medication compliance, and different evaluation approaches. It is likely that case management works better when organised carefully within an integrated programme of services that assumes long-term clinical responsibility for the patient. Given our limited understanding of how to treat severe and persistent illness, it may be unreasonable to expect long-term improvement in clinical status. But case management embedded in a comprehensive system should be able to assist patients and improve social functioning, stability of living situation, satisfaction, and other aspects of quality of life.

ORGANISATIONAL AND FINANCIAL APPROACHES

Stein attributes some of the success of assertive community treatment to Wisconsin's system of financing mental health services and the incentives it established to consider carefully the trade-offs between the use of in-patient care and alternative community services (Stein, 1989). In Wisconsin, the county mental health board receives a global budget for services, whether provided on an in-patient or community basis. To the extent that patients in the PACT programme use in-patient services, the charges must be paid from its budget, so that PACT staff have an incentive to consider carefully the necessity for in-patient care. Should they use too much such care, they substantially reduce their community care budget and threaten their own service system and jobs. However, while the financing system in Wisconsin is an enabling structure, it is insufficient. Many other counties with the same funding system have been slow to modify traditional practice: important explanatory factors for this difference include professional inertia, poor leadership, and traditional college and university training structures that emphasise psychotherapeutic training. A further barrier is the difficulty of obtaining the necessary conversion funding required during the transition period, when it is essential to retain existing funds while new ones are being established.

In the past decade, four strategies have been advocated as ways to organise community services to provide more comprehensive care and improve clients' quality of life. These include: capitation models of various kinds that seek to modify the typical financial incentives that encourage excessive in-patient treatment; development of comprehensive mental health authorities with an improved capacity to take clinical responsibility and control a broader range of resources; design of hospital and out-patient reimbursement systems that seek to change the goals and priorities of treatment; and application of a variety of managed care approaches, designed to broaden the array of available services while keeping costs under control. All of these approaches are early in their evolution, and require continuing evaluation.

Each approach seeks in one way or another to expand the comprehensiveness of services and allow treatment personnel broader choices, to facilitate trade-offs between different types of services. They all seek, in one way or another, to address the fundamental problem of fragmentation and to facilitate coordination in providing the services that a seriously mentally ill person might require. They seek in various ways to break down the rigid separation of funding streams and the segmentation among areas of service. And they do this in a context in which there are many governmental and bureaucratic barriers that make coordination difficult.

CAPITATION APPROACHES

Capitation involves prepayment of a fixed sum for each patient for a defined range of services, regardless of how many services the patient actually uses. For providers, capitation offers the advantage of knowing their budget in advance and providing sufficient capital to develop new services or acquire new equipment. The payers, in turn, know their costs in advance, transfer financial risk to providers, and give providers incentives to use services efficiently. The theory is that being required to function within fixed budgets, providers will make more thoughtful and efficient decisions. Capitation is seen as preferable to global budgets, in that the provider is held responsible for caring for specific patients and not simply for doing the best it can within a catchment area. In the latter case, providers can too easily choose more attractive and less difficult clients and ignore those who may most require services.

The motive behind capitating psychiatric patients is different from the logic of capitation in general medical care, where transfer of financial risk is a central feature (Mechanic & Aiken, 1989). Most seriously mentally ill people who are capitated will need many services, and capitation is valued less for averaging risk than as a device to consolidate resources, to assign clinical responsibility for difficult patients, and to encourage comprehensive systems of care. In most instances where such approaches have been used, the focus has been on long-term hospital patients being returned to the community, but capitation has also been applied to out-patients (Babigian & Marshall, 1989). Typically, health maintenance organisations (HMOs) that specialise in mental health are existing community mental health centres that accept clinical responsibility for providing a specified range of services for specific patients, at an agreed price. Thus, the mental health centre can be held accountable for ensuring that these defined patients receive suitable care. Some of the capitation programmes have been broad in scope, encompassing housing, medical care, social services, psychosocial education, and other services, in addition to basic medical and psychiatric care. However, implementation of the mental health HMO concept has been difficult, because few people in the mental health field have the financial and managerial capacity to develop and administer these entities. It has taken as much as a decade to put such programmes into place. Diagnosis is a poor predictor of the use of resources in psychiatry (Taube et al, 1984), and we lack alternative indicators that are practical for pricing the capitation, so that providers are reluctant to assume financial risk. Most mental health providers are relatively small organisations, and should they unexpectedly enrol a disproportionate number of very expensive patients, they could be put in great financial difficulty. As a result, complex risk-sharing arrangements have to be negotiated. Moreover, garnering the funds for the needed capitation involves cooperation among varying government agencies, each bound by its own legal and bureaucratic criteria, which is no easy task. American experience indicates that capitated programmes can take long-term hospital patients and care for them at much lower cost than the hospital. But there is, as yet, no convincing evidence of superior functional or quality of life outcomes. A number of evaluations of this matter are now in process.

An alternative capitation approach is to "mainstream" persons with severe mental illness into existing HMOs that have been organised to provide medical care for the broader population (Mechanic & Aiken, 1989). These HMOs contract to provide needed medical and mental health services, although most have had only limited experience with the severely mentally ill. These generic HMOs are expected to provide the needed services, either directly or by contract with specialty mental health providers. Mainstreaming is difficult because persons with serious mental illness have high and unpredictable costs for medical as well as mental health needs, and an adequate methodology is lacking for adjusting capitation payments appropriately. In the most ambitious evaluation of mainstreaming, the largest HMO enrolling the greatest number of mentally ill clients withdrew from the project after only seven months because of the uncertain financial risk (Christianson et al, 1989).

While mainstreaming may work well for persons with less severe disorders, generic HMOs are not organised to provide the range of services needed by persons with severe and persistent disorders. Quantitative evidence is difficult to obtain, but experience suggests that the complicated psychiatric patient does not get adequate care in this context (Schlesinger & Mechanic, 1993). There is also some evidence that patients with major depression fare less well in capitated practice than in fee-for-service practice (Rogers et al, 1993). HMOs differ in their organisational structures, however, so that it is difficult to generalise from one situation to another. Some HMOs control referral very stringently, while others may allow patients to refer themselves to mental health providers. In the mainstreaming demonstration project discussed above, mentally ill enrollees were allowed to self-refer. In a randomised study covering about a year of experience, the researchers found that patterns of use of mental health services were comparable in the HMOs where there were no gatekeepers to referral and in fee-for-service situations. A major difference, however, was that mentally ill patients in the HMO were using public sector services, and most of these services were not being reimbursed by the HMOs (Christianson et al, 1992). In short, the HMOs were cost-shifting to the public sector. It is not clear what services would have been available to mentally ill HMO patients, had there not been a broad array of public sector services.

A number of American states are concerned about the high costs of care for disabled persons in Medicaid – a public sector programme that serves poor persons with disabilities. Thus, several are now capitating these patients through community mental health centres, and in some instances by mainstreaming them into generic HMOs. In the coming years, we should learn a great deal more about the potentialities and pitfalls of this approach, but experience thus far suggests the need to proceed carefully. The seriously mentally ill, who are not particularly favoured clients under any circumstances, may do poorly in any organisational setting that is not tailored specifically to meet their special needs.

MENTAL HEALTH AUTHORITIES

Services in large urban areas are especially fragmented, with responsibility often divided among levels of government and medical and welfare bureaucracies that are large, complex, and distant from the life of the individual client. It is often difficult to identify who is responsible for the patient's welfare, and communication among individuals serving the patient in varying service sectors is commonly poor. Because transportation is easily available, patients travel readily from one jurisdiction to another, often using services in a duplicative and uncoordinated fashion.

One possible solution to this fragmentation is to develop effective mental health authorities that have strong managerial capacity and that take clinical responsibility for organising services, to ensure that patients can gain access to the range of services they need. Such authorities, it has been argued, can organise assertive case management programmes and ensure that every patient is appropriately linked, can develop new housing and other community care services and facilities, and can bring together different funding streams in a way that allows clinicians to make trade-offs across a range of services.

To test this concept, the Robert Wood Johnson Foundation and the US Department of Housing and Urban Development provided $125 million in development funds and housing vouchers over five years to nine large American cities including Philadelphia, Baltimore, and Denver. However, experience showed that it was much more difficult to achieve this goal in the complex political environments of these communities than originally anticipated. At the end of five years, most had made progress in developing viable authorities, although the level of accomplishment depended a great deal on where each had started (Morrissey et al, 1994). A careful evaluation of this effort found that these organisations were able to restructure the services environment, and they improved the continuity of care available to patients (Lehmann, 1994).

From the start, those who designed the intervention believed that the only appropriate criterion for success was the ability to demonstrate that patients' levels of function and quality of life would improve as a result of structural reform. The evidence of increased continuity of care would lead to such expectations, but unfortunately, the evaluation could show no direct tangible benefit for patients, as measured individually (Lehman, 1994). One important goal of the demonstration was to have the mental health authorities gain control over some of the massive funding for mental hospitals, so that a better balance could be achieved between hospital and community care and money could more easily follow the patient. For the most part, though, the authorities were not successful, illustrating again the entrenched power of mental hospital interests.

Five years is a short interval for major structural change, but given the efforts and funds that went into this demonstration, the results are disappointing. The cities were selected because of their leadership, favourable environment, and potential for success, yet despite these advantages, their developmental efforts had many false starts and were difficult. More complex cities such as New York, Los Angeles and Chicago were not included in the demonstration, because their potential for developing authorities of this kind seemed less promising. In the light of the careful selection that was made, the accomplishments must be seen as modest, but in retrospect, it seems clear that much more attention should have been directed to the quality of the services themselves. Good structures are enabling frameworks, but ultimately what happens to patients depends on caregivers and the services they provide.

ALTERNATIVE REIMBURSEMENT APPROACHES

Since a dominant assumption of economics is that individuals and institutions will respond to financial incentives, an important approach is to try to build appropriate incentives into reimbursement schemes to achieve particular goals. The single most important example in the American context is Medicare's Prospective Payment System (PPS) that reimburses hospitals by diagnostically related groups (DRGs). Hospitals receive a fixed amount for each case, regardless of the resources they use. The belief is that the incentive of a fixed payment encourages the hospital to be more thoughtful and efficient about how it uses resources than it would be with a cost reimbursement system. The evidence shows that the PPS has saved many billions of dollars (Russell, 1989), without harming the quality of care. However, much of in-patient psychiatric care has been exempt from PPS, because psychiatric diagnosis is a particularly poor predictor of resource utilisation.

Both government and private insurers often use the reimbursement system to attempt to change practice behaviour, and at the most simple level, the relative amount paid for varying procedures affects the mix of services provided. In the United States, technical procedures are reimbursed at much higher rates than cognitive services, giving excessive encouragement to the technological imperative. However, efforts have been made in recent years to modify medical reimbursement so as to change this trend. Similarly, mental health authorities are increasingly experimenting with reimbursement incentives to achieve a variety of objectives.

Modifying reimbursement incentives, however, is more complex than may at first appear. Those who design such systems must clearly understand the values of those they are attempting to influence and must have clear conceptions of how changing institutional incentives will affect individual professional behaviour. Hospitals and mental health programmes are complex behavioural systems, with their own ideologies and norms, and the implicit message of reimbursement systems has to be understandable, focused, clear, and of sufficient force to effect the desired changes in institutional behaviour. This does not always occur.

New York State, for example, initiated complex changes in its in-patient and out-patient psychiatric reimbursement systems, to achieve a variety of objectives. Among the goals were: (1) to increase in-patient capacity, without adding beds, by reducing length of stay; (2) to get hospitals to change their case-mix towards more persons with serious and persistent mental illness; (3) to encourage improved discharge planning and linkage between in-patient and out-patient services; and (4) to increase the intensity of out-patient aftercare to avoid in-patient recidivism.

Thus, the state developed a complex payment system that reimburses hospitals differently for patients with varying diagnostic characteristics and at different rates for varying stages of the in-patient stay. For example, reimbursement was higher for caring for persistent mentally ill patients and for the early part of the in-patient stay. After the average length of stay for a diagnostic category was reached, reimbursement was reduced to 85% of the standard rate, to encourage earlier discharge. Hospitals were also paid an additional sum if a discharged patient in the Medicaid programme received out-patient services within ten days of discharge, as an incentive to improve discharge planning and linkage. Out-patient payments were substantially increased for certain high-priority clients, to encourage greater attention to their needs.

The programme was not successful in achieving its ambitious but complicated goals (Boyer & Mechanic, 1994), and, in retrospect, the reasons are clear. The practice environment was much more complex than those who designed the reimbursement system understood, and its implementation was flawed in many ways. Those who were most responsible for implementing the goals at the service level were not directly affected by the incentives and sometimes were not even aware of them. The reimbursement system did not relay clear and forceful incentives, and also it provided various opportunities for "gaming" the system, which the hospitals understood and used.

Nevertheless, reimbursement approaches remain as viable strategies for achieving some important objectives in mental health services. In most countries in the world, budgeting and reimbursement continues to favour in-patient against out-patient care, and payment approaches are being tried that make it more possible for money to follow the patient. One important approach is to hold the mental health entity responsible for both in-patient and out-patient care within a consolidated budget, thus encouraging thoughtful purchasing of in-patient services. Efforts along these lines continue, and we can anticipate learning a great deal more about how to make financial incentives effective in the years ahead.

MANAGED MENTAL HEALTH CARE

Managed care (MC) is a vague term encompassing some of the concepts already discussed, such as the use of capitation and PACT-like programmes that take broad longitudinal responsibility for patients' care in the home, community, clinic, or hospital. The section that follows, however, focuses primarily on one rapidly growing facet of managed care – utilisation review of mental health services.

In the Clinton health reform plan in the United States, it was assumed that the introduction of managed care would allow substantial broadening of the range of services available. Once a managed care structure was in place, it was argued, all necessary medical and mental health services could be provided within a comprehensive framework, without excessive growth in medical expenditures. The dominant managed care approach affecting most people, and increasingly important in mental health services, is utilisation management (UM).

UM is a customised product, sold by UM companies both to business firms who are self-insured for their own health care costs and to public mental health programmes. Thus, there are many different types of managed care arrangements and it is difficult to generalise about them. The core components of UM are pre-certification of hospital admission or the use of some expensive diagnostic or treatment interventions, concurrent review of in-patient length of stay, and case-management of high-cost cases (Hodgkin, 1992). In pre-certification, doctors or their staff must contact a representative of the UM company and provide information about the case, seeking approval to use an expensive resource such as in-patient care. Should the request be questioned or denied, the clinician typically has an opportunity to discuss the issue with a psychiatrist employed by the UM firm, and they may negotiate about the proper treatment approach. Further methods of appeal are also available to the clinician.

Case management is applied to high-cost cases, where clinicians employed by the UM firm work with the doctor to develop an appropriate treatment plan that makes use of alternatives to in-patient care as much as possible. Case managers can authorise services that are not covered by the services contract, and thus may have a great deal of flexibility. Cynics argue that the only motivation of UM is to reduce costs, whereas UM representatives maintain that the process is motivated by and encourages a more thoughtful and well-integrated treatment plan.

It is difficult to assess these claims because of the rapidly changing character of the UM industry and the enormous variability in their practices (Mechanic et al, 1995). UM firms claim significant cost-savings, but the data are very much biased by the fact that employers who adopt UM typically have high costs, which are then brought closer to the average. It is uncertain that lower-cost companies would have comparable experience. Also, costs are typically measured in terms of cost-savings for the employer, but adequate assessments must also consider costs and social burdens that might be transferred to the patient, the family, the doctor, or even the community. No study has looked at these costs from a broad point of view.

From a theoretical viewpoint, UM offers the potential to develop a treatment plan carefully, to select from a broad menu of possible services, and to design an integrated and longitudinal strategy for the patient's care. It also provides the capacity to reduce costs by denying services without offering suitable alternatives. Examples of both types of practice are readily identified, but it is extraordinarily difficult to ascertain how UM functions on average. A great deal depends on the skill and training of those who carry out the reviews and case management, the quality of their supervision, and the incentives and reward structures of the companies themselves. The only thing fully clear at this point is that managed care and utilisation review are here to stay, and have become a central aspect of the mental health scene.

THE NEED FOR AN INTEGRATED STRATEGY

As emphasised throughout this chapter, there are formidable challenges in organising effective services for persons with severe and persistent mental illness. Each of the major strategies discussed has some potential, but they are often applied in competing and contradictory ways that give confusing messages. Such strategies obviously work better when they are consistent and reinforce one another (Mechanic, 1991). For example, assertive community treatment programmes, organised on capitation and supported by a strong health authority that provides technical assistance and community support, are likely to be more stable and politically resilient than free-standing entities. Strong UM procedures, built-in to the programme, are helpful in ensuring that the team remains thoughtful about alternative treatments and its treatment choices. Finally, the incentives affecting budgeting within the capitation framework can help to ensure that money follows best practice and not simply the routines that have become comfortable.

The strategies discussed all remain uncertain, and they may function differently for varying patient populations and in different organisational environments. Moreover, they may affect differently how treatment programmes affect symptoms, function, and quality of life. Research in this field can only be illustrative and alert us to difficulties (Mechanic, 1996); it cannot provide definitive answers. Situations are too diverse, and practices too varied and changing, to allow easy generalisation from one instance to another. Perhaps the most useful function of all these initiatives is to induce caregivers to be thoughtful about what they do and about the basis for their treatment and care choices. Certainly that in itself, supported by the active participation of patients and their families in treatment choices, can contribute importantly to making services more responsive to client populations and their quality of life.

CHAPTER TWENTY-FOUR

Quality of Life and Mental Disorders: A Global Perspective

Norman Sartorius

INTRODUCTION

Ideally, a mental health programme should have at its disposal a set of measurement tools which will enable it to reduce errors in the identification and diagnosis of mental illness, allow it to control the treatment process and facilitate the assessment of the impact which the illness has on the patients, on their families and communities, and on the health-care system. Table 24.1 shows the domains that should be covered by such a set of tools.

The development of this arsenal of tools has been uneven. While major advances have been made in the construction of methods suitable for the assessment and recording of psychiatric symptoms, the progress of technology for the assessment of other characteristics of the patient's condition has been much less spectacular. Well-written case histories, for example, are still the best way to depict patients' life and the circumstances which are relevant for the understanding of the disease process. Instruments for the assessment of course and outcome of diseases are still not very sophisticated and it is usual to see that investigators restrict themselves to producing global ratings of the course of illness (e.g. "episodic") and that the ratings of outcome are given in summary terms (e.g. "favourable"). Operational definitions of course and outcome that have been proposed by various authors over the years are not generally accepted, and the life of instruments often coincides with the life of the study or, worse still, with the length of funding from a particular source.

Tools suitable for the assessment of the health-care system have grown in numbers, often under the influence of changes in funding structure and the insistence of the authorities on quality assurance. They are still more concerned with the process and input characteristics of a service and less trustworthy when it comes to the measurement of: (1) outcome of service interventions or (2)

Table 24.1   Domains that should be covered by the set of instruments available to the mental health programme

1. Identification and Diagnosis
   - symptoms
   - history of illness
   - life story
   - immediate environment
   - impact of illness
   - course and outcome
   - personality
   - impairments
   - disabilities
   - quality of life

2. Control of the treatment process
   - professional and non-professional caregivers
   - operational features of services (e.g. location of service in relation to catchment area)
   - process of care
   - quality assurance
   - cost
   - quality of life of staff and caregivers

3. Outcome and impact of services
   - on patients' illness
   - on the performance and structure of the health system itself
   - on the satisfaction of the patients and the population with the service

assessment of the impact which a particular set of actions in the health-care system had on the society or patient populations as a whole.

APPROACHES TO THE MEASUREMENT OF QUALITY OF LIFE

For a long time, progress in the development of methods for the assessment of quality of life has been hampered by profound differences in attitudes to its evaluation. While some considered that the only way to measure quality of life was to ask individuals about the goals which they set for themselves and their feeling of how close they had come to them, others felt that the assessment must be based on the measurement of assets and opportunities which people have.

Cell A on Figure 24.1 corresponds to the first of the above attitudes: quality of life will, by "subjectivists", be measured on the basis of statements which the individuals concerned will make on their feeling about the remaining distance to the goals which they have set themselves. In this framework, it does not matter, for example, what material belongings the individual has: the only thing that matters is

		Goals set by		
		Patient	Family	Society
Distance to goals assessed by	Patient	A	B	C
	Family	D	E	F
	Society	G	H	I

Figure 24.1   Approaches to the measurement of quality of life (For explanation of capital letters A–I see text)

whether the individual whose quality of life is being assessed feels that he is close to having all the belongings that he or she aims to have. Cell I shows the other extreme: the wider society and its representatives – the government, for example, or doctors representing it – will have to set the goals (e.g. that everyone should have an apartment) and assess whether the person concerned has reached them. If this has happened (e.g. that the person has been placed in an apartment), his or her quality of life will be judged to be good. In between are other cells: for example, in cell E, the position is that the family should set goals for its members and that the members of the family will have to assess the quality of life of individuals with reference to whether they are close to the goals that their family considers to be most important.

Over the years, the fervour of the advocates of the two extreme positions abated and it became obvious that both an objective assessment – of the individuals' positions in life, their symptoms and their capacities – and a subjective assessment by the individuals themselves are important and complementary. The strategy that the World Health Organization adopted in its effort to develop cross-culturally acceptable and applicable methods for the measurement of quality of life exemplifies this position (Sartorius, 1993; Orley & Kuyken, 1994). The definition of quality of life proposed by the World Health Organization is that quality of life is the people's perception of their position in life in relation to their goals and the value system they have accepted and incorporated in their decision-making. This definition places primary importance on the individuals' willingness and capacity to communicate and participate in the assessment of their quality of life. In the WHO Quality of Life Instrument (WHOQOL), a number of domains of individuals' activities have been selected by consulting a large group of scientists and practitioners from different cultures. For each of the domains, a number of "facets" have been defined and for each of these an *objective assessment* (e.g. of the individuals' capacity to walk) and two *subjective assessments* (i.e. how the individuals feel about their capacity to walk and whether this influences their overall quality of life) have been sought.

WHO was not the only one to produce a tool for the measurement of quality of life. Numerous individual researchers and research networks have also produced methods for this assessment, and it is fair to say that it is now possible to measure quality of life in a variety of health-care situations. Not only have methods used for the purpose been improved: it also appears that there is more willingness to apply them. This is certainly the case in the services providing care to people suffering from malignant tumours, in long-term care institutions, and in services dealing with diseases of long duration, such as cardiovascular disorders.

There has also been an increase in the willingness to measure the quality of life of relatives of severely ill and impaired people. On the other hand, although it has often been recommended that changes in quality of life should be routinely assessed in trials of new medicaments, studies in which this was done are still rare.

MEASURING QUALITY OF LIFE IN PSYCHIATRIC PRACTICE AND RESEARCH

In psychiatric services, the assessment of quality of life is still rarely part of routine practice. There are various reasons that could be responsible for this. First, symptoms of mental disorder may resemble statements about poor quality of life. This is particularly true for symptoms of depressive disorders, of neurotic disorders, and of some types of personality disorders.

Second, in severe mental disorders, the disorder may produce an impairment which makes communication with the assessor difficult. This is clearly the case with certain neurological disorders (e.g. those with aphasia) and mental disorders characterised by cognitive impairment of a severity that makes the comprehension of questions posed by the examiner difficult or impossible.

Third, mental disorders are often accompanied by a stigma which affects all aspects of a patient's life. Stigma will persist even after the symptoms of the disorder have disappeared and may be the main reason for the difficulties which the patient experiences.

Fourth, side-effects of some of the methods of treatment currently used in psychiatry can be serious and can impede a precise measurement of the relationship between a specific psychiatric disorder and quality of life. A further complication is that certain side-effects can be at the origin of "secondary" mental disorders (e.g. depressive disorders emerging as a reaction to tardive dyskinesia or to a severe short-term memory loss after intensive electroconvulsive therapy).

Fifth, the differences between cultures affect the form and severity of mental disorders and the manner in which the information about the disorder is obtained. This makes pooling of data and generalisation difficult from any study of quality of life of people with mental disorders.

Sixth, in some disorders (e.g. schizophrenia), symptoms such as paranoid delusions or suspiciousness may distort the answers or make it impossible to assess quality of life using methods based on patients' statements.

Finally, there is the well-known difficulty in reporting on one's emotional states – that while the emotions last, the individuals experiencing them will not be at their best at observing them, and that once an emotion changes retrospective reporting is bound to be only partially valid – this may be more troublesome in psychiatric patients because it is compounded by the presence of (temporary or permanent) impairments of cognitive function inherent in many mental disorders.

Despite these difficulties, reliable measurements of quality of life of people with psychiatric disorders can be obtained, although, in most instances, the application of currently available methods requires special training and skills. It also takes time and effort, which health staff in general are unlikely to offer unless a dramatic change happens in their estimation of how important quality of life assessment is for their everyday work.

REASONS FOR MEASURING QUALITY OF LIFE IN MENTAL HEALTH PROGRAMMES

Regardless of difficulties, the quality of life of people with a mental disorder should be measured because of several reasons.

First, some forms of mental disorders are long-lasting and their symptoms persist when currently available treatments are applied. This does not mean that the mental health services can cease their efforts to help: rather, that further efforts should be directed to improving the patient's quality of life, despite the continuing presence of symptoms or impairments.

Second, the public health importance of the rehabilitation of the mentally ill and impaired is growing. The number of people disabled because of mental disorders is large – in many industrialised countries, up to 40% of all those disabled owe their disablement to a neurological or mental disorder. Also, there are good reasons to believe that the absolute and relative numbers of people disabled by these disorders will continue to increase. The extension of the life expectancy of those who suffer from chronic mental disorders will increase the prevalence of these disorders, even if incidence rates remain the same. The growing capacity to save people from dying – for example from a parasitic disease involving the brain or from an injury to the central nervous system – may also lead to a greater incidence of organic mental disorders. The ageing of populations increases the numbers of those at risk to become mentally ill.

While treatment of many mental disorders is possible and effective, an important proportion of those affected by a mental disorder will remain impaired and disabled. In current times, it is becoming obvious that their rehabilitation has to be organised, recognising that the central goal of rehabilitation of the mentally ill is the improvement of their overall quality of life, as perceived by the patients and their immediate families. Subsidiary goals could be employment or integration into the community, but these should not be seen as imperative, nor should their attainment be considered as the sole or principal indicator of success of a rehabilitation process. A sizeable proportion of the world's population will not have to be employed in the near future and will not be able to find paid work; economic productivity and technological developments have already made many earlier projections of the size of the labour force obsolete. Many of the earlier goals of rehabilitation have now lost their relevance: the quality of life of people with disability gains in importance in parallel with the changes in society mentioned above and with the overall increase of priority given to improve the quality of life of non-disabled citizens.

Third, the tasks of psychiatry do not stop at the prevention and treatment of mental disorders. Psychiatry is a discipline that should assume the leadership in efforts to make health care in general more humane and inspired by a profound respect for the patient and his feelings. Advocacy of the notion that an improved quality of life is the central goal of health care is therefore clearly within its responsibility.

Fourth, psychiatric skills and knowledge could play a crucial role in the development of methods of assessment of quality of life. The measurement of quality of life has to rely on communication with the individual. Communication skills are clearly in the domain of psychiatry and the disciplines related to it (e.g. psychology), and it is therefore necessary to ensure that these skills and the technical input of mental health programmes are maintained in the process of developing measurements of quality of life in health care.

Fifth, psychiatric work, particularly in dealing with chronic mental disorder, depends on productive and extensive partnership between mental health workers and the patients' families. The participation of the latter in the process of helping the mentally ill will depend on the changes in the quality of their life which this partnership brings to them. Mental health programmes must therefore – if they want to continue to rely on the support of the families and communities of the mentally ill – develop ways of measuring the quality of life of patients' families and incorporate specific measures to improve it in the operation of mental health and other health services.

ADDITIONAL REASONS FOR MEASURING QUALITY OF LIFE IN HEALTH CARE

Measuring quality of life and making its improvement prominent in all health work is an essential corrective to a number of trends in modern health care (see Figure 24.2).

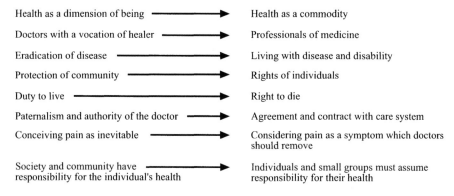

Figure 24.2   Trends in health care

Each of these trends has the potential of dehumanising medical care. When health begins to be conceived as a commodity which should be on the market, purchased, and sold to the highest bidder, the ethical underpinnings of medicine are in danger of being neglected. The chief reason for providing medical care is ethical: a civilised society must help those of its members who are sick, distressed, or disadvantaged. If medical care is provided for economic reasons, health services will be in competition with all others vying for the resources they need to purchase other commodities. If the ethical imperative to provide care is replaced by financial arguments, both society and patients are likely to lose out. Insistence on improved quality of life as a main desirable outcome of health care, on the other hand, lifts health care from the market place to the level of equity – which civilised societies are bound to search for above all else.

The change of health workers' perception of their own roles has similar consequences. As long as health workers see their tasks as part of a humanitarian calling, their satisfaction with the work they do will be high and their motivation to be at the service of their patient will endure. Once they see themselves as health-care professionals performing in relation to the payment they receive, many of the activities they have to perform in order to provide service will be perceived as a burden. In such a situation, health workers will have their sense of purpose stunted. However, being conscious of the inextricable links between the spiritual dimensions of health care and other efforts to increase quality of life can help the care provider and the patient in ways few other strategies can.

The gradual growth of awareness that the optimistic predictions of the early twentieth century about the eradication of all diseases by revolutionary new technologies of treatment and prevention are unlikely to be realised, imposes the duty to think of strategies which will enable patients to continue living a decent life, despite their chronic diseases. The success of such strategies must be measured in terms of quality of life.

The perception of pain as an inevitable part of existence and acceptance of the total authority of the doctor both tend to protect the individual from the diminution of quality of life that disease and medical intervention can bring. However, there are numerous indications that both of these perceptions are losing strength. Patients less and less frequently conceive of pain as an inevitable fact: rather, they see it as a medical problem for which doctors must find a remedy. When this does not happen, it is perceived as a doctor's failure or as an ominous sign. The change in the acceptance of the authority of the doctor has also affected the perception of illness and quality of life. More data about the way in which this change of the doctor–patient relationship affects quality of life would be useful in thinking about strategies of health education and in conceiving curricula for students of medicine and other health-related professions.

The change in the assignment of responsibility for health from the society to the individual also has profound effects on the expectations about care and the motivation to undertake an action to improve health. Coercive mass health measures have often protected the health of individuals. Now that coercion is by and large becoming an unacceptable way to provide care or prevent disease, the acceptance of preventive measures will depend on the motivation of individuals to do something about their health; this will depend on the trade-off in terms of a perceived gain in health and diminished quality of life caused by the measure (e.g. by stopping smoking). The task of public health authorities here will be to assess the impact which the public health measures that they propose will have on the quality of life of individuals, in order to be able to estimate acceptance rates for their interventions.

TASKS BEFORE US

If we decide to use the full potential of the concept of quality of life, a number of methodological and practical challenges await us. The first of the methodological challenges – and perhaps the most difficult one – is to improve methods for the measurement of quality of life in individuals who cannot communicate with the person carrying out the assessment. Children, the demented, and other people suffering from disorders impairing their capacity to communicate are not only very numerous but also the most vulnerable and defenceless. It is clear that, in such instances, we can at best hope for an estimate of quality of life; we have, however, to make this estimate as valid as possible.

Another major methodological challenge is the identification of those aspects of our instruments which are particularly likely to be difficult to apply in a culture different from the one in which they were produced. Transculturally valid instruments are necessary even when the assessments are done in only one institution and when there is no intention to carry out comparative studies involving other investigators in other countries: the millions of migrants and the extraordinary mixture of cultural influences which characterise this century bring different cultures before our door, where we work.

A third methodological challenge is to find ways of incorporating quality of life assessment into other assessment instruments used in health care. The validity of our measurements, when done in the framework of other examinations, will need to be established; what is more, it will be necessary to identify items in currently widely used instruments that could serve as a proxy for quality of life measurement – at least until quality of life assessment becomes a routine examination in medicine.

A fourth methodological challenge resides in the necessity to simplify instruments so as to make them usable by health-care workers rather than only by highly trained researchers. Quality of life instruments should be robust and applicable again and again at relatively short intervals; and they must be constructed in a manner which will make it possible to use them even with people who suffer severe pain or who are otherwise unlikely to participate willingly in evaluation and examination.

There are important practical tasks before us. First, we should ensure that the assessment of quality of life and of its changes under treatment becomes a routine and standard part of the evaluation of any type of new treatment. This requirement is particularly important when new treatments have only marginal advantages over the previously used methods in terms of symptoms, but may be very different in terms of their impact on quality of life.

Second, assessment of quality of life of all those involved in the treatment process – the patient, the family, caregivers, and the health service staff – should be linked to quality assurance procedures. These are likely to be used in most of the health-care institutions and at regular intervals: if they were linked to quality of life assessment, they would gain additional relevance for staff and patients and this assessment would be given much more prominence and importance.

Third, attention to quality of life and its assessment in health care must become an essential part of health-care procedures. This means it will be necessary to introduce instruction about quality of life concepts and measurement into medical schools and other schools of health personnel, and to see insistence on its measurement as a part of the normal supervision process in health services.

Fourth, quality of life research still suffers from disagreements about methods, lack of definitions, insufficiently large samples, and other "childhood diseases" that relatively new branches of research and practice usually have. It will be of great importance to think of ways of reaching agreement about a common language for work on the assessment of quality of life. It is likely that such a language – maybe not in a perfect form, but good enough to be used – could be produced relatively quickly: the chief challenge will not be to produce it, but to make everyone in the field use it. Perhaps we should aim, at least in the beginning, at making the commonly agreed system of measurement of quality of life a "second language", that is, encourage its use *in addition* to whatever practitioners or researchers use to assess symptoms, impairments, and disabilities of quality of life as defined in their own terms at present; it is to be hoped that in this way, and through the education of all concerned, we shall be successful, not only in producing a commonly agreed and generally useful tool, but also in forming attitudes which will ensure that quality of life becomes a central criterion for the success of our work. This will improve medical care, and what is more, it will make a contribution to the search for a better and more humane society in general.

Bibliography

Series of references with more than one author but with the same first author are listed chronologically

Aaronson, N.K., Ahmedzai, S., Bergman, B. et al (1993). The European Organization for Research and Treatment for Cancer QLQ-C30: A quality-of-life instrument for use in international clinical trials in oncology, *J. Natl. Cancer Inst.*, **85**, 365–376.

Abbey, A. & Andrews, F.M. (1985). Modeling the psychological determinants of life quality, *Social Indicators Research*, **16**, 1–34.

Aber, J.L. (1983). Social policy issues in the prevention of burnout: A case study, in *Stress and Burnout in the Human Service Profession* (Ed. B.A. Farber), pp. 213–226, Pergamon Press, New York.

Agbayewa, M.O., Weir, J., Tuokko, H. & Beattie, L. (1991). Depression in dementia: Its impact on functional ability, *Dementia*, **2**, 212–217.

Agosti, V., Stewart, J.W. & Quitkin, F.M. (1991). Life satisfaction and psychosocial functioning in chronic depression: effect of acute treatment with antidepressants, *J. Affective Disorders*, **23**, 35–41.

Aiken, M. & Hage, J. (1966). Organizational alienation: A comparative analysis, *American Sociological Review*, **31**, 497–507.

Akhtar, S. & Samuel, S. (1995). Between the past and the future of psychotherapy research. *Arch. Gen. Psychiatry*, **52**, 642–644.

Akiskal, H. (1988). Personality as a mediating variable in the pathogenesis of mood disorders: Implications for theory, research and prevention, in *Depressive Illness: Prediction of Course and Outcome* (Eds T. Helgason & R. Daly), pp. 131–146, Springer Verlag, Berlin.

Albrecht, G.L. & Fitzpatrick, R. (1994). A sociological perspective on health-related quality of life research, in *Advances in Medical Sociology, Volume 5 Quality of Life in Health Care* (Eds G.L. Albrecht & R. Fitzpatrick), pp. 1–21, Jai Press, Greenwich, CT, London, UK.

Alexopoulos, G.S., Meyers, B.S., Young, R.C., Mattis, S. et al (1993a). The course of geriatric depression with reversible dementia: A controlled study, *Am. J. Psychiatry*, **150**, 1693–1699.

Alexopoulos, G.S., Young, R.C. & Meyers, B.S. (1993b). Geriatric depression: Age of onset and dementia, *Biol. Psychiatry*, **34**, 141–145.

Alexopoulos, G.S., Vrontou, C., Kakuma, T., Meyers, B.S., Young, R.C., Klausner, E. & Clarkin, J. (1996). Disability in geriatric depression, *Am. J. Psychiatry*, **153**, 877–885.

Altmann, J. (1974). Observational study of behaviour: sampling methods, *Behaviour*, **49**, 227–267.

American Psychiatric Association (1980). *Diagnostic and Statistical Manual of Mental Disorders, Third Edition (DSM-III)*, American Psychiatric Association, Washington, DC.

American Psychiatric Association (1994). *Diagnostic and Statistical Manual of Mental Disorders, Fourth Edition (DSM-IV)*, American Psychiatric Association, Washington, DC.

American Psychiatric Association (1987). *Diagnostic and Statistical Manual of Mental Disorders, Third edition, revised, (DSM-III-R)*, Washington, DC.

American Psychiatric Association Commission on Psychotherapies (1982). *Psychotherapy Research, Methodological and Efficacy Issues*, APA, Washington, DC.

Amering, M. & Katschnig, H. (1993a). Die Wirkungen der Psychopharmaka auf das Sexualverhalten und ihre Bedeutung für die Betreuung schizophrener Patienten, in *Brennpunkte der Schizophrenie. Gesellschaft – Angehörige – Therapie* (Ed. T. Platz), pp. 215–222, Springer, Vienna, New York.

Amering, M. & Katschnig, H. (1993b). Psychopharmaka im Spannungsfeld zwischen Patienten, Angehörigen und Betreuern, in *Brennpunkte der Schizophrenie. Gesellschaft – Angehörige – Therapie* (Ed. T. Platz), pp. 223–231, Springer, Vienna, New York.

Amering, M., Hofer, E., Windhaber, J. & Katschnig, H. (1996). Bedürfnisorientierte Psycho- und Sociotherapie in einer Tagesklinik, *Fortschr. Neurol. Psychiatr.*, **64**, Sonderheft 1, p. 2.

Amering, M., Hofer, H. & Rath, I. (In press). Trialog – Ein Erfahrungsbericht nach 2 Jahren "Erster Wiener Trialog", in *Gemeindepsychiatrie in Österreich. Die gemeindenahe Versorgung braucht die Gemeinde, die sich sorgt* (Eds U. Meise, F. Hafner & H. Hinterhuber), VIP Verlag, Innsbruck.

Anderson, J.P., Bush, J.W. & Berry, C.C. (1986). Classifying function for health outcome and quality-of-life evaluation: Self versus interview modes, *Med. Care*, **24**, 454–469.

Andrews, F.M. & Withey, S.B. (1976). *Social Indicators of Well-being. America's Perception of Life Quality*, pp. 1–24, Plenum Press, New York.

Angermeyer, M.C. (1987). Stigma perceived by patients attending modern treatment settings, *J. Nerv. Ment. Dis.*, **175**, 4–11.

Angermeyer, M.C. (1994). Symptomfreiheit oder Lebensqualität: Ziele der Schizophreniebehandlung, in *Schizophrenie und Lebensqualität* (Eds H. Katschnig & P. König), pp. 65–80 Springer Verlag, Vienna, New York.

Angermeyer, M.C., Däumer, R. & Matschinger, H. (1993). Benefits and risks of psychotropic medication in the eyes of the general public: Results of a survey in the Federal Republic of Germany, *Pharmacopsych.*, **26**, 114–120.

Angermeyer, M.C. & Matschinger, H. (1996). Public attitude towards psychiatric treatment, *Acta Psychiat. Scand.*, **94**, 326–336.

Anonymous (1981). First person account: the quiet discrimination, *Schiz. Bull.*, **7**, 736–738.

Anthony, W.A., Cohen, M.R. & Vitalo, R. (1978). The measurement of rehabilitation outcome, *Schiz. Bull.*, **4**, 365–383.

Anthony, W.A. & Farkas, M.A. (1982). A client outcome planning model for assessing psychiatric rehabilitation interventions, *Schiz. Bull.*, **8**, 13–38.

Anthony, W.A., Cohen, M.R. & Cohen, B.F. (1984). Psychiatric rehabilitation, in *The Chronic Mentally Ill; Five Years Later* (Ed. J. Talbott), Grune & Stratton, New York.

Anthony, W.A. & Jansen, M. (1984). Predicting the vocational rehabilitation of the chronically mentally ill, *Am. Psychol.*, **39**, 537–544.

Anthony, W.A., Cohen, M.R. & Marianne, F.D. (1990). *Psychiatric Rehabilitation.* Boston University, Sargent College of Allied Health Professionals, Center for Psychiatric Rehabilitation, Boston, MA.

Anthony, W. & Rogers, S. (1995). Relationships between psychiatric symptomatology, work skills and future vocational performance, *Psychiatric Services*, **46**, 353–358.

Aoki, N., Ishihara, M., Fujita, A. & Inagaki, H. (1990). Usefulness of the DFDL Scale to evaluate the functions of daily living of demented residents in nursing homes. Special Issue: Mental health in the nursing home, *Clin. Gerontol.*, **9**, 19–45.

Arluke, A. (1988). The Sick-Role Concept, in *Health Behavior. Emerging Research Perspectives* (Ed. D.S. Gochman), pp. 169–179, Plenum Press, New York, London.

Arns, P.G. & Linney, J.A. (1993). Work, self, and life satisfaction for persons with severe and persistent mental disorders, *Psychosocial Rehabilitation*, **17**, 63–79.

Arrindell, W.A. & Emmelkamp, P.M.G. (1986). Marital adjustment, intimacy and needs in female agoraphobics and their partners: A controlled study, *Br. J. Psychiatry*, **149**, 592–602.

Arrindell, W.A., Emmelkamp, P.M.G. & Sanderman, R. (1986). Marital quality and general life adjustment in relation to treatment outcome in agoraphobia, *Adv. Behav. Res. Ther.*, **8**, 139–185.

Arsanow, R.F., Brown, W. & Strandburg, R. (1995). Children with a schizophrenic disorder: neurobehavioural studies, *Eur. Arch. Psychiatry Clin. Neurosci.*, **245**, 70–79.

Asen, K., Berkowitz, R., Cooklin, A., Leff, J., Loader, P., Piper, R. & Rein, L. (1991). Family therapy outcome research: A trial for families, therapists and researchers, *Family Process*, **30** 3–20.

Atkinson, J. (1988). *Survey Report*, National Schizophrenia Society, London.

Atkinson, J. (1991). Carers, the community and the White Paper, *Psychiatric Bull.*, **15**, 763.

Atkinson, M., Zibin, S.H. & Chuang, H. (1997). Characterizing quality of life among patients with chronic mental illness: A critical examination of the self-report methodology, *Am. J. Psychiatry*, **105**, 99–105.

Attkisson, C., Cook, J., Karno, M., Lehman, A.F., McGlashan, T.H., Meltzer, H.Y., O'Connor, M., Richardson, D., Rosenblatt, A., Wells, K., Williams, J. & Hohmann, A.A. (1992). Clinical services research, *Schiz. Bull.*, **18**, 561–626.

Aurand, K., Hazard, B.P. & Tretter, F. (Eds) (1993). *Umweltbelastungen und Ängste*, Westdeutscher Verlag, Opladen.

Australian Commonwealth Department of Human Services and Health (ACDHSH) (1995). Guidelines for the pharmaceutical industry of submission to the Pharmaceutical Benefits Advisory Committee: Including submissions involving economic analysis, Australian Government Publishing Service, Canberra.

Avison, W.R. & Speechley, K.N. (1987). The discharged psychiatric patient: A review of social, social-psychological and psychiatric correlates of outcome, *Am. J. Psychiatry*, **144**, 10–18.

Awad, A.G. (1992). Quality of life of schizophrenic patients on medications and implications for new drug trials, *Hosp. Comm. Psychiatry*, **43**, 262–265.

Awad, A.G. (1994). Quality of life of schizophrenic patients on medications – implications for clinical trials, *Neuropsychophar.*, **10**, 3S, 2385.

Awad, A.G. (1995). Quality of life issues in medicated schizophrenics: Therapeutics and research implications, in *The Treatment of Schizophrenia* (eds C.L. Shariqui & H. Nasrallah), American Psychiatric Association Press, Washington, DC.

Awad, A.G. & Hogan, T.P. (1994). Subjective response to neuroleptics and the quality of life: Implications for treatment outcome, *Acta Psychiatr. Scand.*, **89** (suppl 380), 27–32.

Awad, A.G., Voruganti, L.N.P. & Heslegrave, R.J. (1997). A conceptual model of quality of life in schizophrenia: Description and preliminary clinical validation, *Quality of Life Research*, **6**, 21–26.

Babigian, H.M. & Marshall, P. (1989). Rochester: A Comprehensive Capitation Experiment, in *Paying for Services: Promises and Pitfalls of Capitation* (Eds D. Mechanic & L. H.

Aiken), pp. 43–54, New Directions in Mental Health, No. 43, Jossey-Bass, San Francisco.

Bachrach, L.L. (1982). Assessment of outcomes in community support systems: Results, problems and limitations, *Schiz. Bull.*, **8**, 39–61.

Bachrach, L.L. (1987). The homeless mentally ill, *The Chronic Mental Patient/II*, pp. 65–92, American Psychiatric Press, Washington, DC.

Bachrach, H.M., Galatzer-Levy, R., Skolnikoff, A. & Waldron, J.R.S. (1991). On the efficacy of psychoanalysis, *J. Am. Psychoanalytic Association*, **39**, 871–916.

Badía, X. & Rovira, J. (1994). Evaluación económica de medicamentos. Un instrumento para la toma de decisiones en la práctica clínica y la política sanitaria, DuPont Pharma, Barcelona.

Badley, E.M. (1993). An introduction to the concepts and classifications of the International Classification of Impairments, Disabilities and Handicaps, *Disability and Rehabilitation*, **15**, 161–178.

Baines, B., Beecham, J., Hallam, A. & Knapp, M. (1995). Community reprovision: Is it cost-effective? in *Summary of Proceedings of Tenth Annual Conference*, TAPS Research Unit, London.

Baker, F. & Intagliata, J. (1982). Quality of life in the evaluation of community support systems, *Eval. Prog. Planning*, **5**, 69–79.

Baldwin, S., Godfrey, C. & Propper, C. (1990). *Quality of Life. Perspectives and Policies*, Routledge, London.

Bali, L.R. (1979). Long term effect of relaxation on blood pressure and anxiety level in essential hypertensive males. A controlled study, *Psychosom. Med.*, **41**, 637–646.

Bandura, A. (1977). Self efficacy: Toward a unifying theory of behavioural change, *Psychol. Rev.*, **84**, 191–215.

Barberger, G.P., Cormmenges, D., Gagnon, M., Letenneur, L. et al (1992). Instrumental Activities of Daily Living as a screening tool for cognitive impairment and dementia in elderly community dwellers, *J. Am. Geriatrics Soc.*, **40**, 1129–1134.

Barcia, D., Morcillo, L. & Borgonós, E. (1995). Esquizofrenia, calidad de vida y formas clínicas, *An Psiquiatría*, 11, 81–87.

Barcia, D., Ayuso, J.L., Herraiz, M.L. & Fernández, A. (1996). Quality of life of patients treated with Risperidone, *An. Psiquiatría*, **12**, 134–141.

Barge-Schaapveld, D.Q.C.M., Nicolson, N.A., Gerritsen van der Hoop, R. & deVries, M.W. (1995). Changes in daily life experience associated with clinical improvement in depression, *J. Affective Disorders*, **34**, 139–154.

Barham, P. & Hayward, R. (1991). *From the Mental Patient to the Person*, Routledge, London.

Barrowclough, C., Tarrier, N., Watts, S., Vaughn, C., Bamrah, J.S. & Freeman, H.L. (1987). Assessing the functional value of relatives' knowledge about schizophrenia: A preliminary report, *Br. J. Psychiatry*, **151**, 1–8.

Barry, M.M., Crosby, C. & Bogg, J. (1993). Methodological issues in evaluating the quality of life of long-stay psychiatric patients, *J. Mental Health*, **2**, 43–56.

Barry, M.M. & Crosby, C. (1994). Assessing the impact of community placement on quality of life, in *Evaluation of Community Resettlement from the North Wales Psychiatric Hospital* (Eds C. Crosby & M.M. Barry), Community Care Series, Avebury.

Barry, M.M. & Crosby, C. (1995a). Assessing the impact of community placement on quality of life, in *Community Care: Evaluation of the Provision of Mental Health Services* (Eds C. Crosby & M.M. Barry), pp. 137–168, Avebury, Aldershot.

Barry, M.M. & Crosby, C. (1995b). Quality of life and mental health: Evaluating the impact of long-term care, in *Representations of Health, Illness and Handicap* (Eds I. Markova & R.M. Farr), pp. 225–247, Harwood Academic, Reading.

Barry, M.M. & Crosby, C. (1996). Quality of life as an evaluative measure in assessing the impact of community care on people with long-term psychiatric disorders, *Br. J. Psychiatry*, **168**, 210–216.

Bassuk, E.L. & Lamb, H.R. (1986). Homelessness and the implementation of deinstitutionalization, *The Mental Health Needs of Homeless Persons*, pp. 7–14, Jossey-Bass, San Francisco.

Bateson, G. (1979). *Mind and Nature: Necessary Unity*, p. 322, Bantam Books, Toronto.

Baum, C. & Edwards, D.F. (1993). Cognitive performance in senile dementia of the Alzheimer's type: The Kitchen Task Assessment, *Am. J. Occupat. Ther.*, **47**, 431–436.

Baumann, P. (Ed.). (1993). *Biologische Psychiatrie der Gegenwart*, Springer, Vienna, New York.

Baumann, U. & Reinecker-Hecht, C. (1986). Psychotherapie-Evaluation, in *Psychiatrie der Gegenwart 1* (Eds K.P. Kisker, J.E. Meyer, M. Müller & E. Strömgren), pp. 353–372, Springer, Berlin.

Bech, P. (1994). The PCASEE model: An approach to subjective well-being, in *Quality of Life Assessment: International Perspectives* (Eds J. Orley & J. Kuyken), pp. 75–79, Springer Verlag, Berlin.

Bech, P. (1995). Quality of life measurements for patients taking which drugs? *PharmacoEconomics*, **7**, 141–145.

Bech, P. (1996). Quality of life measurements in major depression, *Eur. Psychiatry*, **11**, 123–126.

Bech, P. & Hjortso, S. (1990). Problems in measuring quality of life in schizophrenia, *Nord. Psykiatr. Tidsskr.*, **44**, 77–79.

Beck, A.T. (1976). *Cognitive Therapy and the Emotional Disorders*, International Universities Press, New York.

Beck, A.T., Ward, C.H., Mendelson, M., Mock, J. & Erbaugh, J. (1961). An inventory for measuring depression, *Arch. Gen. Psychiatry*, **4**, 561–571.

Beck, A.T. & Beamesderfer, A. (1974). Assessment of depression: The depression inventory, in *Modern Problems in Pharmacopsychiatry* (Ed. P. Pichot), pp. 151–169, S. Karger, Basel, Switzerland.

Beck, A.T., Rush, A.J., Shaw, B.F. & Emery, G. (1979). *Cognitive Therapy of Depression*, Guilford Press, New York.

Becker, M. (1995). Quality-of-life instruments for severe chronic mental illness. Implications for pharmacology, *PharmacoEconomics*, **7**, 229–237.

Becker, M., Diamond, R. & Sainfort, F. (1993). A new patient focused index for measuring quality of life in persons with severe and persistent mental illness, *Quality of Life Research*, **2**, 239–251.

Becker, M., Diamond, R. & Sainfort, F. (1994). Factors affecting quality of life among people with severe and persistent mental illness, *Mental Health Research Center*, paper series 33, Mental Health Research Center, Madison, WI.

Becker, M. & Feinstein, A.R. (1994). Consumer values and quality of life evaluations, paper presented at *Faculty Residents and Staff Research Division Seminar*, University of Wisconsin Medical School, Madison, Wisconsin.

Beecham, J., Knapp, M. & Fenyo, A. (1991). Costs, needs and outcomes, *Schiz. Bull.*, **17**, 427–439.

Benedetti, G. (1975). *Psychiatrische Aspekte des Schöpferischen und schöpferische Aspekte der Psychiatrie*, Vandenoeck & Ruprecht, Göttingen.

Benesch, C.G., McDaniel, K.D. & Hamill, R.W. (1993). End-stage Alzheimer's disease: Glasgow Coma Scale and the neurological examination, *Arch. Neurol.*, **50**, 1309–1315.

Benson, V. & Marano, M.A. (1994). Current estimates from the National Health Interview Survey, 1992, National Center for Health Statistics, *Vital and Health Statistics*, Series 10, no. 189, pp. 83–113. Government Printing Office, Washington, DC.

Bergin, A.E. & Garfield, S.L. (1994). *Handbook of Psychotherapy and Behavior Change* (4th edn), Wiley, New York.

Berglund, G., Bolund, C., Gustafsson, U. & Sjoden, P. (1994). A randomized study of a rehabilitation program for cancer patients: The "starting again" group, *Psychooncology*, **3**, 109–120.

Bergner, M. (1985). Measurement of health status, *Med. Care*, **23**, 696–704.

Bergner, M. (1989). Quality of care, health status, and clinical research, *Med. Care*, **27** (suppl), 148–156.

Bergner, M., Bobbit, R.A., Canter, W.B. & Gilson, B.S. (1981). The Sickness Impact profile: Development and final revision of a health status measure, *Med. Care*, **19**, 787–805.

Berkeley Planning Associates (1977). Evaluation of child abuse and neglect demonstration project, 1974–1977, Volume IX: *Project Management and Worker Burnout*, Final report, Berkeley, CA.

Berzon, R.A., Simeon, G.P., Simpson Jr., R.L., Donnelly, M.A. & Tilson, H.H. (1995). Quality of life bibliography and indexes: 1993 update, *Quality of Life Res.*, **1**, 53–73.

Biddle, B. (1979). *Role Theory: Expectations, Identities and Behaviour*, Academic Press, New York, London.

Bigelow, D.A., Brodsky, G., Stewart, L. & Olson, M.M. (1982). The concept and measurement of quality of life as a dependent variable in evaluation of mental health services, in *Innovative Approaches to Mental Health Evaluation* (Eds G.J. Stahler & W.R. Tash), pp. 345–366, Academic Press Inc, New York.

Bigelow, D.A., Gareau, M.J. & Young, D.J. (1990). A quality of life interview, *Psychosocial Rehab. J.*, **14**, 94–98.

Bigelow, D.A., McFarland, B.H., Gareau, M.J. & Young, D.J. (1991a). Implementation and effectiveness of a bed reduction project, *Comm. Ment. Hlth. J.*, **27**, 125–133.

Bigelow, D.A., McFarland, B.H. & Olson, M.M. (1991b). Quality of life of community mental health program clients: Validating a measure, *Comm. Ment. Hlth. J.*, **27**, 43–55.

Bigelow, D.A. & Young, D.J. (1991). Effectiveness of a case management program, *Comm. Ment. Hlth. J.*, **27**, 115–123.

Blanchard, E.B. (1994). Behavioral medicine and health psychology, in *Handbook of Psychotherapy and Behavior Change*, 4th edn (Eds A.E. Bergin & S.L. Garfield), pp. 701–733, Wiley, New York.

Blanchard, E.B., Martin, D.J. & Dubbert, P.M. (1988). *Non-drug Treatments for Essential Hypertension*, Pergamon, Elmsford, NY.

Blansjaar, B.A., Takens, H. & Zwinderman, A.H. (1992). The course of alcohol amnestic disorder. A three-year follow-up study of clinical signs and social disabilities, *Acta Psychiat. Scandinav.*, **86**, 240–246.

Blazer, D.G., Kessler, R.C., McGonagle, K.A. & Swartz, M.S. (1994). The prevalence and distribution of major depression in a national community sample: The National Comorbidity Survey, *Am. J. Psychiatry*, **151**, 979–986.

Blumenthal, D.S. (Ed.) (1985). *Introduction to Environmental Health*, Springer, New York.

Blumenthal, J.A. & Emery, C.F. (1988). Rehabilitation of patients following myocardial infarction, *J. Consult. Clin. Psychol.*, **56**, 374–381.

Blumenthal, M. & Dielman, T. (1975). Depressive symptomatology and role function in the general population, *Arch. Gen. Psychiatry*, **32**, 985–991.

Bobes, J., González, M.P., Bousono, M., Munoz, L., G-Quirós, M. & Wallace, D. (1996a). Quality of life in schizophrenic outpatients, *Annual Meeting – New Research Program & Abstracts* (Eds American Psychiatric Association), p. 223, American Psychiatric Association, Washington, DC.

Bobes, J., González, M.P., Wallace, D.H., Bousono, M. & Sáiz, P.A. (1996b). Quality of life instruments in schizophrenia: a comparative study, *Europ. Psychiatry*, **11** (suppl. 4), 228.

Bobes, J., Gonzáles, M.P., Bousono, M. & Sáiz, P.A. (1997a). *Calidad de Vida y Salud Mental*, Aula Médica, Madrid.

Bobes, J., Gutiérrez, M., Gibert, J., González, M.P., Herraiz, M. & Fernández, A. (1997b). Quality of life in 274 schizophrenic outpatients undergoing risperidone maintenance treatment, *Annual Meeting – New Research Program & Abstracts* (Eds American Psychiatric Association), American Psychiatric Association, Washington, DC.

Bobes, J., Gutiérrez, M., Gibert, J., González, M.P., Herraiz, M. & Fernández, A. (1997c). Quality of life in schizophrenia: Long-term follow-up in 362 chronic Spanish schizophrenic outpatients undergoing Risperidone maintenance treatment, *European Psychiatry* (in press).

Bothwell, S. & Weissman, M. (1977). Social impairments four years after an acute depressive episode, *Am. J. Orthopsychiatry*, **47**, 231–237.

Boyer, A.C. & Mechanic, D. (1994). Psychiatric Reimbursement Reform in New York State: Lessons in Implementing Change, *Milbank Quarterly*, **72**, 621–651.

Boyle, P.J. & Callaghan, D. (1993). Minds and hearts: priorities in mental health services, *Hastings Centre Report*, **23**, no. 5, Special Supplement.

Bradburn, N.M. (1969). *The Structure of Psychological Well-Being*, Aldine, Chicago.

Bradburn, N.M. & Caplovitz, D. (1965). *Reports on Happiness*, Aldine, Chicago.

Brandstätter, H. (1994). Well-being and motivational person–environment fit: a time-sampling study of emotions, *Eur. J. Personality*, **8**, 75–93.

Brazier, J. (1993). The SF-36 health survey questionnaire – a tool for economists, *Health Economics*, **2**, 213–215.

Bremer, B.A. & McCauley, C.R. (1986). Quality-of-life measures: Hospital interview versus home questionnaire, *Health Psychology*, **5**, 171–177.

Brewin, C.R., Wing, J.K., Mangen, S.P., Brugha, T.S. & MacCarthy, B. (1987). Principles and practice of measuring needs in the long-term mentally ill: The MRC Needs for Care Assessment, *Psychol. Med.*, **17**, 971–981.

Bridges, K., Davenport, S. & Goldberg, D. (1994). The need for hospital-based rehabilitation services, *J. Ment. Health*, **3**, 205–212.

Broadhead, W.E., Blazer, D.G., George, L.K. & Tse, C.K. (1990). Depression, disability days and days lost from work in a prospective epidemiologic survey, *JAMA*, **264**, 2524–2528.

Brodaty, H. & Hadzi, P.D. (1990). Psychosocial effects on carers of living with persons with dementia, *Australian and New Zealand J. Psychiatry*, **24**, 351.

Bronisch, T. & Hecht, H. (1990). Major depression with and without a coexisting anxiety disorder: Social dysfunction, social integration, and personality features, *J. Affective Disorders*, **20**, 151–157.

Brown, G.W., Birley, J.L.T. & Wing, J.K. (1972). Influence of family life on the course of schizophrenic disorders: A replication, *Br. J. Psychiatry*, **121**, 241–258.

Brown, J., Johnston, K., O'Hanlon, M., Morton, A. & Gerard, K. (1995). Valuing quality of life in an economic evaluation of UK breast screening clinical trials, *Quality of Life Newsletter*, **2**, 10–11.

Browne, S., Roe, M., Lane, A., Gervin, M., Morris, M., Kinsella, A., Larkin, C. & O'Callaghan, E. (1996). Quality of life in schizophrenia: Relationship to socio-demographic factors, symptomatology and tardive dyskinesia, *Acta Psychiatr. Scand.*, **94**, 118–124.

Bühler, Ch. (1969). *Lebenslauf und Lebensziele*, G. Fischer Verlag, Stuttgart.

Bullinger, M. (1991). Quality of life – definition, conceptualization and implications – a methodologist view, *Theor. Surg.*, **6**, 143–148.

Bullinger, M. (1993). Indices versus profiles – advantages and disadvantages, in *Quality of Life Assessment: Key Issues in the 1990s* (Eds S.R. Walker & R.M. Rosser), pp. 209–220, Kluwer Academic, Dordrecht, Boston, London.

Bullinger, M. (1994). Lebensqualität: Grundlagen und Anwendungen, in *Lebensqualität und Asthma* (Eds F. Petermann & K.-C. Bergmann), pp. 17–28, Quintessenz, Munich.

Bullinger, M., Anderson, R., Cella, D. & Aaronson, N. (1993). Developing and evaluating cross-cultural instruments from minimum requirements to optimal models, *Quality of Life Res.*, **2**, 451–459.

Bullinger, M., v. Mackensen, S. & Kirchberger, I. (1994). KINDL – ein Fragebogen zur Erfassung der Lebensqualität von Kindern, *Z. f. Gesundheitspsychol.*, **2**, 64–77.

Bush, J.W. (1984). General Health Policy Model/Quality of Well-Being (QWB) Scale, in *Assessment of Quality of Life in Clinical Trials of Cardiovascular Therapies* (Eds N.K. Wenger, M.F. Mattson & C.D. Furber), LeJacq, New York.

Cacciacarne, M., Resnick, P.J., McArthur, C. & Althof, S. (1986). Burnout in forensic psychiatric staff, *Psychiatry and Law*, **5**, 303–308.

Cadoret, R.J., Troughton, E., Merchant, L.M. & Whitters, A. (1990). Early life psychosocial events and adult affective symptoms, in *Straight and Devious Pathways from Childhood to Adulthood* (Eds L. Robins & M. Rutter), pp. 300–313, Cambridge University Press, Cambridge.

Calman, K.C. (1984). Quality of life in cancer patients – an hypothesis, *J. Med. Ethics*, **10**, 124–127.

Calvocoressi, L., Lewis, B., Harris, M., Trufan, S.J., Goodman, W.K., McDougle, C.J. & Price, L.H. (1995). Family accommodation in obsessive-compulsive disorder, *Am. J. Psychiatry*, **152**, 441–443.

Campbell, A. (1976). Subjective measures of well-being, *Am. Psychol.* (February), 117–124.

Campbell, A. (1981). *The Sense of Well-Being in America: Recent Patterns and Trends*, McGraw-Hill, New York.

Campbell, A., Converse, P.E. & Rodgers, W.L. (1976). *The Quality of American life*, Russell Sage, New York.

Campbell, J. & Schraiber, R. (1989). *The Well-Being Project: Mental Health Clients Speak for Themselves*, California Network of Mental Health Clients, Sacramento, CA.

Campbell, J., Schraiber, R., Temkin, T. & ten Tusscher, T. (1989). *The Well-Being Project: Mental Health Clients Speak for Themselves*, Report to the California Department of Mental Health.

Cantor, N., Smith, E.E., French de Salles, R. & Mezzich, J.E. (1980). Psychiatric diagnosis as prototype categorization, *J. Abnormal Psychology*, **89**, 181–193.

Cantril, H. (1965). *The Pattern of Human Concerns*, Rutgers University Press, New Brunswick, NJ.

Caradoc-Davies, T.H. & Dixon, G.S. (1991). Factor analysis of activities of daily living scores: Culturally determined versus vegetative components, *Clinical Rehabilitation*, **5**, 41–45.

Carpenter, W.T. & Strauss, J.S. (1991). The prediction of outcome in schizophrenia. Eleven Year Followup of the Washington IPSS Cohort, *J. Nerv. Ment. Dis.*, **179**, 517–525.

Carr, D., Jackson, T. & Alquire, P. (1990). Characteristics of an elderly driving population referred to a geriatric assessment center, *J. Am. Geriatrics Society*, **38**, 1145–1150.

Carr-Hill, R. (1991). Allocating resources to health care: Is the QALY (Quality Adjusted Life Year) a technical solution to a political problem? *Int. J. Health Serv.*, **21**, 351–363.

Carson, T. & Carson, R. (1984). The affective disorders, in *Comprehensive Handbook of Psychopathology* (Eds H. Adams & P. Sucker), pp. 349–381, Plenum Press, New York.

Carver, C.S., Scheier, M.F. & Weintraub, J.K. (1989). Assessing coping strategies: A theoretically based approach, *J. Pers. Soc. Psychol*, **56**, 267–283.

Casey P.R., Tyrer P. & Platt S. (1985). The relationship between social functioning and psychiatric symptomatology in primary care, *Soc. Psychiatry*, **20**, 5–9.

Cassano, G.B., Perugi, G., Musetti, L. & Akiskal, H.S. (1989). The nature of depression presenting concomitantly with panic disorder, *Compr. Psychiatry*, **30**, 473–482.

Catalano, R., Dooley, D. & Wilson, G. (1994). Depression and unemployment: Panel findings from the Epidemiologic Catchment Area study, *Am. J. Community Psychol.*, **22**, 745–765.

Cella, D.F. (1990). Health promotion in oncology: A cancer wellness doctrine, *J. Psychosoc. Oncol.*, **8**, 17–31.

Cella, D.F., Sarafian, B., Snider, P.R., Yellen, S.B. & Winicour, P. (1993a). Evaluation of a community-based cancer support group, *Psycho-oncology*, **2**, 123–132.

Cella, D.F., Tulsley, D.S., Gray, G. et al (1993b). Functional Assessment of Cancer Therapy Scale: Development and validation of the general measure, *J. Clin. Oncol.*, **11**, 570–579.

Chamberlin, J. & Rogers, J.A. (1990). Planning a community-based mental health system – Perspective of service recipients, *Am. Psychol.*, **45**, 1241–1244.

Cheng, Sheung-Tak (1988). Subjective quality of life in the planning and evaluation of programs, *Eval. Prog. Planning*, **11**, 123–134.

Cherniss, C. (1980). *Staff Burnout. Job Stress in Human Services*, Sage, Beverly Hills, CA, London.

Cherniss, C. & Egnatios, E. (1978a). Is there job satisfaction in community mental health?' *Comm. Ment. Hlth. J.*, **14**, 309–318.

Cherniss, C. & Egnatios, E. (1978b). Clinical supervision in community mental health, *Social Work*, **23**, 219–223.

Cherniss, C. & Egnatios, E. (1978c). Participation in decision-making by staff in community mental health programs, *Am. J. Comm. Psychol.*, **6**, 171–190.

Cherniss, C. & Krantz, D. L. (1983). The ideological community as an antidote to burnout, in *Stress and Burnout in the Human Service Profession* (Ed. B.A. Farber), pp. 198–212, Pergamon Press, New York.

Chess, S. & Thomas, A. (1992). Interactions between offspring and parents in development, in *Vulnerability and Resilience in Human Development* (Eds B. Tizard & V. Varma), Jessica Kingsley Publishers, London, Philadelphia.

Chisholm, D., Healey, A. & Knapp, M. (1995). QALYs and mental health care, *Ment. Health Res. Rev.*, **2**, 17–19.

Christensen, H. (1991). The validity of memory complaints by elderly persons, *Int. J. Geriatric Psychiatry*, **6**, 307–312.

Christianson, J.B., Lurie, N., Finch, M. & Moscovice, I. (1989). Mainstreaming the mentally ill in HMOs, in *Paying for Services: Promises and Pitfalls of Capitation, New Directions in Mental Health* (Eds D. Mechanic & L.H. Aiken), pp. 19–28, No. 43, Jossey-Bass, San Francisco.

Christianson, J.B., Lurie, N., Finch, M., Moscovice, I.S. & Hartley, D. (1992). Use of Community-Based Mental Health Programmes by HMOs: Evidence from a medicaid demonstration, *Am. J. Pub. Hlth*, **82**, 790–96.

Ciompi, I. (1980). Catamnestic long term study on the course of life and aging of schizophrenics, *Schiz. Bull.*, **6**, 606–618.

Clare, A.W. & Cairns, V.E. (1978). Design, development and use of a standardised interview to assess social maladjustment and dysfunction in community studies, *Psychol. Med.*, **8**, 589–604.

Clark, A. & Fallowfield, L.F. (1986). Quality of life measurements in patients with malignant disease, *J. Roy. Soc. Med.*, **79**, 165–169.

Clark, G.H. Jr. & Vaccaro, J.V. (1987). Burnout among CMHC psychiatrists and the struggle to survive, *Hosp. Comm. Psychiatry*, **38**, 843–847.

Cohen, J.B. (1996). Is expected utility theory normative for medical decision making? *Medical Decision Making*, **16**, 1–6.

Cohen, C.J. & Sokolovsky, J. (1978). Schizophrenia and social networks: ex-patients in the inner city, *Schiz. Bull.*, **4**, 546–560.

Cohen-Mansfield, J., Billig, N., Lipson, S., Rosenthal, A.S. et al (1990). Medical correlates of agitation in nursing home residents, *Gerontology*, **36**, 150–158.

Cohler, B., Woolsey, S., Weiss, J. & Grunbaum, H. (1968). Child rearing attitudes among mothers volunteering and revolunteering for a psychological study, *Psychol. Reports*, **23**, 603–612.

Collins, E.J., Hogan, T.P. & Himansu, D. (1991). Measurement of therapeutic response in schizophrenia. A critical survey, *Schiz. Res.*, **5**, 249–253.

Commonwealth of Australia (1990). Guidelines for the pharmaceutical industry on preparation of submissions to the Pharmaceutical Benefits Advisory Committee: Including submissions involving economic analysis, *Department of Health, Housing and Community Services*, Canberra (ACT).

Cook, J.A. & Pickett, S.A. (1987). Feelings of burden and criticalness among parents residing with chronically mentally ill offspring, *J. Appl. Soc. Sci.*, **12**, 79–107.

Coryell, W., Endicott, J., Keller, M., Klerman, G.L., Maser, J. & Scheftner, W. (1993). The enduring psychosocial consequence of mania and depression, *Am. J. Psychiatry*, **150**, 720–727.

Costa, P.T. & McCrae, R.R. (1980). Influence of extraversion and neuroticism on subjective well-being: Happy and unhappy people, *J. Pers. Soc. Psychol.*, **38**, 668–678.

Cotterill, L. (1993). PhD Thesis, *Schizophrenia and Social Networks*, University of Manchester.

Cox, D., Fitzpatrick, R., Fletcher, A. et al (1992). Quality of life assessment. Can we keep it simple? *J. Roy. Stat. Soc. A.*, **155**, 353–393.

Coyne, J.C. (1976). Depression and the response of others, *J. Abnorm. Psychol.*, **85**, 186–193.

Coyne, J., Kessler, T., Tal, M., Turnbull, J., Wortman, C. & Greden, J. (1987). Living with a depressed person, *J. Cons. Clin. Psychol.*, **55**, 347–352.

Coyne, J., Wortman, C. & Lehman, D. (1988). The other side of support: Emotional overinvolvement and miscarried helping, in *Social Support: Formats, Processes & Effects* (Ed. B. Gottlieb), pp. 137–154, Sage, New York.

Craig, T. & Van Natta, P. (1983). Disability and depressive symptoms in two communities, *Am. J. Psychiatry*, **140**, 598–601.

Cronin-Stubbs, D. & Brophy, E.B. (1985). Burnout. Can social support save the psych nurse? *J. Psychosoc. Nursing Ment. Health Serv.*, **23**, 8–13.

Crosby, C., Barry, M.M., Carter, M.F. & Lowe, C.F. (1993). Psychiatric rehabilitation and community care: Resettlement from North Wales Hospital, *Health and Social Care in the Community*, **1**, 355–363.

Crosby, C., Carter, M.F. & Barry, M.M. (1995). The care process: Care environments, care management and staff attitudes, in *Community Care: Evaluation of the Provision of Mental Health Services* (Eds C. Crosby & M.M. Barry), pp. 59–86, Avebury, Aldershot.

Csikszentmihalyi, M. (1990). *Flow: The Psychology of Optimal Experience. Steps toward Enhancing the Quality of Life*, Harper Perennial, New York.

Csikszentmihalyi, M. & Larson, R. (1984). *Being Adolescent: Conflict and Growth in the Teenage Years*, Basic Books, New York.

Csikszentmihalyi, M. & Larson, R. (1987). Validity and reliability of the Experience Sampling Method, *J. Nerv. Ment. Dis.*, **175**, 526–536.

Csikszentmihalyi, M. & Csikszentmihalyi, I. (1988). *Optimal Experience. Psychological Studies of Flow in Consciousness*, Cambridge University Press, Cambridge.

Culyer, A.J. (1990). Commodities, characteristics of commodities, characteristics of people, utilities and their quality of life, in *Quality of Life. Perspectives and Policies* (Eds S. Baldwin, C. Godfrey & C. Propper), pp. 9–27, Routledge, London.

Cunningham, A.J., Lockwood, G.A. & Edmonds, C.V.I. (1993). Which cancer patients benefit most from a brief, group, coping skills program? *Int. J. Psychiatry Med.*, **23**, 383–398.

Dahrendorf, D. (1965). *Homo Sociologicus. Ein Versuch zur Geschichte, Bedeutung und Kritik der Kategorie der sozialen Rolle*, Fünfte Auflage, Westdeutscher Verlag, Cologne and Opladen.

Davidge, M., Elias, S., Jayes, B. et al (1993). *Survey of English Mental Illness Hospitals*, Health Services Management Centre, Birmingham.

Davidson, J.R.T., Hughes, D.C., George, L.K. & Blazer, D.G. (1993). The epidemiology of social phobia: Findings from the Duke Epidemiologic Catchment Area Study, *Psychol. Med.*, **23**, 709–718.

Davidson, J.R.T., Hughes, D.C., George, L.K. & Blazer, D.G. (1994). The boundary of social phobia: Exploring the threshold, *Arch. Gen. Psychiatry*, **51**, 975–983.

DeBettignies, B.H., Mahurin, R.K. & Pirozzolo, F.J. (1993). Functional status in Alzheimer's disease and multi-infarct dementia: A comparison of patient performance and caregiver report, *Clin. Gerontol.*, **12**, 31–49.

De Jong, A., Giel, R., Slooff, C.J. & Wiersma, D. (1986). Relationship between symptomatology and social disability, *Soc. Psychiatry*, **21**, 200–205.

de Jong, R.G. (1993). Review: Extraaural health effects of aircraft noise, in *Noise and Disease* (Eds H. Ising & B. Kruppa), pp. 259–270, Fischer Verlag, Stuttgart, New York.

De Lisio, G., Maremmani, I., Perugi, G., Cassano, G. B., Deltito, J. & Akiskal, H.S. (1986). Impairment of work and leisure in depressed outpatients: A preliminary communication, *J. Affective Disorders*, **10**, 79–84.

de Neeling, J. (1991). *Quality of Life: Het onderzoek naar welzijnseffecten van medische handelingen*, Wetenschappelijke Uitgeverij Bunge, Utrecht.

Dehlinger, J. & Perlman, B. (1978). Job satisfaction in mental health agencies, *Administration in Mental Health*, **5**, 120–139.

Delespaul, P. (1995). Assessing "Quality of Life" in schizophrenia, *Assessing Schizophrenia in Daily Life: The Experience Sampling Method*, Universitaire Pers, Maastricht.

Delespaul, P.A.E.G., deVries, M.W. & Radstake, D.W.S. (1995). Persoonlijke rehabilitatie: Een "Experience Sampling" casus, in *Rehabilitatie van de Chronische Psychiatrische Patiënt. Op weg naar een gemeenschapspsychiatrie* (Eds G. Pieters & J. Peuskens), pp. 215–234, Garant, Leuven.

Delle Fave, A. & Massimini, F. (1992). The ESM and the measurement of clinical change: A case of anxiety disorder, in *The Experience of Psychopathology* (Ed. M.W. deVries), pp. 280–289, Cambridge University Press, Cambridge.

DeLongis, A., Coyne, J.C., Dakof, G., Folkman, S. & Lazarus, R.S. (1982). Relationship of daily hassles, uplifts and major life events to health status, *Health Psychology*, **1**, 119–136.

Demal, U., Zitterl, W., Lenz, G., Zapotoczky, H-G. & Zitterl-Eglseer, K. (1996). Obsessive compulsive disorder and depression – first results of a prospective study on 74 patients, *Prog. Neuro-Psychopharmacol. & Biol. Psychiat.*, **20**, 801–813.

Denzin, N.K. & Lincoln, Y.S. (1994). *Handbook of Qualitative Research*, Sage, Thousand Oaks, CA.

Department of Health and Social Services Inspectorate (1991). Care Management and Assessment: Practitioners' Guide, HMSO; quoted in M. Slade (1994). Needs assessment – involvement of staff and users will help to meet needs, *Br. J. Psychiatry*, **165**, 293–296.

Dernovsek, M.Z. (1997). The quality of life of schizophrenic outpatients. Poster presented at the European Congress of the World Psychiatric Association, 23–26 April, Geneva.

Derogatis, D.A., Lipman, R.S. & Covi, L. (1973). SCL-90: an outpatient psychiatric rating scale: Preliminary report, *Psychopharmacol. Bull.*, **9**, 13–28.

Detsky, A.S. (1993). Guidelines for economic analysis of pharmaceutical products: A draft document for Ontario and Canada, *PharmacoEconomics*, **3**, 354–361.

Devanand, D.P., Sackeim, H.A. & Mayeux, R. (1988). Psychosis, behavioral disturbance & the use of neuroleptics in dementia, *Comp. Psychiatry*, **29**, 387–401.

deVries, M.W. (1987). Investigating mental disorders in their natural settings, *J. Nerv. Ment. Dis.*, **175**, 509–513.

deVries, M.W. (1992a). *The Experience of Psychopathology: Investigating Mental Disorders in their Natural Settings*, Cambridge University Press, Cambridge.

deVries, M.W. (1992b). The uses of the ESM in psychotherapy, in *The Experience of Psychopathology* (Ed. M.W. deVries), pp. 255–259, Cambridge University Press, Cambridge.

deVries, M.W. & Delespaul, P.A.E.G. (1989). Time, context and subjective experience in schizophrenia, *Schiz. Bull.*, **15**, 233–244.

Dew, M.A., Bromet, E.J., Schulberg, H.C., Parkinson, D.K. & Curtis, E.C. (1991). Factors affecting service utilization for depression in a white collar population, *Soc. Psychiatry Psychiatr. Epidemiol.*, **26**, 230–237.

Deyo, R.A. (1991). The quality of life, research and care, *Ann. Int. Med.*, **114**, 695–696.

Deyo, R. & Carter, W. (1992). Strategies for improving and expanding the application of health status measures in clinical setting, *Med. Care*, MS176–MS186.

Diabetes Control and Complications Trial Research Group. (1985). The DCCT Quality of Life Measure: A preliminary study of reliability and validity, Technical Report, DCCT Coordinating Center, Bethesda, MD.

Diamond, R. (1985). Drugs and the quality of life: The patient's point of view, *J. Clin. Psychiatry*, **46**, 29–35.

Diehl, V., v. Kalle, A.-K., Kruse, T. & Sommer, H. (1990). "Lebensqualität" als Bewertungskriterium in der Onkologie, in *"Lebensqualität" als Bewertungskriterium in der Medizin* (Eds P. Schölmerich & G. Thews), pp. 149–167, Fischer Verlag, Stuttgart.

Diener, E. (1984). Subjective well-being, *Psychol. Bull.*, **95**, 542–575.

Diener, E., Sandvik, E. & Pavot, W. (1991a). Happiness is the frequency, not the intensity, of positive versus negative affect, in *Subjective Well-Being: An Interdisciplinary Perspective* (Eds F. Strack, M. Argyle & N. Schwarz), pp. 119–139, Pergamon, New York.

Diener, E., Sandvik, E., Pavot, W. & Gallagher, D. (1991b). Response artefacts in the measurement of subjective well-being, *Social Indicators Research*, **24**, 35–56.

Dietzen, L. & Bond, G. (1993). Relationships between case manager contact and outcomes for frequently hospitalized psychiatric clients, *Hosp. Comm. Psychiatry*, **4**, 839–43.

Donner, E. (1992). Expanding the experiential parameters of cognitive therapy, in *The Experience of Psychopathology* (Ed. M.W. deVries), pp. 260–269, Cambridge University Press, Cambridge.

Donovan, J., Frankel, S. & Eyles, J. (1993). Assessing the need for health status measures, *J. Epidem. Comm. Hlth.*, **47**, 158–162.

Dorland's Illustrated Medical Dictionary (1974). W.B. Saunders, Philadelphia.

Drachman, D.A., Swearer, J.M., O'Donnell, B.F., Mitchell, A.L. et al (1992). The Caretaker Obstreperous-Behavior Rating Assessment (COBRA) Scale, *J. Am. Geriatrics Society*, **40**, 463–470.

Drake, R.E., Wallach, M.A. & Hoffman, J.S. (1989). Housing instability and homelessness among aftercare patients of an urban state hospital, *Hosp. Comm. Psychiatry*, **33**, 225–227.

Drenowski, J. (1974). *On Measuring and Planning the Quality of Life*, Mouton, The Hague.

Drummond, M.F. (1992). Cost-of-illness studies. A major headache? (Guest editorial) *Pharmacoeconomics*, **2**, 1–4.

Drummond, M.F., Stoddart, G.L. & Torrance, G.W. (1987). Methods for the evaluation of health care programmes, *Oxford Medical Publ.*, Oxford.

Dumont, J. (1996). Personal communication.

Dunn, M., O'Driscoll, C., Dayson, D., Wills, W. & Leff, J. (1990). The TAPS Project. 4: An observational study of the social life of long-stay patients, *Br. J. Psychiatry*, **157**, 842–848.

DuPont, R.L., Rice, D.P., Miller, L.S., Shiraki, S.S., Rowland, C.R. & Harwood, H.J. (1996). Economic costs of anxiety disorders, *Anxiety*, **2**, 167–172.

Dupuy, H.J. (1978). Self-representation of general psychological well-being of American adults, paper presented at the *American Public Association Meeting*, Los Angeles.

Dupuy, H. (1984). The Psychological General Well-Being Index, in *Assessment of Quality of Life in Clinical Trials of Cardiovascular Therapies* (Ed. N. Wenger), pp. 170–183, Le Jacq, New York.

Eaton, W.W., Kessler, R.C., Wittchen, H.-U. & Magee, W.J. (1994). Panic and PD in the United States, *Am. J. Psychiatry*, **151**, 413–420.

Edelwich, J. & Brodsky, A. (1982). Training guidelines: Linking the workshop experience to needs on and off the job, in *Job Stress and Burnout. Research, Theory and Intervention Perspectives* (Ed. W. S. Paine), pp. 133–154, Sage, Beverly Hills, CA, London, New Delhi.

Edgerton, R.B. (1967). *The Cloak of Competence: Stigma in the Lives of the Mentally Retarded*, University of California Press, Berkeley, CA.

Edgerton, R.B. (1984). The participant observer approach to research in mental retardation, *Am. J. Ment. Deficiency*, **5**, 498–505.

Edgerton, R.B. (1990). Quality of life from a longitudinal research perspective, in *Quality of Life. Perspectives and Issues* (Ed. R.L. Schalock), pp. 149–160, American Association on Mental Retardation, Washington, DC.

Edgerton, R.B. & Bercovici, S.M. (1976). The cloak of competence: Ten years later, *Am. J. Ment. Deficiency.*, **80**, 485–497.

Edgerton, R.B., Bollinger, M. & Herr, B. (1984). The cloak of competence: After two decades, *Am. J. Ment. Deficiency*, **88**, 345–351.

Edlund, M.J. & Swann, A.C. (1987). The economic and social costs of PD, *Hosp. Commun. Psychiatry*, **38**, 1277–1288.

Edwards, D.F., Baum, C.M. & Deuel, R.K. (1991). Constructional apraxia in Alzheimer's disease: Contributions to functional loss. Special Issue: The mentally impaired elderly: Strategies and interventions to maintain function, *Physical and Occupational Therapy in Geriatrics*, **9**, 53–68.

Elkin, I., Shea, T., Watkins, J.T., Imber, S.D., Sotsky, S.M., Collins, J.F., Glass, D.R., Pilkonis, P.A., Leber, W.R., Docherty, J.P., Fiester, S.J. & Parloff, M.B. (1989). National Institute of Mental Health Treatment of Depression Collaborative Research Program, *Arch. Gen. Psychiatry*, **46**, 971–982.

Elkinton, J. (1966). Medicine and the quality of life, *Annals Int. Med.*, **64**, 711–714.

Ellwood, P.M. (1988). Outcomes management: A technology of patient experience, *New Eng. J. Med.*, **318**, 1549–1552.

Emerick, R.E. (1991). The politics of psychiatric self-help: Political factions, interactional support, and group longevity in a social movement, *Soc. Sci. Med.*, **32**, 1121–1128.

Endicott, J., Spitzer, R., Fleiss, J. & Cohen, J. (1976). The global assessment scale: A procedure for measuring overall severity of psychiatric disturbance, *Arch. Gen. Psychiatry*, **33**, 766–771.

Endicott, J., Nee, J., Harrison, W. & Blumenthal, R. (1993). Quality of Life Enjoyment and Satisfaction Questionnaire: A new measure, *Psychopharm. Bull.*, **29**, 321–326.

Erickson, R. (1974). Welfare as a planning goal, *Acta Sociologica*, **17**, 32–43.

Erikson, E. (1959). *Identity and the Life Cycle*, Int. Univ. Press, New York.

Erlenmeyer-Kimling, L., Cornblatt, B.A., Bassett, A.S., Moldin, S.O., Hilldoff-Adamo, U. & Roberts, S. (1990). High-risk children in adolescence and young adulthood: Course of global adjustment, in *Straight and Devious Pathways from Childhood to Adulthood* (Eds L. Robins & M. Rutter), pp. 351–364, Cambridge University Press, Cambridge.

Essink-Bot, M.L., Stouthard, M.E.A. & Bonsel, G.J. (1993). Generalizability of valuations on health states collected with the EuroQol-Questionnaire, *Health Economics*, **2**, 237–246.

Estroff, S.E. (1981). *Making it Crazy. An Ethnography of Psychiatric Clients in an American Community*, University of California Press, Berkeley, CA.

Estroff, S.E. (1989). Self, identity, and subjective experiences of schizophrenia: In search of the subject, *Schiz. Bull.*, **15**, 189–196.

Estroff, S.W.S., Lachicotte, L.C., Illingworth, A. & Johnson, A. (1991). Everybody's got a little mental illness: Accounts of illness and self among people with severe, persistent mental illnesses, *Medical Anthropology Quarterly*, **5**, 331–369.

EuroQol Group (1990). EuroQol – a new faculty for the measurement of health-related quality of life, *Health Policy*, **16**, 199–208.

Evans, R.G. (1981). The relationship of two measures of perceived control to depression, *J. Personality Assessment*, **45**, 66–70.

Evans, R.W. (1991). Quality of life, *Lancet*, **338**, 636.

Fabian, E.S. (1990). Quality of life: A review of theory and practice implications for individuals with long-term mental illness, *Rehabilitation Psychology*, **35**, 161–170.

Fabian, E.S. (1991). Using quality of life indicators in rehabilitation program evaluation, *Rehabilitation Counseling Bulletin*, **34**, 344–356.

Fairweather, G.W., Sanders, D.H., Maynard, H. & Cressler, D.L. (1969). *Community Life for the Mentally Ill. An Alternative to Institutional Care*, Aldine Publishing, Chicago.

Farber, B.A. (1983). Introduction: A critical perspective on burnout, in *Stress and Burnout in the Human Service Profession* (Ed. B.A. Farber), pp. 1–20, Pergamon Press, New York.

Farran, C.J., Herth, K.A. & Popovich, J.M. (1994). *Hope and Hopelessness. Critical Clinical Constructs*, Sage Publications, CA.

Fawzy, F.I., Fawzy, N.W., Arndt, L.A. & Pasnau, R.O. (1995). Critical review of psychosocial interventions in cancer care, *Arch. Gen. Psychiatry*, **52**, 100–113.

Feehan, M., Knight, R.G. & Partridge, F.M. (1991). Cognitive complaint and test performance in elderly patients suffering depression or dementia, *Int. J. Geriatric Psychiatry*, **6**, 287–293.

Feinleib, M.F. (Ed.) (1991). Proceedings of 1988 international symposium on data on aging, National Center for Health Statistics, *Vital and Health Statistics*, Series 5, no. 6, pp. 3269, US Government Printing Office, Washington, DC.

Feinstein, A.R. (1967). *Clinical Judgement*, Robert E. Krieger, Huntington, NY.

Feinstein, A.R. (1992). Benefits and obstacles for development of health status assessment measures in clinical settings, *Med. Care*, **30**, MS50–MS56.

Feist, G.J., Bodner, T.E., Jacobs, J.F., Miles, M. & Tan, V. (1995). Integrating top-down and bottom-up structural models of subjective well-being: A longitudinal investigation, *J. Personality Soc. Psychol.*, **68**, 138–150.

Felton, C.J., Stastny, P., Shern, D.L., Blanck, A., Donahue, S.A., Knight, E. & Brown, C. (1995) Consumers as peer specialists on intensive case management teams: Impact on client outcomes, *Psychiatric Services*, **46**, 1037–1044.

Fenton, W.S. & McGlashan, T.H. (1991). Natural history of schizophrenia subtypes: Positive and negative symptoms and long-term course, *Arch. Gen. Psvchiatry*, **48**, 978–986.

Ferrans, C.E. (1990). Quality of life: Conceptual issues, *Seminars Oncology Nursing*, **6**, 248–254.

Ferrans, C.E. & Powers, M.J. (1992). Psychometric assessment of the quality of life index, *Research in Nursing and Health*, **15**, 29–38.

Figurski, T.J. (1992). Everyday self-awareness: implications for self-esteem, depression and resistance to therapy, in *The Experience of Psychopathology* (Ed. M.W. deVries), pp. 304–313, Cambridge University Press, Cambridge.

Fitz, A.G. & Teri, L. (1994). Depression, cognition, and functional ability in patients with, Alzheimer's disease, *J. Am. Geriatrics Society*, **42**, 186–191.

Fitzpatrick, R., Fletcher, A., Gore, S., Jones, D., Spiegelhalter, D. & Cox, D. (1992). Quality of life measures in health care. I: Applications and issues in assessment, *Br. Med. J.*, **305**, 1074–1077.

Flanagan, J.C.A. (1978). A research approach to improving our quality of life, *Am. Psychologist,* **33**, 138–147.

Fletcher, A., Gore, S., Jones, D., Fitzpatrick, R., Spiegelhalter, D. & Cox, D. (1992). Quality of life measures in health care. II: Design, analysis, and intepretation, *Br. Med. J.*, **305**, 1145–1148.

Fletcher, A.E., Hunt, B.M. & Bulpitt, C.J. (1987). Evaluation of quality of life on clinical trials of cardiovascular disease, *J. Chron. Dis.*, **40**, 557–566.

Forsell, Y., Fratiglioni, L., Grut, M., Viitanen, M., et al (1992). Clinical staging of dementia in a population survey: Comparison of DSM-III-R and the Washington University Clinical Dementia Rating Scale, *Acta Psychiat. Scand.*, **86**, 49–54.

Forsell, Y., Jorm, A.F. & Winblad, B. (1994). Outcome of depression in demented and non-demented elderly: Observations from a three-year follow-up in a community-based study, *Int. J. Geriatric Psychiatry*, **9**, 5–10.

Forstl, H., Sattel, H. & Bahro, M. (1993). Alzheimer's disease: Clinical features, *Int. Rev. Psychiatry*, **5**, 327–349.

Foster, J. & Cataldo, J.K. (1994). Protection from clinical depression in medical long-term care facilities: Evidence for psychological adaptation in cognitively intact patients, *Int. J. Geriatric Psychiatry*, **9**, 115–125.

Franklin, J.L., Simmons, J., Solovitz, B., Clemons, J.R. & Miller, G.E. (1986). Assessing quality of life of the mentally ill: a three-dimensional model, *Evaluation and the Health Professions*, **9**, 376–388.

Franklin, J.L., Solovitz, B., Mason, M., Clemons, J.R. & Miller, G.E. (1987). An evaluation of case management, *Am. J. Publ. Health*, **77**, 674–678.

Fredrichs, R., Aneshensel, C., Yokopenic, P. & Clark, V. (1982). Physical health and depression: an epidemic survey, *Preventative Med.*, **11**, 639–646.

Freeman, H.L. (1984). *Mental Health and the Environment*, Churchill Livingstone, London.

Freeman, H. & Henderson, J. (1991). *Evaluation of Comprehensive Care of the Mentally Ill*, Gaskell, London

Freudenberger, H.J. (1974). Staff burn-out, *J. Social Issues*, **30**, 159–165.

Freudenberger, H.J. (1983). Burnout: Contemporary issues, trends, and concerns, in *Stress and Burnout in the Human Service Profession* (Ed. B.A. Farber), pp. 23–28, Pergamon Press, New York.

Fried, M. (1963). Grieving for a lost home, in *The Urban Condition* (Ed. L.J. Duhl), Basic Books, New York.

Friedman, H.S. & Booth-Kewley, S. (1987). The "disease-prone personality": A meta-analytic view of the construct, *Am. Psychol.*, **42**, 539–555.

Friedman, M., Thoresen, C.E., Gill, J., Ulmer, D., Powell, L.H., Price, V.A., Brown, B., Thompson, L., Rabin, D.D., Breall, W.S., Bourg, W., Levy, R. & Dixon, T. (1986). Alteration of Type A behavior and its effect on cardiac recurrences in post-myocardial infarction patients: Summary results of the Recurrent Coronary Prevention Project, *Am. Heart J.*, **112**, 653–665.

Frisch, M.B., Cornell, J., Villanueva, M. & Retzlaff, P.J. (1992). Clinical validation of the Quality of Life Inventory: A measure of life satisfaction for use in treatment planning and outcome assessment, *Psychol. Assessment,* **4**, 92–101.

Fuchs, L. (1986). First person account: Three generations of schizophrenia, *Schiz. Bull.,* **12**, 744–747.

Fulmer, T. & Gurland, B. (1996). Restriction as elder mistreatment: Differences between caregiver and elder perceptions, *J. Ment. Health Aging,* **2**, 89–99.

Fulton, J.P. & Katz, S. (1986). Characteristics of the disabled elderly and implications for rehabilitation, in *Aging and Rehabilitation* (Eds S.J. Brody & G.E. Ruff), pp. 37–41, Springer, New York.

Fulton, J.P., Katz, S., Jack, S.S. & Hendershot, G.E. (1989). Physical functioning of the aged: United States, 1984, Nation-DO, Center for Health Statistics. *Vital and Health Statistics,* Series 10, No. 167, pp. 6–14, US Government Printing Office, Washington, DC.

Furner, S.E. (1993) Health Status, in *Vital and Health Statistics* (Eds R.A. Cohen, J.F. Van Nostrand & S.E. Furner), Chartbook on Health Data on older Americans: United States, 1992. National Center for Health Statistics, Series 3, no. 29, pp. 3–6, 41, US Government Printing Office, Washington, DC.

Garmezy, N. & Masten, A.S. (1994). Chronic Adversities, in *Child and Adolescent Psychiatry: Modern Approaches* (Eds M. Rutter, E. Taylor & L. Hersov), pp. 191–208, Blackwell Scientific Publications, London.

Gasiet, S. (1981). *Menschliche Bedürfnisse. Eine theoretische Synthese,* Campus, Frankfurt.

Gecas, V. (1989). The social psychology of self-efficacy, *Ann. Rev. Sociol.,* **15**, 291–316.

Geigle, R. & Jones, B. (1990). Outcomes measurement: A report from the front, *Inquiry,* **27**, 7–13.

Gill, T.M. & Feinstein, A.R. (1994). A critical appraisal of the quality of life instruments, *JAMA,* **272**, 619–626.

Giner, J., Baca, E., Bobes, J., Ibáñez, E., Leal, C. & Cervera, S. (1995). Calidad de vida en enfermos esquizofrénicos. Desarrollo de un instrumento espanol para su evaluación: el cuestionario 'Sevilla''. Fases iniciales, *An. Psiquiatría,* **11**, 313–319.

Glatzer, W. (1991). Quality of life in advanced industrialised countries: The case of West Germany, in *Subjective Well-Being* (Eds F. Strack, M. Argyle & N. Schwarz), pp. 261–279, Pergamon, Oxford.

Goering, P., Wasylenki, D., Lancee, W. & Freeman, S.J.J. (1983). Social support and post-hospital outcome for depressed women, *Can. J. Psychiatry,* **28**, 612–618.

Goethe, J.W. & Fischer E.H. (1995). Functional impairment in depressed inpatients, *J. Affective Disorders,* **33**, 23–29.

Goffman, E. (1961). *Asylums: Essays on the Social Situation of Mental Patients and other Inmates,* Anchor Books, New York.

Goffman, E. (1963). Stigma. Notes on the management of spoiled identity, Prentice Hall, Englewood Cliffs, NJ.

Goldberg, D. (1979). *Manual of the General Health Questionnaire,* NFER Publishing, Windsor, UK.

Goldstein, J.M. & Caton, C.L.M. (1983). The effects of the community environment on chronic psychiatric patients, *Psychol. Med.,* **13**, 193–199.

Goldstrom, I.D. & Manderscheid, R.W. (1986). The chronically mentally ill: A descriptive analysis from the Uniform Client Data Instrument, *Comm. Supp. Serv. J.,* **2**, 4–9.

Golembiewsky, R.T. (1982). Organizational development (OD) interventions: Changing interaction, structures and policies, in *Job Stress and Burnout. Research, Theory and Intervention Perspectives* (Ed. W.S. Paine), Sage, Beverly Hills, CA, London, New Delhi.

Gonzales, J.J., Lefkowitz, E., McNeil, M., Carter-Campbell, J., Yuan, N., Epstein, S., Schulman, K. & Goldstein, D. (1994). Assessing patient preferences for depression outcomes, Presented at the 3rd Workshop on Costs and Assessment in Psychiatry, *The Economics of Schizophrenia, Depression, Anxiety, Dementias*, ARCAP, Venice, 28–30 October.

Good-Ellis, M.A., Fine, S.B., Spencer, J.H. & DiVittis, A. (1987). Developing a Role Activity Performance Scale, *Am. J. Occupat. Ther.*, **41**, 232–241.

Goodman, W.K., Price, L.H., Rasmussen, S.A., Mazure, C., Fleischmann, R.L., Hill, C.L., Heninger, G.R. & Charney, D. (1989). Yale–Brown Obsessive Compulsive Scale (Y-BOCS) part I: development, use and reliability, *Arch. Gen. Psychiatry,* **46**, 1006–1011.

Gordon, G. (1966). *Role Theory and Illness. A Sociological Perspective*, College & University Press, New Haven, CT.

Gotlib, I.H. (1990). An interpersonal systems approach to the conceptualization and treatment of depression, in *Contemporary Psychological Approaches to Depression* (Ed. R.E. Ingram), pp. 137–154, Plenum Press, New York.

Graham, P., Stevenson, J. & Flynn, D. (1995). *A new measure of health-related quality of life for children: preliminary findings*, unpublished paper, London.

Granger, B. & Baron, R. (1996). *Agency-sponsored entrepreneurial businesses that employ individuals with psychiatric disabilities: Findings from a national survey*, Matrix Institute, Philadelphia.

Grawe, K., Donati, R. & Bernauer, F. (1994). *Psychotherapie im Wandel*, Hogrefe, Göttingen.

Gray, L.C., Farish, S.J. & Dorevitch, M. (1992). A population-based study of assessed applicants to long-term nursing home care, *J. Am. Geriatrics Society*, **40**, 596–600.

Greenley, J.R. & Greenberg, J. (1994). Measuring quality of life: A new and practical survey instrument, *Mental Health Research Center,* paper series 38, Madison, WI.

Gregoire, J., de Leval, N., Mesters, P. & Czarka, M. (1994). Validation of the quality of life in depression scale in a population of adult depressive patients aged 60 and above, *Quality of Life Res.*, **3**, 13–19.

Griefahn, B. (1982). Grenzwerte vegetativer Belastbarkeit. Zum gegenwärtigen Stand der psychophysiologischen Lärmforschung, *Zeitschrift für Lärmbekämpfung*, **29**, 131–136.

Griffin, J. (1986). *Well-Being. Its Meaning, Measurement and Moral Importance*, Oxford University Press, Oxford.

Grønmo, S. (1982). Use of time and quality of life: Dimensions of welfare related to specific activities, in *It's About Time* (Ed. Z. Staikov), pp. 97–117, The Institute of Sociology at the Bulgarian Academy of Science and The Bulgarian Sociological Association, Sofia.

Gruber, B.L., Hall, N.R., Hersh, S.P. & Dubois, P. (1988). Immune system and psychological changes in metastatic cancer patients using relaxation and guided imagery: A pilot study, *Scand. J. Behav. Ther.,* **17**, 25–46.

Grut, M., Jorm, A.F., Fratiglioni, L., Forsell, Y. et al (1993). Memory complaints of elderly people in a population survey: Variation according to dementia stage and depression, *J. Am. Geriatrics Society*, **41**, 1295–1300.

Gudex, C. (1990). The QALY: How can it be used? in *Quality of Life. Perspectives and Policies* (Eds S. Baldwin, C. Godfrey & C. Propper), pp. 218–230, Routledge, London.

Guerrien, B. (1992). Las bases de la teoria económica, *Investigación y Ciencia*, **192**, 64–69.

Gurin, G., Veroff, S. & Feld, S. (1960). *Americans View their Mental Health*, Basic Books, New York.

Gurland, B.J., Yorkston, N.J., Stone, A.R., Frank, J.D. & Fleiss, J.L. (1972). The Structured and Scaled Interview to Assess Maladjustment (SSIAM): Description, rationale and development, *Arch. Gen. Psychiatry*, **27**, 259–264.

Gurland, B., Copeland, J., Kuriansky, J., Kelleher, H., Sharpe, L. & Dean, L.L. (Eds)(1983). *The Mind and Mood of Aging*, pp. 51–52, 105, 121–125, 157–166, Haworth Press, New York.

Gurland, B. & Katz, S. (1992). The outcomes of psychiatric disorder in the elderly:

Relevance to quality of life, in *Handbook of Mental Health and Aging* (Eds J.E. Birren, R.B. Sloane & E.D. Cohen), pp. 230–248, Academic Press, Los Angeles.

Gurland, B., Katz, S., Lantigua, R.A. & Wilder, D.E. (1993). Cognitive function and the elderly, in *U.S. Department of Health and Human Services* (Ed. N. Feinleib), Proceedings of the 1991 International Symposium on Data on Aging, National Center for Health Statistics (NCHS), Series 5, pp. 21–26.

Gurland, B.J., Wilder, D.E., Chen, J., Lantigua, R., Mayeux, R. & Van Nostrand, J. (1995) A flexible system of detection for Alzheimer's disease and related dementias, *Aging Clin. Exp. Res.*, **7**, 165–172.

Gurland, B.J. & Katz, S. (1997). Subjective burden of depression, *Am. J. Geriatric Pyschiatry*, **5**(3), 188–191.

Gurland, B.J., Katz, S. & Chen, J. (1997). Index of affective suffering: Linking a classification of depressed mood to impairment in quality of life, *Am. J. Geriatric Psychiatry* **5**(3), 192–210.

Gurland, B.J., Wilder, D.E., Lantigua, R., Mayeux, R., Stern, Y., Chen, J., Cross, P. & Killeffer, E. (1997). Differences in rates of dementia between ethnoracial groups, in *Racial and Ethnic Differences in the Health of Older Americans* (Eds L.G. Martin & B.J. Soldo), Chapter 8, National Academy Press, Washington, DC..

Gurtman, M.B. (1986). Depression and the response of others: Reevaluating the reevaluation, *J. Abnorm. Psychol.*, **95**, 99–101.

Gutek, B.A., Allen, H., Tyler, T.R., Lau, R.R. & Majchrzak, A. (1983). The importance of internal referents as determinants of satisfaction, *J. Comm. Psychol.*, **11**, 111–120.

Guyatt, G.H., Veldhuyzen Van Zanten, S.J., Feeny, D.H. & Patrick, D.L. (1989). Measuring quality of life in clinical trials; a taxonomy and review, *CMAJ*, **140**, 1441–1448.

Guyatt, G.H., Feeny, D.H. & Patrick, D.L. (1993). Measuring health-related quality of life, *Ann. Int. Med.*, **118**, 622–629.

Hadorn, D.C. (1993). Outcomes management and resource allocation; How should quality of life be measured? *Health Policy Research Unit Discussion Paper HPRU93*, Vol. 7D, pp. 1–56.

Häfner, H. (1995). Epidemiology of schizophrenia. The disease model of schizophrenia in the light of current epidemiological knowledge, *Eur. Psychiatry*, **10**, 217–227.

Häfner, H. & Nowotny, B. (1995). Epidemiology of early-onset schizophrenia, *Eur. Arch. Psychiatry Clin. Neurosci.*, 245, 80–92.

Haley, W.E., Brown, S.L. & Levine, E.G. (1987). Family caregiver appraisals of patient behavioral disturbance in senile dementia, *Clinical Gerontologist*, **6**, 25–34.

Hall, J.N. (1980). Ward rating scales for long stay patients. A review, *Psychol. Med.*, **10**, 277–288.

Halpern, D. (1995). *Mental Health and the Built Environment*, Taylor & Francis, London.

Hamilton, M. (1960). A rating scale for depression, *J. Neurol. Neurosurg. Psychiatry*, **23**, 56–62.

Hamilton, M. & Hoenig, J. (1966). *The Desegregation of the Mentally Ill*, Routledge & Kegan Paul, London.

Hammen, C. (1990). Vulnerability to depression: personal, situational and family aspects, in *Contemporary Psychological Approaches to Depression* (Ed. R. Ingram), pp. 59–70, Plenum Press, New York.

Handy, J. (1991a). Stress and contradiction in psychiatric nursing, *Human Relations*, **44**, 39–53.

Handy, J. (1991b). The social context of occupational stress in a caring profession, *Soc. Sci. Med.*, **32**, 819–830.

Hanninen, T., Reinikainen, K.J., Helkala, E.L., Koivisto, K. et al (1994). Subjective memory complaints and personality traits in normal elderly subjects, Second Congress of the Pan-European Society of Neurology (1991, Vienna, Austria). *J. Am. Geriatrics Soc.*, **42**, 1–4.

Harrison, W.D. (1983). A social competence model of burnout, in *Stress and Burnout in the Human Service Profession* (Ed. B.A. Farber), pp. 29–39, Pergamon Press, New York.

Hatfield, A.B. & Lefley, H.P. (1993). *Surviving Mental Illness*, The Guilford Press, New York, London.

Hatziandreu, E.J., Brown, R.E., Revicki, D.A., Turner, R., Martindale, J., Levine, S. & Siegel, J.E. (1994). Cost utility of maintenance treatment of recurrent depression with sertraline versus episodic treatment with dothiepin, *PharmacoEconomics*, **5**, 249–264.

Hau, E. (1977). Lebensqualität – unter psychoanalytischem Aspekt, *Psychotherapie, Medizin, Psychologie*, **27**, 6–12.

Heady, B. & Wearing, A. (1989). Personality, life events, and subjective well-being: Toward a dynamic equilibrium model, *J. Pers. Soc. Psychol.*, **57**, 731–739.

Heady, B., Veenhoven, R. & Wearing, A. (1991). Top-down versus bottom-up theories of subjective well-being, *Social Indicators Research*, **24**, 81–100.

Health Services Research Institute. (1995). *Quality of Life Toolkit*, Boston, MA.

Hegarty, J.D., Baldessarini, R.J., Tohen, M., Waternaux, C. & Oepen, G. (1994). One hundred years of schizophrenia: A meta-analysis of the outcome literature, *Am. J. Psychiatry*, **151**, 1409–1416.

Heinrich, K. (1967). Zur Bedeutung des postremissiven Erschöpfungs-Syndroms für die Rehabilitation Schizophrener, *Nervenarzt*, **38**, 487–491.

Heinrich, R.L., Schag, C.C. & Ganz, P.A. (1984). Living with cancer: The cancer inventory of problem situations, *J. Clin. Psychol.*, **40**, 972–980.

Heinrich, R.L. & Schag, C.C. (1985). Stress and activity management: group treatment for cancer patients and spouses, *J. Consult. Clin. Psychol.*, **33**, 439–446.

Heinrichs, D.W., Hanlon, E.T. & Carpenter, W.T. Jr (1984). The quality of life scale: an instrument for rating the schizophrenic deficit syndrome, *Schiz. Bull.*, **10**, 388–398.

Helmchen, H. (1990) "Lebensqualität" als Bewertungskriterium in der Psychiatrie, in *"Lebensqualität" als Bewertungskriterium in der Medizin* (Eds P. Schölmerich & G. Thews), pp. 33–115, Fischer, Stuttgart.

Herman, H., Schofield, H., Murphy, B. & Singh, B. (1994). The experiences and quality of life of informal caregivers, in *Quality of Life Assessment: International Perspectives* (Ed. J. Orley), pp. 131–150, Springer, Berlin.

Herz, M., Szymanski, H.E. & Simon, J.C. (1982). Intermittent medication for stable schizophrenic outpatients, *Am. J. Psychiatry*, **139**, 918–922.

Hipwell, A.E., Tyler, P.A. & Wilson, C.M. (1989). Sources of stress and dissatisfaction among nurses in four hospital environments, *Br. J. Med. Psychol.*, **62**, 71–79.

Hirschfeld, R., Klerman, G., Lavori, P., Keller, M., Griffith, P. & Coryell, W. (1989). Premorbid personality assessment of first onset of major depression, *Arch. Gen. Psychiatry*, **46**, 345–350.

Hirst, M. (1990). Multidimensional representation of disablement: A qualitative approach, in *Quality of Life. Perspectives and Policies* (Eds S. Baldwin, C. Godfrey & C. Propper), pp. 72–83, Routledge, London.

Hodgkin, D. (1992). The impact of private utilization management on psychiatric care: A review of the literature, *J. Mental Health Administration*, **19**, 143–157.

Hogan, T.P., Awad, A.G. & Eastwood, M.R. (1983). A self-report scale predictive of drug compliance in schizophrenics: Reliability and discriminative validity, *Psychol. Med.*, **13**, 177–183.

Hogman, G. (1994). *European Questionnaire Survey of Carers*, European Federation of Families of the Mentally Ill (EUFAMI), Groeneweg 151, B-3001 Heverlee, Belgium.

Holcomb, W.R., Morgan, P., Adams, N.A., Ponder, H. & Farrel, M. (1993). Development of a structured interview scale for measuring quality of life of the severely mentally ill, *J. Clin. Psychology*, **49**, 830–840.

Holub, U.M. (1990). *Veränderungsmessung im Rahmen eines stationären verhaltenstherapeutischen Behandlungsprogrammes*, Thesis, University of Vienna.

Hopwood, P., Stephens, R.J. & Machin, D., for the MRC Lung Cancer Working Party (1994). Approaches to the analysis of quality of life data: Experiences gained from a Medical Research Council Lung Cancer Working Party palliative chemotherapy trial, *Qual. Life Res.*, **3**, 339–352.

Hormuth, S.E. (1992). Experience sampling and personality psychology: Concepts and applications, in *The Experience of Psychopathology* (Ed. M.W. deVries), pp. 34–40, Cambridge University Press, Cambridge.

Hoult, J. & Reynolds, J. (1984). Schizophrenia: A comparative trial of community oriented and hospital oriented psychiatric care, *Acta Psych. Scand.*, **69**, 359–372.

Huber, D., Henrich, G. & Herschbach, P. (1988). Measuring the quality of life: a comparison between physically and mentally chronically ill patients and healthy persons, *Pharmacopsychiatry*, **21**, 453–455.

Hughes, C.P., Berg, L., Danziger, W.L., Coben, L.A. & Martin, R.L. (1982). A new clinical scale for the staging of dementia, *Br. J. Psychiatry*, **140**, 566–572.

Hunt, S.M. (1997). The problem of quality of life, *Quality of Life Research*, **6**, 205–212.

Hunt, S.M. & McEwen, J. (1980). The development of a subjective health indicator, *Sociology of Health and Illness*, **2**, 231–246.

Hunt, S.M. & McKenna, S.P. (1992a). The QLDS: A scale for measurement of quality of life in depression, *Health Policy*, **22**, 307–319.

Hunt, S.M. & McKenna, S.P. (1992b). A new measure of quality of life in depression: testing the reliability and construct validity of the QLDS, *Health Policy*, **22**, 321–330.

Hurry, J. & Sturt, E. (1981). Social performance in a population sample: relation to psychiatric symptoms, in *What is a case?* (Eds J.K. Wing, P. Bebbington & L.N. Robins), pp. 202–213, Grant McIntyre, London.

Huxley, P. & Warner, R. (1992). Case management, quality of life, and satisfaction with services of long-term psychiatric patients, *Hosp. Comm. Psychiatry*, **43**, 799–802.

Inouye, S.K., Albert, M.S., Mohs, R., Sun, K. & Berkman, L.F. (1993). Cognitive performance in a high-functioning community-dwelling elderly population, *J. Gerontol. Medical Sciences*, **48**, M146-M151.

Ising, H. & Kruppa, B. (Eds) (1993). *Noise and Disease*. Fischer Verlag, Stuttgart, New York.

Ittelson, W.H., Proshansky, H.M., Rivlin, L.G. & Winkel, G.H. (1974). *An Introduction to Environmental Psychology*, Holt, Rinehart & Winston, New York.

Ivan, T.M. & Glazer, J.P. (1994). Quality of life in pediatric psychiatry: a new outcome measure, *Child and Adolescent Psychiatric Clinics of North America*, Volume 3, pp. 599–611.

Jacobson, A.M., de Groot, M. & Samson, J.A. (1997). The effect of psychiatric disorders and symptoms on quality of life in patients with Type I and Type II diabetes mellitus, *Qual. Life Res.*, **6**, 11–20.

Janca, A., Kastrup, M., Katschnig, H., Lopez-Ibor, J.J., Mezzich, J.E. & Sartorius, N. (1996). The ICD-10 multiaxial system for use in adult psychiatry: structure and application, *J. Nerv. Ment. Dis.*, **184**, 191–192.

Jarema, M., Konieczynska, Z., Jacubiak, A., Glowczak, M. & Meder, J. (1994). First results of quality of life evaluation in treated schizophrenic patients, *Quality of Life Newsletter*, **8**, 10–11.

Jodelet, D. (1991). *Madness and Social Representations*, Harvester Wheatsheaf, Hemel Hempstead.

Johannesson, M., Pliskin, J.S. & Weinstein, M.C. (1994). A note on QALYs, time tradeoff, and discounting, *Medical Decision Making*, **14**, 188–193.

Johnson, D.L. (1990). The family's experience of living with mental illness, in *Families as Allies in the Treatment of the Mentally Ill* (Eds H.P. Lefley & D.L. Johnson), pp. 31–64, American Psychiatric Press, Washington, DC.

Johnson, J., Weissman, M.M. & Klerman, G.L. (1992). Service utilization and social morbidity associated with depressive symptoms in the community, *JAMA*, **267**, 1478–1483.

Johnson, P.J. (1991). Emphasis on quality of life of people with severe mental illness in community-based care in Sweden, *Psychosocial Rehab. J.*, **14**, 23–37.

Jones, H.M. (1953). *The Pursuit of Happiness*. Harvard University Press, Cambridge, MA.

Jones, K., Robinson, M. & Golightly, M. (1986). Long-term psychiatric patients in the community, *Br. J. Psychiatry*, **149**, 537–540.

Joyce, C.R.B. (1987). Quality of life. The state of the art in clinical assessment, in *Quality of Life: Assessment and Application* (Eds S.R. Walker & R.M. Rosser), MTP Press, Lancaster.

Joyce, C.R.B. (1994). Health status and quality of life: What matters to the patient? *J. Cardiovasc. Pharmacol.*, **23** (Suppl. 3), S26–S33.

Juniper, E.F., Guyatt, G.H. & Dolovich, J. (1994). Assessment of quality of life in adolescents with allergic rhinoconjunctivitis: Development and testing of a questionnaire for clinical trials, *J. Allergy Clin. Immunol.*, **93**, 413–423.

Juster, F.T. (1985). The validity and quality of time use estimates obtained from recall diaries, in *Time, Goods, and Well-being* (Eds F.T. Juster & F.P. Stafford), Institute for Social Research, University of Michigan, Ann Arbor.

Juster, F.T., Courant, P.N. & Dow, G.K. (1981). A theoretical framework for the measurement of well-being, *The Review of Income and Wealth*, **27**, 1–31.

Kadushin, Ch. (1969). *Why People go to Psychiatrists*, Atherton Press, New York.

Kahn, R.L., Wolfe, D.M., Quinn, R.P., Snoek, J.D. & Rosenthal, R.A. (1964). *Organizational Stress: Studies in Role Conflict and Ambiguity*, John Wiley, New York.

Kahneman, D. & Tversky, A. (1982). The psychology of preferences, *Scientific American*, **246**, 136–142.

Kamlet, M.S., Wade, M., Kupfer, D.J. & Frank, E. (1992). Cost-utility analysis of maintenance treatment for recurrent depression: A theoretical framework and numerical illustration, in *Economics and Mental Health* (Eds R.G. Frank and W.G. Manning), pp. 267–291, Johns Hopkins University Press, Baltimore, MD.

Kaplan, R., Bush, J. & Berry, C. (1976). Health status: Types of validity and the index of well-being, *Hlth. Serv. Res.*, **11**, 478–507.

Kaplan, R.M. & Bush, J.W. (1982). Health-related quality of life measurement for evaluation research and policy analysis, *Health Psychology*, **1**, 61–80.

Kaplan, H.I. & Sadock, B.J. (1992). *Synopsis of Psychiatry: Behavioral Sciences Clinical Psychiatry* (6th edn), Williams & Wilkins, New York.

Karno, M., Golding, J.M., Sorenson, S.B. & Burnam, M.A. (1988). The epidemiology of obsessive-compulsive disorder in five communities, *Arch. Gen. Psychiatry*, **45**, 1094–1099.

Karnovsky, D.A. & Burchenal, J.H. (1949). The clinical evaluation of chemotherapeutic agents in cancer, in *Evaluation of Chemotherapeutic Agents in Cancer* (Ed. C.M. McLeod), pp. 191–205, Columbia University Press, New York.

Katon, W., von Korff, M., Lin, E., Lipscomb, P., Russo, J., Wagner, E. & Polk, E. (1990). Distressed high utilizers of medical care: DSM-III-R diagnoses and treatment needs, *Gen. Hosp. Psychiatry*, **12**, 355–362.

Katschnig, H. (1983). Methods for measuring social adjustment, in *Methodology in Evaluation of Psychiatric Treatment* (Ed. T. Helgason), pp. 205–218, Cambridge University Press, Cambridge.

Katschnig, H. (1989). *Die andere Seite der Schizophrenie. Patienten zu Hause* (3rd edn), Psychologie Verlags Union, Munich.

Katschnig, H. (1994). Wie läßt sich die Lebensqualität bei psychischen Krankheiten erfassen? in *Schizophrenie und Lebensqualität* (Eds H. Katschnig and P. König), pp. 1–13, Springer Verlag, Vienna.

Katschnig, H. & Nutzinger, D.O. (1988). Psychosocial aspects of course and outcome in depressive illness, in *Depressive Illness: Prediction of Course and Outcome* (Eds T. Helgason and R.J. Daly), pp. 63–75, Springer Verlag, Berlin.

Katschnig, H. & König, P. (Eds) (1994). *Schizophrenie und Lebensqualität*, Springer Verlag, Vienna.

Katschnig. H., Kramer, B. & Simon, M.D. (1993). *Austrian Questionnaire Survey of Relatives of the Mentally Ill*, Ludwig-Boltzmann Institute for Social Psychiatry, 1090 Spitalgasse 11, Vienna, Austria.

Katschnig, H., Simon, M.D. & Kramer, B. (1994). Die Bedürfnisse von Angehörigen schizophreniekranker Patienten – Erste Ergebnisse einer Umfrage, in *Schizophrenie und Lebensqualität* (Eds H. Katschnig & P. König), pp. 241–250, Springer Verlag, Vienna.

Katschnig, H., Simhandl, C., Serim, M., Subasi, B., Zoghlami, A. & Jaidhauser, K. (1996). Depression-specific quality of life scales are flawed, *APA Annual Meeting*, 4–9 May 1996, New York. New Research Abstracts, p. 160.

Katz, S. (1987). Editorial: The science of quality of life, *J. Chronic Disease*, **40**, 459–463.

Katz, S., Branch, L.G., Branson, H.H., Papsidero, J.A., Beck, J.C. & Greer, D.S. (1983). Active life expectancy, *New J. Med.*, **309**, 1218–1224.

Katz, S. & Gurland, B.J. (1991). Science of quality of life of elders: challenges and opportunity, in *The Concept and Measurement of Quality of Life in the Frail Elderly* (Eds J. Birren, J.E. Lubben, J.C. Rowe & D.E. Deutch), pp. 335–343, Academic Press, Los Angeles.

Kay, D.W.K., Beamisch, P. & Roth, M. (1964). Old age mental disorders in Newcastle-upon-Tyne, II. A study of possible social and medical causes, *Br. J. Psychiatry*, **110**, 668–682.

Keilen, M., Treasure, T., Schmidt, U. & Treasure, J. (1994). Quality of life measurements in eating disorders, angina and transplant candidates: Are they comparable? *J. Roy. Soc. Med.*, **87**, 441–444.

Keith, K.D. & Schalock, R.L. (1992). The Quality of Life Questionnaire, *Behavior Ther.*, **15**, 106–107.

Keller, M.B., Lavori, P.W., Friedman, B., Nielson, E., Endicott, J., McDonald-Scott, P. & Andreasen, N.C. (1987). The longitudinal interval follow-up evaluation, *Arch. Gen. Psychiatry*, **44**, 540–548.

Kelloway, E.K. & Barling, J. (1991). Job characteristics, role stress and mental health, *J. Occup. Psychol.*, **64**, 291–304.

Kemmler, G., Holzner, B., Neudorfer, Ch., Schwitzer, J. & Meise, U. (1995). What constitutes overall life satisfaction of chronic schizophrenic outpatients? Results of a pilot study using the Lancashire Quality of Life Profile, *Qual. Life Res.*, **4**, 445–446.

Kentros, M.K., Terkelsen, K., Hull, J., Smith, T.E. & Goodman, M. (1997). The relationship between personality and quality of life in persons with schizoaffective disorder and schizophrenia, *Quality of Life Research*, **6**, 118–122.

Kessler, R.C., McGonagle, K.A., Zhao, S., Nelson, C.B., Hughes, M., Eshleman, M.A., Wittchen, H.-U. & Kendler, K.S. (1994). Lifetime and 12-month prevalence of DSM-III-R psychiatric disorders in the United States, *Arch. Gen. Psychiatry*, **51**, 8–19.

Kim, E. & Rovner, B.V. (1994). Depression in dementia, *Psychiatric Annals*, **24**, 173–177.

Kind, P. (1990). Issues in the design and construction of a quality of life measurement, in *Quality of Life. Perspectives and Policies* (Eds S. Baldwin, C. Godfrey & C. Propper), pp. 63–71, Routledge, London.

Kind, P., Gudex, C. & Godfrey, C. (1990). Introduction: What are QALYs? in *Quality of*

Life. Perspectives and Policies (Eds S. Baldwin, C. Godfrey & C. Propper), pp. 57–62, Routledge, London.

King, W.I. (1930). *The National Income and its Purchasing Power*, NBER, New York.

Klarman, H.E., Francis, J.O. & Rosenthal, G.D. (1968). Cost-effectiveness analysis applied to the treatment of chronic disease, *Med Care*, **6**, 48–54.

Klein, R.G. (1994). Anxiety Disorders, in *Child and Adolescent Psychiatry: Modern Approaches* (Eds M. Rutter, E. Taylor & L. Hersov), pp. 351–374, Blackwell Scientific, London.

Klerman, G.L. (1989). Depressive disorders: Further evidence for increased medical morbidity and impairment of social functioning, *Arch. Gen. Psychiatry*, **46**, 856–858.

Klerman, G.L., Weissman, M.M., Ouellette, R., Johnson, J. & Greenwald, S. (1991). Panic attacks in the community: Social morbidity and health care utilization, *JAMA*, **265**, 742–746.

Kluger, A. & Ferris, S.H. (1991). Scales for Assessment of Alzheimer's Disease, *Psychiatric Clinic of North America*, **14**, 309–326.

Knable, M.B., Kleinman, J.E. & Weinberger, D.R (1995). Neurobiology of schizophrenia, in *Textbook of Psychopharmacology* (Eds A.F. Schatzberg & C.B. Nemeroff), pp. 479–499, American Psychiatric Press. Washington DC.

Knapp, M. (1993). The costing process: Background theory, in *Costing Community Care* (Eds A. Netten & J. Beecham), PSSRU, Ashgate, Aldershot.

Knapp, M. (Ed.) (1995). *The Economic Evaluation of Mental Health Care*, Arena, Ashgate, Aldershot.

Knapp, M., Beecham, J., Anderson, J., Dayson, D., O'Driscoll, C., Leff, J., Margolius, O. & Wills, W. (1990). The TAPS Project. 3: Predicting the community costs of closing psychiatric hospitals, *Br. J. Psychiatry*, **157**, 661–670.

Knapp, M., Beecham, J., Hallam, A. & Fenyo, A. (1993). The TAPS Project.18: The costs of community care for former long-stay psychiatric hospital residents, *Health and Social Care in the Community*, **1**, 4.

Knapp, M., Beecham, J., Koutsogeorgopoulou, V., Hallam, A., Fenyo, A., Marks, I.M., Connolly, J., Audini, B. & Muijen, M. (1994). Service use and costs of home-based versus hospital-based care for people with serious mental illness, *Br. J. Psychiatry*, **165**, 195–203.

Knight, E. (1991). Self-directed rehabilitation, *Empowerment*, **2**, 1–3.

Kocsis, J.H., Frances, A.J., Voss, C., Mann, J.J., Mason, B.J. & Sweeney, J. (1988). Imipramine treatment for chronic depression, *Arch. Gen. Psychiatry*, **45**, 253–257.

Kocsis, J.H., Zisook, S., Davidson, J., Shelton, R., Yonkers, K., Hellerstein, D.J., Rosenbaum, J. & Halbreich, U. (1997). Double-blind comparison of sertraline, imipramine, and placebo in the treatment of dysthymia: Psychosocial outcomes, *Am. J. Psychiatry*, **154**, 390–395.

Koenders, M.E.F., Passchier, J., Teuns, G., van-Harskamp, F. et al (1993). Trait-anxiety and achievement motivation are positively correlated with memory performance in patients who visit a geriatric outpatient clinic with amniotic symptoms, *Psychological Reports*, **73**, 1227–1231.

Kozma, A., Stone, S., Stones, M.J. & Hannah, T.E. (1990). Long- and short-term affective states in happiness: Model, paradigm and experimental evidence, *Social Indicators Research*, **22**, 119–138.

Kraaijkamp, H.J.M. (1992). *Moeilijke rollen. Psychometrisch onderzoek naar de betrouwbaarheid en validiteit van de Groningse Sociale Beperkingenschaal bij psychiatrische patiënten* (Difficult roles. A study into the reliability and validity of the Groningen Social Disability Schedule in psychiatric patients).

Kramer, B., Simon, M. & Katschnig, H. (1996). Die Beurteilung psychiatrischer

Berufsgruppen durch die Angehörigen, *Psych. Praxis*, **23**, 29–32.

Kramer, J., Kluiter, H. & Wiersma, D. (1994). Burden on the family: Day treatment of the acutely mentally ill compared with psychiatric day treatment in a randomized controlled trial, paper read at 7th European Symposium of AEP, Vienna.

Kramer, P. (1993). *Listening to Prozac*, Viking, New York.

Kretschmer, E. (1966). *Mensch und Lebensgrund*, Rainer Wunderlich Verlag Hermann Leins, Tübingen.

Kuyken, W. & Orley, J. (1994). The Development of the World Health Organization Quality of Life Assessment Instrument (The WHOQOL), The WHOQOL Group, in *Quality of Life Assessment: International Perspectives* (Eds J. Orley & W. Kuyken), pp. 41–57, Springer-Verlag, Berlin, Heidelberg, New York, London, Paris, Tokyo, Hong Kong, Barcelona, Budapest.

Kuyken, W., Orley, J., Hudelson, P. & Sartorius, N. (1994). Quality of Life Assessment across Cultures, *Int. J. Ment. Health*, **23**, 5–27.

Kuznets, S. (1941). *National Income and its Composition, 1919–1938*, NBER, New York.

La Puma, J. & Lawlor, E.F. (1990). Quality-adjusted life-years. Ethical implications for physicians and policymakers, *JAMA*, **263**, 2917–2921.

la Rue, A., Watson, J. & Plotkin, D.A. (1993). First symptoms of dementia: A study of relatives' reports, *Int. J. Geriatric Psychiatry*, **8**, 239–245.

Lain-Entralgo, P. (1982). *El Diagnóstico Médico*, Salvat, Barcelona.

Lally, S. J. (1989). Does being in here mean there is something wrong with me? *Schiz. Bull.*, **15**, 253–265.

Lamb, H.R. (1979a). The new asylums in the community, *Arch. Gen. Psychiatry*, **36**, 129–134.

Lamb, H.R. (1979b). Staff burnout in work with long-term patient, *Hosp. Comm. Psychiatry*, **30**, 396–398.

Lamb, H.R. (1981). What did we really expect from deinstitutionalization? *Hosp. Comm. Psychology*, **32**, 105–109.

Lamb, H.R. (1982). *Treating the Long-term Mentally Ill*, Jossey-Bass, San Francisco.

Lance, C.E., Lautenschlager, G.J., Sloan, C.E. & Varca, P.E. (1989). A comparison between bottom-up, top-down and bidirectional models of relationships between global and life facet satisfaction, *J. Personality*, **57**, 601–624.

Larson, E.B. & Gerlach, J. (1996). Subjective experience of treatment, side-effects, mental state and quality of life in chronic schizophrenic out-patients treated with depot neuroleptics, *Acta Psychiatr. Scand.*, **93**, 381–388.

Lauer, G. (1994). The quality of life issue in chronic mental illness, in *Psychology and Promotion of Health* (Ed. J.P. Dauwalder), pp. 28–34, Hogrefe & Huber, Seattle.

Lauer, G. & Stegmüller, U. (1989). Zur Lebensqualität chronisch psychisch Kranker, Paper presented at 15. Kongress für Angewandte Psychologie: Psychologie für Menschenwürde und Lebensqualität, Munich.

Laupacis, A., Feeny, D., Detsky, A.S. & Tugwell, P.X. (1992). How attractive does a new technology have to be to warrant adoption and utilization? Tentative guidelines for using clinical and economic evaluations, *Can. Med. Assoc. J.*, **146**, 473–481.

Lazarus, R.S. (1966). *Psychological Stress and the Coping Process*, McGraw-Hill, New York.

Lazarus, R.S. & Launier, R. (1978). Stress-related transactions between person and environment, in *Perspectives in Interactional Psychology* (Eds L.A. Pervin and M. Lewis), pp. 287–327, Plenum Press, New York.

Lazarus, R.S. & Folkman, S. (1984). *Stress Appraisal and Coping*, Springer, Berlin.

Leader, J.B. & Klein, D.N. (1996). Social adjustment in dysthymia, double depression and episodic major depression, *J. Affective Disorders*, **37**, 91–101.

Lee, J.T., Nielsen, K., Hirsch, J.D. & Michael, L.W. (1994). Assessing the quality of life of patients with generalized anxiety disorder using the SF-36: A comparison with chronic physical conditions, Abstract of Presentation at the 7th European Symposium of the Association of European Psychiatrists Section Committee, Psychiatric Epidemiology and Social Psychiatry, Vienna, Austria, 7–9 April.

Leete, E. (1989). How I perceive and manage my illness, *Schiz. Bull.*, **15**, 197–200.

Leff, J. (1993). All the homeless people – where do they all come from? *Br. Med. J.*, **306**, 669–670.

Leff, J., O'Driscoll, C., Dayson, D., Wills, W. & Anderson, J. (1990). The TAPS Project. 5: The structure of social-network data obtained from long-stay patients, *Br. J. Psychiatry* **157**, 848–852.

Leff, J., Thornicroft, G., Coxhead, N. & Crawford, C. (1994). The TAPS Project. 22: A five-year follow-up of long-stay psychiatric patients discharged to the community, *Br. J. Psychiatry*, **165** (Supplement 25), 13–17.

Leff, J., Dayson, D., Gooch, C., Thornicroft, G. & Wills, W. (1996). The TAPS Project. 19: A comprehensive matched case-control follow-up study of long-stay patients discharged from two psychiatric institutions, *Psychiatric Services*, **47**, 62–67.

Lefley, H.P. (1987). Aging parents as caregivers of mentally ill adult children: An emerging social problem, *Hosp. Comm. Psychiatry*, **38**, 1063–1070.

Lefley, H.P. (1990). Research directions for a new conceptualization of families, in *Families as Allies in the Treatment of the Mentally Ill* (Eds H.P. Lefley & D.L. Johnson), pp.127–162, American Psychiatric Press, Washington, DC.

Lehman, A.F. (1983a). The well-being of chronic mental patients: Assessing their quality of life, *Arch. Gen. Psychiatry*, **40**, 369–373.

Lehman, A.F. (1983b). The effects of psychiatric symptoms on quality of life assessments among the chronically mentally ill, *Eval. Prog. Planning*, **6**, 143–151.

Lehman, A.F. (1988). A Quality of Life Interview for the chronically mentally ill (QOLI), *Eval. Prog. Planning*, **11**, 51–62.

Lehman, A.F. (1992). The effects of psychiatric symptoms on quality of life, *J. Health Soc. Behav.*, **33**, 299–315.

Lehman, A.F. (1994). Continuity of care and client outcomes in the R.W. Johnson Programme on chronic mental illness, *Milbank Quarterly*, **72**, 105–122.

Lehman, A.F. (1995). Promises and problems in assessing quality of life in clinical trials, *Neuropsychopharm.*, **10**(35), 2395.

Lehman, A.F., Ward, N.C. & Linn, L.S. (1982). Chronic mental patients: The quality of life issue, *Am. J. Psychiatry*, **139**, 1271–1276.

Lehman, A.F., Possidente, S. & Hawker, F. (1986). The quality of life of chronic patients in a State hospital and in community residences, *Hosp. Comm. Psychiatry*, **37**, 901–907.

Lehman, A.F. & Burns, B. (1990). Severe mental illness in the community, in *Quality of Life Assessments in Clinical Trials* (Ed. B. Spilker), pp. 357–366, Raven Press, New York.

Lehman, A.F., Slaughter, J.C. & Myers, C.P. (1991). The quality of life of chronically mentally ill persons in alternative residential settings, *Psychiat. Quarterly*, **62**, 35–49.

Lehman, A.F., Slaughter, J.C. & Myers, C.P. (1992). Quality of life of the chronically mentally ill: Gender and decade of life effects, *Eval. Prog. Planning*, **15**, 7–12.

Lehman, A.F., Postrado, L.T. & Rachoba, L.T. (1993). Convergent validation of quality of life assessment for persons with severe mental illness, *Qual. Life Res.*, **2**, 327–333.

Lehman, A.F., Rachuba, L.T. & Postrado, L.T. (1995). Demographic influences on quality of life among persons with chronic mental illnesses, *Eval. Prog. Planning*, **18**, 155–164.

Lehman, A.F. & Burns, B.J. (1996). Severe mental illness in the community, in *Quality of Life and Pharmacoeconomics in Clinical Trials* (Ed. B. Spilker), pp. 919–924,

Lippincott-Raven, Philadelphia.

Lenz-Schmit, V. (1987). *Evaluation des gruppenunterstützten Selbstmodifikations-programms für essentielle Hypertoniker (GSEH)*, Thesis, University of Vienna.

Leon, A.C., Shear, K., Portera, L. & Klerman, G.L. (1992). Assessing impairment in patients with PD: The Sheehan Disability Scale, *Soc. Psychiatry Psychiatr. Epidemiol.*, **27**, 78–82.

Lépine, J.-P., Gastpar, M., Mendlewicz, J., Tylee, A. and on behalf of the DEPRES Steering Committee (1997). Depression in the community: The first pan-European study DEPRES (Depression Research in European Society), *Int. Clin. Psychiatry*, **12**, 19–29.

Levine, S. (1987). The changing terrains in medical sociology: Emergent concerns with quality of life, *J. Health Soc. Behav.*, **28**, 1–6.

Levitt, A.J., Hogan, T.P. & Bucosky, C.M. (1990). Quality of life in chronically mentally ill patients in day treatment, *Psychol. Med.*, **20**, 703–710.

Lewinsohn, P.M. (1974). A behavioral approach to depression, in *The Psychology of Depression: Contemporary Theory and Research* (Eds R.J. Friedman & M.M. Katz), pp. 157–178, Winston–Wiley, New York.

Liang, J. (1985). A structural integration of the affect balance scale and the life satisfaction index A, *J. Gerontology*, **40**, 552–561.

Liberman, R.P. (Ed.) (1988). *Psychiatric Rehabilitation of Chronic Mental Patients*, American Psychiatric Press, Washington, DC.

Liebowitz, M.R., Gorman, J.M., Fyer, A.J. & Klein, D.F. (1985). Social phobia: Review of a neglected anxiety disorder, *Arch. Gen. Psychiatry*, **42**, 729–736.

Linden, M. (1981). Definition of compliance, *Int. J. Clin. Pharmacol. Ther. Toxicol.*, **19**, 86–90.

Link, B.G., Mesagno, F.P., Lubner, M.E. & Dohrenwend, P. (1990). Problems in measuring role strains and social functioning in relation to psychological symptoms, *J. Health Soc. Behav.*, **31**, 354–369.

Linn, M.W., Linn, B.S. & Harris, R. (1982). Effects of counseling for late-stage cancer patients, *Cancer*, **49**, 1048–1055.

Linton, R. (1936). *The Study of Man*, Appleton-Century, New York.

Lipson, J.G. & Koehler, S.L. (1986). The psychiatric emergency room: Staff subculture, *Issues in Mental Health Nursing*, **8**, 237–246.

Llewellyn-Thomas, H., Sutherland, H.J. & Tibshirani, R. (1982). The measurement of patients' values in medicine, *Medical Decision Making*, **2**, 449–456.

Loewenstein, D.A., Amigo, E., Duara, R., Guterman, A., Hurwitz, D., Berkowitz, N., Wilkie, F., Weinberg, G., Black, B., Gittlernan, B. & Eisdorfer, C. (1989). A new scale for the assessment of functional status in Alzheimer's Disease and related disorders, *J. Gerontology, Psychological Sciences*, **44**, 114–121.

Loewenstein, D.A., Ardila, A., Rosselli, M., Hayden, S. et al (1992). A comparative analysis of functional status among Spanish- and English-speaking patients with dementia, *J. Gerontology*, **47**, 389–394.

Lonnqvist, J., Sintonen, H., Syvälahti, E., Appelberg, B., Koskinen, T., Mannikko, T., Loomes, G. & McKenzie, L. (1990). The scope and limitations of QALY measures, in *Quality of Life. Perspectives and Policies* (Eds S. Baldwin, C. Godfrey & C. Propper), pp. 84–102, Routledge, London.

Lonnqvist, J., Sintonen, H., Syvälahti, E., Appelberg, B., Koskinen, T., Mannikko, T., Mehtonen, O.P., Naarala, M., Sihvo, S., Auvinen, J. & Pitkanen, H. (1994). Antidepressant efficacy and quality of life in depression: A double blind study with moclobemide and fluoxetine, *Acta Psychiat. Scand.*, **89**, 363–369.

Loomes, G. & McKenzie, L. (1990). The scope and limitations of QALY measures, in *Quality of Life Perspectives and Policies* (Eds S. Baldwin, C. Godfrey & C. Propper), pp. 84–102, Routledge, London.

Lubeck, D.P. & Fries, J.F. (1991). Health status among persons with HIV infection: A community-based study (Abstract), *American Public Health Association, Annual Meeting*, Atlanta.

Luborsky, L., Singer, B. & Luborsky, L. (1975). Comparative studies of psychotherapies: Is it true "everyone has won and all must have prizes?" *Arch. Gen. Psychiatry*, **32**, 995–1008.

Lueken, V. (1995). Ich in der Spiegelstadt. Die autobiographische Fiktion der Neuseeländerin Janet Frame, *Psychotherapeutin*, **2**, 89–93.

Lyles, J.N., Burish, T.G., Krozely, M.G. & Oldham, R.K. (1982). Efficacy of relaxation training and guided imagery in reducing the aversiveness of cancer chemotherapy, *J. Consult. Clin. Psychol.*, **50**, 509–524.

Lyness, J.M., Caine, E.D., Conwell, Y., King, D.A. & Cox, C. (1993). Depressive symptoms, medical illness, and functional status in depressed psychiatric inpatients, *Am. J. Psychiatry*, **150**, 910–915.

Magee, W.J., Eaton, W.W., Wittchen, H.-U., McGonagle, K.A. & Kessler, R.C. (1996). Agoraphobia, simple phobia and social phobia in the National Comorbidity Survey, *Arch. Gen. Psychiatry*, **52**, 159–168.

Mahurin, R.K., DeBettignies, B.H. & Pirozzolo, F.J. (1991). Structured Assessment of Independent Living Skills: Preliminary report of a performance measure of functional abilities in dementia, *J. Gerontology*, **46**, 58–66.

Malm, U., May, P.R.A. & Dencker, S.J. (1981). Evaluation of the quality of life of the schizophrenic outpatient: A checklist, *Schiz. Bull.*, **7**, 477–487.

Mangone, C.A., Hier, D.B., Gorelick, P.B., Ganellen, R.J. et al (1991). Impaired insight in Alzheimer's disease, *J. Geriatric Psychiatry and Neurology*, **4**, 189–193.

Markowitz, J.S., Weissman, M.M., Puellette, R., Lish, J.D. & Klerman, G.L. (1989). Quality of life in panic disorder, *Arch. Gen. Psychiatry*, **46**, 984–992.

Marks, I.M., Connolly, J., Muijen, M., Audini, B., McNamee, G. & Lawrence, R.E. (1994). Home-based versus hospital-based care for people with serious mental illness, *Br. J. Psychiatry*, **165**, 179–194.

Martin, C., Genduso, L., Revicki, D., Hamilton, S., Tran, P. & Beasley, C. (1996). *Quality of life outcomes of olanzapine*, Presentation at Summer University, Hertfordshire.

Maser, J.D. & Kaelber, C. (1991). International use and attitude towards DSM-III and DSM-III-R: Growing consensus in psychiatric classification. Special issue: Diagnosis, dimensions, and DSM-IV: The science of classification, *J. Abnormal Psychology*, **100**, 271–279.

Maslach, C. (1976). Burned-out, *Human Behaviour*, **5**, 16–22.

Maslach, C. (1978a). The client role in staff burn-out, *J. Social Issues*, **34**, 111–124.

Maslach, C. (1978b). Job burn-out: How people cope, *Public Welfare*, **36**, 56–58.

Maslach, C. (1979). The burn-out syndrome and patient care, in *Stress and Survival: The Emotional Realities of Life-threatening Illness* (Ed. C.A. Garfield), C.V. Mosby, St Louis, MO.

Maslach, C. & Pines, A. (1977). The burnout syndrome in the day care setting, *Child Care Quarterly*, **6**, 100–113.

Maslach, C. & Jackson, S.E. (1978). Lawyer burn-out, *Barrister*, **5**, 52–54.

Maslach, C. & Jackson, S.E. (1979). Burned-out cops and their families, *Psychology Today*, **12**, 59–62.

Maslach, C. & Jackson, S.E. (1981). The measurement of experienced burnout, *J. Occupat. Behav.*, **2**, 99–113.

Maslow, A.H. (1954). *Motivation and Personality*, Harper & Row, New York.

Mason, J.M. (1994). Cost-per-QALY league tables. Their role in pharmaeconomics analysis,

PharmacoEconomics, **5**, 472–481.

Massimini, F., Csikszentmihalyi, M. & Carli, M. (1987). The monitoring of optimal experience. A tool for psychiatric rehabilitation, *J. Nerv. Ment. Disease*, **175**, 545–549.

Massimini, F. & Carli, M. (1988). The systematic assessment of flow in daily life experience, in *Optimal Experience: Psychological Studies of Flow in Consciousness* (Eds M. Csikszentmihalyi & I. Csikszentmihalyi), pp. 266–287, Cambridge University Press, New York.

Massion, A.O., Warshaw, M.G. & Keller, M.B. (1993). Quality of life and psychiatric morbidity in PD and generalized anxiety disorder, *Am. J. Psychiatry*, **150**, 600–607.

Mauskopf, J.A., Simeon, G.P., Miles, M.A., Westlund, R.E. & Davidson, J.R.T. (1996). Functional status in depressed patients: the relationship to disease severity and disease resolution, *J. Clin. Psychiatry*, **57**, 588–592.

Maynard, A. (1993). Cost management: The economist's viewpoint, *Br. J. Psychiatry*, **163** (supplement 20), 7–13.

Mayou, R. (1990). Quality of life in cardiovascular disease, *Psychother. Psychsom.*, **54**, 99–109.

Mayou, R.A., Macmahon, D., Sleight, P. & Florencio, M.J. (1981). Early rehabilitation after myocardial infarction, *Lancet*, **2**, 1399–1402.

McCabe, S. & Unzicker, R. (1995). Changing roles of consumer/survivors in mature mental health systems, *New Directions in Mental Health Services*, No. 66, 61–73.

McCarthy, P. (1985). Burnout in psychiatric nursing, *J. Advanced Nursing*, **10**, 305–310.

McDowell, I. & Newell, C. (1987). *Measuring Health: A Guide to Rating Scales and Questionnaires*, Oxford University Press, New York.

McGill, T.M. (1995). Quality of life assessment: values and pitfalls, *J. Roy. Soc. Med.*, **88**, 680–683.

McGlone, J., Gupta, S., Humphrey, D., Oppenheimer, S. et al (1990). Screening for early dementia using memory complaints from patients and relatives, *Arch. Neurol.*, 47, 1189–1193.

McKenna, S.P. (1997). Measuring quality of life in schizophrenia, *Eur. Psychiatry*, **12**, (supplement 3), 267s–274s.

McKenna, S.P. & Hunt, S.M. (1992). A new measure of quality of life in depression: Testing the reliability and construct validity of the QLDS, *Health Policy*, **22**, 321–330.

McLean, A. (1995). Empowerment and the psychiatric consumer/ex-patient movement in the United States: Contradictions, crisis and change, *Soc. Sci. Med.*, **40**, 1053–1071.

Mechanic, D. (1986). The challenge of chronic mental illness: A retrospective and prospective view, *Hosp. Comm. Psychiatry*, **37**, 891–896.

Mechanic, D. (1991). Strategies for Integrating Public Mental Health Services, *Hosp. Comm. Psychiatry*, **42**, 797–801.

Mechanic, D. (1996). Can research on managed care inform practice and policy decisions? in *Controversies in Managed Mental Health Care* (Ed. A. Lazarus), pp. 197–211, American Psychiatric Press, Washington, DC.

Mechanic, D. & Aiken, L.H. (1989). Capitation in mental health: potentials and cautions, in *Paying for Services: Promises and Pitfalls of Capitation* (Eds D. Mechanic and L.H. Aiken), pp. 5–18, New Directions Series, MHS, 43, Jossey-Bass, San Francisco.

Mechanic, D., McAlpine, D., Rosenfield, S. & Davis, D. (1994). Effects of illness attribution and depression on the quality of life among persons with serious mental illness, *Soc. Sci. Med.*, **39**, 155–164.

Mechanic, D., Schlesinger, M. & McAlpine, D. (1995). Management of mental health and substance abuse services: State of the art and early results, *Milbank Quarterly*, **73**, 19–55.

Meenan, R.F., Gertman, P.M. & Mason, J.M. (1980). Measurement of health status in arthritis: The Arthritis Impact Measurement Scales, *Arthritis Rheum.*, **23**, 146.

Megone, C. (1990). The quality of life. Starting from Aristotle, in *Quality of Life. Perspectives and Policies* (Eds S. Baldwin, C. Godfrey & C. Propper), pp. 84–102, Routledge, London.

Mehrez, A. & Gafni, A. (1991). The healthy-years equivalents: How to measure them using the standard gamble approach, *Medical Decision Making*, **11**, 140–146.

Mehtonen, O.P., Naarala, M., Sihvo, S., Auvinen, J. & Pitkanen, H. (1994). Antidepressant efficacy and quality of life in depression: A double-blind study with moclobemide and fluoxetine, *Acta Psychiat. Scand.*, **89**, 363–369.

Meltzer, H.Y. (1992). Dimensions of outcome with clozapine, *Br. J. Psychiatry*, **160** (suppl. 17), 46–53.

Meltzer, H.Y., Bastani, B., Young Kwon, K., Ramirez, L.F., Burnett, S. & Sharpe, J. (1989). A prospective study of clozapine in treatment-resistant schizophrenic patients. I. Preliminary report, *Psychopharmacol.*, **99**, S68–S72.

Meltzer, H.Y., Burnett, S., Bastani, B. & Ramirez, L.F. (1990). Effects of six months of clozapine treatment on the quality of life of chronic schizophrenic patients, *Hosp. Comm. Psychiatry*, **41**, 892–897.

Meltzer, H.Y., Cola, P., Way, L., Thompson, P.A., Bastani, B., Davies, M.A. & Snitz, B. (1993). Cost effectiveness of clozapine in neuroleptic-resistant schizophrenia, *Am. J. Psychiatry*, **150**, 1630–1638.

Meltzer, H., Gill, B., Petticrew, M. & Hinds, K. (1996). *OPCS Survey of Psychiatric Morbidity in Great Britain*, Report 1: The prevalence of psychiatric morbidity among adults living in private households, Report 3: Economic activity and social functioning of adults with psychiatric disorders, HMSO, London.

Mercier, C., Renaud, C., Desbiens, F. & Gervais, S. (1990). *The Contribution of Services to the Quality of Life of Psychiatric Patients in the Community*, Health and Welfare Canada, Ottawa.

Mercier, C. & King, S. (1994). A latent variable causal model of the quality of life and community tenure of psychotic patients, *Acta Psychiatr. Scand.*, **89**, 72–77.

Merikangas, K. (1984). Divorce and assertive mating among depressed patients, *Am. J. Psychiatry*, **141**, 74–76.

Meyer, A. (1907). Fundamental conceptions of dementia praecox, *J. Nerv. Ment. Dis.*, **34**, 331–336.

Mezzich, J.E. (1994). Multiaxial diagnosis: Purposes and challenges, in *Psychiatric Diagnosis. A World Perspective* (Eds J.E. Mezzich, Y. Honda & M.C. Kastrup), Springer, New York.

Mezzich, J.E. (1995). International perspectives on psychiatric diagnosis, in *Comprehensive Textbook of Psychiatry*, 6th edn (Eds H.I. Kaplan & B.J. Sadock), Williams & Wilkins, Baltimore.

Mezzich, J.E., Fabrega, H. & Mezzich, A.C. (1985). An international consultation on multiaxial diagnosis, in *Psychiatry: The State of the Art* (Eds P. Pichot, P. Berger, R. Wolf & K. Thau), Plenum Press, London.

Mezzich, J.E. & Jorge, M.R. (1993). Psychiatric nosology: Achievements and challenges, in *International Review of Psychiatry*, Volume 1 (Eds J.A. Costa e Silva & C.C. Nadelson), American Psychiatric Press, Washington, DC.

Mezzich, J.E. & Schmolke, M.M. (1995). Multiaxial diagnosis and psychotherapy planning: On the relevance of ICD-10, DSM-IV and complementary schemas, *Psychother. Psychosom.*, **63**, 71–80.

Michalos, A.C. (1985). Multiple discrepancies theory (MDT), *Social Indicators Research*, **16**, 347–443.

Miesen, B.M. (1993). Alzheimer's disease, the phenomenon of parent fixation and Bowlby's attachment theory, *Int. J. Geriatric Psychiatry*, **8**, 147–153.

Mike, V. (1992). Quality of life research and the ethics of evidence, *Qual. Life Res.*, **1**, 273–276.

Milbrath, L.W. (1982). A conceptualization and research strategy for the study of ecological aspects of the quality of life, *Social Indicators Research*, **10**, 133–157.

Mintz, J., Mintz, L.I., Arruda, M.J. & Hwang, S.S. (1992). Treatment of depression and the functional capacity to work, *Arch. Gen. Psychiatry*, **49**, 761–768.

Mittleman, G. (1985). First person account. The pain of parenthood in the mentally ill, *Schiz. Bull.*, **11**, 300–303.

Monroe, S.M. & Steiner, S.S. (1986). Social support and psychopathology: Interrelations with preexisting disorders, stress, and personality, *J. Abnorm. Psychol.*, **95**, 29–39.

Moos, R.H. & Lemke, S. (1984). *Multiphasic Environmental Assessment Procedure Manual*, Social Ecology Laboratory, Veterans Administration and Stanford University Medical Center, Palo Alto CA.

Mor, V. & Guadogoli, E. (1988). Quality of life measurement: A psychometric Tower of Babel, *J. Clin. Epidemiol.*, **41**, 1055–1058.

Mor, V., Murphy, J., Masterson-Allen, S., Willey, C., Razmpour, A., Jackson, N.E., Greer, D. & Katz, S. (1989). Risk of functional decline among well elders, *J. Clin. Epidemiol.*, **42**, 895–904.

Morcillo, L., Barcia, D. & Borgoñós, E. (1995). Esquizofrenia: calidad de vida y años de evolución, *Actas Luso-Esp. Neurol. Psiquiatr.*, **23**, 293–298.

Morgado, A., Smith, M., Lecrubier, Y. & Widlocher, D. (1991). Depressed subjects unwittingly overreport poor social adjustment which they reappraise when recovered, *J. Nerv. Ment. Dis.*, **179**, 614–619.

Morrissey, J.P., Calloway, M., Bartko, W.T., Ridgely, M.S., Goldman, H.H. & Paulson, R.L. (1994). Local Mental Health Authorities and Service System Changes: Evidence from the Robert Wood Johnson Programme on Chronic Mental Illness, *Milbank Quarterly*, **72**, 49–80.

Morrow, G.R., Chiarello, R.J. & Derogatis, L.R. (1978). A new scale for assessing patients' psychological adjustment to medical illness, *Psychol. Med.*, **8**, 605–610.

Morss, S.E., Lenert, L.A. & Faustman, W.O. (1993). The side effects of antipsychotic drugs and patients' quality of life: Patient education and preference assessment with computers and multimedia, *Proc. Annu. Symp. Comput. Appl. Med. Care*, **17**, 17–21.

Mortimer, J.A., Schuman, L.M. & French, L.R. (1981). Epidemiology of dementing illness, in *The Epidemiology of Dementia* (Eds J.A. Hortimer & L.N. Schuman), pp. 6–9, Oxford University Press, New York.

Moum, T. (1988). Yea-saying and mood-reporting quality of life, *Social Indicators Research*, **20**, 117–139.

Mukherjee, R. (1989). *The Quality of Life: Valuation in Social Research*, Sage, London.

Mulkern, V., Agosta, J.M. Ashbaugh, J.W., Bradley, V.J., Spence, R.A., Allein, S., Nurczynski, P. & Houlihan, J. (1986). Community Support Program Client Follow-up Study, Report to NIMH.

Müller, Ch. (1993). *Die Gedanken werden handgreiflich*, Springer Verlag, Berlin, Heidelberg, New York.

Murray, C.J.L. (1994). Quantifying the burden of disease: The technical basis for disability-adjusted life years, in *Global Comparative Assessment in the Health Sector: Disease Burden, Expenditures and Intervention Packages* (Eds C.J.L. Murray & A.D. Lopez), pp. 3–19, World Health Organization, Geneva.

Musil, R. (1930). *Der Mann ohne Eigenschaften*, Rowohlt, Reinbeck bei Hamburg.

Myers, D.G. & Diener, E. (1996). The pursuit of happiness, *Scientific American*, May, 54–56.

Myers, G.C. (1993). International research on healthy life expectancy, in *Proceedings of the*

1991 International Symposium on Data on Aging (Ed. H. Feinleib), National Center for Health Statistics. *Vital and Health Statistics*, Series 5, no. 7, pp. 33–41, US Government Printing Office, Washington, DC.

Naber, D. (1994). Subjective effects of neuroleptic drugs. Relationships to compliance and quality of life, in *Quality of Life and Disabilities in Mental Disorders. Abstract* (Ed. Association of the European Psychiatrists), p. 104, Vienna.

Naber, D. (1995). A self-rating to measure subjective effects of neuroleptic drugs, relationships to objective psychopathology, quality of life, compliance and other clinical variables, *Int. Clin. Psychopharmacol.*, **10**, Suppl. 3, 133–138.

Nader, R. (Ed.) (1973). *The Consumer and Corporate Accountability*, Harcourt, Brace, Jovanovich, New York.

Nadler, J.D., Richardson, E.D., Malloy, P.F., Marran, M.E. et al (1993). The ability of the Dementia Rating Scale to predict everyday functioning, *Arch. Clin. Neuropsychol.*, **8**, 449–460.

Nagi, S.Z. (1969). *Disability and Rehabilitation*, Ohio State University Press, Columbus.

Nagi, S.Z. (1991). Disability Concepts revisited: implications for prevention, in *Disability in America. Toward a National Agenda for Prevention* (Eds A.M. Pope & A.R. Tarlov), pp. 309–327, Institute of Medicine, National Academy Press, Washington D.C.

National Institute of Mental Health (1985). Special feature: Rating scales and assessment instruments for use in pediatric psychopharmacology research, *Psychopharm. Bull.*, **21**, 839–843.

Netten, A. & Beecham, J. (Eds) (1993). *Costing Community Care*, PSSRU, Ashgate, Aldershot.

New South Wales Department of Health (1983). *Psychiatric Hospital Versus Community Treatment: A Controlled Study*, Sydney, Australia (HSR 83–046).

Newman, O. (1972). *Defensible Space*, Macmillan, New York.

Nietzsche, F. (1872). Die Geburt der Tragödie aus dem Geiste der Musik, *Nietzsche's Complete Works*, critically edited by G. Colli & M. Montinari, 30 vols, 1967ff.

Nikkel, R.E., Smith, G. & Edwards, P. (1992). A consumer operated case management project, *Hosp. Comm. Psych.* **43**, 577–579.

Nishimura, T., Kobayashi, T., Hariguchi, S., Takeda, M. et al (1993). Scales for mental state and daily living activities for the elderly: Clinical behavioral scales for assessing demented patients, *Int. Psychogeriatrics*, **5**, 117–134.

Nord, E. (1992). An alternative to QALYs: the saved young life equivalent (SAVE), *Br. Med. J.* **305**, 875–877.

Nüchterlein, K.H. (1987). Vulnerability models for schizophrenia. State of the art, in *Search for the Causes of Schizophrenia* (Eds H. Häfner, W.F. Gattaz & W. Janzarik), pp. 297–316, Springer, New York.

Nyth, A.L. & Brane, G. (1992). Principal component analysis of the GBS scale, *Dementia*, **3**, 193–199.

O'Brien, J.T., Beats, B.H., Katie, H.R. et al (1992). Do subjective memory complaints precede dementia? A three-year follow-up of patients with supposed "benign senescent forgetfulness", *Int. J. Geriatric Psychiatry*, **7**, 481–486.

O'Brien, J.T., Ames, D. & Schweitzer, I. (1993). HPA axis function in depression and dementia: A review, *Int. J. Geriatric Psychiatry*, **8**, 887–898.

O'Connor, D.W., Pollitt, P.A., Roth, M., Brook, P.B. et al (1990). Memory complaints and impairment in normal depressed, and demented elderly persons identified in a community survey, *Arch. Gen. Psychiatry*, **47**, 224–227.

O'Connor, D.W., Pollitt, P.A., Roth, M. & Brook, C.P. (1991). Problems reported by relatives in a community study of dementia, *Br. J. Psychiatry*, **156**, 835–841.

Oakle, F., Sunderland, T., Hill, J.L., Phillips, S.L. et al (1991). The Daily Activities Questionnaire: A functional assessment for people with Alzheimer's disease, *Physical and Occupational Therapy in Geriatrics*, **10**, 67–81.

Olfson, M. (1990). Assertive community treatment: An evaluation of the experimental evidence, *Hosp. Comm. Psychiatry*, **41**, 634–641.

Oliver, J.P.J. (1991a). The quality of life in community care, in *Residential Needs for Severely Disabled Psychiatric Patients: The Case for Hospital Hostels* (Ed. R. Young), HMSO, London.

Oliver, J.P.J. (1991b). The social care directive: development of a quality of life profile for use in community services for the mentally ill, *Soc. Work Soc. Sci. Rev.* **3**, 5–45.

Oliver, J. & Mohamad, H. (1992). The quality of life of the chronically mentally ill: a comparison of public, private and voluntary residential provisions, *Br. J. Social Work*, **22**, 391–404.

Oliver, J., Huxley, P., Bridges, K. & Mohamad, H. (1996). *Quality of Life and Mental Health Services*, Routledge, London.

OMH (Office of Mental Health) (1996). Quarterly Newsletter, Albany, New York.

Ordway, S.H. Jr (1953). *Resources and The American Dream*, Ronald Press, New York.

Orley, J. & Kuyken, W. (1994) (Eds). *Quality of Life Assessment: International Perspectives*, Proceedings of the Joint Meeting organized by the World Health Organization and the Foundation IPSEN in Paris, 2–3, July, 1993, Springer, Heidelberg, New York, London, Paris, Tokyo, Hong Kong, Barcelona, Budapest.

Orlinsky, D.E., Grawe, K. & Parks, R. (1994). Process and outcome in psychotherapy, in *Handbook of Psychotherapy and Behavior Change* (Eds A.E. Bergin & S.L. Garfield), 4th edn, Wiley, New York.

Ormel, J., Oldehinkel, T., Brilman, E. & van den Brink, W. (1993a). Outcome of depression and anxiety in primary care, *Arch. Gen. Psychiatry*, **50**, 759–766.

Ormel, J., Von Korff, M., Van Den Brink, W., Katon, W., Brilman, E. & Oldehinkel, T. (1993b). Depression, anxiety and social disability show synchrony of change in primary care patients, *Am. J. Public Health*, **83**, 385–390.

Ormel, J., Von Korff, M., Ustun, T.B., Pini, S., Korten, A. & Oldehinkel, T. (1994). Common mental disorders and disability across cultures: Results from the WHO Collaborative Study on Psychological Problems in General Health Care, *JAMA*, **272**, 1741–1748.

Overall, J.E. & Gorham, D.R. (1962). The brief psychiatric rating scale, *Psychol. Reports*, **10**, 799–812.

Overall, J.E., Scott, J., Rhoades, H.M. & Lesser, J. (1990). Empirical scaling of the stages of cognitive decline in senile dementia, *J. Geriatric Psychiatry and Neurology*, **3**, 212–220.

Oyebode, F. (1994). Ethics and resource allocation: Can health care customers be qualified? *Psychiatric Bull.*, **18**, 395–398.

Oyebode, F., Cumella, S., Garden, G. & Nicholls, J. (1992). Development of outcome measures in acute psychiatry, *Psychiatric Bull.*, **16**, 618–619.

Packer, S. (1994). Psychopathology and quality of life in schizophrenia, *Neuropsychopharm.*, **10**, 35 (Supplement), 2405.

Parasuraman, R. & Nestor, P.G. (1991). Attention and driving skills in aging and Alzheimer's disease, *Special Issue: Safety and Mobility of Elderly Drivers: Part I. Human-Factors*, **33**, 539–557.

Parkerson, G.R., Broadhead, W.E. & Tse, C.K.J. (1990). The Duke Health Profile, *Med. Care*, **28**, 1056–1072.

Parsons, T. (1951). *The Social System*, Free Press, Glencoe, IL.

Parsons, T. (1958). Definitions of health and illness in the light of American values and social structure, in *Patients, Physicians, Illnesses* (Ed. E.G. Jaco), Free Press, Glencoe, IL.

Patel, C. (1973). Yoga and biofeedback in the management of hypertension, *Lancet*, 1053–1055.

Patel, C. & Marmot, M.G. (1987). Stress management, blood pressure and quality of life, *J. of Hypertension*, **5**, 21–28.

Patrick, D.L. (1992). Health-related quality of life in pharmaceutical evaluation: Forging progress and avoiding pitfalls, *PharmacoEconomics*, **1**, 76–78.

Patrick, D.L. & Erickson, P. (1993). *Health Status and Health Policy: Quality of Life in Health Care Evaluation and Resource Allocation*, Oxford University Press, New York.

Pattie, A.H. & Gilleard, C.J. (1979). *Manual of the Clifton Assessment Procedures for the Elderly (CAPE)*, Hodder & Stoughton, Sevenoaks, Kent.

Paykel, E.S., Weissman, M.M. & Prusoff, B. (1978). Social maladjustment and severity of depression, *Comp. Psychiatry*, **19**, 121–128.

Pearlin, L.I. (1967). Alienation from work: A study of nursing personnel, in *The Professional in the Organization* (Ed. M. Abrahamson), Rand McNally, Chicago.

Pearlin, L.I., Lieberman, M.A., Menaghan, E.G. & Mullan, J.T. (1981). The stress process, *J. Health. Soc. Behav.*, **22**, 337–356.

Penn, D.L., Guynan, K., Daily, T., Spaulding, W., Garbin, C.P. & Sullivan, M. (1994). Dispelling the stigma of schizophrenia: What sort of information is best? *Schiz. Bull.*, **20**, 567–578.

Perlman, B. & Hartman, E.A. (1982). Burnout: Summary and future research, *Human Relations*, **4**, 283–305.

Perugi, G., Akiskal, H.S., Musetti, L., Simonini, E. & Cassano, G.B. (1994). Social adjustment in panic-agoraphobic patients reconsidered, *Br. J. Psychiatry*, **164**, 88–93.

Petermann, F. (1991). Asthmafragebogen für Kinder und Jugendliche, *Dem Asthma auf der Spur*, Psychologisches Institut der Universität, Bonn.

Petermann, F. & Bergmann, K.-C. (Eds) (1994). *Lebensqualität und Asthma*, Quintessenz, Munich.

Peters, R.K., Benson, H. & Porter, D. (1977). Daily relaxation response breaks in a working population. I. Effects on self-reported measures of health, *Am. J. Publ. Health*, **67**, 946–953.

Pfeffer, R.I., Kurosaki, T.T., Harrah, C.H., Chance, J.M. & Filos, S. (1982). Measurement of functional activities in older adults in the community, *J. Gerontology*, **37**, 3, 323–329.

Phelan, M., Slade, M., Thornicraft, G., Dunn, G., Holloway, F., Wykes, T., Strathdee, G., Loftus, L., McCrone, P. & Hayward, P. (1995). The Camberwell Assessment of Need: The validity and reliability of an instrument to assess the needs of people with severe mental illness, *Br. J. Psychiatry*, **167**, 589–595.

Pickney, A.A., Gerber, G.J. & Lafave, H.G. (1991). Quality of life after psychiatric rehabilitation: The client's perspective, *Acta Psychiat. Scand.*, **83**, 86–91.

Pines, A. (1982). Changing organizations: Is a work environment without burnout an impossible goal? in *Job Stress and Burnout. Research, Theory, and Intervention Perspectives* (Ed. W.S. Paine), pp. 189–212, Sage, Beverly Hills, London, New Delhi.

Pines, A. (1983). On Burnout and the buffering effects of social support, in *Stress and Burnout in the Human Service Profession* (Ed. B.A. Farber), pp. 155–174, Pergamon Press, New York.

Pines, A. & Maslach, C. (1978). Characteristics of staff burnout in mental health settings, *Hosp. Comm. Psychiatry*, **29**, 233–237.

Pines, A. & Maslach, C. (1980). Combatting staff burn-out in a day care center: A case study, *Hosp. Comm. Psychiatry*, **9**, 5–16.

Platt, S. (1981). Social adjustment as a criterion of treatment success: Just what are we measuring? *Soc. Psychiatry*, **44**, 95–112.

Platt, S., Weyman, A., Hirsch, S.R. & Hewett, S. (1980). The Social Behaviour Assessment Schedule (SBAS): Rationale, contents, scoring and reliability of a new interview schedule, *Soc. Psychiatry*, **15**, 43–55.

Plog, U. (1976). *Differentielle Psychotherapie II*, Huber, Bern.

Pogue-Geile, M.F. & Harrow, M. (1984). Negative and positive symptoms in schizophrenia and depression: A followup, *Schiz. Bull.*, **10**, 371–376.

Pope, A.M. & Tarlov, A.R. (1991). *Disability in America. Toward a National Agenda for Prevention*, Institute of Medicine, National Academy Press, Washington, DC.

Poster, E.C. & Ryan, J. (1994). A multiregional study of nurses' beliefs and attitudes about work safety and patient assault, *Hosp. Comm. Psychiatry*, **45**, 1104–1108.

Poustka, F. (1982). Graduelle Entlassungen als teilstationäre Behandlung, *Psychiat. Prax.*, **9**, 155–159.

Poustka, F. (1991). Psychische Auffälligkeiten bei Kindern in Gebieten unterschiedlicher Tiefflugaktivitäten, in *Die physiologischen und psychischen Auswirkungen des militärischen Flugbetriebes* (Ed. F. Poustka), Huber, Berne.

Poustka, F., Eckermann, P. & Schmeck, K. (1992). Effect of aircraft noise and psychosocial stressors on mental disturbances of children and adolescents – an epidemiological survey in Westphalia, in *Developmental Psychopathology* (Eds H. Remschmidt and M.H. Schmidt), Hogrefe, Göttingen.

Priebe, S., Gruyters, T., Heinze, M., Hoffmann, C. & Jäkel, A. (1995). Subjektive Evaluationskriterien in der psychiatrischen Versorgung – Erhebungsmethoden für Forschung und Praxis, *Psychiat. Prax.*, **22**, 140–144.

Prior, L. (1993). *The Social Organization of Mental Illness*, Sage, London, Newbury Park, CA, New Delhi.

Prochaska, T., Mermelstein, R. & Hiller, B. (1993). Functional status and living arrangements, in *Health data on older Americans: United States, National Center for Health Statistics, Vital and Health Statistics* (Eds J.E. Van Nostrand, S.E. Furner & R. Suzman) (1993), Series 3, no. 27, pp. 23–39, Government Printing Office, Washington, DC.

Puig-Antick, J., Lukens, E., Davies, M., Goetz, C., Brennan-Quattrock, J. & Todak, G. (1985a). Psychosocial functioning in prepubertal major depressive disorders. I. Interpersonal relationships during the depressive episode, *Arch. Gen. Psychiatry*, **42**, 500–507.

Puig-Antick, J., Lukens, E., Davies, M., Goetz, C., Brennan-Quattrock, J. & Todak, G. (1985b). Psychosocial functioning in prepubertal major depressive disorders: 2. Interpersonal relationships after sustained recovery from affective episode, *Arch. Gen. Psychiatry*, **42**, 511–517.

Pyne, J.M., Patterson, T.L., Kaplan, R.M., Gillin, J.C., Koch, W.L. & Grant, I. (1997). Assessment of the quality of life of patients with major depression, *Psychiatric Services*, **48**, 224–230.

Random House Dictionary for the English Language, The Unabridged Edition (1971). Random House, New York.

Read, J.L., Quinn, R.J. & Hoefer, M.A. (1987). Measuring overall health: An evaluation of three important approaches, *J. Chron. Diseases*, **40** (Suppl. 1), 7S–21S.

Reimer, C. (1994). Lebensqualität von Psychotherapeuten, *Psychotherapeut*, **39**, 73–78.

Reisberg, B. (1990). Alzheimer disease: The clinical syndrome: Diagnostic and etiologic importance, *Acta Neurol. Scand.*, **82**, 2–4.

Reisberg, B., Ferris, S.H., De Leon, M.J. & Crook, T. (1982). The Global Deterioration Scale for assessment of primary degenerative dementia, *Am. J. Psychiatry*, **139**, 9, 1136–1139.

Remschmidt, H. & Schmidt, M.H. (Eds). (1988). *Kinder- und Jugendpsychiatrie in Klinik und Praxis*, Thieme Verlag, Stuttgart, New York.

Rescher, N. (1972). *Welfare. The Social Issues in Philosophical Perspective*, University of Pittsburgh Press, Pittsburgh.

Revicki, D.A. (1995). Measuring health outcomes for cost-effectiveness studies: Are all quality adjusted life-years created equal? *Drug Information J.*, **29**, 1459–1467.

Revicki, D.A. (1989). Health-related quality of life in the evaluation of medical therapy for chronic illness, *J. Family Practice*, **29**, 377–380.

Revicki, D.A., Turner, R., Brown, R. & Martindale, J.J. (1992). Reliability and validity of a health-related quality of life battery for evaluating outpatient antidepressant treatment, *Qual. Life Res.*, **1**, 257–266.

Revicki, D.A., Brown, R., Borowitz, M. & Murray, M. (1994). Cost-effectiveness of nefazodone compared to imipramine or fluoxetine treatment for major depression disorder. Presented at the 3rd Workshop on Costs and Assessment in Psychiatry, *The Economics of Schizophrenia, Depression, Anxiety, Dementias, ARCAP*, Venice, 28–30 October.

Revicki, D.A. & Murray, M. (1994). Assessing health-related quality of life outcomes of drug treatments for psychiatric disorders, *CNS Drugs*, **1**, 465–476.

Revicki, D.A., Brown, R.E., Palmer, W., Bakish, D., Rosser, W.W., Anton, S.F. & Feeny, D. (1995). Modelling the cost-effectiveness of antidepressant treatment in primary care, *PharmacoEconomics*, **8**, 524–540.

Rhode, P., Lewinsohn, P. & Seeley, J. (1990). Are people changed by the experience of having an episode of depression? A further test of the scar hypothesis, *J. Abnorm. Psychol.*, **99**, 264–271.

Ritchie, K., Robine, J.M., Letenneur, L. & Dartigues, J.F. (1994). Dementia-free life expectancy in France, *Am. J. Public Health*, **84**, 232–236.

Robins, L.N. & Regier, D.A. (1991). *Psychiatric Disorders in America. The Epidemiologic Catchment Area Study*, The Free Press, Maxwell Macmillan International, New York, Oxford, Singapore, Sydney.

Robinson, J. (1977). *How Americans Use Time: A Social-psychological Analysis of Everyday Behaviour*, Praeger, New York.

Robinson, J. (1987). Microbehavioural approaches to monitoring human experience, *J. Nerv. Ment. Dis.*, **175**, 514–518.

Robson, P.J. (1988). Self-esteem – A psychiatric view, *Br. J. Psychiatry*, **153**, 6–15.

Rodgers, W.L. & Converse, P.E. (1975). Measures of the perceived overall quality of life, *Social Indicators Research*, **2**, 127–152.

Rodin, J. (1986). Aging and health: Effects of the sense of control, *Science*, **233**, 1271–1276.

Rogers, W.H., Wells, K.B., Meredith, L.S., Sturm, R. & Burnam, M. (1993). Outcomes for adult outpatients with depression under prepaid or fee-for-service financing, *Arch. Gen. Psychiatry*, **50**, 517–525.

Romme, M.A. & Escher, A.D. (1989). Hearing voices, *Schiz. Bull.*, **15**, 209–216.

Romney, D.M. & Evans, D.R. (1996). Toward a general model of health-related quality of life, *Qual. Life Res.*, **5**, 235–241.

Rosen, A., Hadzi-Pavlovic, D. & Parker, G. (1989). The life skills profile: A measure assessing function and disability in schizophrenia, *Schiz. Bull.*, **15**, 325–337.

Rosen, M., Simon, E. & McKinsey, L. (1995). Subjective measure of quality of life, *Mental Retardation*, **33**, 31–34.

Rosenfield, S. (1987). Services organization and quality of life among the seriously mentally ill, *New Directions for Mental Health Services*, **36**, 47–59.

Rosenfield, S. (1992). Factors contributing to the subjective quality of life of the chronic mentally ill, *J. Health Soc. Behav.*, **33**, 299–315.

Rosenfield, S. & Neese-Todd, S. (1993). Elements of a Psychosocial Clubhouse Programme Associated with a Satisfactory Quality of Life, *Hosp. Comm. Psychiatry*, **44**, 76–78.

Rosenmann, R.H., Brand, R.J., Jenkins, D., Friedman, M., Straus, R. & Wurm, M. (1975).

Coronary heart disease in the Western Collaborative Group Study: Final follow-up experience of 8 years, *JAMA*, **233**, 872–877.

Rosser, R. & Kind, P. (1978). A scale of evaluations of states of illness: Is there a social consensus? *Int. J. Epidemiol.*, **7**, 347–358.

Rosser, R., Cottee, M., Rabin, R. & Selai, C. (1992). Index of health-related quality of life, in *Measures of the Quality of Life* (Ed. A. Hopkins), pp. 81–89, Royal College of Physicians, London.

Rossi, H. & Wright, J.D. (1987). The determinants of homelessness, *Health Affairs*, **6**, 19–32.

Rost, K., Smith, G.R., Burnman, M.A. & Burns, B.J. (1992). Measuring the outcomes of care for mental health problems: The case of depressive disorders, *Med. Care*, **30** (Suppl. 5), S266–S273.

Rotering-Steinberg, S. (1989). *Hypertonie – Prävention und Therapie: Gruppenunterstützte Selbstmodifikation für essentielle HypertonikerInnen (GSEH)*, Materialie 21, Deutsche Gesellschaft für Verhaltenstherapie, Tübingen.

Rotter, J.B. (1966). Generalized expectancies for internal versus external control of enforcement, *Psychological Monographs: General and Applied*, **80**, 1–28.

Rotter, J.B. (1982). *The Development and Applications of Social Learning Theory*, Springer, New York.

Roy-Byrne, P.P., Milgrom, P., Khoon-Mei, T. & Weinstein, P. (1994). Psychopathology and psychiatric diagnosis in subjects with dental phobia, *J. Anx. Disorders*, **8**, 19–31.

Rubin, E.H., Morris, J.C., Storandt, M. & Berg, L. (1987). Behavioral changes in patients with mild senile dementia of the Alzheimer's type, *Psychiatry Res.*, **21**, 55–62.

Rubin, H.C., Rabin, A.S., Levine, B., Auerbach, M. Kaplan, R. & Rapaport, M. (1995). Measuring quality of life in panic disorder, Oral presentation at the Annual Meeting of the American Psychiatric Association, Miami, FL.

Russell, L.B. (1989). *Medicare's New Hospital Payment System: Is it Working?* The Brookings Institution, Washington, DC.

Rutter, M. (1987). Psychological resilience and protective mechanisms, *Am. J. of Orthopsychiatry*, **57**, 316–331.

Rutter, M. & Quinton, D. (1977) Psychiatric disorder – ecological factors and concepts of causation, in *Ecological Factors in Human Development*, Chapter 3 (Ed. M. McGurk), pp. 173–187, North-Holland, Amsterdam.

Rutter, M., Shaffer, D. & Sturge, C. (1975). *A Guide to a Multi-Axial Classification Scheme for Psychiatric Disorders in Childhood and Adolescence*, Dep. of Child and Adolescent Psychiatry, Institute of Psychiatry, London.

Rutter, M., Taylor, E. & Hersov, L. (Eds) (1994). *Child and Adolescent Psychiatry: Modern Approaches*, Blackwell Scientific, London.

Ryff, C.D. (1995). Psychological well-being in adult life, *Current Directions in Psychological Science*, **4**, 99–104.

Ryff, C.D. & Keyes, C.L.M. (1995). The structure of psychological well-being revisited, *J. Personality Soc. Psychol.*, **69**, 719–727.

Sackett, D.L. & Torrance, G.W. (1979). The utility of different health states as perceived by the general public, *J. Chron Dis.*, **31**, 697–704.

Sainfort, F., Becker, M. & Diamond, R. (1996). Judgments of quality of life of individuals with severe mental disorders: Patient self-report versus provider perspectives, *Am. J. Psychiatry*, **153**, 497–502.

Salvador-Carulla, L., Segui, J., Fernandez-Cano, P. & Canet, J. (1995). Costs and offset effect in panic disorders, *Br. J. Psychiatry*, **27** (Suppl.) 23–28.

Sandman, P.O., Norberg, A., Adolfson, R., Eriksson, S. et al (1990). Prevalence and characteristics of persons with dependency on feeding at institutions for elderly, *Scand. J.*

Caring Sci., **4**, 121–127.

Sarata, B.P.V. (1974). Employee satisfactions in agencies serving retarded persons, *Am. J. Mental Deficiency*, **79**, 434–442.

Sarata, B.P.V. & Jeppesen, J.C. (1977). Job design and staff satisfaction in human service settings, *Am. J. Comm. Psychol.*, **5**, 229–236.

Sartorius, N. (1987). Cross-cultural comparisons of data about the quality of life: A sample of issues, in *The Quality of Life of Cancer Patients* (Eds N.K. Aaronson & J. Beckmann), pp. 19–24, Raven Press, New York.

Sartorius, N. (1990). Preface – *The Public Health Impact of Mental Disorder* (Eds D. Goldberg & D. Tantam), Hogrefe & Huber, Toronto, Lewiston, NY, Berne, Göttingen, Stuttgart.

Sartorius, N. (1993). A WHO method for the assessment of health-related quality of life (WHOQOL), in *Quality of Life Assessment: Key Issues in the 1990s* (Eds S.R. Walker & R.M. Rosser), pp. 201–207, Kluwer Academic, Dordrecht, Boston, London.

Sartorius, N. (1994). Progress in the development of the classification of mental disorders in the ICD-10, in *Psychiatric Diagnosis: A World Perspective* (Eds J.E. Mezzich, Y. Honda & M.C. Kastrup), Springer, New York.

Sartorius, N. (1995). Rehabilitation and quality of life, *Int. J. Ment. Health*, **24**, 7–13.

Sartorius, N. & Kuyken, W. (1994). Translation of Health Status Instruments, in *Quality of Life Assessment: International Perspectives*, Proceedings of the Joint Meeting organized by the World Health Organization and the Foundation IPSEN in Paris, 2–3 July, 1993 (Eds J. Orley & W. Kuyken), Springer Verlag, Berlin, Heidelberg, New York, London, Paris, Tokyo, Hong Kong, Barcelona, Budapest.

Schalock, R.L., Keith, K.D., Hoffman, K. & Karan, U.D. (1989). Quality of life: Its measurement and use, *Mental Retardation*, **27**, 25–31.

Scheff, T.J. (1966). *Being Mentally Ill. A Sociological Theory*, Aldine, Chicago.

Scheibe, G., Albus, M., Walter, A.U. & Schmauß, M. (1993). Gruppenpsychotherapie bei Patienten mit Panikstörung und Agoraphobie, *Psychotherapie, Psychosomatik, Medizin Psychologie*, **43**, 238–244.

Schene, A.H. & van Wijngaarden, B. (1994). Quality of life of family members of psychotic patients, paper read at 7th European Symposium of AEP, Vienna.

Scheper-Hughes, N. (1981). Dilemmas in deinstitutionalization: A view from inner city Boston, *J. Operational Psychiatry*, **12**, 90–99.

Schiller, L. & Bennett, A. (1996) *Quiet Room: Journey Out of the Torment of Madness*, Warner, New York.

Schipper, H., Clinch, J., McMurray, A. & Levitt, M. (1984). Measuring Quality of Life of cancer patients: the Functional Living Index – Cancer, development and validation, *J. Clin. Oncol.*, **2**, 472–483.

Schipper, H., Clinch, J. & Powell, V. (1990). Definition and conceptual issues, in *Quality of Life Assessments in Clinical Trials* (Ed. B. Spilker), Raven Press, New York.

Schipper, H., Clinch, J.J. & Olweny, C.L.M. (1996). Quality of life studies: Definitions and conceptual issues, in *Quality of Life and Pharmacoeconomics in Clinical Trials* (Ed. B. Spilker), pp. 11–23, Lippincott-Raven, Philadelphia, New York.

Schlesinger, M. & Mechanic, D. (1993). Challenges for managed competition from chronic illness, *Health Affairs*, **12** (Supplement), 123–137.

Schmeck, K. (1992). *Beeinträchtigung von Kindern durch Fluglärm*, Klotz Verlag, Eschborn.

Schmeck, K. & Poustka, F. (1993). Psychophysiological and psychiatric tests with children and adolescents in a low-altitude flight region, in *Noise and Disease* (Eds H. Ising & B. Kruppa), pp. 301–306, Fischer Verlag, Stuttgart, New York.

Schmidt, L., Reinhardt, A., Kane, R. & Olsen, M. (1977). The mentally ill in nursing homes: New back wards in the community, *Arch. Gen. Psychiatry*, **34**, 687–691.

Schmidt, M.H., Schultz, E., Blanz, B. & Lay, B. (1994). Verlauf schizoaffektiver Psychosen in der Adoleszenz, *Zeitschrift für Kinder- und Jugendpsychiatrie*, Volume 22, Part 4, pp. 253–261.

Schmidt, M., Blanz, B., Dippe, A., Koppe, T. & Lay, R. (1995). Course of patients diagnosed as having schizophrenia during first episode occurring under age 18 years, *Eur. Arch. Psychiatry Clin. Neurosci.*, **245**, 93–110.

Schneier, F.R., Johnson, J., Hornig, C.D., Liebowitz, M.R. & Weissman, M.M. (1992). Social phobia: Comorbidity and morbidity in an epidemiologic sample, *Arch. Gen. Psychiatry*, **49**, 282–288.

Schneier, F.R., Heckelman, L.R., Garfinkel, R., Campeas, R., Fallon, B.A., Gitow, A., Street, L., DelBene, D. & Liebowitz, M.R. (1994). Functional impairment in social phobia, *J. Clin. Psychiatry*, **55**, 322–331.

Schulberg, H. & Bromet, E. (1981). Strategies for evaluating the outcome of community services for the chronically mentally ill, *Am. J. Psychiatry*, **138**, 930–935.

Schulz, E., Martin, M. & Remschmidt, H. (1994). Zur Verlaufsdynamik schizophrener Erkrankungen in der Adoleszenz, *Zeitschrift für Kinder- und Jugendpsychiatrie*, Volume 22, Part 4, pp. 262–274.

Schwarz, N. & Clore, G.L. (1983). Mood, misattribution, and judgments of well-being: Informative and directive functions of affective states, *J. Personality Soc. Psychol.*, **45**, 513–523.

Sclan, S.G., Foster, J.R., Reisberg, B., Franssen, E. et al (1990). Application of Piagetian measures of cognition in severe Alzheimer's disease, *Psychiatric J. University Ottawa*, **15**, 221–226.

Scott, J.E., Lehman, A.F., Dixon, L.B. Postrado, L., Lyles, A., Skinner, A. & Fahey, M. (1997). Quality of life and its relationship to patterns of service use among individuals with schizophrenia. Poster presented at the International Congress on Schizophrenia Research, 12–16 April, Colorado.

Scully, R. (1983). The work-setting support group: A means of preventing burnout, in *Stress and Burnout in the Human Service Profession* (Ed. B.A. Farber), pp. 188–197, Pergamon Press, New York.

Searight, H.R., Dunn, E.J., Grisso, T., Margolis, R.B. et al (1989). The relation of the Halstead–Reitan Neuropsychological Battery to ratings of everyday functioning in a geriatric sample, *Neuropsychology*, **3**, 135–145.

Seedhouse, D. (1995). The way around health economics' dead end, *Health Care Analysis*, **3**, 205–220.

Seelhorst, R.M. (1984). Psychisch Kranke in der Familie – aus der Sicht der Angehörigen, in *Die Angehörigengruppe. Familie mit psychisch Kranken auf dem Weg zur Selbsthilfe* (Eds M.C. Angermeyer & A. Finzen), pp. 11–16, Enke Verlag, Stuttgart.

Segall, A. (1988). Cultural factors in sick-role expectations, in *Health Behavior: Emerging Research Perspectives* (Ed. D.S. Gochman), pp. 249–260, Plenum Press, New York, London.

Seguin, C.A. (1946). The concept of disease, *Psychosom. Med.*, **8**, 252–257.

Seligman, M.E.P. (1975). *Helplessness*, Freeman, San Francisco.

Shadish, W. & Bootzin, R. (1981). Nursing homes and chronic mental patients, *Schiz. Bull.*, **7**, 488–498.

Shaffer, H. & Gambino, B. (1978). Psychological rehabilitation, skills-building, and self-efficacy, *Am. Psychol.*, **33**, 394–396.

Shapiro, C.H. (1982). Creative supervision: An underutilized antidote, in *Job Stress and*

Burnout. Research, Theory, and Intervention Perspectives (Ed. W.S. Paine), pp. 213–228 Sage, Beverly Hills, CA, London, New Delhi.

Shea, M.T., Elkin, I., Imber, S.D., Sotsky, S.M., Watkins, J.T., Collins, J.F., Pilkonis, P.A., Beckham, E., Glass, D., Dolant, R.T. & Parloff, M.B. (1992). Course of depressive symptoms over follow-up: findings from the National Institute of Mental Health Treatment of Depression Collaborative Research Program, *Arch. Gen. Psychiatry*, **49**, 782–787.

Shear, M.K. & Maser, J.D. (1994). Standardized assessment for PD research, *Arch. Gen. Psychiatry*, **51**, 346–354.

Sheehan, D.V. (1986). *The Anxiety Disease*, p. 138, Bantam Books, New York.

Shepherd, G., Muijen, M., Dean, R. & Cooney, M. (1996). Residential care in hospital and in the community – quality of care and quality of life, *Br. J. Psychiatry*, **168**, 448–456.

Sherbourne, C.D., Wells, K.B. & Judd, L.L. (1996). Functioning and well-being of patients with panic disorder, *Am. J. Psychiatry*, **153**, 213–218.

Shiell, A., Pettipher, C., Raynes, N. & Wright, K. (1990). Economic approaches to measuring quality of life, in *Quality of Life. Perspectives and Policies* (Eds S. Baldwin, C. Godfrey & C. Propper), Routledge, London.

Shtasel, P.L., Gur, R.E., Gallacher, F., Heimberg, C. & Gur, R. (1992). Gender differences in the clinical expression of schizophrenia, *Schizophr. Res.*, **7**, 225–231.

Siegel, L., Jones, W.C. & Wilson, J.O. (1990). Economic and life consequences experienced by a group of individuals with PD, *J. Anx. Disorders*, **4**, 201–211.

Siegrist, J. & Junge, A. (1989). Conceptual and methodological problems in research on the quality of life in clinical medicine, *Soc. Sci. Med.*, **29**, 463–468.

Simon, M.D. (1994). Psychiatriereform und die Lebensqualität von Angehörigen von Schizophreniekranken, in *Schizophrenie und Lebensqualität* (Eds H. Katschnig & P. König), pp. 231–240, Springer, Vienna, New York.

Simpson, C.J. (1996). Quality of life in a new hospital hostel, *Psychiatric Bull.*, **20**, 275–276.

Simpson, C.J., Hyde, C.E. & Faragher, E.B. (1989). The chronically mentally ill in community facilities – a study of quality of life, *Br. J. Psychiatry*, **154**, 77–82.

Skantze, K. (1993). *Defining Subjective Quality of Life Goals in Schizophrenia: the Quality of Life Self-Assessment Inventory, QLS-100, A New Approach to Successful Alliance and Service Development*, Department of Psychiatry, Sahlgrenska Hospital, University of Gothenburg, Gothenburg, Sweden.

Skantze, K., Malm, U., Dencker, S.J. & May, P.R. (1990). Quality of life in schizophrenia, *Nord. Psykiatr. Tidsskr.*, **44**, 71–75.

Skantze, K., Malm, U., Dencker, S.J., May, P.R. & Corrigan, P. (1992). Comparison of quality of life with standard of living in schizophrenic outpatients, *Brit. J. Psychiatry*, **161**, 797–801.

Skantze, K. & Malm, U. (1994). A new approach to facilitation of working alliances based on patients' quality of life goals, *Nord. Psykiatr. Tidsskr.*, **48**, 37–55.

Skodol, A.E., Link, B.G., Shrout, P.E. & Horwath, E. (1988). The revision of axis V in DSM-III-R: Should symptoms have been included? *Am. J. Psychiatry*, **145**, 825–829.

Skoog, I. (1993). The prevalence of psychotic, depressive and anxiety syndromes in demented and non-demented 85-year-olds, *Int. J. Geriatric Psychiatry*, **8**, 247–253.

Skurla, E., Rogers, J.C. & Sunderland, T. (1988). Direct assessment of activities of daily living in Alzheimer's disease: A controlled study, *J. Am. Geriatrics Society*, **36**, 97–103.

Slade, M. (1994). Needs assessment – involvement of staff and users will help to meet needs, *Br. J. Psychiatry*, **165**, 293–296.

Slaughter, J.C., Lehman, A.F. & Myers, C.P. (1991). Quality of life of severely mentally ill adults in residential care facilities, *Adult Residential Care J.*, **5**, 97–111.

Slovic, P., Kraus, N., Lappe, H., Letzel, H. & Malmfors, T. (1989). Risk perception of prescription drugs: Report on a survey in Sweden, in *The Perception and Management of Drug Safety Risks* (Eds B. Horisberger and R. Dinkel), pp 90–111, Springer, Berlin, Heidelberg, New York, London, Paris, Tokyo.

Smith, A.L. & Weissman, M.M. (1992). Epidemiology, in *Handbook of Affective Disorders* (Ed. E.S. Paykel), pp. 111–129, Churchill Livingston, Edinburgh.

Smith, M.L., Glass, G.V. & Miller, T.I. (1980). *The Benefits of Psychotherapy*, Johns Hopkins University Press, Baltimore, MD.

Solomon, P. (1992). The closing of a state hospital: What is the quality of patients' lives one year post-release? *Psychiatry Quarterly*, **63**, 279–296.

Sontag, S. (1979). *Illness as Metaphor*, Allan Lane, Penguin Press, London.

Sontag, S. (1989). *AIDS and its Metaphors*, Allan Lane, Penguin Press, London.

Spaniol, L., Jung, H. & Zipple, A.M. (1985). Families as a central resource in the rehabilitation of the severely psychiatrically disabled: Report of a national survey, *unpublished manuscript*, Boston University.

Spiegelhalter, D.J., Gore, S.M., Fitzpatrick, R., Fletcher, A.E., Jones, D.R. & Cox, D.R. (1992). Quality of life measures in health care. III: resources allocation, *Br. Med. J.*, **305**, 1205–1209.

Spilker, B. (1990). *Quality of Life Assessments in Clinical Trials*, Raven Press, New York.

Spilker, B. (1992). Standardization of quality of life trials: An industry perspective, *PharmacoEconomics*, **I** (2), 73–75.

Spilker, B. (1996). *Quality of Life and Pharmacoeconomics in Clinical Trials*, Lippincott–Raven Press, New York.

Spitz, B. (1978). A National Survey of Medicaid Case-management Programmes, *Health Affairs*, **6**, 61–70.

Spitzer, R.L., Williams, J.B.W., Kroenke, K., Linzer, M., deGruy, F.V., Hahn, S.R., Brody, D. & Johnson, J.G. (1993). Utility of a new procedure for diagnosing mental disorders in primary care. The PRIME-MD 1000 Study, *JAMA*, **272**, 1749–1756.

Spitzer, R.L., Kroenke, K., Linzer, M., Hahn, S.R., Williams, J.B., deGruy, F.V. III, Brody, D. & Davies, M. (1995). Health-related quality of life in primary care patients with mental disorders. Results from the PRIME-MD 1000 Study, *JAMA*, **274**, 1511–1517.

Spitzer, W.O., Dobson, A., Hall, J., Chesterman, E., Levi, J., Shepherd, R., Battista, R.N. & Catchlove, B.R. (1981). Measuring the quality of life in cancer patients: A concise Q/L index for use by physicians, *J. Chronic Dis.*, **34**, 585–597.

Spreng, M. (1984). Risikofaktor Lärm – physiologische Aspekte, *Therapiewoche*, **34**, 3765–3772.

Stanton, A.H. & Schwartz, M.S. (1954). *The Mental Hospital. A Study of Institutional Participation in Psychiatric Illness and Treatment*, Basic Books, New York.

Stein, L. (1989). Wisconsin's System of Mental Health Financing, in *Paying for Services: Promises and Pitfalls of Capitation* (Eds D. Mechanic & L.H. Aiken), pp. 29–41, New Directions for Mental Health Services No. 43, Jossey-Bass, San Francisco.

Stein, L.I. & Test, M.A. (Eds) (1978). *Alternatives to Mental Hospital Treatment*, Plenum Press, New York, London.

Stein, L.I. & Test, M.A. (1980). Alternative to mental hospital treatment: I. Conceptual model, treatment program and clinical evaluation, *Arch. Gen. Psychiatry*, **37**, 392–397.

Stein, L.I. & Test, M.A. (1985). *The Training in Community Living Model: A Decade of Experience*, Jossey-Bass, San Francisco.

Stein, L.I. & Test, M.A. (1987). Training in community living: Research design and results, in *Alternatives to Mental Hospital Treatment* (Eds L.I. Stein and M.A. Test), pp. 57–74, Plenum Press, New York, NY.

Stein, L.I., Diamond, R.J. & Factor, R.M. (1990). A system approach to the care of persons with schizophrenia, *Handbook of Schizophrenia: Psychosocial Therapies* (Eds M.I. Herz,

S.J. Keith & J.P. Docherty), Volume 5, pp. 213–246, Elsevier Science, Amsterdam.

Stein, M.B., Walker, J.R. & Forde, D.R. (1994). Setting diagnostic thresholds for social phobia: Considerations from a community survey of social anxiety, *Am. J. Psychiatry*, **151**, 308–312.

Stevens, A. & Gabbay, J. (1991). Needs assessment needs assessment, *Health Trends*, **23**, 20–23.

Stewart, A.L., Hays, R.D. & Ware, J.E. (1988). The MOS Short-Form General Health Survey: reliability and validity in a patient population, *Med. Care*, **26**, 724–735.

Stewart, A.L., Hays, R.D. & Ware, J.E. (1994). The Medical Outcomes Study Short-Form General Health Survey, in *Psychiatric Epidemiology. Assessment Concepts and Methods* (Eds J.E. Mezzich, M.R. Jorge & I.M. Salloum), Johns Hopkins University Press, Baltimore, MD.

Stewart, J.W., Quitkin, F.M., McGrath, P.J., Rabkin, J.G., Markowitz, J.S., Tricamo, E. & Klein, D.F. (1988). Social functioning in chronic depression: Effect of 6 weeks of antidepressant treatment, *Psychiatric Res.*, **25**, 213–222.

Stoker, M.J., Dunbar, G.C. & Beaumont, G. (1992). The SmithKline Beecham "Quality of Life" Scale: A validation and reliability study in patients with affective disorder, *Qual. Life Res.*, **1**, 385–395.

Strauss, A. (1987). *Qualitative Analysis for Social Scientists*, Cambridge University Press, Cambridge.

Strauss, J.S. (1989). Subjective experiences of schizophrenia: Toward a new dynamic psychiatry, *Schiz. Bull.*, **15**, 179–187.

Strauss, J.S. & Carpenter, W.T. (1974). The prediction outcome in schizophrenia: II. Relationships between predictor and outcome variables: A report from the WHO international pilot study of schizophrenia, *Arch. Gen. Psychiatry*, **31**, 37–42.

Strauss, J.S. & Carpenter, W.T. (1977). The prediction of outcome in schizophrenia: five-year outcome and its predictors, *Arch. Gen. Psychiatry*, **34**, 159–163.

Sturt, E. & Wykes, T. (1986). The Social Behaviour Schedule: A validity and reliability study, *Br. J. Psychiatry*, **148**, 1–11.

Sullivan, G., Wells, K.B. & Leake, B. (1991). Quality of life of seriously mentally ill persons in Mississippi, *Hosp. Comm. Psychiatry*, **4**, 752–755.

Sullivan, G.S., Wells, K.B. & Leake, B. (1992). Clinical factors associated with better quality of life in a seriously mentally ill population, *Hosp. Comm. Psychiatry*, **43**, 794–798.

Sullivan, I.G. (1989). Burnout – A study of a psychiatric center, *Loss, Grief and Care*, **3**, 83–93.

Swales, J.D. (1995). Quality of life data: How can we get best quality from them? *J. Roy. Soc. Med.*, **88**, 125.

Sweeting, H.N. & Gilhooly, M.L. (1991–1992). Doctor, am I dead? A review of social death in modern societies, *Omega J. Death and Dying*, **24**, 251–269.

Szasz, T.S. (1970). *The Manufacture of Madness. A Comparative Study of the Inquisition and the Mental Health Movement*, Harper & Row, New York.

Tamminga, C. (1996). Quality of life profile in schizophrenic patients under sertindol treatment. Presented at 20th CINP Congress, Melbourne.

Tantam, D. (1988). Review article: Quality of life and the chronically mentally ill, *Int. J. Soc. Psychiatry*, **34**, 243–247.

Taube, C., Eun, S.L. & Forthofer, R. (1984). Drugs in psychiatry: An empirical evaluation, *Med. Care*, **22**, 597–610.

Taylor, E. (1994). Physical treatments in *Child and Adolescent Psychiatry: Modern Approaches* (Eds M. Rutter, E. Taylor & L. Hersov), pp. 880–899, Blackwell Scientific, London.

Teri, L. (1986). Severe cognitive impairments in older adults, *Behavior Therapist*, **9**, 51–54.

Teri, L., Larson, E.B. & Reifler, B.V. (1988). Behavioral disturbance in dementia of the Alzheimer's type, *J. Am. Geriatrics Society*, **36**, 1–6.

Teri, L., Borson, S., Kiyak, H.A. & Yamagishi, M. (1989). Behavioral disturbance, cognitive dysfunction and functional skill: Prevalence and relationship in Alzheimer's disease, *J. Am. Geriatrics Society*, **37**, 109–116.

Teri, L., Hughes, J.P. & Larson, E.B. (1990). Cognitive deterioration in Alzheimer's disease: Behavioral and health factors, *J. Gerontology*, **45**, 58–63.

Teri, L., Truax, P., Logsdon, R., Uomoto, J., Zarit, S. & Vitaliano, P.P. (1992). Assessment of behavioral problems in dementia: The revised memory and behavior problems checklist, *Psychol. Aging*, **7**, 622–631.

Test, M.A. & Stein, L.I. (1978). Training in community living: Research design and results, in *Alternatives to Mental Hospital Treatment* (Eds L.I. Stein & M.A. Test), Plenum Press, New York, London.

The Lancet (1995). Quality of life and clinical trials, *Lancet*, **346**, 1–2 (Editorial).

The WHOQOL Group (1994). The development of the WHO quality of life assessment instrument (The WHOQOL), in *Quality of Life Assessment: International Perspectives* (Eds J. Orley & W. Kuyken), pp. 41–57, Springer, Heidelburg, New York, London, Paris, Tokyo, Hong Kong, Barcelona, Budapest.

Thepa, K. & Rowland, L. (1995). Quality of life perspectives in long-term care: Staff and patient perceptions, *Acta Psychiat. Scand.*, **80**, 267–271.

Thomas, A. & Chess, S. (1977). *Temperament and Development*, Brunner & Mazel, New York.

Thornicroft, G., Gooch, C., O'Driscoll, C. & Reda, S. (1993). The TAPS Project. 9: The reliability of the Patient Attitude Questionnaire, in (Ed. J. Leff) Evaluating community placement of long-stay psychiatric patients, *Br. J. Psychiatry*, **162** (Supplement 19), 25–29.

Torrance, G.W., Blaker, D., Detsky, A., Kennedy, W., Schubert, F., Menon, D., Tugwell, P., Konchak, R., Hubbard, E. & Firestone, T. (1996). Canadian guidelines for economic evaluation of pharmaceuticals, *PharmacoEconomics*, **9**, 535–559.

Tremmel, L. & Spiegel, R. (1993). Clinical experience with the NOSGER (Nurses' Observation Scale for Geriatric Patients): Tentative normative data and sensitivity to change, *Int. J. Geriatric Psychiatry*, **8**, 311–317.

Trieman, N. & Leff, J. (1996). Difficult to place patients in a psychiatric closure programme: The TAPS Project, *Psychol. Med.*, **26**, 765–774.

Tschuschke, V., Kächele, H. & Hölzer, M. (1994). Gibt es unterschiedlich effektive Formen von Psychotherapie? *Psychotherapeut*, **39**, 281–297.

Tubesing, N.L. & Tubesing, D.A. (1982). The treatment of choice: Selecting stress skills to suit the individual and the situation, in *Job Stress and Burnout. Research, Theory and Intervention Perspectives* (Ed. W.S. Paine), pp. 155–172, Sage, Beverly Hills, CA, London, New Delhi.

Turner, J.A., Deyo, R.A., Loeser, J.D., Von Korff, M. & Fordyce, W.E. (1994). The importance of placebo effects in pain treatment and research, *JAMA*, **271**, 1609–1614.

Turner, S.M., Beidel, D.C., Dancu, C.V. & Keys, D.J. (1986). Psychopathology of social phobia and comparison to avoidant personality disorder, *J. Abnormal Psychol.*, **95**, 389–394.

Tweed, D.L. (1993). Depression-related impairment: Estimating concurrent and lingering effects, *Psychol. Med.*, **23**, 373–386.

Tyrer, P.J. (1990). Personality disorder and social functioning, in *Measuring Human Problems. A Practical Guide* (Eds D.F Peck & C.M. Shapiro), pp. 119–142, Wiley, Chichester.

Tyrer, P.J. & Casey, P. (1993). *Social Function in Psychiatry. The Hidden Axis of Classification Exposed*, Wrightson Biomedical.

Uehara, E.A. (1994). Race, gender and housing inequality: An exploration of the correlates of low-quality housing among clients diagnosed with severe and persistent mental illness, *J. Health Soc. Behav.*, **35**, 309–321.

Uttaro, C.T. & Mechanic, D. (1994). The NAMI Consumer Survey: Analysis of unmet Needs, *Hosp. Comm. Psychiatry*, **45**, 372–374.

Vaccaro, J.V. & Clark, G.H. Jr (1987). A profile of community mental health center psychiatrists: Results of a national survey, *Comm. Ment. Health J.*, **23**, 282–289.

Van Dam, F.S.A.M., Somers, R. & Van Beek-Couzijn, A.L. (1981). Quality of life: Some theoretical issues, *J. Clin. Pharmacol.*, **21**, 166–168.

van der Poel, E.G.T. & Delespaul, P.A.E.G. (1992). The applicability of ESM in personalized rehabilitation, in *The Experience of Psychopathology* (Ed. M.W. deVries), pp. 290–303, Cambridge University Press, Cambridge.

Van Deusen, J. (1992). Perceptual dysfunction in persons with dementia of the Alzheimer's type: A literature review, *Physical and Occupational Therapy in Geriatrics*, **10**, 33–46.

van Goor-Lambo, G., Orley, J., Poustka, F. & Rutter, M. (1990). Classification of abnormal situations: Preliminary report of a revision of a WHO Scheme, *J. Child Psychol. Psychiatry*, **31**, 229–241.

van Goor-Lambo, G., Orley, J., Poustka, F. & Rutter, M. (1994). Multiaxial classification of psychiatric disorders in children and adolescents: Axis five – associated abnormal psychosocial situations. Preliminary results of a WHO and a German multicenter study, *European Child Adolescent Psychiatry*, **3**, 229–241.

Van Putten, T., Crumpton, E. & Yale, C. (1975). Drug refusal in schizophrenia and the wish to be crazy, *Arch. Gen. Psych.*, **33**, 1443–1446.

van Tosh, L. (1995). An analysis of consumers as peer specialists on intensive case management teams: Impact on client outcomes, *Psychiatric Services*, **46**, 1037–1044.

Veenhoven, R. (1991). Is happiness relative? *Social Indicators Research*, **24**, 1–34.

Voll, R., Allehoff, W.H., Esser, G., Poustka, F. & Schmidt, M.H. (1982). Widrige familiäre und soziale Bedingungen und psychiatrische Auffälligkeit bei 8-Jährigen, *Zeitschrift für Kinder- und Jugendpsychiatrie*, **10**, 100–109.

Voll, R. & Poustka, F. (1994). Coping with illness and coping with handicap during the vocational rehabilitation of physically handicapped adolescents and young adults, *Int. J. of Rehabilitation Research*, **17**, 305–318.

Volmer, T. (1994). Klinische Studien zur Lebensqualität bei Asthma, in *Lebensqualität und Asthma* (Eds F. Petermann & K.-C. Bergmann), pp. 83–98, Quintessenz, Munich.

von Korff, M., Ormel, J., Katon, W. & Lin, E. (1992). Disability and depression among high utilizers of health care: A longitudinal analysis, *Arch. Gen. Psychiatry*, **49**, 91–100.

Wadden, T.A. (1984). Relaxation therapy for essential hypertension: Specific or non-specific effects, *J. Psychosom. Res.*, **28**, 53–61.

Wahl, O.F. & Harman, Ch.R. (1989). Family views of stigma, *Schiz. Bull.*, **25**, 131–139.

Walker, S.R. & Ascher, W. (Eds) (1986). *Medicine and Risk/Benefit Decisions*, MTP Press, Lancaster.

Wallace, C.J. (1986). Functional assessment in rehabilitation, *Schiz. Bull.*, **12**, 604–630.

Ware, J.E., Brook, R.H., Davies, A.R. & Lohr, K.N. (1981). Choosing measures of health status for individuals in general populations, *Am. J. Public Health*, **71**, 620–625.

Ware, J.E., Manning, G.W., Duan, N. et al (1984). Health status and the use of out-patient mental health services, *Am. Psychol.*, **30**, 1090–1100.

Ware, J.E. & Sherbourne, C.D. (1992). The MOS 36-Item Short-Form Health Survey (SF-36), *Med. Care*, **30**, 473–483.

Warner, R. (1985). *Recovery from Schizophrenia: Psychiatry and Political Economy*, Routledge & Kegan Paul, London and New York.

Warner, R. & Huxley, P. (1993). Psychopathology and quality of life among mentally ill patients in the community, British and US samples compared, *Br. J. Psychiatry*, **163**, 505–509.

Warren, E.J., Grek, A., Conn, D., Herrmann, N. et al (1989). A correlation between cognitive performance and daily functioning in elderly people, *J. Geriatric Psychiatry Neurology*, **2**, 96–100.

Warshaw, M.G., Fierman, E., Pratt, L., Hunt, M., Yonkers, K.A., Massion, A.O. & Keller, M.B. (1993). Quality of life and dissociation in anxiety disorder patients with histories of trauma or PTSD, *Am. J. Psychiatry*, **150**, 1512–1516.

Weber, E. (1990). Pharmakotherapie, Compliance und "Lebensqualität", in *"Lebensqualität" als Bewertungskriterium in der Medizin* (Eds P. Schölmerich & G. Thews), pp. 133–148, Fischer Verlag, Stuttgart.

Weber, I. (1995). Lebensqualität: Messung und Ergebnisbeurteilung, *Deutsches Ärzteblatt*, **92**, Part 18, pp. 961.

Webster's Seventh New Collegiate Dictionary (1976). G. & R. Merriam, Springfield, MA.

Weiden, P. (1994). Neuroleptics and quality of life – the patient's perspective, *Neuropsychopharm.*, **10**, 35, S415.

Weinstein, R.M. (1979). Patient attitudes towards mental hospitalization: A review of quantitative research, *J. Health Soc. Behav.*, **20**, 237–258.

Weisbrod, B.A., Test, M.A. & Stein, L. (1980). Alternatives to Mental Hospital Treatment II. Economic Benefit-cost Analysis, *Arch. Gen. Psychiatry*, 37, 400–402.

Weissman, M.M. (1975). The assessment of social adjustment. A review of techniques, *Arch. Gen. Psychiatry*, **32**, 357–365.

Weissman, M.M., Paykel, E.S., Siegel, R. et al (1971). The social role performance of depressed women: comparisons with a normal group, *Am. J. Orthopsychiatry*, **41**, 390–405.

Weissman, M.M. & Paykel, E.S. (1974) *The Depressed Women: A Study of Social Relationships*, University of Chicago Press, Chicago.

Weissman, M.M. & Bothwell, S. (1976). Assessment of social adjustment by patient self-report, *Arch. Gen. Psychiatry*, **33**, 1111–1115.

Weissman, M.M., Prusoff, B.A., Thompson, W.D., Harding P.S. & Myers, J.K. (1978). Social adjustment by self-report in a community sample and in psychiatric outpatients, *J. Nerv. Ment. Dis.* **166**, 317–326.

Weissman, M.M., Prusoff, B.A., Di Mascio, A., Neu, C., Gohlaney, M. & Klerman, G.L. (1979). The efficacy of drugs and psychotherapy in the treatment of acute depressive episodes, *Am. J. Psychiatry*, **136**, 555–558.

Weissman, M.M., Klerman, G.L., Prusoff, B.A., Sholomskas, D. & Padian, N. (1981a). Depressed outpatients: Results 1 year after treatment with drugs and/or interpersonal psychotherapy, *Arch. Gen. Psychiatry*, **38**, 51–55

Weissman, M.M., Sholomskas, D. & John, K. (1981b). The assessment of social adjustment. An update, *Arch. Gen. Psychiatry*, **38**, 1250–1258.

Weissman, M.M., Bland, R.C., Canino, G.J., et al (1996). Cross-national epidemiology of major depression and bipolar disorder, *JAMA*, **276**, 293–299.

Wells, K.B., Stewart, A., Hays, R.D., Burnam, A., Rogers, W., Daniels, M., Berry, S., Greenfield, S. & Ware, J. (1988). The functioning and well-being of depressed patients: Results from the medical outcomes study, *JAMA*, **262**, 914–919.

Wells, K.B., Burnam, M.A., Rogers, W., Hays, R. & Camp, P. (1992). The course of depression in adult outpatients. Results from the Medical Outcomes Study, *Arch. Gen. Psychiatry*, **49**, 788–794.

Wenger, N.K., Matteson, M.E., Furberg, C.D. & Ellison, J. (1984). Assessment of quality of life in clinical trials of cardiovascular therapies, *Am. J. Cardiol.*, **54**, 908–913.

Westermeyer, J. (1980). Psychosis in a peasant society: social outcomes, *Am. J. Psychiatry*, **137**, 1390–1394.

Wheeler, L. & Reis, H.T. (1991). Self-recording of everyday life events: Origins, types and uses, *J. Personality*, **59**, 339–354.

Whiting, B.B. & Whiting, J.W.M. (1975). *Children of Six Cultures: A Psycho-cultural Analysis*, Harvard University Press, Cambridge, MA.

Whynes, D.K. & Neilson, A. (1993). Convergent validity of two measures of the quality of life, *Health Economics*, **2**, 229–235.

Wiener, J.M. (Ed.) (1991). *Textbook of Child and Adolescent Psychiatry*, American Psychiatric Press, Washington, DC.

Wiersma, D. (1986). Psychological impairments and social disabilities on the applicability of the ICIDH to psychiatry, *Int. J. Rehab. Med.*, **8**, 3–7.

Wiersma, D., De Jong, A. & Ormel, J. (1988). The Groningen Social Disabilities Schedule: Development, relationship with the ICIDH and psychometric properties, *Int. J. Rehab. Res.*, **3**, 213–224.

Wiersma, D., De Jong, A., Kraaijkamp, H.J.M. & Ormel, J. (1990). *GSDS-II. The Groningen Social Disabilities Schedule, second version. Manual, questionnaire and rating form*, Department of Social Psychiatry, University of Groningen.

Wiersma, D. & Chapireau, F. (1991). *The Use of the International Classification of Impairments, Disabilities and Handicaps in Mental Health*, Council of Europe, Strasbourg.

Wiersma, D., Giel, R. & Kluiter, H. (1994). Day treatment and Community Care: Policy and research in the Netherlands, in *Psychiatry in Europe: Directions and Developments* (Eds C. Katone, S. Montgomery & T. Sensky), pp. 152–160, Gaskell, London.

Wiersma, D., Kluiter, H., Nienhuis, F.J. & Giel, R. (1995). Costs and benefits of hospital and day treatment with community care of affective and schizophrenic disorders. A randomized trial with a follow up of two years, *Br. J. Psychiatry*, **166** (Supplement 27), 52–59.

Wilkinson, G., Croft-Jeffreys, C., Krekorian, H. et al (1990). QALYs in psychiatric care, *Psychiatric Bull.*, **14**, 582–585.

Wilkinson, G., Williams, B., Krekorian, S., McLees, S. & Falloon, I. (1992). QALYs in mental health: A case study, *Psychol. Med.*, **22**, 725–731.

Williams, A. (1985). Economics of coronary artery bypass grafting, *Br. Med. J.*, **291**, 326–329.

Williams, B. & Wilkinson, G. (1995). Patient satisfaction in mental health care. Evaluating and evaluative method, *Br. J. Psychiatry*, **166**, 559–562.

Williams, G.H. (1987). Quality of life and its impact on hypertensive patients, *Am. J. Med.* **82**, 98–105.

Wills, W. & Leff, J. (1996). The TAPS Project 30: Quality of Life for elderly mentally ill patients: A comparison of hospital and community settings, *Int. J. Geriatric Psychiatry*, (in press).

Wilson, I.B & Cleary, P.D. (1995). Linking clinical variables with health-related quality of life: A conceptual model of patient outcomes, *J. Am. Med. Assoc.*, **4**, 59–65.

Wilson, W. (1967). Correlates of avowed happiness, *Psychol. Bull.*, **67**, 294–306.

Wing, J.K. (1986). Psychosocial factors affecting the long-term course of schizophrenia, in *Psychosocial Treatment of Schizophrenia* (Eds J.S. Strauss, W. Boker & H.D. Brenner), Hans Huber, Berne.

Wing, J.K. (1989). The measurement of social disablement. The MRC social behaviour and social role performance schedules, *Soc. Psychiatry Psychiat. Epidemiol.*, **24**, 173–178.

Wing, J. (1993). Institutionalism Revisited, *Criminal Behaviour and Mental Health*, **3**, 441–451.

Wing, J.K. & Brown, G.W. (1970). *Institutionalism and Schizophrenia: A Comparative Study of Three Mental Hospitals 1960–68*, Cambridge University Press, London.

Wing, J.K., Cooper, J.E. & Sartorius, N. (1974). *Description and Classification of Psychiatric Symptoms*, Cambridge University Press, London.

Wise, T.N. & Berlin, R.M. (1981). Burnout: Stresses in consultation-liaison psychiatry, *Psychosomatics*, **22**, 744–751.

Wittchen, H.-U. & von Zerssen, D. (1987). *Verläufe behandelter und unbehandelter Depressionen und Angststörungen. Eine klinisch-psychiatrische und epidemiologische Verlaufsuntersuchung*, Springer Verlag, Berlin, Heidelberg, New York, London, Paris, Tokyo.

Wittchen, H.-U., Essau, C.A., von Zerssen, D., Krieg, J.-C. & Zaudig, M. (1992). Lifetime and six-month prevalence of mental disorders in the Munich Follow-Up Study, *Eur. Arch. Psychiatry Clin. Neurosci.*, **241**, 247–258.

Wittchen, H.-U. & Beloch, E. (1996). The impact of social phobia on quality of life, *Int. Clin. Psychopharmacol.*, **11**, 15–23.

Wohlfarth, T.D., van den Brink, W., Ormel, J., Koeter, M.W.J. & Oldehinkel, A.J. (1993). The relationship between social dysfunctioning and psychopathology among primary care attenders, *Br. J. Psychiatry*, **163**, 37–44.

World Bank. (1993). *World Development Report 1993*, Oxford University Press, Washington, DC.

World Health Organization (1948). *Constitution of the World Health Organization*. Basic Documents, Geneva.

World Health Organization (1978). *Mental Disorders: Glossary and Guide to their Classification in Accordance with the Ninth Revision of the International Classification of Diseases*, WHO, Geneva.

World Health Organization (1979). *Schizophrenia: An International Follow-up Study*, Wiley, Chichester.

World Health Organization (1980). *International Classification of Impairments, Disabilities and Handicaps (ICIDH)*, WHO, Geneva.

World Health Organization (1988). *WHO Psychiatric Disability Assessment Schedule (WHO/DAS) with a Guide to its Use*, WHO, Geneva.

World Health Organization (1988a). *Psychiatric Disability Assessment Schedule (DAS)*, Who, Geneva.

World Health Organization (1988b). Draft multiaxial classification of child psychiatric disorders. Axis five: Associated abnormal psychosocial situations *(WHO Document MNH/PRO/86. 1, REV. 1)*, WHO, Geneva.

World Health Organization (1991). Multiaxial version of ICD-10 prepared for use by clinicians dealing with child and adolescent psychiatric disorders, Draft, WHO, Geneva.

World Health Organization (1992a). *International Classification of Diseases and Related Health Problems, Tenth Revision (ICD-10)*, WHO, Geneva.

World Health Organization (1992b). *The ICD-10 Classification of Mental and Behavioral Disorders. Clinical Description and Diagnostic Guidelines*, WHO, Geneva.

World Health Organization (1993a). *The Development of the WHO Quality of Life Assessment Instrument*, WHO, Geneva.

World Health Organization (1993b). *WHOQOL Study Protocol* (MNH/PSF/93.3), WHO, Geneva.

World Health Organization (1994). *Qualitative Research for Health Programmes*, Division of Mental Health, WHO, Geneva.

World Health Organization (1997). *The Multiaxial Presentation of the ICD-10 for Use in Adult Psychiatry*, Cambridge University Press, Cambridge.

Wyman, P.A., Cowen, E.L., Work, W.C., Raoof, A., Gribble, P.A., Parker, G.R. & Wannon, M. (1992). Interviews with children who experienced major life stress: Family and child attributes that predict resilient outcomes, *J. Am. Acad. Child Adolesc. Psychiatry*, **31**, 5,

904–910.

Zanetti, O., Bianchetti, A., Frisoni, G.B., Rozzini, R. et al (1993). Determinants of disability in Alzheimer's disease, *Int. J. Geriatoric Psychiatr.*, **8**, 581–586.

Zapotoczky, H.G. (1994). Quality of life and OCD, Abstract of Presentation at the 7th European Symposium of the *Association of European Psychiatrists Section Committee Psychiatric Epidemiology and Social Psychiatry*, Vienna, Austria, 7–9 April.

Zautra, A. & Goodhart, D. (1979). Quality of life indicators: A review of the literature, *Comm. Mental Health Review*, **4**, 1–10.

Zeiss, A. & Lewinsohn, P. (1988). Enduring deficits after remission of depression: A test of the "scar" hypothesis, *Behav. Res. Ther.*, **26**, 151–158.

Zigmond, A.S. & Snaith, R.P. (1983). The Hospital Anxiety and Depression Scale, *Acta Psychiat. Scand.*, **67**, 361–370.

Zimmermann, M.A. & Rappaport, J. (1988). Citizen participation, perceived control and psychological empowerment, *Am. J. Comm. Psychol.*, **16**, 725–749.

Zissi, A. & Barry, M.M. (1997). From Leros asylum to community-based facilities: Levels of functioning and quality of life among hostel residents in Greece, *Int. J. Soc. Psychiat.*, **43**, 104–115.

Zubin, J. & Spring, B. (1977). Vulnerability: A new view of schizophrenia, *J. Abnormal Psychology*, **86**, 103–123.

Index

Index compiled by A. Campbell Purton